SYLVIA PLATH: THE CRITICAL HERITAGE

THE CRITICAL HERITAGE SERIES

GENERAL EDITOR: B. C. SOUTHAM, M.A., B. LITT. (OXON.)
Formerly Department of English, Westfield College, University of London

For a list of books in the series see the back endpaper

SYLVIA PLATH

THE CRITICAL HERITAGE

Edited by
LINDA W. WAGNER

Professor of English
Michigan State University
East Lansing, Michigan

ROUTLEDGE
LONDON AND NEW YORK

First published in 1988 by
Routledge
11 New Fetter Lane, London EC4P 4EE

Published in the USA
by Routledge, Chapman and Hall Inc.
29 West 35th Street, New York, NY 10001

Photypesetting by
Thomson Press (India) Limited, New Delhi
and printed in Great Britain
by T J Press (Padstow) Ltd
Padstow, Cornwall

Library of Congress Cataloging in Publication Data

Sylvia Plath, the critical heritage.

(The Critical Heritage series)
Bibliography: p.
Includes index.
1. Plath, Sylvia—Criticism and interpretation.
I. Wagner-Martin, Linda. II. Series.
PS3566.L27Z919   1988   811'.54   88–4501

British Library CIP Data also available
ISBN 0–415–00910–3

General Editor's Preface

The reception given to a writer by his contemporaries and near-contemporaries is evidence of considerable value to the student of literature. On one side we learn a great deal about the state of criticism at large and in particular about the development of critical attitudes towards a single writer; at the same time, through private comments in letters, journals or marginalia, we gain an insight upon the tastes and literary thought of individual readers of the period. Evidence of this kind helps us to understand the writer's historical situation, the nature of his immediate reading-public, and his response to these pressures.

The separate volumes in the *Critical Heritage Series* present a record of this early criticism. Clearly, for many of the highly productive and lengthily reviewed nineteenth- and twentieth-century writers, there exists an enormous body of material; and in these cases the volume editors have made a selection of the most important views, significant for their intrinsic critical worth or for their representative quality—perhaps even registering incomprehension!

For earlier writers, notably pre-eighteenth century, the materials are much scarcer and the historical period has been extended, sometimes far beyond the writer's lifetime, in order to show the inception and growth of critical views which were initially slow to appear.

In each volume the documents are headed by an Introduction, discussing the material assembled and relating the early stages of the author's reception to what we have come to identify as the critical tradition. The volumes will make available much material which would otherwise be difficult of access and it is hoped that the modern reader will be thereby helped towards an informed understanding of the ways in which literature has been read and judged.

B.C.S.

For Bob

Contents

ACKNOWLEDGMENTS   xiii

INTRODUCTION   1

ABBREVIATIONS   25

NOTE ON THE TEXT   26

Meeting Sylvia Plath

1 ELINOR KLEIN   27

2 JANE BALTZELL KOPP   28

3 IRENE V. MORRIS   28

4 CHRISTOPHER LEVENSON   29

5 ANNE SEXTON   30

The Colossus and Other Poems (1960)

6 BERNARD BERGONZI, 'The Ransom Note,' *Manchester Guardian*, November 1960   32

7 JOHN WAIN, 'Farewell to the World,' *Spectator*, January 1961   33

8 A. ALVAREZ, 'The Poet and the Poetess,' *Observer*, December 1960   34

9 ROY FULLER, review, *London Magazine*, March 1961   35

10 A. E. DYSON, review, *Critical Quarterly*, Summer 1961   36

11 Unsigned review, *Times Literary Supplement*, August 1961   41

The Colossus and Other Poems (1962)

12 E. LUCAS MYERS, 'The Tranquilized Fifties,' *Sewanee Review*, January–March 1962   42

13 JUDSON JEROME, 'A Poetry Chronicle—Part I,' *Antioch Review*, Spring 1963   44

14 RICHARD HOWARD, review, *Poetry*, March 1963   45

15 MARK LINENTHAL, 'Sensibility and Reflection from the Poet's Corner,' *San Francisco Sunday Chronicle, This World*, March 1963   47

16 NICHOLAS KING, 'Poetry: A Late Summer Roundup,' *New York Herald–Tribune Book Review*, August 1962   48

17 IAN HAMILTON, 'Poetry,' *London Magazine*, July 1963   48

The Bell Jar (Victoria Lucas, 1963)

18 Unsigned review, 'Under the Skin,' *Times Literary Supplement*, January 1963   52

19 LAURENCE LERNER, 'New Novels,' *Listener*, January 1963   53

Ariel (1965)

20 A. ALVAREZ, 'Poetry in Extremis,' *Observer*, March 1965   55

21 Unsigned review, 'Along the Edge,' *Times Literary Supplement*, November 1965   58

22 M. L. ROSENTHAL, 'Poets of the Dangerous Way,' *Spectator*, March 1965   60

23 Unsigned review, 'Poems for the Good-Hearted,' *The Times*, November 1965   62

24 PETER DALE, '"O Honey Bees Come Build,"' *Agenda*, Summer 1966   62

25 STEPHEN SPENDER, 'Warnings from the Grave,' *New Republic*, June 1966   69

26 P. N. FURBANK, 'New Poetry,' *Listener*, March 1965,   73

27 HUGH KENNER, 'Arts and the Age, On *Ariel*,' *Triumph*, September 1966   74

28 JOHN MALCOLM BRINNIN, 'Plath, Jarrell, Kinnell, Smith,' *Partisan Review*, Winter 1967   78

29 RICHARD TILLINGHAST, 'Worlds of Their Own,' *Southern Review*, Spring 1969   79

30 PETER DAVISON, 'Inhabited by a Cry: The Last Poetry of Sylvia Plath,' *Atlantic Monthly*, August 1966   80

31 IRVING FELDMAN, 'The Religion of One,' *Book Week*, June 1966   84

32 Unsigned review, 'Russian Roulette,' *Newsweek*, June 1966   88

33 ROBIN SKELTON, review, *Massachusetts Review*, Autumn 1965   90

The Colossus and Other Poems (reissue, 1967, 1968)

34 Unsigned review, 'Chained to the Parish Pump,' *Times Literary Supplement*, March 1967   92

35 M. L. ROSENTHAL, 'Metamorphosis of a Book,' *Spectator*, April 1967   92

37 JAMES TULIP, 'Three Women Poets,' *Poetry Australia*, December 1967   95

The Bell Jar (Sylvia Plath, reissue, 1966)

37 C. B. COX, 'Editorial,' *Critical Quarterly*, Autumn 1966   99

38 STEPHEN WALL, review, *Observer*, September 1966   100

The Bell Jar (Sylvia Plath, New York, 1971)

39 J. D. O'HARA, 'An American Dream Girl,' *Washington Post Book World*, April 1971   101

40 SAUL MALOFF, 'Waiting for the Voice to Crack,' *New Republic*, May 1971   103

41 MASON HARRIS, '*The Bell Jar*,' *West Coast Review*, October 1973   107

42 GEOFFREY WOLFF, '*The Bell Jar*,' *Newsweek*, April 1971   113

43 MARGARET L. SHOOK, 'Sylvia Plath: The Poet and the College,' *Smith Alumnae Quarterly*, April 1972   114

44 TERESA DE LAURETIS, 'Rebirth in *The Bell Jar*,' *Women's Studies*, 1976   124

Crossing the Water (1971)

45 DOMENICA PATERNO, 'Poetry,' *Library Journal*, October 1971   135

46 EILEEN M. AIRD, review, *Critical Quarterly*, Autumn 1971   136

47 DOUGLAS DUNN, 'Damaged Instruments,' *Encounter*, August 1971   139

48 VICTOR HOWES, 'I am Silver and Exact,' *Christian Science Monitor*, September 1971   142

49 ROBERT BOYERS, 'On Sylvia Plath,' *Salmagundi*, Winter 1973   144

50 TERRY EAGLETON, 'New Poetry,' *Stand*, 1971-2 152

51 PETER PORTER, 'Collecting Her Strength,' *New Statesman*, June 1971 155

52 PAUL WEST, '*Crossing the Water*,' *Book World (Chicago Tribune)*, January 1972 157

53 VICTOR KRAMER, 'Life-and-Death Dialectics,' *Modern Poetry Studies*, 1972 161

Winter Trees (1971, 1972)

54 Unsigned review, 'A World in Disintegration,' *Times Literary Supplement*, December 1971 165

55 LINDA RAY PRATT, '"The Spirit of Blackness is in Us...,"' *Prairie Schooner*, Spring 1973 168

56 ROGER SCRUTON, 'Sylvia Plath and the Savage God,' *Spectator*, December 1971 171

57 JOYCE CAROL OATES, '*Winter Trees*,' *Library Journal*, November 1972 175

58 DAMIAN GRANT, '*Winter Trees*,' *Critical Quarterly*, Spring 1972 177

59 RAYMOND SMITH, 'Late Harvest,' *Modern Poetry Studies*, 1972 179

60 JAMES FINN COTTER, 'Women Poets: Malign Neglect?' *America*, February 1973 182

61 INGRID MELANDER, review, *Moderna Språk*, 1971 184

62 ERIC HOMBERGER, 'The Uncollected Plath,' *New Statesman*, September 1972 187

63 EILEEN M. AIRD, '"Poem for a Birthday" to *Three Women*: Development in the Poetry of Sylvia Plath,' *Critical Quarterly*, Winter 1979 191

Letters Home by Sylvia Plath, Correspondence 1950-1963 (1975)

64 ERICA JONG, 'Letters Focus Exquisite Rage of Sylvia Plath,' *Los Angeles Times Book Review*, November 1975 204

65 ANNE TYLER, '"The Voice Hangs On, Gay, Tremulous,"' *National Observer*, January 1976 210

66 JO BRANS, '"The Girl Who Wanted to be God,"' *Southwest Review*, Summer 1976 213

67 MARTHA DUFFY, 'Two Lives,' *Time*, November 1975   216

68 CAROL BERE, '*Letters Home: Correspondence 1950–1963*,' *Ariel*, October 1977   219

69 ROSE KAMEL, '"Reach Hag Hands and Haul Me In": Matrophobia in the Letters of Sylvia Plath,' *Northwest Review*, 1981   223

Johnny Panic and the Bible of Dreams: Short Stories, Prose and Diary Excerpts (1977, 1979)

70 DOUGLAS HILL, 'Living and Dying,' *Canadian Forum*, June 1978   234

71 LORNA SAGE, 'Death and Marriage,' *Times Literary Supplement*, October 1977   237

72 G. S. FRASER, 'Pass to the Centre,' *Listener*, October 1977   243

73 MELODY ZAJDEL, 'Apprenticed in a Bible of Dreams: Sylvia Plath's Short Stories,' *Critical Essays on Sylvia Plath*, 1984   245

The Collected Poems of Sylvia Plath (1981)

74 LAURENCE LERNER, 'Sylvia Plath,' *Encounter*, January 1982   259

75 WILLIAM H. PRITCHARD, 'An Interesting Minor Poet?' *New Republic*, December 1981   262

76 DAVE SMITH, 'Syliva Plath, the Electric Horse,' *American Poetry Review*, January 1982   268

77 MICHAEL KIRKHAM, 'Sylvia Plath,' *Queen's Quarterly*, Spring 1984   276

78 MICHAEL HULSE, 'Formal Bleeding,' *Spectator*, November 1981   291

79 MARJORIE PERLOFF, 'Sylvia Plath's *Collected Poems*,' *Resources for American Literary Study*, Autumn 1981   293

The Journals of Sylvia Plath, 1950–1962 (1982)

80 MARNI JACKSON, 'In Search of the Shape Within,' *Maclean's Magazine*, May 1982   304

81 LINDA W. WAGNER, '*The Journals of Sylvia Plath*,' *Contemporary Literature*, Winter 1983   306

CONTENTS

82 MIRIAM LEVINE, '*The Journals of Sylvia Plath,*' *American Book Review*, May–June 1983   308

83 STEVEN GOULD AXELROD, 'The Second Destruction of Sylvia Plath,' *American Poetry Review*, March–April 1985   313

SELECT BIBLIOGRAPHY   320

INDEX   323

Acknowledgments

For permission to reprint copyright material, and for answering queries, acknowledgment is due to the following: *Agenda* for No. 24; Eileen M. Aird for Nos 46 and 63; *Antioch Review* for No. 13, first published in the *Antioch Review*, vol. 23, no. 1 (Spring 1963) (Copyright © 1963 by The Antioch Review, Inc. Reprinted by permission of the editors); *Ariel* for No. 68; Steven Gould Axelrod for No. 83; Bernard Bergonzi for No. 6; Robert Boyers for No. 49; Jo Brans and the *Southwest Review* for No. 66; *Canadian Forum* for No. 70; *Christian Science Monitor* for No. 48 (© 1971 The Christian Science Publishing Society. All rights reserved); James Finn Cotter and *America* for No. 60; C. B. Cox and the *Critical Quarterly* for No. 37; Peter Davison for No. 30; A. E. Dyson for No. 10; P. N. Furbank for No. 26; Damian Grant for No. 58; Mason Harris and *West Coast Review* for No. 41; Eric Homberger for No. 62; Richard Howard and *Poetry* for No. 14; Erica Jong for No. 64; Rose Kamel for No. 69; Hugh Kenner for No. 27; Michael Kirkham and *Queen's Quarterly* for No. 77; Elinor Klein for No. 1; Laurence Lerner for Nos 19 and 74; Miriam Levine for No. 82; *Library Journal* for Nos 45 and 57; *London Magazine* for Nos 9 and 17; *Maclean's Magazine* for No. 80; *Massachusetts Review* for No. 33 (© 1965 The Massachusetts Review, Inc.); *Modern Poetry Studies* for Nos 53 and 59; *Moderna Språk* for No. 61; the Registrar of the Roll, Newnham College, Cambridge, for No. 3, from *Newnham College Roll Letter*; *New Republic* for Nos 25, 40, and 75 (© 1966, 1971, 1981, The New Republic, Inc. Reprinted by permission); *Newsweek* for Nos 32 and 42 (Copyright 1966 and 1971 by Newsweek, Inc. All rights reserved. Reprinted by permission); *Observer* for Nos 8, 20, and 38; *Partisan Review* for No. 28; *Poetry Australia* for No. 36; *Resources for American Literary Study* for No. 79; M. L. Rosenthal for Nos 22 and 35; *San Francisco Chronicle* for No. 15 (© *San Francisco Chronicle*, 1963); *Sewanee Review* for No. 12, first published in the *Sewanee Review*, vol. 70, no. 2 (Spring 1962) (Copyright 1962 by the University of the South. Reprinted with the permission of the editor); Margaret L. Shook and *Smith*

Alumnae Quarterly for No. 43; Dave Smith for No. 76; *Spectator* for Nos 7, 56, and 78; *Stand* for No. 50; Richard Tillinghast for No. 29; *Time* for No. 67 (Copyright 1975 Time Inc. All rights reserved. Reprinted by permission); Times Newspapers Ltd for Nos 11, 18, 21, 34, 54, and 71 from the *Times Literary Supplement* and No. 23 from *The Times*; Anne Tyler for No. 65; University of Nebraska Press for No. 55, from *Prairie Schooner* (Copyright © 1973 University of Nebraska Press); *Washington Post* for No. 39; *Women's Studies* (Gordon & Breach Science Publishers) for No. 44.

It has proved difficult in some cases to locate the owners of copyright material. However, all possible care has been taken to trace ownership of the selections included and to make full acknowledgment for their use.

Introduction

Few modern or contemporary writers have had the quantity of criticism dedicated to their writing that Sylvia Plath's work has received. Generally positive, that criticism has fluctuated widely, depending on when it was written. In the early 1960s, when her first poetry collection, *The Colossus and Other Poems*, and her novel, *The Bell Jar*, appeared, most criticism was highly encouraging. Critics recognized a sure new voice, speaking in tightly wrought patterns and conveying a definite sense of control. The more traditional critics responded to Plath's work with enthusiasm. Plath was obviously a well-educated, disciplined writer who usually avoided the sentimentalities of some female writers. She wrote tidy poems, reminiscent of those by Richard Eberhart, Karl Shapiro, Randall Jarrell, and Richard Wilbur. She wrote fiction—at least part of *The Bell Jar*—with a wry voice somewhat like that of J. D. Salinger. In retrospect, that same taut humor was evident in many of the poems from *The Colossus*.

The Bell Jar was published on 14, January 1963, under the pseudonym of 'Victoria Lucas.' No one knew it was Sylvia Plath's work; it stood on its own completely unknown feet—yet it was favorably reviewed. On 11 February 1963, Plath committed suicide, and the second stage of criticism of her work began immediately. Within a week eulogies and laments appeared that, of necessity, changed the tenor of reader response for years to come. For a young woman to kill herself at the beginning of a successful writing career posed an intriguing—and frightening—mystery. All kinds of equations between art and life began to be suggested. Had Plath written so personally that she had somehow crossed the boundary between art and life? Was full exploration of the creative process dangerous? Why would a woman with two small children choose to leave not only her successful practice of her art but also those dependents? Controversy was rampant, and criticism of Plath's work would never again be untouched by biography.

THE COLOSSUS AND OTHER POEMS

When Heinemann published *The Colossus and Other Poems* in London, in late fall of 1960, very near Plath's twenty-eighth birthday, the collection was well received. The first half-dozen reviews were almost entirely positive. Peter Dickinson's comment in *Punch* set the tone. He called the book 'a real find...exhilarating to read.' Dickinson commented on Plath's being an American but said that she was 'different.' (In an adjoining review of Richard Eberhart's *Collected Poems*, Dickinson mentioned that the older poet's work was 'hard going...in the American manner' and equated a high proportion of abstractions with that national style.) He saw Plath's strength as her ability to avoid the abstract, to arrange concrete experience in 'clean, easy verse.'

Bernard Bergonzi's tactic in his *Manchester Guardian* review (No. 6) was similar. He began by discussing generally the work of women poets and then pointed out that Plath's poetry differed from that body of writing because of its 'outstanding technical accomplishment,' its 'virtuoso' quality. He identified Plath's influences as Theodore Roethke and John Crowe Ransom, but claimed that neither her poems nor her vision was derivative, and that she wrote with a rare degree of assurance. John Wain, in the *Spectator* (No. 7), agreed that Plath already had an individual manner and voice. He enjoyed what he called her 'clever, vivacious poetry' and humor. Roy Fuller, however, in the *London Magazine* (No. 9), objected to the fact that Plath was twenty-eight rather than twenty-three. For her age, he thought she was too dependent on voices other than her own 'controlled and rather ventriloquial' one. Even this review, however, was largely positive.[1]

The most accurate of the early comments on *The Colossus and Other Poems* appeared in the *Observer* for 18 December 1960 (No. 8). A. Alvarez described Plath's work as 'good poetry,' regardless of her nationality, gender, or age, and pointed out how concentrated—and how mysterious—some of her work was. Alvarez saw Plath's reluctance to express herself directly as a 'sense of threat, as though she were continually menaced by something she could see only out of the corners of her eyes' as the distinction of her work. According to Alvarez, at Plath's best, 'her tense and twisted language preserves her and she ends with something ominous, odd, like one of the original tales from Grimm.'[2] Plath clearly was a presence on the London poetry scene.

As reviewers recognized, *The Colossus and Other Poems* was a strong book. Nearly all the poems in it had already been published in leading American and British journals. The book had, in one form or another, several times been the runner-up in the prestigious Yale ·Younger Poets book competition. (The winning manuscript in the competition was published as a book in the Yale series of that name.) Plath was hardly unknown. During the previous ten years she had published in *Harper's*, *Atlantic Monthly*, the *Christian Science Monitor*, the *London Magazine*, the *Kenyon Review*, *Chelsea*, the *Critical Quarterly*, the *Antioch Review*, *Mademoiselle*, *Seventeen*, the *Listener*, *Encounter*, the *New Statesman*, the *Observer*, the *Nation*, the *Spectator*, the *Sewanee Review*, *Poetry*, *Granta*, the *Hudson Review*, the *Partisan Review*, and the *Times Literary Supplement*. She had a 'first-reading' contract with the *New Yorker*, which meant that that magazine was sent all new writing and had first right of either acceptance or rejection. Somewhat like Wallace Stevens' *Harmonium*, the first book Stevens published although he had been writing poetry for many years, Plath's *The Colossus* included the core of her poetic aesthetic and a good many poems that would remain seminal.

In April of 1962, *The Colossus* was published in the United States by Alfred A. Knopf. In agreeing to publish the book, Knopf had asked that Plath shorten the collection by ten poems, and that the closing sequence, 'Poem for a Birthday,' be omitted because of its resemblance to Theodore Roethke's work. Plath agreed, but then replaced two of the seven parts of the latter poem, 'Flute Notes from a Reedy Pond' and 'The Stones,' to close the American text.

American reviewers seemed somewhat less excited about the book than British readers, thinking that Plath's derivative qualities were more noticeable than her originality. William Dickey objected to what he called her narrow range of tone, as did Reed Whittemore, who opened his comments by identifying Plath as 'Mrs. Ted Hughes.' E. Lucas Myers' review (No. 12) stressed the impersonal nature of Plath's poems, even though they appeared to be about personal subjects. He praised Plath for her technical skill and suggested that her next collection would be even more

3

rewarding if she could get rid of that sense of objectivity that kept readers from feeling that the poems mattered. M. L. Rosenthal recalled later that the American reviews recognized Plath's promise but thought her academic: 'her work seemed "craft"-centered and a bit derivative.' (No. 35)[3]

PLATH'S BIOGRAPHY

All her life, Sylvia Plath had known she wanted to become either an artist or a writer. The older child of well-educated Boston parents, Aurelia Schober and Otto Plath, Sylvia collected a number of academic awards during her childhood and adolescence. An English major at Smith College, she won all the major prizes for writing and scholarship, but she was also very much an American woman of the 1950s. She was plagued with the notion that she had to marry and have children, as well as having a career. Some of these conflicts over her life direction (career vs. marriage, sexual experience vs. chastity) combined with a strain of depression in her father's family to cause a breakdown in the summer of 1953, shortly after she had come home from a month on the *Mademoiselle* College Board in New York. The out-patient electroconvulsive shock treatments she received probably led to her suicide attempt in late August, and she spent the next six months under psychiatric care before returning to Smith College. In June 1955, she graduated *summa cum laude* and then studied for an MA on a Fulbright fellowship at Newnham College, Cambridge.

On 16 June 1956, she married the British poet Ted Hughes. She completed her work at Newnham and then in 1957 she and Hughes returned to the United States and Plath taught freshman English for a year at Smith. She and Hughes then lived for another year in Boston, establishing themselves as professional writers. Sylvia studied briefly with Robert Lowell; she and Ted spent the fall of 1959 at Yaddo. Late in 1959 they returned to England and lived for more than a year in London. In the next three years, Plath bore two children, published *The Colossus and Other Poems*, established a home in an ancient Devon house, separated from Hughes, and was living with her children in a flat in Yeats' house in London when she committed suicide, just a few weeks after *The Bell Jar* was published in England.

THE BELL JAR

Published under a pseudonym, *The Bell Jar* was greeted as the work of a female Salinger. Reviewers were struck with parallels in tone with *The Catcher in the Rye*. Robert Taubman preferred *The Bell Jar* to James Jones' *The Thin Red Line* and John Updike's *Pigeon Feathers*, calling it 'an intensely interesting first novel' and terming Lucas 'astonishingly skillful.' Laurence Lerner (No. 19) made no comparisons and, seemingly, had no reservations. He called it 'a brilliant and moving book' which triumphed in both language and characterization. Similarly, the unnamed reviewer for the *Times Literary Supplement* (No. 18) praised Lucas (Plath) for her skill in creating a different world, particularly with so keen a wit. The review concluded that the novel is 'a considerable achievement.' For Rupert Butler, *The Bell Jar* was 'intensely interesting,' 'brave,' 'astonishingly skillful,' 'honest,' and 'terribly likeable.'[4]

Later reviewers knew that Sylvia Plath had written *The Bell Jar*, so in commenting on the novel, they discussed both her suicide and her poems. When the novel was reissued in England under Plath's name, and finally appeared in 1971 in the United States, it was usually reviewed as being inferior to Plath's late poems. In his 1966 editorial in *Critical Quarterly* (No. 37) for example, C. B. Cox praised the novel as an 'extremely disturbing narrative' that made 'compulsive reading.' He then compared *The Bell Jar* with Plath's late poetry and concluded, 'The novel seems a first attempt to express mental states which eventually found a more appropriate form in the poetry. But throughout there is a notable honesty' and 'something of that fierce clarity so terrifying in the great poems of *Ariel*.'[5] Even though *The Bell Jar* came to take a secondary place to Plath's poetry, it was responsible for much of her reputation, especially her international reputation. Prose translates more easily than does poetry, and a readership existed for Plath's novel that only much later came to her poems. Thematically, *The Bell Jar* was accessible to women readers the world over.

There were good late reviews of the novel as well. M. L. Rosenthal, writing in the *Spectator*, spoke of the book's 'magnificant sections whose candour and revealed suffering will haunt anyone's memory.' He then introduced a theme which became a touchstone for criticism of Plath's work, that of cultural alienation—and the resulting frustration—of talented women.

Rosenthal spoke of 'the sense of having been judged and found wanting for no externally discernible reason, and the equally terrifying sense of great power gone to waste or turned against oneself.'[6] Patricia Meyer Spacks took that direction in her 1972 *Hudson Review* essay when she called *The Bell Jar* a good survey of the limited possibilities for women:

the sensibility expressed is not dismissible. The experience of the book is that of electrocution.... Female sexuality is the center of horror: babies in glass jars, women bleeding in childbirth, Esther herself thrown in the mud by a sadist, hemorrhaging after her single sexual experience. To be a woman is to bleed and burn.... Womenhood is entrapment, escaped from previously by artistic activity, escaped from surely only by death.[7]

Lucy Rosenthal, writing in the *Saturday Review*, compared *The Bell Jar* to Joan Didion's *Play It as It Lays* but pointed out that 'the Plath mode is gentler.' She praised the novel as 'a deceptively modest, uncommonly fine piece of work...in its own right a considerable achievement. It is written to a small scale, but flawlessly—an artistically uncompromising, witty account.' Juxtaposed to these reviews came Melvin Maddocks' caustic note that he found an abrupt break between the first half of the book ('Bobbsey Twins on Madison Avenue, gradually being disenchanted') and the second half, 'less a contrast than a discontinuity.' Martha Duffy, however, said in *Time* that the novel was an American best-seller because of its 'astonishing immediacy.' Simultaneous with the American reviews in the early 1970s came Tony Tanner's opinion in his *City of Words, American Fiction 1950–1970* (1971) that *The Bell Jar* was 'perhaps the most compelling and controlled account of a mental breakdown to have appeared in American fiction.' He also called it 'a very distinguished American novel.'[8]

ARIEL

While criticism of *The Bell Jar* has continued to be positive, and while it may be the work by Plath that is most read, most critics and reviewers today think of her as primarily a poet. The reviews of her major collection, *Ariel*, the book edited by Hughes and published in 1965, two years after her death, marked the beginning of her present critical reputation.

John Malcolm Brinnin, reviewing the American edition of *Ariel*, said that Plath was

a marvel.... what we have here is not, as some bewildered critics have claimed, the death rattle of a sick girl, but the defiantly fulfilling measures of a poet.... If Sylvia Plath's performance were not so securely knowledgeable, so cannily devised, so richly inventive and so meticulously reined, it would be intolerable. Many of these poems are magnificent.[9]

Samuel F. Morse, too, in *Contemporary Literature* called *Ariel* 'an absolute achievement' and Derek Parker, in the British *Poetry Review*, said, 'Criticism is disarmed, finally, by these poems... remarkable poems... immensely varied in tone.' Parker described Plath's ability to celebrate 'life and her children, in some tender, loving and laughing poems' and noted that 'one has the impression of a control so complete and natural that it never inhibits.'[10] Praise came even from comparatively staid reviewers. Richard Tillinghast (No. 29) called *Ariel* 'the most interesting new poetic development of recent years.... here nothing is wasted, everything is a diamond.' He was pleased with 'the intensity, the economy, the emphasis on originality, the ability to combine seemingly unrelated things and to separate the expected combinations'[11]—again, with Plath's craft as poet.

Yet—for all the attention to craft—there was already a strong strain of biography in criticism of Plath's work. *Ariel* was difficult to separate from the events of her life because so many of its poems seemed to speak about those events, and its production had been a part of them. At the time of her suicide, Plath had left a manuscript by the title of *Ariel* ready for publication.* Unfortunately Hughes—who was her literary executor because she died intestate—chose to omit a number of the poems Plath had chosen for the book (among those omitted 'The Detective,' 'The Jailer,' 'Purdah,' 'The Rabbit Catcher,' 'The Courage of Shutting-Up,' 'A Secret,' and others). The collection, however, contained many powerful later poems—'Daddy,' 'Lady Lazarus,' 'Ariel,' 'Elm,' 'The Applicant,' and the sequence of bee poems.

---

* Compiled in mid-November 1962, the collection earlier was titled *The Rival, The Rabbit Catcher, A Birthday Present,* and *Daddy.* Each of these titles focused on the separation, the failed marriage and possible reasons for it. In changing the focus to the spirit of Ariel, Plath was leaving some of her personal history behind, and emphasizing the power of art to transform life.

In Hughes' role as editor, he also changed the arrangement Plath had planned for the book. Her conception of *Ariel* was that it would be an affirmation. In keeping with the spirit Ariel from Shakespeare's *The Tempest*, who was freed from imprisonment in a tree because of his potential for good, the book Plath titled *Ariel* would suggest a coming to freedom for its equally androgynous poet persona. It would open with the beautiful 'Morning Song' and its first word would be 'Love.' It would close with the powerful five-poem bee sequence, making the poem 'Wintering' the last in the collection. The closing word, in that case, would have been 'Spring.'

The positioning of the bee sequence was important because that group of poems (reminiscent of Plath's 'Poem for a Birthday' sequence, which closed *The Colossus and Other Poems* in its British edition) is a masterful summation of the diverse emotional strands in her late poems—suspicion, sorrow, anger, vengeance, pride, love, self-confidence, and joy. In the group of the bee poems, the themes of self-knowledge and self-possession dominate. The endurance and wisdom of the tattered old queen bee become the speaker's ideal.

The bee poems also suggest Otto Plath, Sylvia's father, who was an entomologist who specialized in bees. She had written about her relationship with him (and his death when she was only eight) in 'The Colossus,' 'The Bee Keeper's Daughter,' 'Electra on the Azalea Path,' 'Full Fathom Five,' and 'Daddy,' many of her best poems. She also brought the father–daughter relationship to mind in her allusions to *The Tempest*, where the primary story is that of Prospero, the deposed duke of Milan, and his loving daughter Miranda. In contrast to *The Tempest*, in Plath's poems the absence of a protective father is a haunting theme.

For whatever reasons, the affirmative progression that Plath had planned for *Ariel* was destroyed in the somewhat random order Hughes gave the book. The emphases that accrued naturally from the placement of key poems, their images or themes repeated in other poems, no longer existed. Had the collection been published as Plath had intended, praise for it would have been even louder.

The importance of *Ariel* in the Plath canon cannot be over-emphasized. Even though she had been a professional writer for over a decade, she had written very little that pleased her as much as the *Ariel* poems did. After a dozen years of being a poet, a time during which she read voraciously and knew well the works of a number of poets and novelists (chief among them Dylan Thomas, Wallace Stevens, E. E. Cummings, Theodore Roethke, William Butler Yeats, Gerard Manley Hopkins, Shakespeare, John Donne, D. H. Lawrence, William Blake, W. H. Auden, Anne Sexton, Stevie Smith, and many other contemporary poets), Plath knew her craft. She had written poems in every stanza form and every rhyme pattern available; she knew what was possible in her art.

After finishing her two years of study at Cambridge, living in the United States, and then returning to England during the 1959–60 winter, she began developing her own style in poetry as well as in prose. Writing *The Bell Jar* during the spring of 1961 may have helped her find the voice that was right for her poetry—somewhat cynical, sorrowful, wry, but also incisive and truthful. At times it was a voice of raucous, not very ladylike, humor. Many of the poems that Plath wrote during 1961 and early 1962, including the long radio play *Three Women*, spoke with this voice. It had occurred only intermittently earlier in her career: 'Poem for a Birthday' had some touches of it, as did 'The Colossus' and 'Mushrooms.' By the fall of 1962, when Plath and Hughes had decided to separate, she found in her poems a means of expressing her emotions while yet creating expert and moving poems.

Plath's so-called 'October poems' number twenty-five. They include the entire bee sequence as well as 'Daddy,' 'Lady Lazarus,' 'The Detective,' 'Purdah,' 'Fever 103°,' 'The Applicant,' and others. Because she was troubled by insomnia and woke up early in the morning, Plath wrote most of these poems (which she called her dawn poems) between 4 and 7 a.m., when the children awoke. The consistent excellence of Plath's fall poems derived, of course, not from their being written early in the day, or in a single month, or after marital problems; but rather from her ability to create a poetic voice that could express the wide range of emotions she was struggling with. During the fall of 1962, Plath's life experience and art experience coalesced, and the results were poems uniquely her own. No one else had ever written poems that told such depressing narratives in macabre yet jaunty comedy. She called such poems as 'Daddy' and 'Lady Lazarus' 'light verse.' The cinematic progression from image to image, the use of unexpected rhymes, the defiant tone had little antecedent in any poetry, and might have been closer to the early plays of Arthur Kopit than to any poems

9

Plath knew. A devotee of Beckett, Camus, and Ionesco, Plath had borrowed the elliptical gallows humor of their prose and drama for her poems during what she thought of as her own 'absurd' autumn.

In mid-November of 1962 Plath arranged the manuscript she called *Ariel*. She wrote other poems during December, January, and early February, as she closed down the Devon house and moved her family into their new flat—the upper two floors of Yeats' house—in London. Those very late poems were poignant, sad, and mercilessly controlled. The anger which had flamed so brilliantly in the October poems had changed into a meditative austerity, almost impersonal in tone. Although Plath had been planning a new collection for these late poems, Hughes published a dozen of them in *Ariel*. The resulting mixture of styles and themes kept some readers from seeing the consistent development of Plath's poetry.*

THE PLATH LEGEND

So great was the critical response to the publication of *Ariel*, however, when it appeared in England in 1965 and in the United States in 1966, that a virtual Plath legend developed. It began with Alvarez's review of *Ariel* along with Robert Lowell's collection, *For the Union Dead* (No. 20), and his use of the term 'extremist art' to describe a poetry in which the poet's perceptions are pushed to the edge of breakdown. Alvarez credited Lowell with the creation of such a poetry, and saw *Ariel* as heavily influenced by Lowell's earlier poems. He spoke of Plath's poems as 'nearly all...about dying,' a somewhat misleading description, and included accounts of her 'extraordinary outburst of creative energy in the months before her death' which led to the intense last poems. According to Alvarez, Plath's art left her no direction except death. As he wrote, 'when her death finally came it was prepared for and, in some degree, understood. However wanton it seemed, it was also, in a way, inevitable, even justified, like some final unwritten poem.'[12]

* That achievement is, however, clear for the first time in the dating and arranging of Plath's work as she intended it, now available in *The Collected Poems* (New York: Harper & Row, 1981).

Even before the publication of *Ariel*, there had been much notice of Plath's last poems, published separately and in groups as they were soon after her death. In 1964, *Critical Quarterly* published an essay by C. B. Cox and A. R. Jones which announced Plath and James Baldwin as the writers to influence the future. In 'After the Tranquilized Fifties, Notes on Sylvia Plath and James Baldwin,' they created the paradigm that Plath and Baldwin were mirroring the violent chaos that life in the 1960s was, much as Eliot's *The Waste Land* had echoed his culture in the 1920s. The authors had only praise for Plath's work, and singled out her poem 'Daddy' to illustrate the way her poetry went beyond

the expression of a personal and despairing grief. The poem is committed to the view that this ethos of love/brutality is the dominant historical ethos of the last thirty years. The tortured mind of the heroine reflects the tortured mind of our age. The heroine carefully associates herself and her suffering with historical events. For instance, she identifies herself with the Jews and the atrocities of 'Dachau, Auschwitz, Belsen' and her persecutors with Fascism and the cult of violence. The poem is more than a personal statement for, by extending itself through historical images, it defines the age as schizophrenic, torn between brutality and a love which in the end can only manifest itself, today, in images of violence. This love, tormented and perverse, is essentially life-denying: the only escape is into the purifying freedom of death.

Controversy raged: A. E. Dyson had called attention to the essay and the issues in a two-page editorial that opened the number, and several letters from important critics appeared, challenging the assumptions, in a subsequent issue of *Critical Quarterly*. Plath's work, even before its appearance in *Ariel*, was of interest, compelling interest, in the world of British letters.[13]

Alvarez was not the only critic who reviewed the Robert Lowell and Sylvia Plath collections in tandem. Many readers reached the same conclusions, and used the term 'confessional' to describe the work. The comparison was encouraged because when Plath's *Ariel* was published in the United States the following year, 1966, it included a Foreword written by Lowell himself. He described Plath's poems as 'personal, confessional, felt,' although he also qualified his praise of her by saying that her tone was one of 'controlled hallucination' and was therefore impersonal. Lowell clearly understood the audacity of Plath's late technique. He admired the *Ariel* poems and wrote, 'These poems are playing

Russian roulette with six cartridges in the cylinder.'[14] In this comment, too, the implication is that the practice of such an art can be fatal.

Coupling Plath and Lowell (and W. D. Snodgrass, John Berryman, and Anne Sexton) into a 'confessional' school of poetry was a critical event of the mid-1960s that had far-reaching repercussions. M. L. Rosenthal used the term in his 1967 book, *The New Poets*, including Theodore Roethke and Allen Ginsberg in that category. The term was attacked as being imprecise and inaccurate, but it had currency for the next twenty years. Because confessional poets were said to write about the extremes of human behavior, many of them having experienced mental breakdown, and because several of these poets were women, the term 'confessional' became pejorative. It signalled the end of control, the opposite of craft. The use of the term also fed into a current of resistance that surfaced when the Lowell foreword to *Ariel* was published: that of women readers and critics who objected to the somewhat patronizing tone of the established male poet praising Plath by setting her apart from other women writers. Lowell had written that, in her amazing production, 'Sylvia Plath becomes herself, becomes something imaginary, newly, wildly and subtly created—hardly a person at all, or a woman, certainly not another "poetess."' (Erica Jong's poem 'Bitter Pills for the Dark Ladies,' which quotes Lowell's line, is an aptly famous answer to his undermining statement.)

The battle over what confessional poetry is or was, and how influential it is or was to more contemporary poetry, did not hinge entirely on the merits of Sylvia Plath's work. Her reputation developed as an integral part of this larger issue, however, and the focus in discussing Plath's work remained, for the next decade, on those personal elements in her art that so intrigued many of her readers. A. Alvarez's 1971 book, *The Savage God, A Study in Suicide*, acted as a catalyst to prompt even more attention to the personal elements in Plath's art. Published despite objections from the Hughes family, Alvarez's book presented an erstwhile biography of Plath as the driven writer, whose brilliance derived from her psychological daring in testing the known limits of a person's involvement in creativity. (Parts of this book had appeared in the special Plath issue of *Tri-Quarterly*, edited by Charles Newman and published in 1966. It was later reissued in book form by Indiana

University Press in 1970. This special issue gave much credence to the art of Plath, including many fine essays, worksheets from unpublished poems, and some of Plath's drawings.) For despite the sensational kinds of attention Plath had received since the publication of *Ariel* in the mid-sixties, there was also a strong and steady current of critical essays appearing in a variety of academic and poetry publications.

CROSSING THE WATER AND WINTER TREES

In 1971 Hughes published a second posthumous collection of Plath's late poems. *Crossing the Water* was frequently reviewed in light of the Alvarez study; to a certain extent, the third posthumous collection, *Winter Trees*, published a year later, also shared that fate. Critics seemed caught between trying to balance the invidious image of Plath the suicidal, destructive, and destroying woman with that of Plath as artist, mother, and friend.

Helen Vendler, for example, in a *New York Times Book Review* essay on *Crossing the Water*, denies that Plath is 'schizophrenic,' claiming that 'her sense of being several people at once never here goes beyond what everyone must at some time feel.' She also deals with Plath as 'confessional,' stating that the poet is never out of control. Rather,

an undeniable intellect allegorizes the issues before they are allowed expression. Even in the famous 'Daddy,' the elaborate scheme of Prussian-and-Jew has been constructed to contain the feelings of victimization, and the decade-by-decade deaths in 'Lady Lazarus' are as neat a form of incremental repetition as any metaphysical poet could have wanted.[15]

With the perspicuity of hindsight, Robin Skelton finds the poems in *Crossing the Water* 'perturbing' for their evidence of 'neurotic self-absorption.' Such sophistry as Plath evinces leads to flawed structures, Skelton finds, and so 'dangerous distortions' of philosophy. He admits that Plath writes a 'poetry of extreme verbal brilliance,' using 'imagery that is more vital and surprising than that of any other poet of her generation. . . . *Crossing the Water* goes some way towards beginning to justify the high reputation her work has already been given.'[16]

Both Victor Kramer and Linda Ray Pratt (Nos 53 and 55) stress the 'transitional' nature of the poems in this collection, a label more misleading—now that Plath's poems have been arranged in *The Collected Poems* according to her dating of them—than was guessed at the time. In reviews of both *Crossing the Water* and *Winter Trees*, critics attempted to sort out patterns, and pieces, of the Plath career. Joyce Carol Oates, for example, notes that 'it is evident that the bulk of *Winter Trees* does not constitute so finished a work as *Ariel* or *The Colossus* (No. 57). Nevertheless,' Oates continues, 'the volume is fascinating in its preoccupation with formlessness, with dissolving, with a kind of premature posthumous disappearance of the poet's personality.' Both Oates and Raymond Smith (No. 59) stress the importance of the radio play *Three Women*, partly as a major coherent piece and partly for its subject matter, the consciousness of three women in a maternity ward. Oates closes her brief review with the affirmation that Plath's poems maintain their 'existential authority': 'it seems incontestable to me that her poems, line by line, image by image, are brilliant.'[17]

James Finn Cotter, writing in *America* about the neglect of most women poets (No. 60), notices Plath's 'spiritual dimension' in poems such as 'Mystic,' 'Brasilia,' and 'Winter Trees.' He finds her 'a reflexive poet,' searching for answers that are not clichés. What negative criticism exists of these latter collections builds on the premise of Plath as demonic poet, as when Roger Scruton (No. 56) remarks that, 'In the later poetry we find no attempt to *say* anything. Images enter these later poems as particulars only, without symbolic significance, and however much the poet may borrow the emotional charge from distant and surprising sources...it is never with any hint of an intellectual aim.'[18]

Soon after the publication of *Crossing the Water* and *Winter Trees*, the cry that had been comparatively small in the late 1960s for the full publication of Plath's work grew larger. One of the most articulate voices was that of Eric Homberger who, in an important *New Statesman* essay (No. 62), gave details of the profitability of the limited editions of unpublished Plath poems, and called for a complete collected poems at once. 'Sylvia Plath means big business. Ninety thousand copies of the American edition of *The Bell Jar* were sold by Harper & Row at $6.95; the paperback edition sold one million copies between April and July of this year [1972]; and it was chosen by the Literary Guild.'[19]

LETTERS HOME

If criticism of Plath's later poems during the early 1970s could be characterized as having a sense of dutifulness—critics having to take one side or the other of the discourse about this controversial poet—the response that greeted *Letters Home by Sylvia Plath, Correspondence 1950–1963*, selected and edited with commentary by the poet's mother, Aurelia Schober Plath (1975) was revitalized by firm convictions. Critics maligned Plath's mother for her role as editor (omissions, presenting the poet as a sugary daughter who never lost her temper, trying to disguise the psychological problems that must have been apparent). In fact, critics seemed to disbelieve the Plath persona as it appeared in these hundreds of letters written from Smith College and the subsequent locations in England; and were ready to blame their own disbelief on any likely explanation. Jo Brans' remarks (No. 66) are typical of many of the reviews: 'we can learn very little of the Sylvia of the poetry, the only Sylvia in whom we can take a legitimate interest, from these letters,' 'the most consistent tone of the letters is bright insincerity, indicated by all kinds of giveaways to anyone conscious of style.' Brans also criticized Mrs Plath for her editing, although it later became clear that there were some passages that the Hugheses would not permit to be reprinted.[20]

Other reviews were more solicitous of Aurelia Plath. Martha Duffy wrote with sympathy of the life of this sacrificing mother, and even attributed Plath's suicide to her distance from Mrs Plath (No. 67). Marjorie Perloff also defends the mother figure in *The Bell Jar*, saying, 'It will not do to think of Aurelia Plath as the "Mrs. Greenwood" of *The Bell Jar*, that hopeless Polly-anna-Mother.' Perloff makes some striking points in her review, among them that Plath 'seems to be on an eternal treadmill: she *must* excel, she *must* be popular, she *must* decide. . . .' Perloff's conclusion, after reading the 400-odd letters of the book, is that 'Sylvia Plath had, in Laingian terms, no sense of identity at all.' That, for Perloff, is the reason *Letters Home* traces 'the American Dream Gone Sour,' the bright, promising person, aimed at ostensible success, who fails in the most visible, futile way possible.[21]

The publication of these letters seemed to clarify many of the lines of argument about Plath and the Plath persona in the poems, even while reviewers were arguing about 'the real Plath.' Subsequent books of criticism and essays made use of the letters; and the relative merits of studies by Mary Lynn Broe, Jon Rosenblatt, and Lynda Bundtzen (published in 1980, 1979, and 1983, respectively), when compared with those by Eileen Aird (1973), Edward Butscher (1976), and David Holbrook (1976), seem to bear out the sense that something valuable was implicit in the process of reading Plath's letters.[22]

PLATH AS WOMAN WRITER

One of the most important directions Plath criticism took after the publication of *Letters Home* in the mid-seventies was toward defining and assessing Plath as a woman writer. Such treatment gave new prominence to work such as *Three Women*, the bee sequence, and the poems about children. Given impetus by critics such as Ellen Moers, Suzanne Juhasz, Patricia Meyer Spacks, Elaine Showalter, Tillie Olsen, Sandra M. Gilbert, and Susan Gubar, the study of writing by women began to assume intelligible patterns. Gilbert and Gubar's phrase, 'the anxiety of authorship,' spoke to the difficulties women had in finding their roles as writers; Suzanne Juhasz's 'double-bind situation' suggested the mixture of aggression and passivity women writers must encompass. Carol Christ noted, 'The simple act of telling a woman's story from a woman's point of view is a revolutionary act.' When Hughes says, writing about Plath's late work, 'A real self, as we all know, is a rare thing. The direct speech of a real self is rarer still...,'[23] his praise is greater than he knows. For a woman writer to come to such validity is the rarest achievement of all.

Rather than emphasizing the angers Plath expressed late in her life, the best of this feminist criticism attempts to piece together the reasons for her angers, her skillful manipulation of art forms that could be useful to her in her newly discovered voice, and the resulting impact her art evoked on modern-day readers. To categorize her as another Richard Brautigan, immersed in the definition (or denial) of the power of death, misses the mark; as does the notion that Ernst Becker's theories of anomie rise from the holocaust of war-riddled life. Arthur Oberg, in his own posthumously published study of the contemporary lyric, described

Plath as 'perhaps a poet who lived and wrote almost before what might have been her time.'[24] There is an exciting sense of this—of a mystery not yet solved—in recent criticism on Plath's work and, perhaps more importantly, on studies of those readers who have found Plath on their own. Plath's work speaks to an audience that has mushroomed on its own, that has not been instructed in academic classrooms to read Plath (if anything, her work has been treated like that of Allen Ginsberg, as something to shy away from). We have yet to discover the multiple roots of its seemingly great appeal.

Valuable is Anne Cluysenaar's study of Plath as

a typical 'survivor' in the psychiatric sense. Her work shows many traits which are recognized as marking the psychology of those who have, in some bodily or psychic sense, survived an experience of death...extreme vulnerability to danger. As an element in this complex of emotions, imagining death has a life-enhancing function. It is an assertion of power, over death but also (less attractive but psychologically authentic) over other human beings.

Cluysenaar concludes, 'That is the crux of her message—the retention of discrimination and the will to speak, the will to communicate. Her determination not to accept relief from any ready-made dogma is admirable.'[25] This broader appeal may account for the ready acceptance of Plath in feminine circles as well.

JOHNNY PANIC AND THE BIBLE OF DREAMS

This collection of short stories, prose, and journal excerpts was published in 1977 in Britain and two years later in the United States. Again edited by Hughes, the material provided the first short fiction available to readers. It was, however, generally criticized as being apprentice work. Lorna Sage (No. 71) commented on Plath's being 'surprisingly inept at inventing structures, even ordinary plots, taking refuge instead in archaic, would-be wry, O. Henry "twists" to rescue directionless narratives.' William Dowie remarks about the 'remarkable control which is almost too tense.' Even though Douglas Hill (No. 70) finds the best of the work here as 'indelibly distinctive' as the poems, most reviews expressed disappointment.[26] It was left to Margaret Atwood, writing in the *New York Times Book Review*, to note that Plath had tried for many years to be a commercial fiction writer: 'To this end she slogged away in the utmost self-doubt and agony, composing more than 70 stories.' Atwood also points out, accurately, how incredibly hard Plath worked at her writing.

On one level 'Johnny Panic' is the record of an apprenticeship. It should bury forever the romantic notion of genius blossoming forth like flowers. Few writers of major stature can have worked so hard, for so long, with so little visible result. The breakthrough, when it came, had been laboriously earned many times over.[27]

THE COLLECTED POEMS

Published in 1981, after almost a decade of promises that such a volume would soon appear, Plath's *Collected Poems* were edited and arranged by Ted Hughes. The volume was an immediate critical and commercial success; reviews were almost uniformly positive, and the book surprisingly won the Pulitzer Prize for Poetry in 1982 (an award seldom given posthumously). The 274 poems in the volume show *why* Plath changed the direction of contemporary poetry. They prove repeatedly that a versatile structure—the poet's ability to reflect mood in every nuance of the poem, from image to single line to patterns of sound repetition—is more important than any prescriptive technique. And they show with even more surprising consistency how successful Plath was in shifting those structures, molding tone and pace and language to reflect the poem in its unique form—both tragic and comic. Called by a wide range of distinguished reviewers 'the most important collected volume of the last twenty years,' 'a triumph of hard work and artifice,' and 'the most important book of poetry this year,' *The Collected Poems* showed clearly that Plath was, indeed, 'one of the most remarkable poets of her time.' As Katha Pollitt concluded, 'by the time she came to write her last seventy or eighty poems, there was no other voice like hers on earth.'[28]

Several of the reviews echoed William H. Pritchard's *New Republic* comment, entitled, ironically, 'An Interesting Minor

Poet?' (No. 75). Pritchard acknowledges that his earlier assessment of Plath's work—until the publication of this collection—had been an endorsement of Irving Howe's 'interesting but minor' categorization. He now considers Plath truly central, 'an altogether larger and more satisfying poet' than he had thought previously: a poet to be studied and learned from, poem by poem.[29]

Just as Pritchard stresses the lessons to be learned from the poems, so Laurence Lerner (No. 74) sees Plath's work as a continuum. He points out that poems in *The Colossus* might well have been included in *Ariel* (discounting the sense of rigid separation most critics believed existed between the two collections), and that many of the *Ariel* poems are not the best-known pieces, but rather poems that 'stand back a little,' that work through

greater formality...half-rhymes and regular stanzas.... It undercuts at least one popular view of Sylvia Plath, that her early work is controlled, formal, even superficial, and the later poems make true contact with her anxieties, and so are imbued with a new power. There is some truth in this, but it should not be taken too rigidly.

Michael Hulse (No. 78) repeats this injunction, that *The Collected Poems* 'is a corrective to many myths and misunderstandings.' For Dave Smith (No. 76), writing in *American Poetry Review*, Plath's collection is a 'cranky, beautiful, maudlin, neurotic, soaring book...the record of a life.' '*The Collected Poems* is that shimmering change, a gothic fairy tale with the properties of dry ice: it keeps, it burns, it lives.' And beyond Smith's exuberant praise for the poems, when he deals with the issue of Plath's suicide, he says, accurately,

Poetry became Sylvia Plath's life. It did not kill her except where it failed her.... Poetry kept Sylvia Plath alive; her poems are ectoplasmic with the will to live, to be as right as poetry can be, to be unequivocally, seriously, perfectly the voice of the poem as magical as a heartbeat. That is a burden no poet can bear forever, and it surprises any poet who bears it at all.[30]

The widespread surprise at the excellence of this volume—the ability it had to penetrate the clichés about Plath's poetry by presenting readers with nearly 300 poems of varied and expert authority—was followed the next year by the publication, again in the United States, of her journals.

THE JOURNALS OF SYLVIA PLATH

In the spring of 1982, just a few weeks before Plath's *Collected Poems* won the Pulitzer Prize, the excerpted *Journals* were published. Many reviews of this book also mention the Pulitzer, conveying to the readers the sense of wasted promise that her journals in themselves also evinced.

For Marni Jackson (No. 80), the journals express Plath's

vulnerability: not only is the writer's love of the world here, but so is the fearful '50s woman driven to be everything to everyone .... She managed... but in her own mind she was always falling short. Her private writing is one long ache of self-recrimination.

Jackson points out, too, the bursts of 'radiant well-being,' Plath's thirst for life and experience. As Nancy Milford notes in her review, however, full self-expression as a woman is at odds with being someone's wife, and Plath's journal charts long years of her understanding that dilemma. As Milford describes the pervasive themes: 'the twin thrusts of sex and vocation, which are, unfortunately for her, linked to idealized domesticity and female dependence.' In the words of Le Anne Schreiber, Plath's 'pagan relish for life' was all but subsumed in her fears that her 'true deep voice' will never be allowed to speak. Schreiber finds that late-poem voice intermittently in the journal entries, and writes,

The irony is that the voice she was looking for... is present in these diaries from the beginning. In a raw state, to be sure. And only fitfully. But while she was looking to D. H. Lawrence, Dylan Thomas, Theodore Roethke and, of course, Mr. Hughes, and practicing a kind of ventriloquism that made her doubt her talent and even her existence, her own voice was pouring itself out in these journals.[31]

In reviewing the journals, too, several critics stress the apprenticeship Plath served as writer, and Walter Clemons finds that emphasis one of the most important of the book.

The revelation of how unremittingly she works makes this a book I recommend to any aspiring writer, particularly to a novice who thinks of Plath as a special case—a star clothed in the glamour of suicide... the journals help us appreciate the protracted, hard-working apprenticeship that led to her final blazing utterance.[32]

While it is unfair to assess the hundreds of critical reviews and essays, not to mention numerous books, as 'transitional,' tentative, revealing only the impression Plath's work evoked at certain times in the past thirty years, still the body of criticism that now exists does have that flavor. There is a tone of hesitancy about even the surest pronouncements; there is still some mystery about the Plath *oeuvre*. And rightly. Her journals of the last three years of her life are not available. Several collections of materials are housed in the Smith Library Plath collection, sealed until either the year 2013 or the years of the deaths of both her mother and her younger brother. Plath's last novel, titled *Double Exposure*, has never been found, though 130 pages of it—at least—were known to exist at the time of her death. One cannot be sure that all the poems have been published, although there is no immediate reason to believe that they have not been included in *The Collected Poems*. There is good reason, consequently, to feel that the materials Plath wrote are yet incomplete, and that a full and just assessment of her work would be impossible at the present time.

NOTES

1 Peter Dickinson, 'Some Poets,' *Punch*, 239 (7 December 1960), p. 829; Bernard Bergonzi, 'The Ransom Note,' *Manchester Guardian* (25 November 1960), p. 9; John Wain, 'Farewell to the World,' *Spectator*, 206 (13 January 1961), p. 50; and Roy Fuller, review, *London Magazine*, 8 (March 1961), pp. 69–70.

2 A. Alvarez, 'The Poet and the Poetess,' *Observer* (18 December 1960), p. 12.

3 William Dickey, 'Responsibilities,' *Kenyon Review*, 24 (Autumn 1962), pp. 756–64; Reed Whittemore, '*The Colossus and Other Poems*,' *Carleton Miscellany*, 3 (Fall 1962), p. 89; E. Lucas Myers, 'The Tranquilized Fifties,' *Sewanee Review*, 70 (January-March 1962), pp. 212–20; M. L. Rosenthal, 'Metamorphosis of a Book,' *Spectator*, 218 (21 April 1967), pp. 456–7.

4 Robert Taubman, 'Anti-heroes,' *New Statesman*, 65 (25 January 1963), pp. 127–8; Laurence Lerner, 'New Novels,' *Listener*, 69 (31 January 1963), p. 215; 'Under the Skin,' *Times Literary Supplement* (25 January 1963), p. 53; Rupert Butler, 'New American Fiction: Three Disappointing Novels—But One Good One,' *Time and Tide*, 44 (31 January 1963), p. 34.

5 C. B. Cox, 'Editorial,' *Critical Quarterly*, 8 (Autumn 1966), p. 195.

6 M. L. Rosenthal, 'Blood and Plunder,' *Spectator*, 217 (30 September 1966), p. 418.

7 Patricia Meyer Spacks, 'A Chronicle of Women,' *Hudson Review*, 25 (Spring 1972), pp. 157–70.

8 Lucy Rosenthal, '*The Bell Jar*,' *Saturday Review*, 54 (24 April 1971), p. 42; Melvin Maddocks, 'A Vacuum Abhorred,' *Christian Science Monitor* (15 April 1971), p. 11; Martha Duffy, 'Lady Lazarus,' *Time*, 97 (21 June 1971), pp. K7–K9; Tony Tanner, *City of Words, American Fiction 1951–1970* (London: Jonathan Cape, 1971).

9 John Malcolm Brinnin, 'Plath, Jarrell, Kinnell, Smith,' *Partisan Review*, 34 (Winter 1967), pp. 156–60.

10 Samuel F. Morse, 'Poetry 1966,' *Contemporary Literature*, 9 (Winter 1968), pp. 112–29; Derek Parker, '*Ariel*, Indeed,' *Poetry Review*, 56 (Summer 1965), pp. 118–20.

11 Richard Tillinghast, 'Worlds of Their Own,' *Southern Review*, 5 (Spring 1969), pp. 582–96.

12 A. Alvarez, 'Poetry in Extremis,' *Observer* (14 March 1965), p. 26.

13 C. B. Cox and A. R. Jones, 'After the Tranquilized Fifties,' *Critical Quarterly*, 6 (Summer 1964), pp. 107–22; A. E. Dyson, 'Editorial,' *Critical Quarterly*, 6 (Summer 1964), pp. 99–100. *Critical Quarterly*, 7 (Autumn 1964), pp. 276–7.

14 Robert Lowell, 'Foreword' to Sylvia Plath's *Ariel* (New York: Harper & Row, 1966), pp. vii–ix.

15 Helen Vendler, '*Crossing the Water*,' *New York Times Book Review* (10 October 1971), pp. 4, 48.

16 Robin Skelton, 'Poetry,' *Malahat Review*, 20 (October 1971), pp. 137–8.

17 For the best assessment of the misdating of Plath's poems, see Marjorie Perloff, 'On the Road to *Ariel*: The "Transitional" Poetry of Sylvia Plath,' *Iowa Review*, 4 (Spring 1973), pp. 94–110. Victor Kramer, 'Life-and-Death Dialectics,' *Modern Poetry Studies*, 3 (1972), pp. 40–2; Linda Ray Pratt, '"The Spirit of Blackness is in Us...,"' *Prairie Schooner*, 67 (Spring 1973), pp. 87–90; Raymond Smith, 'Late Harvest,' *Modern Poetry Studies*, 3 (1972), pp. 91–3; Joyce Carol Oates, '*Winter Trees*,' *Library Journal*, 97 (1 November 1972), p. 3595.

18 James Finn Cotter, 'Women Poets: Malign Neglect?' *America*, 128 (17 February 1973), p. 140; Roger Scruton, 'Sylvia Plath and the Savage God,' *Spectator*, 227 (18 December 1971), p. 890.

19 Eric Homberger, 'The Uncollected Plath,' *New Statesman* (22 September 1972), pp. 404–5.

20 Jo Brans, '"The Girl Who Wanted to be God,"' *Southwest Review*, 61 (Summer 1976), p. 325.

21 Martha Duffy, 'Two Lives,' *Time*, 106 (24 November 1975), pp.

101–2; Marjorie Perloff, 'Review of *Letters Home*,' *Resources for American Literary Study*, 7 (Spring 1977), pp. 77–85.

22 Jon Rosenblatt, *Sylvia Plath, The Poetry of Initiation* (Chapel Hill: University of North Carolina Press, 1979); Mary Lynn Broe, *Protean Poetic, The Poetry of Sylvia Plath* (Columbia: University of Missouri Press, 1980); and Linda Bundtzen, *Plath's Incarnations, Woman and the Creative Process* (Ann Arbor: University of Michigan Press, 1983). Other useful books are Nancy Hunter Steiner, *A Closer Look at Ariel: A Memory of Sylvia Plath* (New York: Harper's Magazine Press, 1973); Judith Kroll, *Chapters in a Mythology, The Poetry of Sylvia Plath* (New York: Harper & Row, 1976); two bibliographies, Thomas P. Walsh and Cameron Northouse, *Sylvia Plath and Anne Sexton: A Reference Guide* (Boston, Mass.: G. K. Hall, 1974) and Gary Lane and Maria Stevens, *Sylvia Plath: A Bibliography* (Metuchen, NJ: Scarecrow Press, 1978); and five collections of essays, that from 1970 edited by Charles Newman; another from 1977 edited by Edward Butscher (*Sylvia Plath, The Woman and the Work*, New York: Dodd, Mead, & Co.); from 1979, Gary Lane, ed., *Sylvia Plath, New Views on the Poetry* (Baltimore, Md.: Johns Hopkins University Press); in 1984, *Critical Essays on Sylvia Plath*, ed. Linda W. Wagner (Boston, Mass.: G. K. Hall), and *Ariel Ascending, Writings about Sylvia Plath*, ed. Paul Alexander (New York: Harper & Row, 1984).

23 Sandra M. Gilbert and Susan Gubar, *Madwoman in the Attic* (New Haven, Conn.: Yale University Press, 1979) and their introduction to *Shakespeare's Sisters, Feminist Essays on Women Poets* (Bloomington: Indiana University Press, 1979); Suzanne Juhasz, *Naked and Fiery Forms, Modern American Poetry by Women: A New Tradition* (New York: Harper Colophon, 1976); Carol Christ, *Diving Deep and Surfacing, Women Writers on Spiritual Quest* (Boston, Mass.: Beacon Press, 1980); Elaine Showalter, *A Literature of Their Own* (Princeton, NJ: Princeton University Press, 1977); Tillie Olsen, *Silences* (New York: Delacorte Press/Seymour Laurence, 1978); Patricia Meyer Spacks, *The Female Imagination* (New York: Alfred A. Knopf, 1975); and Ellen Moers, *Literary Women* (Garden City, New York: Doubleday, 1976). Ted Hughes' comment appears in the 'Foreword' to *The Journals of Sylvia Plath, 1950–1962*, ed. Frances McCullough and Ted Hughes (New York: Dial Press, 1982), p. xii.

24 Arthur Oberg, *Modern American Lyric—Lowell, Berryman, Creeley, and Plath* (New Brunswick, NJ: Rutgers University Press, 1978), p. 177.

25 Anne Cluysenaar, 'Post-culture: Pre-culture?' in *British Poetry Since 1960: A Critical Survey*, ed. Michael Schmidt and Grevel Lindop (Oxford, England: Carcanet Press, 1972), pp. 219–21.

26 Lorna Sage, 'Death and Marriage,' *Times Literary Supplement* (21

October 1977), p. 1235; William Dowie, 'A Season of Alarums and Excursions: "Johnny Panic and the Bible of Dreams,"' *America*, 140 (3 March 1979), p. 165; Douglas Hill, 'Living and Dying,' *Canadian Forum*, 58 (June 1978), pp. 323–4.

27 Margaret Atwood, 'Poet's Prose,' *New York Times Book Review* (28 January 1979), pp. 10, 31.

28 Michael Hulse, 'Formal Bleeding,' *Spectator*, 247 (14 November 1981), p. 20; John Bayley, 'Games with Death and Co.,' *New Statesman*, 102 (2 October 1981), p. 19; Laurence Lerner, 'Sylvia Plath,' *Encounter*, 58 (January 1982), p. 53; Katha Pollitt, 'A Note of Triumph,' *Nation*, 234 (16 January 1982), p. 54.

29 William H. Pritchard, 'An Interesting Minor Poet?' *New Republic*, 185 (30 December 1981), pp. 32–5.

30 Dave Smith, 'Sylvia Plath, The Electric Horse,' from 'Some Recent American Poetry: Come All Ye Fair and Tender Ladies,' *American Poetry Review*, 11 (January 1982), p. 46.

31 Marni Jackson, 'In Search of the Shape Within,' *Maclean's Magazine*, 95 (17 May 1982), p. 57; Nancy Milford, '*The Journals of Sylvia Plath*,' *New York Times Book Review* (2 May 1982), pp. 30–2; Le Anne Schreiber, '*The Journals of Sylvia Plath*,' *New York Times* (21 April 1982).

32 Walter Clemons, 'A Poet's Rage for Perfection,' *Newsweek*, 99 (3 May 1982), p. 77.

Abbreviations

CP *The Collected Poems of Sylvia Plath*, New York and London, 1981

J *The Journals of Sylvia Plath*, New York, 1982

LH *Letters Home by Sylvia Plath, Correspondence, 1950–1963*, ed. Aurelia Schober Plath, New York and London, 1975

Note on the Text

Save for some silent corrections, texts are printed verbatim. Deletions are marked by the use of ellipsis or indicated with square brackets. Original notes are numbered 1, 2, 3 etc. Editorial notes are indicated with asterisks.

MEETING SYLVIA PLATH

1. Elinor Klein

Taken from 'A Friend Recalls Sylvia Plath,' *Glamour* (November 1966), p. 168.

Elinor Friedman Klein, a friend of Sylvia's from Smith College, visited Plath in England and throughout the remaining years of her life. They met in the fall of 1954.

The first time I met Sylvia Plath, I remember thinking ungenerously, 'It's too much. She's pretty too!' Admiring her work and her easy brilliance, I automatically assumed that such genius would have the grace to take a clichéd form—the shy, spectacled, unattractive kid in the corner clutching her Dostoevski for dear life. But Sylvia was lovely, willowy-lithe with great soft dark eyes, wide laughing mouth and a tumble of light hair....

The first afternoon we spent together, perhaps to dispel any worshipful attitudes I might hold about her being a much-heralded 'published writer,' she showed me her rejection slips. 'I've got hundreds,' she said. 'They make me proud of myself. They show me I try.' That afternoon was the first of many glorious afternoons we shared, talking nonstop until twilight. Sylvia was not only brilliant, incisive and perceptive, she was funny. Her sense of humor, unique and effortless, bubbled around her.... Even our most serious conversations were invariably punctuated with laughter. It seems apparent to me, reading her posthumous poems, that she did not lose that humor.

2. Jane Baltzell Kopp

Excerpted from ' "Gone, Very Gone Youth," ' in *Sylvia Plath, The Woman and the Work*, ed. Edward Butscher (New York: Dodd, Mead, 1977), pp. 62–3.

Jane Baltzell Kopp (b. 1935) was also studying at Cambridge in 1955 when Plath began her two-year Fulbright stay there. She received a PhD from the University of California at Berkeley in 1965 and has had an academic career, specializing in medieval literature and narrative.

...she was ambitious in many directions, and she rarely did anything without striving (I choose the word with care) to excel. During the first year I knew her she variously pursued horseback riding, sketching, and amateur dramatics, as well as, always, poetry. Every one of these things she did *hard*, not so much giving herself pleasure as somehow trying (so it seemed) to satisfy someone very difficult to please. The variety of the things she concerned herself with meant that her activity tended to be disintegral; yet when I think back now, it was as though her momentum was somehow along a vector into space, as though she was frantically trying to 'get somewhere' in an almost literal sense. One vivid memory I have, a sight I must have seen a thousand times, is of Sylvia riding a bicycle. She was 'goal oriented,' to say the least, and would peddle vehemently, head and shoulders straining forward, as though pure will power rather than her legs propelled her. She rode, say, like a passionate little girl.

3. Irene V. Morris

Excerpted from 'Sylvia Plath at Newnham, A Tutorial Recollection,' *Newnham College Roll Letter* (1975).

I. V. Morris, who is now retired, was Sylvia's tutor while she was a student at Newnham College, Cambridge, and has written warmly of her American student.

...throughout her two years at Newnham Sylvia gave every indication of being happy and of coping successfully with her life and work. In fact in retrospect she seemed to me to be almost too happy, even ecstatic, but at the time I thought she was just being more 'American' than usual in her capacity for enthusiastic reactions. I can recall a specific instance: it was my practice soon after the academic year had begun and when the new students had time to settle in to go over to Whitstead one morning and have breakfast there...; I would also call on the individual students and see if they were happily settled. There were ten or eleven rooms in Whitstead and Sylvia had one of the smaller ones at the top of the house; rather pretty and picturesque with a slanting roof, dormer window and window seat and a fine view over the Whitstead garden and the broad expanse of the College grounds. She expressed her delight in the room and particularly in the window seat where she would sit and write poems, she told me; I was a bit surprised and touched at the intensity of her delight. I asked about her poems and writing, but I did not register the fact particularly: so many students write poems and want to be writers, and Sylvia seemed to be so youthfully and touchingly enthusiastic. This is the impression she made on me of being very young and spontaneous in her reactions, even somewhat naive and over-emotional. She also struck me as possessing a unique gentleness and charm....

4. Christopher Levenson

From a letter to Linda W. Wagner, 27 October 1984.

Christopher Levenson (b. 1934) was editor of the influential magazine *Delta* when Plath was a student in England. He is currently Professor of English at Carleton University, Ottawa, Canada.

My main impression remains one of a combination of intensity and sophistication. For me at least she came across as a strong, confident, experienced young woman: I remember her on one occasion describing driving through, or very close to, a tornado. I remember the vividness and intensity of her gestures and eyes, the way certain words, like the word 'strong' itself, were elongated to our English ears, almost physically savoured in the telling. I think she must have been aware of the sense of power, and of a larger, less controllable world, that she projected...in her personal appearance it is her well-groomed appearance, sleek hair, an air of affluence (by our mid fifties standards at least) and of ease, that I recall...at the time she struck me at least almost as a golden girl, gifted and poised, energetic, serious and intent.

5. Anne Sexton

From Sexton's essay about Plath, 'The Barfly Ought To Sing,' in *The Art of Sylvia Plath, A Symposium*, ed. Charles Newman (Bloomington: Indiana University Press, 1970), p. 177.

Anne Sexton (1928–74) won a Pulitzer Prize in 1963 for her collection of poems *All My Pretty Ones*. She published more than a dozen books before her death in 1974. She and Plath were friends during the spring of 1959, when they both sat in Robert Lowell's poetry workshop at Boston University.

I have heard since that Sylvia was determined from childhood to be great, a great writer at the least of it. I tell you, at the time I did not notice this in her. Something told me to bet on her but I never asked it why. I was too determined to bet on myself to actually notice where she was headed in her work. Lowell said, at the time, that he liked her work and that he felt her poems got right to the point. I didn't agree. I felt they really missed the whole point. (These were early poems of hers—poems on the way, on the working toward way.) I told Mr. Lowell that I felt she dodged the point and did so perhaps because of her preoccupation with form. Form was important for Sylvia and each really good poet has one of his own. No matter what he calls it—free verse or what. Still, it belongs to you or it doesn't. Sylvia hadn't then found a form that belonged to her. Those early poems were all in a cage (and not even her own cage at that). I felt she hadn't found a voice of her own, wasn't, in truth, free to be herself. Yet, of course, I knew she was skilled—intense, skilled, perceptive, strange, blonde, lovely, Sylvia.

THE COLOSSUS AND OTHER POEMS

London, October 1960

---

6. Bernard Bergonzi, 'The Ransom Note,' *Manchester Guardian*

25 November 1960, 9

Bernard Bergonzi (b. 1929) is an MA Oxford graduate. A leading 'Movement' poet and critic, he teaches now at the University of Warwick.

As a rule the work of women poets is marked by intensity of feeling and fineness of perception rather than by outstanding technical accomplishment. Miss Sylvia Plath is, however, a young American poetess whose work is most immediately noticeable for the virtuoso qualities of its style. In *The Colossus*, which is her first collection of poems, she writes with a degree of assurance that would be rare in her contemporaries of either sex on this side of the Atlantic. It is evident that she has learnt a good deal from such poets as John Crowe Ransom and Theodore Roethke, yet their influence is assimilated to Miss Plath's highly personal tone and way of looking at the world. She writes of people or natural objects in a detached yet sympathetic way, with a fastidious vocabulary and a delicate feeling for the placing of the individual word. Here is the first stanza of 'Spinster,' one of her most successful poems:

> Now this particular girl
> During a ceremonious April walk
> With her latest suitor
> Found herself, of a sudden,
>   intolerably struck
> By the birds' irregular babel
> And the leaves' litter.

The Ransom note is apparent; yet he is a profitable master. Miss

Plath also has a number of odd but convincing poems about lower forms of natural life, animal or vegetable. 'Mushrooms' is an admirable piece on an unpromising subject, and 'Frog Autumn' is exquisitely poignant:

[Quotes stanzas 1 and 3, *CP*, p. 99.]

I read this collection with considerable pleasure, and I can happily recommend it to those inquiring spirits who demand at intervals if there are any new poets worth reading nowadays.

7. John Wain, 'Farewell to the World,' *Spectator*

13 January 1961, 50

John Wain (b. 1925) is a poet, novelist, and critic, who writes widely about British and American literature, especially modernist and contemporary writing.

Sylvia Plath writes clever, vivacious poetry, which will be enjoyed most by intelligent people capable of having fun with poetry and not just being holy about it. Miss Plath writes from phrase to phrase as well as with an eye on the larger architecture of the poem; each line, each sentence, is put together with a good deal of care for the springy rhythm, the arresting image and—most of all, perhaps—the unusual word. This policy ought to produce quaint, over-gnarled writing, but in fact Miss Plath has a firm enough touch to keep clear of these faults. Here and there one finds traces of 'influences' not yet completely assimilated ('Snakecharmer,' for instance, is too like Wallace Stevens for comfort, and the sequence 'Poem For a Birthday' testifies too flatly to an admiration for Theodore Roethke), but, after all, this is a first book, and the surprising thing is how successful Miss Plath has already been in finding an individual manner.

8. A. Alvarez, 'The Poet and the Poetess,' *Observer*

18 December 1960, 12

A(lfred) Alvarez (b. 1929) is a novelist, poet, and critic, who wrote accurately about Plath's poetry during her lifetime and after. He accepted many of her poems for publication in the *Observer* during the early 1960s, and wrote about her lifetime as an artist in *The Savage God, A Study of Suicide*.

Sylvia Plath's *The Colossus* needs none of the usual throat-clearing qualifications, to wit: 'impressive, considering, of course, it is a *first* volume by a *young* (excuse me), *American* poet*ess*.' Miss Plath neither asks excuses for her work nor offers them. She steers clear of feminine charm, deliciousness, gentility, supersensitivity and the act of being a poetess. She simply writes good poetry. And she does so with a seriousness that demands only that she be judged equally seriously. She makes this plain in the first stanza of her first poem:

> The fountains are dry and the roses are over.
> Incense of death. Your day approaches.
> The pears fatten like little buddhas.
> A blue mist is dragging the lake.

There is an admirable no-nonsense air about this; the language is bare but vivid and precise, with a concentration that implies a good deal of disturbance with proportionately little fuss.

I think Miss Plath can allow herself this undemonstrativeness because most of her poems rest secure in a mass of experience that is never quite brought out into daylight:—

> ...the students stroll or sit,
> Hands laced, in a moony indolence of love—
> Black-gowned but unaware
> How in such mild air
> The owl shall stoop from his turret,
> the rat cry out.

34

It is this sense of threat, as though she were continually menaced by something she could see only out of the corners of her eyes, that gives her work its distinction.

She is not, of course, unwaveringly good. At times her feeling weakens, the language goes off on its own and she lands in blaring rhetoric. At other times she hovers close to the whimsy of fairy stories. But here her tense and twisted language preserves her and she ends with something ominous, odd, like one of the original tales from Grimm. But it would be a strange first book that had no faults; *The Colossus* has more than enough excellent poems to compensate for them.

9. Roy Fuller, review, *London Magazine*

March 1961, 69–70

Roy Fuller (b. 1912), an English poet and Professor of Poetry at Oxford for a term of three years, was educated at Blackpool High School. His *Collected Poems* appeared in 1962.

Miss Plath is a young American poet who was at Cambridge and is married to a Yorkshireman, and English subjects—Grantchester, Hardcastle Crags—fit as naturally into her verse as American ones. But her sensibility is wholly transatlantic—her sensibility and poise, and the cool connoisseur's acceptance of experience which nevertheless does not preclude a tenderness of feeling that in a lesser poet might become sentimental:

> Soft fists insist on
> Heaving the needles,
> The leafy bedding,
>
> Even the paving.
> Our hammers, our rams,
> Earless and eyeless,
>
> Perfectly voiceless,
> Widen the crannies,
> Shoulder through holes...

('Mushrooms')

The language of this poetry is unusual but not eccentric, with a great gift for the right epithet, the metaphoric noun. The following examples come from an excellent poem called 'The Ghost's Leave-taking': 'sulphurous dreamscapes', 'meat-and-potato thoughts', 'rocky gizzard of the earth', 'crisp cusp' (of the moon). Miss Plath's descriptive power is brilliant, too. But the strongest impression these poems leave is of cleverness, a quality that I for one admire inordinately, and which gives the book its extraordinary enjoyableness. And yet it is this aspect of the verse that prompts a slight unease. How excited we would be about Miss Plath if we—and she—had never read Mr Ransom and Miss Moore. Or if she were 23 and not 28. No experience seems, as yet, to have drawn out other than this controlled and rather ventriloquial voice: too many poems have no other point than their own skill. For all the strangeness and power, the book exudes taste—taste in the tradition that puts a good poet in an academic sinecure.

Perhaps these are too cautious reservations. Certainly even when one is not enamoured of Miss Plath's subject or approach one must admire the choice of metre, the stanza organization, the complex but beautifully clear syntax. Even her half rhymes grow on one and she makes one see that full rhymes would not do for her. And though the themes of these poems are the traditional deep ones of poetry—time, death and the curiousness of the physical world— the poet is always well in control. Possibly too well. If Miss Plath can let things slip a bit without gushing her next book may remove all one's doubts.

10. A. E. Dyson, review, *Critical Quarterly*

Summer 1961, 181–5

A(nthony) E(dward) Dyson (b. 1929) is a poet and critic who, with C. B. Cox, edited *Critical Quarterly* for much of its twenty-six-year history.

It is true, but not especially important, to notice that Sylvia Plath is influenced by Theodore Roethke and by Ted Hughes; what is more to the point is that on the evidence of these poems she has to be mentioned in the same breath with them. *The Colossus* is a volume that those who care for literature will wish to buy, and return to from time to time for that deepening acquaintance which is one of the rewards of the truest poetry. It established Miss Plath among the best of the poets now claiming our attention: the most compelling feminine voice certainly, that we have heard for many a day.

The title poem is as significant as we now expect title poems to be; a sense of the huge and the continuing dominates Sylvia Plath's sensibility. But the grandeur of nature oppresses as well as impresses her; apprehensions of lurking menace, more likely to test our endurance than our joy, are seldom far below the surface. In 'Hardcastle Crags' the young woman who walks by night through a bleak landscape is offered nothing, unless it be the action of putting flesh and blood against the iron of the universe itself.

> All the night gave her, in return
> For the paltry gift of her bulk and the beat
> Of her heart was the humped indifferent iron
> Of its hills, and its pastures bordered by black stone set.

In battling with the encroachments of rock, wind, the sea which is 'brutal endlessly,' a temporary, almost humdrum heroism may be earned, as poems like 'Point Shirley' and 'The Hermit at Outermost House' suggest; but Nature outlasts man, and wins again in the end.

> A labour of love, and that labour lost.
> Steadily the sea
> Eats at Point Shirley.

When Miss Plath encounters a landscape that has been tamed and reduced by man, she feels it as a type of trifling. Walking in Grantchester Meadows, the very touchstone of English, and *a fortiori* Cambridge nostalgia, she notes that 'Nothing is big or far.' The birds are 'thumb-size,' the cygnets 'tame,' the Granta 'bland,' the water rat 'droll.' Even the students, lost in a 'moony indolence of love,' are unmenaced and therefore somewhat unreal. 'It is a country on a nursery plate,' a pretty place, but Sylvia Plath is more at home when she senses behind Nature its naked inhospitality to man.

Wind and sea are only the more natural of the forces she detects waiting to better and supplant the human race, or patiently take over when it is gone. In 'Ouija' there is an eerie evocation of 'those unborn, those undone' as they crowd into the seance room, drawn to the living by envy

> Imagine their deep hunger, deep as the dark
> For the blood-heat that would ruddle or reclaim.

In 'The Thin People' the threat comes from devitalised humanity itself; from those who in Blake's words 'restrain Desire... because theirs is weak enough to be restrained,' and who having resisted energy, put the 'Giants who formed this world into its sensual existence' in chains. Sylvia Plath sees the thin folk as a menace, as Blake does, but she fears too 'their talent to persevere/In thinness, to come, later, / Into our bad dreams.' In 'Mushrooms,' the quality of menace is even more chillingly detected in the sinister, almost cancerous proliferation of fungus. This macabrely ironic vision of a form of life infinitely lower than man simply waiting in endless patience to 'Inherit the earth' has the vividness of science fiction at its best, without being in the least sensational. (The associations which the word 'mushroom' have for us since Hiroshima may enhance the effectiveness, which is not, however, dependent upon them.) In 'Sculptor,' by a further surprising stroke, the forms the sculptor is about to create are felt as bodiless realities waiting to use him for incarnation, after which they will both dwarf and outlast him

> His chisel bequeathes
> Them life livelier than ours.

The theme sounds again in 'Frog Autumn,' and in the longer 'Mussel Hunter at Rock Harbour.' Perhaps the most remarkable variation, however, is in 'All The Dead Dears,' a poem which starts, as a note informs us, from the Archeological Museum in Cambridge, where there is 'a stone coffin of the fourth century A.D. containing the skeletons of a woman, a mouse and a shrew. The ankle-bone of the woman has been slightly gnawn.' From the stark statement

> These three, unmasked now, bear
> Dry witness
> To the gross eating game

the poet goes on to sense, in the long dead, a host waiting to revisit the living in memories, and later claim them to itself. There is first the suggestion of vampirish affinity between dead and living

> How they grip us through thick and thin,
> These barnacle dead!
> This lady here's no kin
> Of mine, yet kin she is: she'll suck
> Blood and whistle my marrow clean
> To prove it...

and then this inexorable community is still more strikingly explored, in a manner that reminds us again of 'Ouija' and 'Mushrooms,' whilst perhaps reaching even nearer to the heart of the thematic menace

> All the long gone darlings: they
> Get back, though, soon,
> Soon: be it by wakes, weddings,
> Childbirths or a family barbecue:
> Any touch, taste, tang's
> Fit for those outlaws to ride home on,
>
> And to sanctuary: usurping the armchair
> Between tick
> And tack of the clock, until we go,
> Each skulled-and-crossboned Gulliver
> Riddled with ghosts, to lie
> Deadlocked with them, taking root as cradles rock.

The affinity which Sylvia Plath feels with the dead and the alien is not unlike a type of pity; a conviction of kinship with everything that lives or has lived, however inaccessible or sinister. Her feeling for the animal world is similar in kind, not only in 'Frog Autumn' and 'Mussel Hunter at Rock Harbour,' but in one of the most moving of the poems, 'Blue Moles.' And the same may be said of her feeling for human outcasts, in 'The Beggars' for instance, a poem published in the *Critical Quarterly*, but unaccountably omitted from this volume.

One further theme running through Sylvia Plath's poems is her occasional sense of being teased by glimpses of better worlds, also lurking just beyond the surfaces of things, but this time in the realm of fantasy rather than fact. Syren voices from under water, at Lorelei,

> sing
> Of a world more full and clear
> Than can be...

The 'lost otherworld' of dreams presents itself like 'hieroglyphic/of some godly utterance,' yet the sleeper 'merely by waking up' comes to know its lack of substance. In the fine early poem 'Black Rook In Rainy Weather' Sylvia Plath reflects, half philosophically, half ironically on the nature of her own poetic gift. She does not expect 'miracles,' but nonetheless 'a certain minor light' might still at times shine out, transfiguring the everyday world in a manner

> to seize my sense, haul
> My eyelids up, and grant
> A brief respite from fear
> Of total neutrality.

Continuing the logic of this she moves, consciously and delicately tentative, to a limited claim for poetry itself

> With luck,
> Trekking stubborn through the seasons
> Of fatigue, I shall
> Patch together a content
>
> Of sorts. Miracles occur,
> If you care to call those spasmodic
> Tricks of radiance miracles.

The differences between this sensibility, and that of Ted Hughes, scarcely need underlining, even after so brief a survey. There are, one admits, similarities—forceful narrative skill; verbal precision of high order; effective use of homely events and observations as taut but unstrained allegory; several poems, about animals, and so on. But the sensibility itself is different. Ted Hughes is heroic and violent in his dominating mood, Sylvia Plath brooding and tentative. Their gods are also different. Ted Hughes's is the god of the tiger, Sylvia Plath's 'a chilly god, a god of shades.' He is Neptune, the inscrutable Father of the endlessly brutal sea, an alien

and useless deity, whom she half believes in, half worships. He
defies questions, defies other godhood, yet still she can call him
'Father.' The application of this supremely religious word to a god
so far removed from the personal or the approachable, so
intermingled with hallucination and conjecture—an application
ironic in overtones, yet wholly serious and central to Miss Plath's
sense of life—is very profoundly characteristic of this fine body of
work.

11. Unsigned review, *Times Literary Supplement*

18 August 1961, 550

Miss Plath is a much more variously ambitious poet.... She has a
real gift for creating images which are at once sensuously vivid and
dramatically disturbing:

> As the gods began one world, and man another,
> So the snakecharmer begins a snaky sphere
> With moon-eye, mouth-pipe. He pipes. Pipes green.
> Pipes water.

The difficulty in this vivid poem, in which water is turned to
snakes, snakes into trees and people, and then back into water
again, is to know how deep the meaning is meant to be. Is the
poem just a fantasy based, say, on the snakiness of the movement
of water or the shapes of branches? Miss Plath tends to be elusive
and private in this way, as if what the poem were 'about' in a prose
sense were very much her own business. Thus this first volume is a
stimulating one but also, combining as it does fine surface clarities
with a deeper riddling quality, it is a teasing one. Here certainly,
however, is a talent.

THE COLOSSUS AND OTHER POEMS

New York, 1962

12. E. Lucas Myers, 'The Tranquilized Fifties,' *Sewanee Review*

January–March 1962, 212–13, 216

E. Lucas Myers was a close friend of Ted Hughes during the mid-fifties in Cambridge. He came to know Sylvia Plath through her marriage to Hughes, and wrote frequently for the *Sewanee Review* once he and his wife had returned to live in the United States. Poet and critic.

The poets who first appeared during the fifties have some distinction: the best of them write with technical skill, intelligence, and resourcefulness. Yet a stack of their books, read through, leaves a sense of dissatisfaction, just as living through the decade did, especially in those whose minds were still being formed. What fails to emerge is a statement, in some measure coherent, of the experience of a decade, such as can be made out from the poetry of the twenties or the thirties. (The beat writers essay something like this, of course—it is symptomatic of the temper of the decade that more accomplished ones do not.) The young poets, in fact, share a conceptual framework handed down almost unmodified from the twenties and thirties, which can not serve them as well as it served their predecessors; beyond that, no important relations can be established among the worlds they evoke, and, more often than not, the world of the individual practitioner is itself without substantial unity of thought or attitude. No confluences of new ideas which would sweep things along in one direction appear. It was a time for spinning from the belly, not of cross-fertilization or mutual aid in growth. There are a great many poems (especially from the British) about incidentals of daily life, completed by the metaphysical or psychological observations they occasion, and a

42

great many more (especially from Americans) about Rome, Florence, Granada, etc., seen through expatriates' or tourists' eyes, and similarly completed. Neither topic delivers many of the poems to generally significant ground; they tend to remain private. Many poets seem to feel that further protest against the state of our sensibility is pointless, and aim to write as positively as possible, but the search for renewal of passion too often follows a long cerebral detour and issues in verse with an unmistakable dryness and air of fatigue about it, and a mechanical quality in the motions of its sense. Curiously enough, in some of the most telling performances, one feels that the poet is experientially or psychologically detached from what he or she is writing about....

There is not an imperfectly finished poem in Sylvia Plath's book. She is impressive for control of form and tone, appropriateness of rhythmic variation within the poem, and vocabulary and observation which are often surprising, and always accurate: 'The waves' / Spewed relics clicker masses in the wind,' or (the place is a laboratory), 'In their jars the snail-nosed babies moon and glow.' 'Poem for a Birthday,' in seven parts, concludes the volume, and catalogues the sensation of pregnancy in rich images altogether astonishing to the mere male, even though he may have heard described the parti-colored dreams of pregnant women. In 'Metaphors,' a shorter (nine-line) but equally engaging poem about pregnancy, she is 'a melon strolling on two tendrils,' has 'boarded the train there's no getting off.' I am struck, in reading a lot of her poems together, by her posture *vis-à-vis* her material, which is one of considerable objectivity, even when the material is her childhood, her Muses, her pregnancy. The focus of the emotions, like the visual focus, is sharp and is found at medium distance or more, the perspective in which we see her spinster, her strumpet, her suicide, the perspective which, in the following from 'Blue Moles,' is characteristically restored from the initial close-up by the words 'easy' and 'often': 'What happens between us / Happens in darkness, vanishes / Easy and often as each breath.' Poems should be criticized as they are, not as the critic thinks they might have been, and these poems, as they are, merit anybody's reading; but I can not help wondering what will happen if, in Miss Plath's second volume of poems, the emotional distance is shortened—no melting of the moulds her craftsmanship has created, I think, but a lesser frequency of phrases like, 'Now, this particular girl,' 'Mark, I cry,' 'gimcrack relics,' and more of the pressure of 'Lorelei,' of the close of 'The Colossus,' or of 'Departure,' which is an example of her finest writing.

13. Judson Jerome, 'A Poetry Chronicle—Part I,' *Antioch Review*

Spring 1963, 110–11

Judson Jerome (b. 1927) is an American poet and critic who writes widely on the practice of poetry.

Thankfully, just when I am deeply questioning whether I know what poetry is or how to read English, a book in English comes along and restores my confidence a little. Such is *The Colossus and Other Poems* by Sylvia Plath. She writes a plump and stumping line that jolts with imagination and clarity: 'Stars grinding, crumb by crumb, / Our own grist down to its bony face.' The poems are full of seascapes (a little more animated than Bly's snowfields), in which 'the slutting, rutted sea' lays into leaden shores with brackish stubbornness, perfectly and variously realized. But she never stops with description: she pushes on to wisdom, mystery, often (like her husband, the English poet Ted Hughes) to horror, to life quavering as fresh intestines in a wet hand. I love her animals—especially goats and pigs. And she is a good allegorist—as in the title poem she imagines living on 'The Colossus,'

> Scaling little ladders with gluepots and pails of lysol
> I crawl like an ant in mourning
> Over the weedy acres of your brow
> To mend the immense skull plates and clear
> The bald, white tumuli of your eyes.

Playing along even in the eeriest and most grotesque of the poems is a bubble of unabashed humor: she likes life—oh rare response! Her forms are knotty but controlled, her ear exquisite, her vision lucid. An exciting discovery in this heap of books! In the fad-ridden and mandarin-dominated world of poetry it is unusual to find a book one simply enjoys reading.

14. Richard Howard, review, *Poetry*

March 1963, 412–13

Richard Howard (b. 1929) is a Cleveland, Ohio, poet and critic educated at Columbia University and the Sorbonne. A prolific translator as well as poet, his book *Alone with America* maps post-war American poetry.

Sylvia Plath's eye is sharp ('spotted cows revolve their jaws and crop / red clover') and her wits responsive to what she sees. She prefers, though, to make you *hear* what she sees, the texture of her language affording a kind of analogue for the experience she presents. In the brilliant 'Hardcastle Crags,' event is reproduced in the aural imagery: 'a racket of echoes tacking in crooks from the black town...gave way to fields and the incessant seethe of grasses....' Once in a while this concern for texture as the dramatization of experience blurs the poem's movement or even its intelligibility ('the waves' spewed relics clicker masses in the wind'), but in most poems what catches in the ear is governed, checked, and we grasp what it is she wishes us to know because of the way we hear it. Miss Plath's burden is, throughout, the disaster inscribed within the surface of life and landscape (if she is a 'nature poet' it is not because she runs ahead down the path and holds out her hand: she makes us push through the weeds with her every step of the way, and occasionally snaps a bramble back in the most unlady-like way: 'What happens between us / happens in darkness,

45

vanishes / easy and often as each breath'); her poems, though there are no people in them, are instinct with Presences, which best arrive of themselves through the accurate evocation of their site. She has a genius for the *genius loci*. Sometimes the Spirit is summoned too brutally, as in 'Lorelei,' and all we get is stage properties. Yet in her modesty, Miss Plath is best content to let the Event disclose itself without too much prompting, and when 'nothing happens' she has still submitted the world to order: 'They are unloading three barrels of little crabs. / The pier pilings seem about to collapse / and with them that rickety edifice / of warehouses, derricks, smokestacks and bridges / in the distance.' This preference for the bleak and the unpromising suggests another poet of estrangement:

> From thence a length of burning sand appears
> Where the thin harvest waves its withered ears,
> Rank weeds, that every art and care defy,
> Reign over the land, and rob the blighted rye:
> There thistles stretch their prickly arms afar
> And to the ragged infant threaten war.

This is the same mode as Miss Plath's:

> Behind him the hotdogs split and drizzled
> On the public grills, and the ochreous salt flats,
> Gas tanks, factory stacks—that landscape
> Rippled and pulsed in the gleaming updraft.
> A mongrel working his legs to a gallop
> Hustled a gull flock to flap off the sandspit.

Sylvia Plath has not Crabbe's humor or his ease (the rhymes in her poems are all slant, and the end-stop she avoids like a reproach). But like him she has been shaken by life and takes the trouble to say so; the tenacity of her hard syllables is the measure of her success. The last poem, 'The Stones', is what I take to be a new departure: 'My mendings itch. There is nothing to do. / I shall be good as new.' Here there is more than the Pythoness's expectancy as she broods over a broken landscape: here is a vividly human voice, speaking from 'the city of spare parts, the city where men are mended.' I look forward to hearing more about that.

15. Mark Linenthal, 'Sensibility and Reflection from the Poet's Corner,' *San Francisco Sunday Chronicle, This World*

10 March 1963, 33

Sylvia Plath's *The Colossus* is a fine, decisive first collection by a young woman whose work has appeared here and in England and who is surely, among the best poets of her generation.

Her poems are impressive because of their firm wedding of technique to statement and because her work is feminine, never effeminate. Critics have called her language masculine, probably in response to the force with which it takes hold of its subject, its uncluttered unsentimental quality, its decisive rhythms.

But these are simply qualities of superior writing, and the experiences Miss Plath offers are those of a serious young woman who can take account of the pressure of the world out there as well as the world within.

Miss Plath is not bemused by the delicacy of her own sensibility. Nor is she ready yet, it appears, to make a large conclusive pronouncement; but if the craft of poetry continues to be what it is here, a means of experiment and discovery, she may well become a major American voice.

The title poem is a record of her ambitious devotion to her art; its opening stanzas are characteristic of her assurance, her modesty, her arresting imagination:

Quotes 'The Colossus,' ll. 1–10, *CP*, p. 129.

47

16. Nicholas King, 'Poetry: A Late Summer Roundup,' *New York Herald-Tribune Book Review*

26 August 1962, 4

Sylvia Plath's observation bores through the landscapes and details of daily life with an objective language that is pure, drama-less and often arresting.

Her objectivity is more subtle and embracing than one first supposes, but it is still more of an attitude than a conviction. Conviction will undoubtedly grow in her with time. In her first book she shows exceptional promise.

17. Ian Hamilton, 'Poetry,' *London Magazine*

July 1963, 54–7

Ian Hamilton (b. 1938) is a poet and biographer whose most recent book is a biography of J. D. Salinger.

Sylvia Plath died on February 11, aged 30. An American, Miss Plath lived in England for a number of years and her book of poems, *The Colossus*, was published here in 1960. It is a clever, remarkably sophisticated first volume, displaying a real gift for the exotically arresting single phrase or image without in the end carrying more than a few wholly impressive poems. Its debts—to Wallace Stevens, Theodore Roethke and, most pervasively, to Marianne Moore—seem somewhat too obtrusive and there are times when her pursuit of the odd word, the glittering simile that resonates, or throws its sparks, into areas that have too marginal a

bearing on the poem's subject, seems too deliberate, too whimsical even. The subjects themselves—and they are always, at bottom, the perennial important ones—often seem bricked up with a tasteful hand, or glanced at from too many directions too quaintly; the assured, leisured accent that is so attractive in a *tour de force* like 'Mushrooms' seems to diminish the seriousness of, say, 'The Ghost's Leavetaking,' a poem that is dense with disturbances of an important kind, all demanding to be followed through differently, more tentatively perhaps; certainly with less literary gusto.

Several of her poems—'Night Shift', for example, and 'Sow'—remind one of Valéry's comment on the confident realist, the confronter of things as they are: 'the universe cannot for one instance endure to be only what it is ... the mistakes, the appearances, the play of the dioprics of the mind deepen and quicken the world's miserable mass .... the idea introduces into what is, the leaven of what is not.' Frank Kermode has very appropriately quoted this statement in his book on Stevens and it has relevance to Sylvia Plath in a similar way. It is a peculiar perception because it can encourage poetry to ends that are quite antithetical; it can make poetry into a high-class game or it can see it as a vitally necessary instrument for controlling and bodying into consciousness a whole puzzled quality of experiencing. The danger, maybe, is in systematizing it too narrowly in the way that Valéry seems to; he implies that everyone really knows what the universe is and that poetry is a way of telling lively fictions about it, of pretending that it is something else, something more entertaining. It could be that this is, in effect, what poetry does with our experience but one ought not to feel that sure about it. In Sylvia Plath's 'Sow', for instance, the experience is approached in terms of the appearances that it might conceivably assume; it assumes a number of these, one by one, and they form the bulk of the poem, acting as an appetizing prelude to the appearance of the 'real'. This is a dangerous method, it seems to me, because it sets up no available scheme for discriminating between the various illusions, nor is there any way of limiting their number; the 'real' is known to the poet from the beginning and the spirit in which it is withheld from the reader is the spirit of fun-and-games; the strategy can easily come to seem like a way of using up powers of invention for which no more serious function can, meantime, be found.

This feeling that Miss Plath has great gifts but that she is marking time with them runs through *The Colossus*; there are notable exceptions, such as the excellent 'A Winter Ship', in which the experience absorbs and vitalizes the range of her curiosity, but these are largely successes of an orthodox, descriptive kind; they are concentrated and very accurately detailed, but there is a minimum of personal involvement in them.

In her poems published since *The Colossus*, and particularly in those that have been appearing very recently, Miss Plath has certainly developed. I hesitate before welcoming the achievement of these last poems as enthusiastically as A. Alvarez has in *The Observer*; I am not at all sure that in them 'The peculiar intensity of her genius found its perfect expression', nor that they represent a 'totally new breakthrough for modern verse'. There has certainly been an enormous gain in intensity and, one suspects, in seriousness of purpose. But it is as if she has taken that Valéry quotation and re-written it as the subject that her skills have been in search of; that is to say it is the impossibility of 'seeing things as they are', and the blank horror this provokes, that preoccupies her in these poems. There is a kind of nightmarish panic beneath their tough, enigmatic surfaces; the concrete world fragments into emblems of menace that are denoted in a tone of flat surrender:

> This man makes a pseudonym
> And crawls behind it like a worm
>
> This woman on the telephone
> Says she is a man, not a woman
>
> The mask increases, eats the worm,
> Stripes for mouth and eyes and nose.

Now and then the tone is one of barely controlled malevolence, as if experience has in some way cheated by seeming to be coherent; this is her most powerful note mainly because it does set up a relation between the world of organized human endeavour and her own terribly disorganized subjective world. It is a peculiar, slightly arid relation, perhaps, but it can breed the powerfully chilling hostilities of a poem like 'Kindness':

> Kindness glides about my house.
> Dame Kindness, she is so nice!
> The blue and red jewels of her rings smoke
> In the windows, the mirrors
> Are filling with smiles.

What is so real as the cry of a child?
A rabbit's cry may be wilder
But it has no soul.
Sugar can cure everything, so Kindness says.
Sugar is a necessary fluid.

The danger facing a poetry that commits itself to the recreation of nightmare experience is that it will be no less fragmentary and arbitrary than the experience that occasions it. That is to say, there must be some kind of coherent reflection upon experience, some effort of understanding it in terms of the urban, civilized world that its readers inhabit; this need not narrow nor constrict what it re-creates—on the contrary, it should simply extend its relevance. When Alvarez, in his *Observer* tribute to Miss Plath, says that 'in these last poems she was systematically probing that narrow, violent area between the viable and the impossible, between experience that can be transmuted into poetry and that which is overwhelming' I think he must surely be pointing out a danger rather than a legitimate mode. If we are to finally settle that there is experience which is too overwhelming to be transmuted into poetry then it is the poets who must assume the blame. In the best of her work Miss Plath has demonstrated, with formidable assurance, that she is aware of this; the less successful poems, those in which 'the world buckles and warps like a flame in mad draft', in which 'there is no sure objective ground—stillness and motion, near and far, telescope upsettingly, and become one'—they testify to the appalling difficulties she faced.

THE BELL JAR

(Victoria Lucas, Pseudonym)

London, January 1963

---

18. Unsigned review, 'Under the Skin,' *Times Literary Supplement*

25 January 1963, 53

Few writers are able to create a different world for you to live in; yet Miss Lucas in *The Bell Jar* has done just this. She writes in the first person the story of a girl who has a breakdown and is sent to a mental hospital. The story begins in a heat-wave in New York and she is already in her private world, the Bell Jar, with a wall of glass between herself and the other winners of a magazine contest. When she goes home to Boston it becomes more and more difficult to find a reason even for washing her hair: sleep becomes impossible; her nerves twang, and at last she tries to commit suicide and is taken to a private home from which she is finally discharged.

Miss Lucas can certainly write and the book is convincing. It reads so much like the truth that it is hard to disassociate her from Esther Greenwood, the 'I' of the story, but she has the gift of being able to feel and yet to watch herself: she can feel the desolation and yet relate it to the landscape of everyday life. There is a dry wit behind the poetic flashes and the zany fiascos of her relationships, and when the last part of the book begins to trail a little and details seem both ugly and irrelevant, one finds oneself thinking 'but this is how it happened.' Miss Lucas is exploring as she writes and if she can learn to shape as well as she imagines, she may write an extremely good book. *The Bell Jar* is already a considerable achievement.

19. Laurence Lerner, 'New Novels,' *Listener*

31 January 1963, 215

Laurence Lerner (b. 1925) is a widely published novelist, poet, and critic. Formerly of the University of Sussex, he is currently a chaired professor in the Department of English at Vanderbilt University.

I recommend *The Bell Jar* strongly. It is the story of Esther Greenwood, who wins a fashion magazine contest and gets, with eleven other girls, a free trip to New York, with free clothes, free meals, free entry to fashion shows, previews, and perhaps a career. Esther feels uncomfortable about it all. New York must have secrets it hasn't yielded to her—in the next taxi, perhaps, in the night club she wasn't asked to. Esther is a nice girl, she appreciates what people are doing for her, but somehow the deputy editor has to ask her if she is really interested in her work. She is gloriously and convincingly young: she sees through everyone, is influenced by everyone.

Slowly, then more quickly, we realize that Esther's ruthless and innocent wit is not just the result of youth and intelligence. It is the sign of a detachment, a lack of involvement, so complete that it leads to neurosis. From satirist she becomes a patient, yet so imperceptibly that after realizing she is sick we don't feel at all tempted to discount her previous shrewdness, or even cease to find her funny, in a rather frightening way. There are criticisms of American society that the neurotic can make as well as anyone, perhaps better, and Miss Lucas makes them triumphantly.

This book has another triumph: its language. The bell jar is Esther's image for her neurosis: 'wherever I sat, on the deck of a ship or at a street cafe in Paris or Bangkok—I would be sitting under the same glass bell jar, stewing in my own sour air.' Sharp, pungent, brittle, her images catch at almost indescribable states of mind for an instant, then shift restlessly to catch others. The novelist who deals with these elusive states of being usually has to choose between apt and elaborate imagery, or a simplifying and readable clarity. But Miss Lucas is tremendously readable, and at the same time has an almost poetic delicacy of perception. This is a brilliant and moving book.

ARIEL

Edited by Ted Hughes

London, 1965

20. A. Alvarez, 'Poetry in Extremis,' *Observer*

12 March 1965, 26

In this review, Alvarez continues his consistent helpful readings of Plath's work, here linking her with the older American poet Robert Lowell and coining the term which became used to describe poets who used personal experience in their art.

It is over two years now since Sylvia Plath died suddenly at the age of 30, and in that time a myth has been gathering around her work. It has to do with her extraordinary outburst of creative energy in the months before her death, culminating in the last few weeks when, as she herself wrote, she was at work every morning between four and seven, producing two, sometimes three, poems a day. All this last verse was intensely personal, nearly all was about dying. So when her death finally came it was prepared for and, in some degree, understood. However wanton it seemed, it was also, in a way, inevitable, even justified, like some some final unwritten poem.

All this last work is something quite new in poetry. I wrote at the time in the *Observer* that 'she was systematically probing that narrow, violent area between the viable and the impossible, between experience which can be transmuted into poetry and that which is overwhelming.' In order to tap knowingly the deep reservoirs of feeling that are released usually only in breakdown she was deliberately cutting her way through poetic conventions, shedding her old life, old emotions, old forms. Yet she underwent this process as an artist. If the poems are despairing, vengeful and destructive, they are at the same time tender, open to things, and also unusually clever, sardonic, hardminded:—

> Dying
> Is an art, like everything else.
> I do it exceptionally well.
>
> I do it so it feels like hell.
> I do it so it feels real.
> I guess you could ·say I've a call.

The myth, then, is a diversion from the objective achievement. For the verse has an originality that keeps it apart from any poetic fads. It is too concentrated and detached and ironic for 'confessional' verse, with all that implies of self-indulgent cashing-in on misfortunes; and it is violent without any deliberate exploitation of horrors and petty nastiness. If these last poems could never have been predicted from her first collection, *The Colossus*, this is not simply because such a leap into originality is always unforeseeable, but because her earlier absorption with style would, in the usual order of things, have made it doubly hard for her to bore through the crust of mere craftsmanship and release the lava below. As it worked out, the preparation was essential: when the wrenching crisis took place she had the art to handle it.

Technically, the basic difference between the earlier and later poems is that the first were written for the eye, the second for the ear. They need to be read aloud; they are original because she discovered in them her own speaking voice, her own identity. So the poems run with an inner rhythm which alters with the pressure of feeling and allows the images, which came crowding in with an incredible fertility and accuracy, to shift into one another, define and modify one another, and rub off colours each on the next. To take a straightforward example from 'The Arrival of the Bee Box':—

> I put my eye to the grid.
> It is dark, dark,
> With the swarmy feeling of African hands
> Minute and shrunk for export.
> Black on black, angrily clambering.
>
> How can I let them out?
> It is the noise that appals me most of all,

The unintelligible syllables.
It is like a Roman mob,
Small, taken one by one, but my god, together!

I lay my ear to furious Latin.
I am not Caesar.
I have simply ordered a box of maniacs.
They can be sent back.
They can die, I need feed them nothing, I am the owner.

It starts as simple narrative description; but as 'dark' is repeated it is somehow made to reverberate inwardly, crystallising into a metaphor which voices her underlying sense of threat. That menace carries over into the next bit of description (of the noise) and shifts, through another image, into wry helplessness ('I am not Caesar'); at which point a sense of proportion reasserts itself: 'They can die...I am the owner.' So a trivial incident gathers into itself a whole complicated nexus of feelings about the way her life is getting out of control. It is a brilliant balancing act between colloquial sanity and images which echo down and open up the depths.

Many of the poems are more difficult than that, rawer, more extreme. But all have that combination of exploratory invention, violent, threatened personal involvement and a quizzical edge of detachment. The poems are casual yet concentrated, slangy yet utterly unexpected. They are works of great artistic purity and, despite all the nihilism, great generosity.

Ariel is only a selection from a mass of work she left. Some of the other poems have been printed here and there, some have been recorded, some exist only in manuscript. It is to be hoped that all this remaining verse will soon be published. As it is, the book is a major literary event.

Sylvia Plath learned a great deal from the extremist art—the perceptions pushed to the edge of breakdown—that Robert Lowell first handled in 'Life Studies.'

In one of the most memorable lines in *Ariel*, in a poem called
'Getting There,' Sylvia Plath wrote

> All the gods know is destinations.

Nearly all her poems are full of these gods, inexorable and often
terrible forces driving through her mind and body regardless of any
consequences; and the first accomplishment of *Ariel* is that it makes
their existence real. The short, stabbing sentences, like stage
directions in the first person, draw one into the intense, claustrophobic present the speaker is living in—perceiving acutely, yet
enclosed, acted upon and powerless:

> I am red meat. His beak
>
> Claps sidewise: I am not his yet.
> He tells me how badly I photograph.
> He tells me how sweet
> The babies look in their hospital
> Icebox, a simple
>
> Frill at the neck....
> I do not stir....

> ('Death & Co.')

The forces are fears, or nightmarish impulses towards brutality or
suicide; or often they are simply obsessive images of death that
press a confused set of feelings, horror and fascination and pain, on
her:

> They propped his jaw with a book until it stiffened
> And folded his hands, that were shaking: goodbye, goodbye.
>
> Now the washed sheets fly in the sun,
> The pillow cases are sweetening.
>
> It is a blessing, it is a blessing:
> The long coffin of soap-coloured oak,

> The curious bearers and the raw date
> Engraving itself in silver with marvellous calm.
>
> ('Berck-Plage')

The stillness and purity of death sometimes present themselves as the only riposte to the horror of man's being a creature that dies.

Yet there is another quality in some of the poems: an ability—ability with language, ability of spirit—to confront the horrors not only with a precise description of them but also with a slangy bravado, to make mocking caricatures out of them at the very moment that they threaten to suffocate her. One of the most remarkable poems, 'Lady Lazarus,' is a statement—one can hardly describe it as an utterance, on the face of it, any more emotional than that—of having tried to commit suicide for the third time. But the insistent dryness of the comment, when the circumstances are so cogently presented, is what makes it such an extraordinarily moving poem:

['Lady Lazarus,' ll. 24–6, 45–50, *CP*, p. 245.]

We do not learn a great deal from the poems about the happenings in her life that exposed Sylvia Plath to these sufferings—and, of course, the power that she had to write about them is as mysterious in its origins as such gifts always are. But one or two of the poems grapple with her relationship with her German father, and one of them, 'Daddy,' is perhaps the greatest poem in the book. The father in the poem is a Fascist, who died when his daughter, who is the thirty-year-old 'I' of the poem, was ten. It is about the fear and love, the hatred and the longing, that the girl has felt for twenty years for this stranger, and about her terrible final rejection of him in her heart—the 'pretty red heart' that he 'bit in two.' The five-line stanzas have the grim rhythm—in the context—of a children's poem (almost exactly the form, in fact, of Kipling's poem on the camel's hump: 'We all get the hump / Camelious hump / The Hump that is black and blue'). The child's rhyme with its tortured content itself stands as a metaphor for the whole experience that the poem is about. It is both a powerful historical poem—a 'Daughter in the Sixties,' answering Auden's 'A Bride in the Thirties' across the decades which saw Auschwitz at their mid-point—and as anguished a personal poem as any in the book. In its overwhelming last line all trace of the nursery rhythm is finally drained away from the dragging anapaests:

> Daddy, daddy, you bastard, I'm through.

There are also, scattered about the book, a few poems of comparatively happy intensity—of wondering pleasure in her children, or of gratitude when 'the world / Suddenly turns, turns colour.' There are, too, a number of poems that seem like parodies of a Sylvia Plath poem, where the sinister trappings are mounted one on the other without carrying any conviction at all. But such duds are of no importance, just relics of a bid for intensity that on those occasions failed. The bids that came off make this one of the most marvellous volumes of poetry published for a very long time.

22. M.L. Rosenthal, 'Poets of the Dangerous Way,' *Spectator*

19 March 1965, 367

M.L. Rosenthal (b. 1917), a poet and critic, and Professor of English at New York University, has done a great deal to chart the development of modern and contemporary poetry. His most recent book, with Sally M. Gall, is *The Modern Poetic Sequence*.

Sylvia Plath, with her narrower range of technical resource and objective awareness than Lowell's, and with her absolute, almost demonically intense commitment by the end to the confessional mode, took what seems to me the one alternative advance position open to her. Only a few poems in her first book, *The Colossus* (1960), hint that she was destined to fulfil the implied suicidal programme of irreversible anguish beyond his limits. She was only thirty when, two years later, she threw herself into that last passionate burst of writing that culminated in *Ariel* and in her death, now forever inseparable. We shall never be able to sort out clearly the unresolved, unbearably exposed suggestibility and agitation of these poems from the purely aesthetic energy that shaped the best of them. Reading 'Daddy' or 'Fever 103°,' you would say that if a poet is sensitive enough to the age and brave enough to face it directly it will kill through the exacerbation of his awareness alone. Sometimes Sylvia Plath could not distinguish between herself and the facts of, say, Auschwitz or Hiroshima. She was victim, killer, and the place and process of horror all at once.

This is not the whole picture. Though Sylvia Plath may become a legend, we ought not to indulge in over-simplification. There are some lovely poems in the book ('Poppies in October,' for instance) that are cries of joy despite a grim note or two. There is rhythmic experimentation looking to the future, in particular with an adaptation of Whitman's characteristic line; and beyond that, the sheer wild leap into absolute mastery of phrasing and the dynamics of poetic movement in the title-poem alone, despite its tragic dimension, cannot but be considered an important kind of affirmation. But there are poems too that are hard to penetrate in their morbid secretiveness, or that make a weirdly incantatory black magic against unspecified persons and situations, and these often seem to call for biographical rather than poetic explanation.

Under all other motifs, however, is the confusion of terror at death with fascination by it. The visions of the speaker as already dead are so vivid that they become yearnings toward that condition. 'Death & Co.' is one of several nearly perfect embodiments of this deeply compulsive motif. It moves from a revolted imagery of death as a condor-like predator, a connoisseur of the beauty of dead babies, to a disgusted yet erotic picture of him as would-be lover, and at last to a vision of the speaker's own death such as I have mentioned:

> I do not stir.
> The frost makes a flower,
> The dew makes a star,
> The dead bell,
> The dead bell.
>
> Somebody's done for.

Thinking of this pitifully brief career, it is hard not to ask whether the cultivation of sensibility is after all worth the candle.

The answer is yes, for reasons that I hope we all know—yet it seems important to raise the question anyway.

23. Unsigned review, 'Poems for the Good-Hearted,' *The Times*

4 November 1965, 15

The two most important volumes of American poetry of late are books that deal with violence in a different way. One is *Ariel*, by Sylvia Plath, who also died in 1963, when she was living in London. Her poems at their best combine an exact and powerful delineation of cruel or self-destructive emotion, with a brave wit or a determined hanging-on to happiness. They are noble poems....

24. Peter Dale, ' "O Honey Bees Come Build," ' *Agenda*

Summer 1966, 49–55

Peter Dale (b. 1938), an Oxford-educated poet and teacher, is best known for his own poems and his translations of Villon. He has been an associate editor of *Agenda* for some time.

These poems were composed in circumstances which, for a number of reasons, make criticism difficult. They were written at such a whitehot intensity of feeling and imagination that, life and death as they are, to cast a cold critical eye on them would be to mistake their ultimate meaning. Further, a natural sympathy for the artist who dies young tends to give the poems a powerful, though perhaps extra-poetic, effect. A critic is almost driven to find them successful so that the immortality of the work may compensate for the tragedy of the death. Next, the question of the inter-relation of art with life intrudes itself inescapably. The poems are condensed, elliptical, and autobiographical. Many are impenetrable without at least as much information as Alvarez provides in the special Plath issue of *The Review*. Some suppress matter which seems necessary to proper understanding; others are so personal that the reader senses he has overheard something not intended for his ears. This falling between two stools is a constant danger of the autobiographical approach in poetry. There is no satisfactory resolution. Although one seeks clear understanding there remain privacies and reticences that, more than ever in our publicity-mad world, one is reluctant to intrude upon. These are therefore not readily subject to literary treatment. For example, 'Berck-Plage' presents many attitudes, opinions and bitternesses which have no causative explanation within the poem. A widow mourning is seen with a bitterness uncaused and unexplained:

> A widow with her black pocket book and three daughters...

We are presented with the dramatic creation of the results of a breakdown in relations, rather than with the actual cause and effect. Poetry is not created until those bitternesses are 'caused' in the poem sufficiently enough to seem justifiable and inevitable. Yet to ask for more detail is to join the 'peanut-crunching crowd'.

But many of these poems must have been written in conditions of almost total breakdown where the injunction 'look in thy heart and write' entails a self-inflicted surgery which must nearly always remove most of the detached critical faculty, an operation from which no one should require formal objectivity. Poems of such abnormal states of being must be next to impossible to write well. The critic wishes he might concentrate on the 'art' and gloss over these nigglings for autobiography to 'complete' this poetry of fragments. Yet to do so would deny the central 'living' qualities of the poems. With what reticence he can, he has to admit that the circumstances of their composition must influence his judgement; poetry is probably and finally the most autobiographical of the arts. Keats' sonnet 'Bright Star,' not a particularly 'perfect' poem, draws strength from its place in the tragedy of his life and can hardly be criticised with complete objectivity. Yet Keats was only half in love with easeful death whereas Sylvia Plath's death obtrudes more directly, almost as a conscious act, to shatter forever our critical detachment. Nor was she accustomed to half measures.

The main conflict in the book lies between her ambitions and pretensions as a poet and the soul-destroying mundanity of life as a mother and wife. She sees herself cut out for something greater than this:

> but I
> Have a self to recover, a queen.

But life is destroying her distinction:

> I stand in a column
>
> Of winged, unmiraculous women,
> Honey-drudgers.
> I am no drudge
> Though for years I have eaten dust
> And dried plates with my dense hair
>
> And seen my strangeness evaporate,
> Blue dew from dangerous skin.

Even when ostensibly one in purpose with other people she still feels this sense of alienation and distinction which she is reluctant to surrender:

> Now they are giving me a fashionable white straw hat
> And a black veil that moulds to my face, they are making
> me one of them.

She is isolated from relationships and satisfactions that make life for others worth living. In the poem 'Morning Song,' successful in its sympathetic, ironic self-mockery, she feels detached from her child:

> I'm no more your mother
> Than the cloud that distils a mirror to reflect its own slow
> Effacement at the wind's hand.

Other people become 'The peanut-crunching crowd' which 'shoves in to see / Them unwrap me hand and foot—The big strip tease.' Her loved ones are seen with a chilling detachment:

> Are those the faces of love, those pale irretrievables?
> Is it for such I agitate my heart?

At other times she feels unable to cope. The children with demands have 'hooks and cries' which she cannot deal with. In 'The Hanging Man' she comments:

> A vulturous boredom pinned me to this tree.
> If he were I, he would do what I did.

Even kindness is seen with a detached mockery:

> Sugar can cure everything, Kindness says.
> Sugar is a necessary fluid,
>
> Its crystals a little poultice.

In the same poem the wound to be poulticed is poetry:

> The bloodjet is poetry,
> There is no stopping it.
> You hand me two children, two roses.

The ordinary blessings of life were not enough to staunch the flow, the poetry poured out, mortally.

One attempted solution to her conflict is in violent physical activity and the appreciation of natural things. In 'Ariel' she achieves a joy in living by riding her favourite horse but still there is a dubious note at the close:

> And I
> Am the arrow,
>
> The dew that flies
> Suicidal, at one with the drive
> Into the red
> Eye, the cauldron of morning.

In 'Poppies in October' she cries out about them:

> O my God, What am I
> That these late mouths should cry open
> In a forest of frost, in a dawn of cornflowers.

and the conflict is again met in the ambiguities of that 'cry open'. In its accessibility and directness this is one of her best poems, along with 'Sheep in Fog' where the conflict balances in the word 'threaten', and she has probably come out in favour of life:

> My bones hold a stillness, the far
> Fields melt my heart.
>
> They threaten
> To let me through to a heaven
> Starless and fatherless, a dark water.

Yet perhaps the most reposed poem in this group is the slightly Roethkean 'Letter in November' about a day in the garden:

> I am flushed and warm,
> I think I may be enormous,
> I am so stupidly happy,
> My Wellingtons
> Squelching and squelching through the beautiful red.

The most frequent way out of her dilemma, however, seems to be death. The difficulty here is that death is seen in romantic terms, unsupported by expressed religious beliefs, as a purification, a peace, and in some ways a triumph. It is not the defiant, self-proclaiming absurd act of existentialism à l'Anouilh etc, nor l'acte gratuit. Nor is it seen with any consistency, the classical Lethe crops up and the vague, now Christian term, Paradise.

> ...I only wanted
> To lie with my hands turned up and be utterly empty.
> How free it is, you have no idea how free—
> The peacefulness is so big it dazes you,
> And it asks nothing, a name tag, a few trinkets.
> It is what the dead close on, finally...

In another instance it is seen as a purification:

> And I, stepping from this skin
> Of old bandages, boredoms, old faces
>
> Step to you from the black car of Lethe
> Pure as a baby

Discussing the kind of gift she would like she says:

> If it were death
>
> I would admire the deep gravity of it, its timeless eyes,
> I would know you were serious.
>
> There would be a nobility then, there would be a birthday.
> And the knife not carve but enter

> Pure and clean as the cry of a baby,
> And the universe slide from my side.

Yet there is no religious belief to support her idea of death:

> Eternity bores me,
> I never wanted it.

Finally, in 'Edge', she imagines herself dead:

> The woman is perfected.
> Her dead
>
> Body wears a smile of accomplishment.

Certain poems go some way to give cause and reason to this persistent death-urge. 'Lady Lazarus' reveals that she had felt it before:

> I have done it again.
> One year in every ten
> I manage it.

and show that it has to do with her German father and her doubts over his role in war-time Germany, though there is little exact meaning the reader can attach to its final ecstatic stanza:

> Out of the ash
> I rise with my red hair
> And I eat men like air.

In 'Daddy' she returns to this theme in powerful nursery-rhyme mockery, closing with the ambiguous triumph of:

> Daddy, daddy, you bastard, I'm through.

These two poems, along with 'Little Fugue', are essential to an understanding of her recurrent symbols and images but they are ultimately unsuccessful.

The best poems in the book are those where her highly private fears, guilts, failures and neuroses are made objective in concrete situations such as in the beekeeping poems, or in the hospital of 'Tulips'. Where this concreteness is lacking there remain obscure associations on an unexplained theme. In such poems as 'Fever 103'; 'Medusa'; 'The Couriers' the reader is lost in a welter of private associations.

But for reasons given earlier it is difficult to come to a final criticism of these poems. What is certain is that they are a major technical achievement; the short lines and occasional rhymes and assonances bring the speaking voice directly across, and, if they have not the finish of poetry, they have the life of drama. Though many of them do not properly articulate their final intentions as poems, all of them move in the process, the main source of poetry in them being the drama of soliloquy, of exclamation, clipped phrase, metaphor and ironic parenthesis set in juxtaposition. Something may be lost in the exclusion of the five acts, but, outside novel or casehistory, this was the only way to go about it.

As it is the reader can share to some extent her distaste, even hatred of the daily chores of life, the pettiness of things, and, occasionally, even her detachment from her own circle. He also may share her hatred of the peanut-crunching crowd—though in reading these poems he becomes one of that mob. The one nagging reservation, however, is an inability to comprehend from the poems, and to understand and share, her view of death. In its most direct and unexplained expression, in 'Edge', there seems to be more idealisation than actuality and the poem is based ultimately on a poetic cliché. This kind of objection, subconscious almost, raises itself to several of her references to death, and is only met and faced in the poem 'Death and Co'. In the poem 'Contusion' and the witty 'Cut', though admirably done, it is difficult not to feel a slight nausea at the morbidity of the sensibility upsetting the aesthetic balance. But lastly, it is difficult not to feel that the circumstances of their composition should exclude them from critical niggling.

When all is said and done, it is clear that in all senses Lorca's 'duende' is in these poems. Perfect they could not be, but polish without 'duende' is nothing. They will be read forever, like Keats' 'Letters'.

25. Stephen Spender, 'Warnings from the Grave,' *New Republic*

18 June 1966, 23, 25–26

Stephen Spender (b. 1909), a distinguished poet, playwright, critic, autobiographer, and travel writer, was Professor of English at University College, London. His work has consistently influenced world-wide literary opinion, as in *Love-Hate Relations: A Study of Anglo-American Sensibilities* and *The Thirties and After.*

Poetry is a balancing of unconscious and conscious forces in the mind of the poet, the source of the poetry being the unconscious, the control being provided by the conscious. If the poet thinks about his poetic ego, he visualizes, I suppose, a point at which consciousness and unconsciousness meet. The unconscious forces are below the threshold at which he becomes aware of himself as having an identity; but his 'name' also is below the threshold where it requires attributes of character, performer, reputation, family, and all those things. That is why labels attached by chairmen, editors and award givers to poets are so irrelevant. Today, it is true, they have become the apparatus whereby the poet keeps himself afloat in life for the purpose of writing his poetry. But that as much importance is attached to labels is part of the general disgrace attached to the life of the imagination in our time.

If you consider the quality suggested by the name 'Keats' in a poem by that poet, it has little to do with his biography, his critical reputation, his place in the anthologies. It has, rather, two aspects. First, 'Keats' is a suffusing quality of sensibility in a poem of Keats, a climate, or like the colour of a sunset, a glow affecting all objects seen in that light. Secondly, though, there is something more personal that this, something like the feel of a pulse on the wrist, the throb of blood in the rhythm of:

> Forlorn! The very word is like a bell
> To toll thee back from thee to my sole self!

69

Today, true poets must feel, I think, a growing distrust of their own 'names' which are to an ever-increasing extent sold to the reading public, or listening audience, on grounds totally irrelevant to poetry (the poet's achievements, academic status, or unacademic misdemeanours, etc.). The result is that poets find themselves forced to escape from their public persona, either into their unconscious pre-named-and-labelled activity, or into an intellectualism which rises superior to the givers of labels. Sometimes, as with Robert Lowell, these two opposites seem combined: an extreme intellectuality is fused with an ability to plunge into the subconscious depths. Reading Berryman, Jarrell, Lowell, Roethke, and now this posthumous collection of Sylvia Plath, one is forced to take note that with some of the best recent poets, even though one does not immediately connect them with Rimbaud, a programme of the poet 'cultivating his hysteria' seems to have become very serious indeed.

Sylvia Plath's poems in this volume (which were written immediately after the birth of a child, and shortly before she committed suicide) come out of a consciousness which is unique, immensely forceful, but which is below the threshold of what I have here described as the second kind of poetic naming, in which you can put your finger on a line and say 'this is Sylvia Plath'. Their power, their decisiveness, the positiveness and starkness of their outline, are decided not by an identifiable poetic personality expressing herself, but by the poet, a woman finding herself in a situation, out of which she produces these disconcerting, terrifying poems. The guarantees of the authenticity of the situation are insanity (or near-insanity) and death. All the way through we feel that the last thing the poet cares about is her book, her name, whether she will get a critical accolade, a Book Award, a Pulitzer, a Guggenheim, or whatever. She is writing out of a pure need of expression, certified, as I say, by death. The miracle is an effect of controlled uncontrolledness. As one reads on, one begins to seek the dark places which provide the structure of the control, the landmarks among which the poetry is moving. There is the German and Austrian background (Sylvia Plath was born in Boston in 1932 of German and Austrian parents), feelings about her German father (which correspond rather to those of Theodore Roethke about his), concentration camps, her daughter, and her son, her husband (the English poet, Ted Hughes), the Devonshire landscape, villagers, the sea. Probably at some later stage, critics will chart this autobiographic territory. One will be grateful when they do this, but one can be grateful also that they have not done so already. Part of the impressiveness of these poems is the feeling they give the reader of finding his way darkly through a dark and ominous landscape.

The landscape is an entirely interior, mental one in which external objects have become converted into symbols of hysterical vision:

> This is my property,
> Two times a day
> I pace it, sniffing
> The barbarous holly with its viridian
> Scallops, pure iron,
>
> And the wall of old corpses.
> I love them.
> I love them like history.
> The apples are golden,
> Imagine it—
>
> My seventy trees
> Holding their gold-ruddy balls
> In a thick grey death-soup,
> Their million
> Gold leaves metal and breathless.
>
> 'Letter in November'

One can enjoy the 'description' in this, the autumn-golden apples in the grey-soup mist. All the same, this nature is not in the least alleviating, it is not outside the poet, it is not the great furniture of the continuity of the seasonal earth, on which the distraught mind can rest. Or if there are some externals in these poems (they do give one a strong panicky feeling of kitchens, utensils, babies, gardens) they exist in an atmosphere where the external is in immediate process of becoming the internal, opposites identical with one another.

The same fusion of opposites applies to the feelings expressed. Sylvia Plath's imagination does not, like D.H. Lawrence's, merely oscillate between feelings of love and of hatred. With her the two attitudes seem completely fused. How else can one take lines like these?

Darling, all night
I have been flickering, off, on, off, on.
The sheets grow heavy as a lecher's kiss.

Three days. Three nights.
Lemon water, chicken
Water, water make me retch.

I am too pure for you or anyone.
Your body
Hurts me as the world hurts God.

'Fever 103°'

Considered simply as art, these poems have line to line power and rhythm which, though repetitive, is too dynamic to be monotonous. Beyond this, they don't have 'form'. From poem to poem they have little principle of beginning or ending, but seem fragments, not so much of one long poem, as of an outpouring which could not stop with the lapsing of the poet's hysteria. In this respect they have to be considered emotional-mystical poetry, like the poems of St. John of the Cross, in which the length of the poem is decided by the duration of the poet's vision, which is far more serious to the poet than formal considerations.

They are like nothing more than poems of prophecy, written by some priestess cultivating her hysteria, come out of Nazi and war-torn Europe, gone to America, and then situated on the rocky Cornish Atlantic coast. One does not think of Clytemnestra as a *hysteric*; one thinks of her as hysterical for very good reasons, against which she *warns*. Sylvia Plath would have agreed with Wilfred Owen that 'all a poet can do today is to warn'. But being a woman, her warning is more shrill, penetrating, visionary than Owen's. Owen's came out of the particular circumstances of the trenches, and there is nothing to make us think that if he had not been on the Western Front—the mud and blood into which his nose was rubbed—he would not have warned anyone about anything at all. He would have been a nice chap and a quiet poet. With Sylvia Plath, her femininity is that her hysteria comes completely out of herself, and yet seems about all of us. And she has turned our horrors and our achievements into the same witches' brew. In the following lines one feels that a spaceman promenading in space is not too distant a relation from a man in a concentration camp, and that everything is a symptom of the same holocaust:

The same fire

Melting the tallow heretics,
Ousting the Jews.
Their thick palls float

Over the cicatrix of Poland, burnt-out
Germany.
They do not die.

Grey birds obsess my heart,
Mouth-ash, ash of eye.
They settle. On the high

Precipice
That emptied one man into space
The ovens glowed like heavens incandescent.

It is a heart,
This holocaust I walk in,
O golden child the world will kill and eat.

'Mary's Song'

As with all visionary poetry, one can sup here on horror even
with enjoyment.

26. P. N. Furbank, 'New Poetry,' *Listener*

11 March 1965, 379

P(hilip) N(icholas) Furbank (b. 1920) is a Cambridge-
educated critic and educator. Formerly an editor for Macmillan, he has held a variety of university appointments.

Nothing could be healthier than Lowell's poetry... and likewise it
is no good pretending that Sylvia Plath's is not sick verse. The
poem 'Lady Lazarus' is frank enough; she obviously felt, in these
poems of her last year, like someone brought back from death to
disturb and terrify us. There is something essentially desperate in

her using her old wild child-like fantasy to express her new anguish and horror. The *persona* of the last poems is still recognizably the limbless fairy-tale homunculus 'All-mouth' (of 'Poem for a Birthday') muttering and mythologizing to itself. The poems are an attempt to give words to what the psychiatrists call 'the non-me.' They are a brilliantly successful attempt up to a point. The myth-creating power is certainly extraordinary. No more Gothic lines could be conceived than

> The moon is no door. It is a face in its own right,
> White as a knuckle and terribly upset.
> It drags the sea after it like a dark crime; it is quiet
> With the O-gape of complete despair.

And the whole form of 'Berck-Plage,' a poem about a seaside funeral, is a most remarkable piece of black cinema. Consider this short sequence:

> This black boot has no mercy for anybody.
> Why should it, it is the hearse of a dead foot,
>
> The high, dead, toeless foot of this priest
> Who plumbs the well of his book.
>
> The bent print bulging before him like scenery.
> Obscene bikinis hide in the dunes....

One sees Bergman's camera creeping up from that horrible boot, to the priest's face, to the obscene landscape.

You feel, though, that she is playing a losing game in these poems. They are Pyrrhic victories, not really defeating the horror and life-hatred. The gaiety, such as it is, is helpless, and the art, for all its power, is an hysterical bravado in the face of insuperable calamity.

27. Hugh Kenner, 'Arts and the Age, On *Ariel*,' *Triumph*

September 1966, 33–34

Hugh Kenner (b. 1923), a Canadian critic whose writing about the modern literary scene became a touchstone, is best known for his books on T.S. Eliot, James Joyce, Ezra Pound, and such comprehensive studies as *The Pound Era* and *A Homemade World*.

There's a lot of nonsense being talked about these poems, as if, for instance, they were unmediated shrieks from the heart of the fire. (They make such assertions themselves: 'The blood jet is poetry, / There is no stopping it.') But like Villon, whom legend has writing *Le Testament* under the shadow of the hangman, Sylvia Plath was counting her lines and governing her rhetoric. She comments on this fact too:

> Dying
> Is an art, like everything else.
> I do it exceptionally well
>
> I do it so it feels like hell.
> I do it so it feels real.
> I guess you could say I've a call.

Sparse rhymes come and go nearly at random, and the number of syllables in a line swings with the vertigo of her thought. Still, these are shaped poems, all but two of them measured out, in stanzas, by preference with an odd number of lines (5 or 3). Not that they resemble in the least Villon's ceremonious ballades. Perhaps some of them only play the desperate game of repeating again and again the stanza the opening fell into; there's more of compulsion neurosis than mathematics in those forms; the breaks between stanzas are like cracks in the sidewalk, on which she is careful never to step.

The resulting control, sometimes *look* of control, is a rhetoric, as cunning in its power over our nerves as the stream of repulsions. It in fact enacts its own inability to govern. Naked negation spilling down the sides of improvised vessels, that is the formal drama of poem after poem. Being formal, it saves them from shrillness.

The negation, liquid, labile, repudiates with the gleeful craft of a mad child, other persons, the poet's own body, the entire created universe. She cuts her thumb: 'What a thrill— / My thumb instead of an onion. / The top quite gone / Except for a sort of a hinge / / Of skin, / A flap like a hat, Dead white.' Or she slips easily into the identity of an as-if-entombed paralytic: 'My god

75

the iron lung / / That loves me, pumps / my two / Dust bags in and out, / Will not / / Let me relapse / While the day outside glides by like ticker tape.' This seems to be an optical pun: the glass dome of the stock ticker, like the panes of the iron lung, house a mechanized process the unenlightened world takes for vital. The same principle gobbles up whole communities: 'These are the people that were important— / Their round eyes, their teeth, their grimaces / On a stick that rattles and clicks, a counterfeit snake.' The stick, the counterfeit snake, is a train, eating up its track; and 'There is no terminus, only suitcases / Out of which the same self unfolds like a suit.' She longs for a lethal birthday present:

> Only let down the veil, the veil, the veil.
> If it were death
>
> I would admire the deep gravity of it, its timeless eyes.
> I would know you were serious.
>
> There would be a nobility then, there would be a birthday.
> And the knife not carve, but enter
>
> Pure and clean as the cry of a baby,
> And the universe slide from my side.

This is insidious nausea; Robert Lowell writes in his foreword of the serpent he hears whispering from her lines, 'Come, if you only had the courage, you too could have my rightness, audacity and ease of inspiration.' But most of us, he adds, will turn back: 'These poems are playing Russian roulette with six cartridges in the cylinder.'

Lowell has put his finger on the appeal that seems to be propelling *Ariel* toward best-sellerdom (15,000 copies sold in England; American bookstores sold out in city after city). The book's nausea is insidious because the denizen of an IBM-Playtex-Cadillac world has been coached, as much by his mentors as by his psyche, to accept as sincerity nothing less than repudiation. 'And the knife not carve, but enter / Pure and clean as the cry of a baby'; this is one way of becoming as a little child. The key-word is 'pure,' and we encounter it more than once; she hopes to step to Death 'from the black car of Lethe, / Pure as a baby.' Another poem poises the purity of high fever, verging on death ('I / Am a pure acetylene / Virgin / Attended by roses') against the body's 'aguey tendon, the sin, the sin.'

This is bogus spirituality; and for all that it's a phase of the despair that brought Miss Plath's head finally into a gas oven, it passes for unarguable virtue in a time of beats (pop Franciscans) and psychedelics (pop mysticism). It goes with Zen, inertia, sandals, beards and a disinclination to wash. Miss Plath passed through it in an agony we cannot begin to comprehend; but her readers, one gathers, half envy her. The pathology of the modern secular world is a religious pathology, in quest of spiritual shortcuts to spiritual virtues, but preferring to see someone else try them out. The dry accidia of the Cumaean Sibyl when small boys poked at her and asked 'What do you want?' ('I want to die.') belonged to an order willing to extract banquet entertainment from any tale, but still in touch with Stoical virtues. The overtoppling luxury of Keats, 'half in love with easeful death,' was framed and stabilized by intricate stanzas within which, as within a system of coordinates, the mind can recall where the waking world is, and return to it. Miss Plath's 'blood jet,' which Keats would have read as the fever-chart of a terrible madness, pulsates in the only world there is, where all is always now, and not self-abnegation but self-annihilation wears the mask of ultimate purity. A Manichaean hysteria (matter is dirty, existence itself is foul) mesmerizes Miss Plath's deeply shaken readers.

Hence the strange need to play down the poem's art and mix up their nature with a tasteless Plath Legend to which readers can respond not as celebrants of a rhetoric but with the voyeur's intimate purity of participation. The details, as with most legends, don't jibe. For instance the account in *Time* (June 10) differs from the one on the book jacket not only in tone but in pertinent fact. It's clear the poems were written in the months before Sylvia Plath killed herself; but in the three months? (blurb) the six months? (*Time*) throughout most of every night? (*Time*) or just from 4 a.m. till the baby cried? (blurb). And 'two, three, six complete poems night after night?' (*Time*). If so, what happened to most of them? There are just 43 in the book.

Obviously no one is meant to wonder how much work-over the poems in *Ariel* received. My guess would be, a good deal; and I'd add that some of them (notably the first and last in the volume) read rather like expert contrivances than like dictations from the black angel. On the death-poems, moreover, fingerprints of contrivance don't show, and I'd point to her mustering of the craft that was necessary in that harrowing time as the victory for which she deserves to be celebrated: that, and not the shrieking 'sincerity.' It is much to have illustrated, *in articulo mortis*, William Carlos Williams' remark about Villon, that he 'could not exist now if there were the faintest feeling about his writing that he had sought to be effective.'

28. John Malcolm Brinnin, 'Plath, Jarrell, Kinnell, Smith,' *Partisan Review*

Winter 1967, 156–7

John Malcolm Brinnin (1916–86) was best known for his writing about Dylan Thomas. A poet and critic, he was an important anthologist and understood well patterns in both British and American poetry.

If Sylvia Plath's performance were not so securely knowledgeable, so cannily devised, so richly inventive and so meticulously reined, it would be intolerable. Many of these poems are magnificent; a whole book of them is top-heavy, teetering on that point where the self-created figure threatens to topple over into self-expression and the diversions of psychopathology. Reaching for a poet with whom to compare her, or in whose sphere of influence to 'place' her—and only the illustrious will do—one hesitates before Blake (too 'big,' too masculine. too mythopoeic), before Baudelaire (too much the *poseur*, too *raffiné*, perhaps too comfortable in his rancor), and stops at Emily Dickinson. But anguish in Emily Dickinson is a consequence; it partakes of a classical notion of anguish: the great heart victimized by its own humanity. In Sylvia Plath, by contrast, anguish is not a consequence but the whole relentless subject itself. In her vision the primary colors of anguish, the myopic eye of anguish, not only seriously distort the observed world but threaten to obliterate it. The exhibition of an obsession may, for a time, provide a reader with a voyeuristic *frisson*. But in the long run any fixation is apt to alienate its witness. The old cliché is inevitable: Miss Plath's strength is her weakness; impulses that individuate her thrilling talent are the same impulses that shrink the limits of a commanding achievement. Anything pursued far enough is likely to turn into its opposite: a shriek maintained for eighty-five pages becomes, to say the least, a bore. Nevertheless, what we have here is not, as some bewildered critics have claimed, the death rattle of a sick girl, but the defiantly fulfilling measures of a poet. Taken in small—one is almost forced to say, medicinal—doses, she is a marvel.

29. Richard Tillinghast, 'Worlds of Their Own,' *Southern Review*

Spring 1969, 582–3

Richard Tillinghast (b. 1940) is a poet and critic who teaches at the University of Michigan. His recent book is a collection of poems.

Sylvia Plath's *Ariel* is the most interesting new poetic development of recent years. The American edition has four poems not in the English edition, and an introduction by Robert Lowell. *Ariel* seems to be by someone different from the author of her first book, *The Colossus*, which might have been written by any of a dozen or so poets. Her autobiographical novel, *The Bell Jar* (by 'Victoria Lucas') gives a certain answer: these are poems of schizophrenia, or rather poems by a schizophrenic who had painstakingly, over a period of years, mastered the craft of poetry. Anyone who has heard schizophrenics talk or has read things they have written will be familiar with the crystal-clear shatterings of logical order that form Sylvia Plath's style: 'It is shimmering, has it breasts, has it edges?' The difference, of course, is that here nothing is wasted, everything is a diamond; clinical schizophrenic writing has pages of platitudes, cheap thrills, dullness, for every striking passage. So this is not material for the clinician, but, as Robert Lowell describes it in the Introduction, 'controlled hallucination, the autobiography of a fever,' taking its place alongside such psychotic visual art as the demonic fantasies of Bosch, Goya's *Pinturas Nigras*, Piranesi's *Carceri d'Invenzione*, and Louis Wain's kaleidoscopic cats. When the rest of her poems are published, it will be interesting to see how they compare in quality and lucidity with these.

If one can free oneself from the spell of these terrifyingly beautiful poems (presumably too well-known to need quoting), perhaps something can be gained by considering the aesthetic problems raised by them. It is impossible, I think, to distinguish between the kind of images in *Ariel* and those used by other, very good, modern poets. The intensity, the economy, the emphasis on originality, the ability to combine seemingly unrelated things and to separate the expected combinations—all of these are accepted goals of contemporary art. Some critics believe that a poetry of breakdown is needed as an 'early warning system' for a world headed for total breakdown—that we need to be shocked into seeing that our familiarity with, and acceptance of, the 'logic' of our civilization hides a dangerous irrationality. Everyone is aware that underlying the 'normal' mental state is insanity and chaos. But Sylvia Plath went farther. She seems to have accepted her madness as not only inevitable, but even a triumph—as the means to writing great poetry. 'Health' became an illusion. As Lowell puts it, 'This poetry and life . . . tell that life, even when disciplined, is simply not worth it.' This is where her poetry must leave the rest of us behind: 'health,' though tenuous, must be within our grasp; and life must be possible.

30. Peter Davison, 'Inhabited by a Cry: The Last Poetry of Sylvia Plath,' *Atlantic Monthly*

August 1966, 76–7

Peter Davison (b. 1928) is a poet and critic who writes about Plath in his memoir, *Half-Remembered*. He is currently an editor with Atlantic Monthly Press.

Only rarely, and almost never when still alive, does a poet become the object of a cult. Sylvia Plath, age thirty, died in London in 1963, leaving behind her a sheaf of terrifying poems. Since then, and especially in the past year, poem after poem has been written to her memory by people who never knew her work while she was alive. The fable of her 'abrupt, defiant death,' as Robert Lowell puts it, sees her as immolated on the altar of a cruel society, her poems the outraged by-product of her last agony. But to oversimplify her life, making her into the James Dean of modern poetry, would also be to oversimplify and vulgarize the development of her work.

Sylvia Plath was a greatly but unevenly gifted woman who took the trouble, and had the intellectual resources, to train herself for a decade as a poet. The *Atlantic* and other periodicals published a fair amount of her early work, written in her twenties, and it showed an unusual sense of rhythm, a vocabulary that had a long, accurate reach, and a protean talent kept under severe control.

The early poems, many of them published in a collection called *The Colossus* (published first in London; then in a shortened version by Knopf, 1962), seemed to have no absolute necessity for being: they read like advanced exercises. She wrote a lot of prose as well, including a novel, but none that I have read seemed to me much out of the ordinary. Sylvia Plath's talent, though intensely cultivated, did not bloom into genius until the last months of her life, when, if we may take the internal evidence of the poems in *Ariel* (also published first in London) as our guide, she stood at the edge of the abyss of existence and looked, steadily, courageously, with holy curiosity, to the very bottom. It is not a matter for personal praise or personal blame that she did so; but the resultant poetry has a bone-chilling authority that could not have been achieved except by steady staring. No artifice alone could have conjured up such effects; yet such is the paradox of art, these poems would never have come into being without the long, deliberate, technical training that had preceded them. We can only perform with true spontaneity what we have first learned to do by habit.

Every artist, and almost everyone else, at one time or another fetches up against the stark facts of life and death. No one can avert his gaze at such a time without some degree of self-betrayal, even though he may be turned to stone if he continues looking. The greatest writers have been able to record these terrible moments against the larger canvas of ordinary life, adjusting the threatened catastrophes of death and destruction among related and contrasting themes of life and hope and renewal. It has become fashionable—or if not fashionable, at least common—for poets to set down their autobiographical crises, first person and second person and all, as a qualifying confession to admit them to the fraternity—a kind of professional good-conduct pass. All the difference in the world, however, lies between such antics, performed always with an audience in mind, whether explicitly in the poem or implicitly in its tone, and, on the other hand, such terrifying lines as these, from several of the poems in *Ariel*. No matter to whom these may be addressed, they are written for nobody's ears except the writer's. They have a ritual ring, the inevitable preface to doom.

From 'Lady Lazarus'

[Quotes ll. 43–8, 79–84, *CP*, p. 245.]

From 'Lesbos' (one mother speaks to another)

> You say you can't stand her,
> The bastard's a girl.
> You who have blown your tubes like a bad radio
> Clear of voices and history, the staticky
> Noise of the new.
> You say I should drown the kittens. Their smell!
> You say I should drown my girl.
> She'll cut her throat at ten if she's mad at two.
> The baby smiles, fat snail,
> From the polished lozenges of orange linoleum.
> You could eat him. He's a boy.
> You say your husband is just no good to you.

From 'Death & Co

> I do not stir.
> The frost makes a flower
> The dew makes a star,
> The dead bell,
> The dead bell.
>
> Somebody's done for.

From 'Elm'

> I know the bottom, she says. I know it with
>   my great tap root:

It is what you fear.
I do not fear it: I have been there...

I am inhabited by a cry.
Nightly it flaps out
Looking, with its hooks, for something to love.

From 'The Applicant'

First, are you our sort of person?
Do you wear

A glass eye, false teeth or a crutch.
A brace or a hook,
Rubber breasts or a rubber crotch,

Stitches to show something's missing? No, no? Then
How can we give you a thing?...

A living doll, everywhere you look.
It can sew, it can cook,
It can talk, talk, talk.

It works, there is nothing wrong with it.
You have a hole, it's a poultice.
You have an eye, it's an image.
My boy, it's your last resort.
Will you marry it, marry it, marry it.

To be given over to poems like these is to stand at the poet's side frozen, but powerless to reach a hand out as she falls. Though the poems have humor in them ('I guess you could say I've a call'), it is gallows humor. They carry little of the playfulness that is contained in most poetry. Their hectic, breathless rhythms give plenty of evidence that they were written in dead earnest, as stays against confusion that were at best only momentary. What else is there to do when you are 'inhabited by a cry'? Nothing but to set down what you see, what strikes you, without compunction or consideration. That is what these poems have done. It is all poetry *can* do in the situation.

The poems in *Ariel* are poems of defeat except in one sense: that they exist at all. It would be preposterous to suggest that the experience embodied here is unique; but it would be a lie to suggest that experience alone could have written these poems, that they could have been written by anyone but a true poet. They are a triumph for poetry, in fact, at the moment that they are a defeat for their author.

To have prepared, with all the devices and techniques of an art, for the awful catastrophe which you alone were fitted to face is to have sacrificed for art more victims than life can dispense with. One even infers, from the grim joy of some of these poems, that at the moment of writing, Sylvia Plath's life was eagerly consuming all its careful preparations. The candle is burnt out, and we have nothing left but the flame.

31. Irving Feldman, 'The Religion of One,' *Book Week*

19 June 1966, 3

Irving Feldman (b. 1928) is a poet and critic who teaches at the State University of New York at Buffalo.

There is a spirit of puffery that seems entirely natural to reviewing new books of poetry. It responds to and complements the tenuousness of the enterprise of lyric poetry: which is to sustain the power of inspirations and to summon into existence a world and a community in which the poems will be meaningful.

In the case of *Ariel*, this second and posthumous collection of Sylvia Plath's poems, the spirit of puffery is likely to turn to cult of homage. Sylvia Plath died, a suicide, in 1963 at the age of 31, and the equivocal completion of her life rests like a seal on these confessional poems, affirming the authenticity of their gestures by their eruption into life itself and drawing its own meaning from them. The death and the work fuse into one another and achieve the authority of a naked fact, which is all the more compelling in contrast to the recent parade of confessional poets and novelists whose 'nakedness' is largely cosmetic, who are in fact merely 'interesting,' intent on suffering beautifully. Sylvia Plath, then, is the stuff of myth, and she and *Ariel* come to exist as such in England.

Brilliant, vivid, hysterical, insane, isolated, bursting with revulsion, pain, and hatred, with no scope but that of their intensity, these poems cannot fail to fascinate and compel readers who are harassed by a sense of the inactuality of action, of its enclosure within artificial rôles. As our literature increasingly tells us, ours is a culture that seeks to be branded by a direct and final experience of power, and to be cleansed and renewed by the reductions and reversals of madness. Glamorous with misery (hers and ours), enclosed in the circle where she is both murderer and victim, Sylvia Plath looms up as our infirm prophet, and her poems, which demand neither praise nor blame—this sort of collaboration is forbidden the reader—stand as the acts of her encounter with power.

I have been speaking of madness, of a cultural madness (for better or for worse) and of a personal madness. Yet I don't want to imply that these lack genuine aesthetic and religious impulses—to which can be traced both the strengths and the weaknesses of *Ariel*. Aesthetically, the madness within which these poems locate themselves is the ultimate term of the subjectivity and narrowness of the lyric poem, which tends to view the world as an aspect of the self. Religiously, this madness dissolves the neutral objectifications of the universe and uncovers its bare power and will, for 'universe' (and 'god') is a concept of the will and as such is always implicit with will. 'God' cannot, as the current literary cliché has it, 'die.' As Dostoyevsky understood in one way or Yeats in another, God can only be killed (or obeyed), for He is ultimately not an object to be known but a will to be engaged; and the 'universe' is 'meaningless' or 'absurd' only because someone has declared it so. So long as the conceiving will exists, somebody, whether an 'I' or a 'God,' must wield the power. The primary religious question, then, is, Whose is this will and power?

The strength of *Ariel* is that it isolates and, from moment to moment, sustains the power and forces this question. Its weakness is that its answer is the answer of madness—that religion of one—which cannot distinguish between the self and the world. The power—the 'blue volts' that fitfully sizzle and crackle through these poems—leaps in an immediate arc between these poles and confounds them in its alternations. Now one is one and now the

other. Unmediated, uncontainable, irresistible, this power becomes a will too murderous to be engaged. Take, for example, the
shifting identifications and murderous atmosphere of 'Getting
There,' one of the 10 or 12 impressive poems in this volume. There
is a war; aboard a train, she aches for her destination, conscious of
the 'gigantic gorilla interiors / Of the wheels' which 'eat' and
become

> Fixed to their arcs like gods,
> The silver leash of the will—
> Inexorable. And their pride!
> All the gods know is destinations.

Suddenly, she then becomes a message, 'a letter in this slot,' and
then a messenger. There is a trainstop, and then the wounded and
mutilated, their 'legs, arms piled outside / The tent of unending
cries.' But she freezes them out; in the next line the tent has become
'A hospital of dolls.' Now she is on the ground slipping in the
reddened mud, in an agony to 'undo myself' under the 'train's teeth
/ Ready to roll, like a devil's.' Beset by the 'obstacles' of body and
her mourners, she wants to reach a 'still place.... Untouched and
untouchable.' The train, now 'insane for its destination,' labors to
give birth to her. For a moment, the very moment before her
rebirth, she is herself the murderous train:

> I shall count and bury the dead.
> Let their souls writhe in a dew,
> Incense on my track.
> The carriages rock, they are cradles.

And she steps forth 'to you from the black car of Lethe, / Pure as a
baby.'

'Ariel,' the title poem, hurtles through the same trajectory, but
more economically and without the pat and unconvincing rebirth
that mars 'Getting There.' It begins:

> Stasis in darkness.
> Then the substanceless blue
> Pour of tor and distances.

Their blueness shows these distances already charged with the
murderous volts. And God is announced immediately: 'God's
lioness, / How one we grow.' But, mysteriously, the lioness has
become another, cannot be caught, and the blood-filled darkness

presses into the poet's mouth. Suddenly, she is lifted into the air, becomes 'white Godiva' unpeeling 'dead hands, dead stringencies.' This purification doesn't work; now she is herself the lioness (and perhaps the wheat and dew as well): 'And now I/Foam to wheat, a glitter of seas.' A child is murdered ('a child's cry/Melts in the wall')—and she is released into the free flight compelled to dive (beyond the possibility of innocence) into the power's burning center, the sun, the eye of the lioness:

> And I
> Am the arrow,
>
> The dew that flies
> Suicidal, at one with the drive
> Into the red
>
> Eye, the cauldron of morning.

'Getting There' and 'Ariel' are memorable poems: bold, powerful, grotesque, appalling, for they show her universe, infected with the self, as a devilish will; salvation requires murder and murder requires damnation, and the damned must seek salvation.

Haunted by this universal taint and this ravenously dissolving power, the poems try to escape their dilemma by 'flying off into nothing,' into the only gift the murderous power can make: not the static perfection of death, but disembodied motion, the voltage rushing through the void, the great lyric dream of song and dance become a nightmare of flight. The short-circuit is complete. Precisely here the larger part of the poems of *Ariel* go weak, for the disembodiment takes the form of a sort of pure style, of words released from their weight of meaning of moral concern. 'Poppies in October,' for example, begins:

> Even the sun-clouds this morning cannot
>   manage such skirts
> Nor the woman in the ambulance
> Whose red heart blooms through her
>   coat so astoundingly—
>
> A gift, a love gift
> Utterly unasked for...

Is this really a woman in an ambulance? Has someone's chest been torn open? Is this a heart? No, they are only metaphors arranged to serve the idea of late-blooming poppies. The poem goes on to dwindle into the apotheosis of its falsity, and all this might be dismissed as literary chatter, if we didn't know the terrible process behind it. These words, mere words, are the motions of the disembodied will—arbitrary, capricious, arch, hysterical—on its own in the void, unsupported by any pressure of circumstance. Even the poems themselves are not permitted to supply, as poems do, such a containing pressure, and the hysterical blaze of the voice must, with its exclamations, sweep the inert and rhythmless words into their brief vivid lives. Elsewhere, the words appear as rôles, to be taken up and impatiently discarded. But we are again in the void, without any pressure of rules, for the name of this game is not, as some critics have put it, control; it is evasion. As a result, the rôle-playing becomes self-referring and arch, develops a sad hideous coquetry.

There is, however, a group of six poems—centering on bees and bee-keeping—that give us the poet this side of madness. Mechanical and yet vital, inert in winter (the hive then almost a sleeping baby armed with murderous stings), honey-makers, largely female—the bees provide a little world complex in its possibilities and willful enough to resist the volatilizations of madness, strong enough to drive off even death, the 'third person [who] is watching.' The bees are very small, they require care, they are dangerous. Their intense infinitesimal life yields a measurable and human fright and a dramatically defined (not infinite) self from which Miss Plath can reach toward her universal terror.

32. Unsigned review, 'Russian Roulette,' *Newsweek*

20 June 1966, 110–11

Poetry used to be a matter of life and death. 'Every healthy man,' said Baudelaire, 'can do without food for two days—but without poetry, never!' Today, as language slips away on one hand into the binary burps of technology, and on the other into the stereophonic nagging of the mass media (including most works of fiction and nonfiction), it is tougher than ever for a real poet to hang on to the battered nucleus of language—modern poets like Hart Crane, Dylan Thomas and the late Theodore Roethke have demonstrated how devastating such dedication can be. Sylvia Plath died in 1963 at 30, an apparent suicide after a life of tension and release that only poetry could express or transcend. As with Dylan Thomas, she may well become a mythic martyr of poetry, a scapegoat who earned illumination only through the light cast by her own immolation.

Her second and posthumous book of poems, *Ariel*, has already sold 15,000 copies in England (her husband, Ted Hughes, is an outstanding English poet). The importance of its American publication is signaled by a moving introduction by Robert Lowell, who remembers her as 'a brilliant, tense presence... willowy, long-waisted, sharp-elbowed, nervous, giggly, gracious....' The poems in *Ariel* were 'written in the last months of her life and often rushed out at the rate of two or three a day... These poems,' adds Lowell, 'are playing Russian roulette with six cartridges in the cylinder.'

Plasma: Indeed, the general effect of the book is that of a symphony of death and dissolution, scored in language so full of blood and brain that it seems to burst on the page and spatter the reader with the plasma of life. Pain and exacerbation were for Sylvia Plath what voluptuousness was for Keats. 'I must shriek,' she writes, and, 'I am red meat.' For her, 'health' is 'a country far away,' and even nature is painful in the power of its presence. This, for example, is what it feels like to look at the sea: 'The lines of the eye, scalded by these bald surfaces,/Boomerang like anchored elastics, hurting the owner.'

The universe is a planetarium of shocks for the sophisticated vulnerability of Sylvia Plath. In 'Lady Lazarus,' she speaks, almost boastingly, of her once-a-decade attempts at suicide: 'The first time it happened I was ten./It was an accident./The second time I meant/To last it out and not come back at all./I rocked shut/As a seashell./They had to call and call/And pick the worms off me like sticky pearls.'

Daughter, wife, mother—the births and entrances of a woman

are rendered with hair-raising palpability in these poems. It is almost as if Sylvia Plath feels too sharply for mere love or hate. She addresses her German father in 'Daddy,' a fantastic, Oedipal, tin-drumming nursery rhyme:

> I have always been scared of you,
> With your Luftwaffe, your gobbledygoo.
> And your neat moustache
> And your Aryan eye, bright blue.
> Panzer-man, panzer-man, O You—.

And even her baby with a balloon is seen in a bloodshot, sinister perspective, 'A red/Shred in his little fist.'

Sylvia Plath created a powerful, clinical lyricism—it cuts so insistently that a certain ecstatic numbness sets in. But she does the job of the poet as few today have done it—she makes her readers feel the amplified sense of their humanity, which for our time involves shock and loss and the flexible armor of frustration. An age that has not ceased to drink blood must appreciate her apocalyptic matter-of-factness: 'Somebody's done for.' And, in an unforgettable line, she re-creates herself as a lovable creature tethered to doom: 'I am the magician's girl who does not flinch.'

33. Robin Skelton, Review, *Massachusetts Review*

Autumn 1965, 834–5

Robin Skelton (b. 1925) is a British poet and critic who has for some time taught in Canada, and has edited the *Malahat Review*.

Sylvia Plath's posthumous collection, *Ariel*, is also filled with violence, but it is the violence of the disturbed mind rather than that of society. It is clear that these last poems belong to the 'confessional' school of poets, of whom Robert Lowell and Anne Sexton are the most brilliant members. Sylvia Plath was, of course, an American. She owes much to Theodore Roethke, and her work occasionally suffers from this debt. Her best poems, however, have an urgency, originality, and drive which place them among the most disturbing of our century. She chose, in many of her later poems, to explore a nightmare world of intense sensation and intense emotion, and made use of first person narration with increasing simplicity of diction and ferocity of imagery. Her imagery is unusual also in that she does not confine it to one category, but switches from one kind to another with a speed and certainty that remind me of the intellectual vigor and passion of Donne, as well as of the 'fragmented' poetry of Roethke. A good example is the following passage from 'Fever 103°':

[Quotes ll. 34–48, CP, p. 232.]

Although the imagery moves rapidly each new image is lucidly related to the theme, so that structural strength is never lost. Sometimes the poems have a simplicity and a bareness that bring them very close to anti-poetry, but never too close: the rhythms are always assured, though not always emphatic. Thus 'Death & Co.' ends with a flatness that is more terrible than any rhetoric:

[Quotes ll. 26–31, CP, p. 255.]

Sylvia Plath is dead herself now, but she has left us poetry that seems to me central to the fifties and sixties in which poetry of violence and 'confessional' poetry became more in evidence than ever before, and many poets began to explore the nightmare worlds of hysteria, fear, and neurotic tension.

THE COLOSSUS AND OTHER POEMS
(reissue)

London, 1967; New York, 1968

---

34. Unsigned review, 'Chained to the Parish Pump,' *Times Literary Supplement*

16 March 1967, 220

Sylvia Plath's first volume of poems, *The Colossus*, originally published by Heinemann in 1960, has now been reissued by Faber. In it one sees all the sure sophistication, all the rich image-creating energy, which were her early gifts. It is not yet an entirely original voice—there are touches of Ransom and Roethke—and it is not yet pushing itself over the edge. 'Spinster,' 'Mushrooms,' and 'The Disquieting Muses' are among the best things she ever wrote.

35. M.L. Rosenthal, 'Metamorphosis of a Book,' *Spectator*

21 April 1967, 456–7

Sylvia Plath's *The Colossus* was first published in 1960 by Heinemann, and then was issued two years later in the United States by Knopf in a new edition with ten of the original poems omitted. Miss Plath's promise was quickly recognised, despite a general impression of academic precisionism. Except for a few poems whose bitter, concentrated force made them unlike the rest, her work seemed 'craft'-centred and a bit derivative. In 1963 came the shocking news of her suicide. Soon afterwards we began to read in the *Observer* and elsewhere those extraordinary last poems that went into the 1965 volume *Ariel* and all but swamped the memory of the earlier book.

Now *The Colossus* has been reissued in its original form, though Miss Plath's cuts for the American edition had actually improved the book. For me at least, it has become almost an entirely different organism. After one has experienced *Ariel*, the poet's death-obsession and its deep link with her fear of yielding to the impersonal processes of her body stand out in *The Colossus* with morbid emphasis. The way in which many of the poems are haunted by images of cold terror, and the empathy involved in her poems about dead animals, are more striking now, and the theme of suicide is seen to be more pervasive than was at first evident.

The psychological horror of 'Daddy' is revealed to have a less drastic forerunner in the title poem of the earlier book. Familiarity with later poems like 'Lady Lazarus' and with the autobiographical novel *The Bell Jar* has sensitised me to the orientation of much of *The Colossus*. *Ariel* was not a completely new direction for its author, but the realisation and clarification of irresistible motives that were seeking their way to the surface from the start. I do not mean that *The Colossus* is artistically on the same level as *Ariel*, but that it has become far more interesting than it was at first. It has flashes of Sylvia Plath's final, and special, kind of awareness. We see it, for instance, in one macabre line in her 'Two Views of a Cadaver Room,' with its grisly echo of 'Prufrock:' 'In their jars the snail-nosed babies moon and glow.'

We see it, in fact, in the whole of this poem. The first of its two sections is about a girl's visit to a dissecting room, where she sees 'white-smocked boys' working on four cadavers, 'black as burnt turkey,' and where her friend (one of these boys) hands her 'the cut-out heart like a cracked heirloom'—a gross love-token that seems to foreshadow the morbidity of the lover hinted at in 'Lady Lazarus.' The second section describes a Brueghel painting of a war scene, but with a romantic love-scene painted in the lower right-hand corner showing two lovers absorbed in one another and 'deaf to the fiddle in the hands of the death's head shadowing their song.'

Her attempt here to relate by simple juxtaposition her painful private experience in the dissecting room to the general theme of war represented in Brueghel's 'panorama of smoke and slaughter and to Brueghel's other implied themes of love and of the transcendent character of art points to Sylvia Plath's major preoccupations just a short time later. So does her attempt in 'Suicide off Egg Rock' to reconstruct exactly how the protagonist of the poem felt at the moment when he drowned himself and how it was with him afterwards when his body was an inert object.

Sylvia Plath was a true 'literalist of the imagination.' When we use the word 'vision' about her poems, it must have a concrete, not a philosophically general, sense. Thus 'The Disquieting Muses' gives us a literal account of her 'muses'. After her death, her husband, Ted Hughes, said in a memorial note that in her later poems 'there is a strange muse, bald, white, and wild in her hood of bone, floating over a landscape like that of the primitive painters, a burningly luminous vision of Paradise. A Paradise which is at the same time eerily frightening, an unalterably spotlit vision of death.' The evolution of her muse is one sign of the growth and clarification, within a brief span of months, of Sylvia Plath's peculiar awareness of the burden of her sensibility in the whole context of the lifelong 'association' with such visions.

The happier side of her poetic character is revealed in poems and passages of entrancement within nature, moments of the sub-ordination of that sensibility to the pure rapture of existence. A marvellous moment of such entrancement comes at the beginning of 'The Eye-Mote':

> Blameless as daylight I stood looking
> At a field of horses, necks bent, manes blown,
> Tails streaming against the green
> Backdrop of sycamores....

It is all turned into merely nostalgic, rueful memory, however, by a splinter that flies into the speaker's eye, as if with the deliberate intention of knocking the Wordsworth out of her—leaving only a doleful, Larkin-like sense of loss behind. Only one poem of this volume, 'Flute Notes from a Reedy Pond,' ends more joyfully than it began.

More characteristic are 'Hardcastle Crags,' a poem of absolute alienation from town and landscape both, without an ounce of self-pity or sentimentality, but as concrete and irrefutable as the rocks of which it speaks, and 'The Stones.' This last poem, with which the book closes, is one of those whose bearing is clearer and more harshly moving now that *Ariel* and *The Bell Jar* have illuminated the mind behind them for us. I feel rebuked not to have sensed all these meanings in the first place, for now they seem to call out from nearly every poem.

36. James Tulip, 'Three Women Poets,' *Poetry Australia*

December 1967, 35–7

The reissue of Sylvia Plath's first book of poems, *The Colossus* (1960), pointedly reminds us that a new poetry has taken hold in the 1960's. A new style has come of age, one that has had its prophets, patron saints, apostates, disciples—and in Miss Plath its first martyr. It has 'happened'. First in America, and now everywhere. Usefully, but not adequately, it has been called a 'confessional' poetry. More pertinently, it has made the personal self of the poet the subject of the poem. Put in this way it may seem too simple to be true, or new. Yet the problem of how to make the 'I' presence in a poem the real subject in itself—and not merely a mask for the real subject, or a mere device, or some unexamined vantage point for observation and feeling—has required in the contemporary context of letters as radical a breakthrough as in any previous revolution of poetry. Of the three women poets to be considered here Anne Sexton most clearly illustrates the new style *qua* style; but the real issues underlying the change are issues of perception, attitude and craft, and are germane to all three.[1]

What we feel when we go to such a focus for the new poetry as Robert Lowell's *Life Studies* is the peculiar kind of balance and sanity achieved in his verse, and the way his subject-object relations enact a new perception of our situation. Yet, at first introduction to Lowell, this must seem to many people to be a peculiar kind of imbalance and disturbance.

The 'things' of Lowell's experience (his own terribly ordinary

95

experience) stand out in his writing precisely because they are no longer mere 'things' but 'objects' perceived by a 'subject', himself. It is the *relation* that matters, and that makes for the poem's stability over and against the material's instability. An instinctive shaping of a dozen possibilities is happening before our eyes. His 'confessional' method is, then, only a method; ultimately, it becomes absorbed in the scene, the confession being a necessary precondition of the perception. A freedom occurs in his poetry as a recognition and enactment of a loss of freedom; what he is in the present is a matter of what he has been in the past.

I

The Colossus shows Sylvia Plath poised in between the possibilities of releasing subject and object poetically in this same way, but holding back from the dramatic enactment that is so central in Lowell. She instinctively resists the loss of rational control, the emptying of self and immersion in objects of which he is capable; and yet the logic of her short and tragic career as a poet was pointing with an ever increasing intensity in this direction. 'This intense breakthrough', she has said of *Life Studies*, 'into very serious, very personal emotional experience which I feel has been partly taboo'. And why her imagination could not ultimately break out of its contemplative mould into this dramatic utterance she admired so much is the problem that defines her special power and genius as a poet. We hear echoes of herself in the poem she dedicates to Leonard Baskin, 'Sculptor':

> To his house the bodiless
> Come to barter endlessly
> Vision, wisdom, for bodies
> Palpable as his, and weighty.
>
> Hands moving move priestlier
> Than priest's hands, invoke no vain
> Images of light and air
> But sure stations in bronze, wood, stone.
>
> Obdurate, in dense-grained wood,
> A bald angel blocks and shapes
> The flimsy light; arms folded
> Watches his cumbrous world eclipse

> Inane worlds of wind and cloud.
> Bronze dead dominate the floor,
> Resistive, ruddy-bodied,
> Dwarfing us....

She is the gentle outsider wishing to come inside, a disembodied soul in search of a body, a bald angel in love with Falstaffian life. As in her title poem, 'The Colossus':

> I shall never get you put together entirely,
> Pieced, glued, and properly jointed.
> Mule-bray, pig-grunt and bawdy cackles
> Proceed from your great lips.
> It's worse than a barnyard.

'No frown of mine', she writes elsewhere, 'will betray the company I keep.' Reticence of this sort holds her back from depicting more than the *idea* of objects, and there is an allusiveness to the poems of *The Colossus* that makes them seem to be standing at arm's length from their meanings. Yet this condition, still, seems genuine in Sylvia Plath's world. Her poems for all their detachment have both a hardness and a delicacy to them; and, above all, a charismatic clarity of utterance and outline.

After *The Colossus* the issue for Miss Plath was to break out of the magic circle of her own making. It is fascinating to see in the *Ariel* volume, that follows, how she is subjecting her own character and selfhood to an intense scrutiny and a range of attitudes; the result is something of Lowell's sharp and jagged, even gauche, sense of individuality. But the problem remains that Miss Plath's poetry can never make a full and vital connection with objects. Her relation with the things of her world is a willed and self-conscious one. She is projecting herself into existence, however, with such energy and penetration that whether it be object or not-object she is aiming at her poetry is always enabled to enact her particular and peculiar kind of faith and character.

> And I
> Am the arrow,
>
> The dew that flies
> Suicidal, at one with the drive
> Into the red
>
> Eye, the cauldron of morning.
>
>   'Ariel'.

Such exactness of rhythm and metaphor elsewhere in poetry would find support and nurture from objects, attitudes, beliefs. Here, there is a total isolation of the person in her universe of perception. The words are held together only in a desperate act of will, and all that can eventuate from such a process, apart from the process itself, is exhaustion and oblivion. It seems to be a fallacy of the subjective correlative.

NOTE

1 See M. L. Rosenthal, *The New Poets* (New York: OUP, 1967) for a recent penetrating and wide ranging study of the contemporary scene in poetry.

THE BELL JAR
(Sylvia Plath) (reissue)

London, 1966

---

37. C. B. Cox, 'Editorial,' *Critical Quarterly*

Autumn 1966, 195

C. B. Cox (b. 1929), editor of *Critical Quarterly*, is a poet and critic in his own right. He was responsible for Plath's editing the magazine supplement *American Poetry Now* in 1961.

Sylvia Plath's novel, *The Bell Jar*, first published under a pseudonym in 1963, has now been reissued by Faber and Faber. It's not easy to evaluate this semi-autobiographical story. The heroine, Esther Greenwood, wins a prize which gives her a month working on a magazine in New York, suffers extreme stresses that end in attempts to commit suicide, and finishes up undergoing treatment in a mental hospital. As I read this extremely disturbing narrative, the heartbreaking intensity of the last poems in *Ariel* became so involved with the scenes in the novel that aesthetic detachment was not really possible. From the first sentence *The Bell Jar* makes compulsive reading: 'It was a queer, sultry summer, the summer they electrocuted the Rosenbergs, and I didn't know what I was doing in New York'. In a slick, professional style the novel recreates the falsity of New York glamour, but as Esther Greenwood breaks down, the tone becomes more personal, and I don't think these later sections are completely successful. It's not clear how far Esther, who tells her own story, properly understands her motives, and the tone wavers between detachment and involvement. The novel seems a first attempt to express mental states which eventually found a more appropriate form in the poetry. But throughout there is a notable honesty—the intellectual woman's conflicting attitudes to her body, desiring to be attractive to men, and yet a little resentful of the feminine rôle. And the hospital world of breakdown and operation is presented with something of that fierce clarity so terrifying in the great poems in *Ariel*.

38. Stephen Wall, review, *Observer*

11 September 1966, 27

The late Sylvia Plath's novel, first published under another name and now reissued as *The Bell Jar*,★ does deal with mental crisis in the accents of literary authority. This terse account of an American girl's breakdown and treatment gains its considerable power from an objectivity that is extraordinary considering the nature of the material. Sylvia Plath's attention had the quality of ruthlessness, and here—even more perhaps than in her last poems—imagery and rhetoric is disciplined by an unwinking intelligence.

NOTE

★ Evidently Mr Wall thought the title of the book had changed, not the name of its author.

THE BELL JAR
(Sylvia Plath)

New York, 1971

39. J. D. O'Hara, 'An American Dream Girl,' *Washington Post Book World*

11 April 1971, 3

'Victoria Lucas' first published *The Bell Jar* in England in 1963. But Victoria Lucas was really the American poet Sylvia Plath—or had been; the novel's characters and settings were equally American; and the time of action was the mid-Fifties, not the Sixties. Never much publicized, *The Bell Jar* became something of an unknown favorite, especially among the young. In 1965 Faber & Faber published a paperback edition under Sylvia Plath's name, and now Harper & Row are finally bringing the book back home.

The novel is a curious combination of stories. It begins in high spirits as a cheerful, shallow, fast-moving, and satirical account of the author's barely fictionalized summer in New York as one of the undergraduate guest editors of *Mademoiselle*. The Barbizon Hotel becomes the Amazon, *Mademoiselle* is simply 'a fashion magazine,' and Esther Greenwood, a cheerful female Holden Caulfield, tells us about her terrible blind dates, her interest in sex ('When I was nineteen, pureness was the great issue'), and her memories of college and of her Yale boyfriend Buddy Willard. The anecdotes are very well told: after all, Sylvia Plath was a poet (*The Colossus*; *Ariel*), which means that she knew how to use words economically and unostentatiously. But the narrator's voice is a nineteen-year-old's, pure and simple. When eleven of the twelve guest editors came down simultaneously with ptomaine poisoning, pure and simple Esther comments cheerfully that 'there is nothing like puking with somebody to make you into old friends.' Remembering the time when Buddy Willard took it upon himself to show her what a naked man looked like, she says:

He just stood there in front of me and I kept on staring at him. The only thing I could think of was turkey neck and turkey gizzards and I felt very depressed.

But then the New York adventures end, Esther returns to quiet, suburban Connecticut, and a strange new book begins. The funny incidents are funny in a different way, and suddenly Esther is undergoing psychiatric treatment, and suddenly she's in an asylum.

(The question of where exactly the tone of the novel shifts, where exactly the madness begins, can provoke some very curious discussions, complete with many a sidelong glance. Contestants are likely to take almost any position, some insisting that Esther was never crazy at all, that she was merely the victim of a Communist plot, and others insisting that they knew it from the start, that Esther was crazy to have accepted that first blind date.)

Esther's story of her six months of madness and treatment—the novel ends as she's about to return to Smith College—is bound to be compared, nowadays, to Hannah Green's *I Never Promised You a Rose Garden*. Esther's story is better, partly because Sylvia Plath was a better writer, partly because the story is told more swiftly, and partly because the first-person narration fixes us there, in the doctor's office, in the asylum, in the madness, with no reassuring vacations when we can keep company with the sane and listen to their lectures.

Of course the subject matter of the two stories is necessarily similar: asylums, like happy families, are much alike. The interviews and treatments, the less fortunate and the luckier fellow patients, and the incompetent and the godlike psychiatrist appear in both. In *Rose Garden*, Deborah's mind created a complicated fictional world; fortunately for the reader of *The Bell Jar*, Esther never gets past the opening stages of hers: 'My heroine would be myself, only in disguise. She would be called Elaine. Elaine.'

Sylvia Plath was herself as two-sided as her novel. She was tall, blonde, beautiful, intelligent, witty, and talented—everyone's dream girl, the American ideal. But we've begun to learn, nowadays, that the safest thing to do in the presence of an Eagle Scout is to turn and run, screaming; and we have also begun to realize that to be a beautiful, intelligent, witty, and talented girl, at least here in mid-century America, is considerably more dangerous than shooting heroin. For such an illness, cures are less common than delays. Born in 1932, Sylvia Plath committed suicide in 1963.

40. Saul Maloff, 'Waiting for the Voice to Crack,' *New Republic*

8 May 1971, 33–5

Saul Maloff (b. 1922) is a novelist, editor, and college teacher. He has been books editor for *Newsweek*.

Apparent reasons for the eight-year delay in importing *The Bell Jar* from England (publication there, 1963) are not in themselves convincing. The pseudonym of Victoria Lucas was a hedge, but against what? Sylvia Plath made no secret of her authorship. Her suicide followed publication by a month, but such things have never stopped the wheels of industry from turning: she was a 'property' after all, certainly following the publication of *Ariel* in 1966. Nor can we take seriously her having referred to it as a 'potboiler' and therefore to be kept separate from her serious work: the oldest and most transparent of all writers' dodges. All the evidence argues against it: as early as 1957 she had written a draft of the novel; she completed the final version on a Eugene Saxton Fund fellowship and felt toward its terms an urgent sense of commitment and obligation; the painstaking quality of the writing—but above all, its subject: her own pain and sickness, treated with literal fidelity, a journal done up as a novel, manifestly re-experienced, and not from any great distance of glowing health. One of her motives was the familiar one of getting her own back, to (as her heroine says) 'fix a lot of people'—among others of smaller significance, to lay the ghost of her father, and tell the world she hated her mother (the exact words of her protagonist-surrogate, spoken to her psychiatrist in a key passage).

Only the names were changed, nothing else: as much as a novel can be, it was recorded rather than imagined. Evidently she panicked as publication drew near and displayed more than the usual terror of reviewers, who were on the whole generous and patronizing in a chuckling avuncular way, though she mis-read their intention, as toward the end, one supposes, she mis-read everything. Her last awful year was marked by a miscarriage, an appendectomy, the birth of her second child, as well as a series of plaguing minor illnesses, to say nothing of separation from her husband. According to her mother, Mrs. Aurelia Plath, whose 1970 letter to her daughter's Harper & Row editor is included in a 'Biographical Note' appended to the novel, Miss Plath told her brother that the book must in no circumstances be published in the U.S.

Mrs. Plath's letter is a noteworthy document, and an oddly touching one. She pleads her case by telling the editor she knows no pleas will help, though publication here will cause 'suffering' in the lives of several persons whom Sylvia loved and who had 'given freely of time, thought, affection, and in one case, financial help during those agonizing six months of breakdown in 1953.' To them, the book as it stands in itself 'represents the basest ingratitude.' But, Mrs. Plath argues, her daughter didn't mean for the book to stand alone; she herself told her mother in 1962 that she'd merely 'thrown together events from my own life, fictionalizing to add color,' a 'potboiler' to show 'how isolated a person feels when he is suffering a breakdown... to picture my world and the people in it as seen through the distorting lens of a bell jar.' Her second novel, she assured her mother, 'will show that same world as seen through the eyes of health.' Ingratitude was 'not the basis of Sylvia's personality'; the second novel, presumably, would have been one long, ingratiating, fictionalized thank-you note to the world. Of course the publisher is right to publish; but since the persons who may be slightly scorched are still alive, why eight years?

The novel itself is no firebrand. It's a slight, charming, sometimes funny and mildly witty, at moments tolerably harrowing 'first' novel, just the sort of clever book a Smith summa cum laude (which she was) might have written if she weren't given to literary airs. From the beginning our expectations of scandal and startling revelation are disappointed by a modesty of scale and ambition and a jaunty temperateness of tone. The voice is straight out of the 1950's: politely disenchanted, wholesome, yes, wholesome, but never cloying, immediately attractive, nicely confused by it all, incorrigibly truthtelling; in short, the kind of kid we liked then, the best product of our best schools. The hand of Salinger lay heavy on her.

But this is 1971 and we read her analyst, too wily to be deceived by that decent, smiling, well-scrubbed coed who so wants to be liked and admired. We look for the slips and wait for the voice to crack. We want the bad, the worst news; that's what we're here for, to be made happy by horror, not to be amused by girlish chatter. Our interests are clinical and prurient. A hard case, she confounds us. She never raises her voice. To control it, she stays very close to the line of her life in her twentieth year, telling rather than evoking the memorable events; more bemused than aghast. That year she came down to New York from Smith one summer month to work as an apprentice-editor for *Mademoiselle* (here *Ladies Day*) for its college issue, a reward for being a good, straight-A girl and promising young writer; and had exactly the prescribed kind of time, meeting people and going places, eating out and dressing up, shopping and sightseeing, and thinking maybe it was about time she got laid. The closest she came to it was sleeping chastely, quite dressed and untouched, beside an inscrutable UN simultaneous translator. Throughout, the tone is prevailingly unruffled, matter-of-fact, humorously woebegone.

Prevailingly, but not quite. What should have been exciting—she was a small-town girl living in NYC for the first time on her own—was dreary, trivial, flat. She was beginning to doubt herself, her talent, her prospects. Mysteriously, as if from another work, period of life, region of the mind, images and memories startlingly appear, and just as quickly vanish; colors and events we recognize from the late poems: darkness and blackness; the world perceived as misshapen and ominous; her father (the figure of her marvelous poem 'Daddy') remembered with love and fury, the source of her last 'pure' happiness at the age of nine before he perversely left her bereft one day by cruelly dying; foetuses and blood, fever and sickness, the obsession with purity and the grotesque burden of her body, of feeling itself. In the poems the pressure is terrific; she screams her pain, in a final effort to contain it; yet here it is duly noted, set down serially, linearly, as possibly interesting to those in the business of making connections, scrupulously recorded as in a printed clinical questionnaire by a straight-A girl in the habit of carefully completing forms. When she sees the dumb, staring 'goggle-eyed head lines' monstrously proclaiming the execution of the Rosenbergs, she 'couldn't help wondering what it would be like, being burned alive all along the nerves' and concludes flatly, 'I thought it must be the worst thing in the world.' A silent china-white telephone sits like a 'death's head.' Her hometown boy-friend, a medical student, takes her to see cadavers at the morgue and a foetus with a 'little piggy smile' that reminds her of Eisenhower; and then, to round things off, they go to watch a child-birth. The woman on the 'awful torture-table, with these metal stirrups sticking up in mid-air' seems to her 'to have nothing but an enormous spider-fat stomach and two little ugly spindly legs propped in the high stirrups' and 'all the time the baby was being born she never stopped making this unhuman wooing noise' and 'all the time, in some secret part of her, that long, blind, doorless and windowless corridor of pain was waiting, to open up and shut her in again.' A silly, simpering girl, a hat-designer idiotically pleased at the good news of the Rosenbergs' execution, reveals a 'dybbuk' beneath her plump, bland exterior. But these darker notes do not accumulate to thematic density save in retrospect; they seem accidental dissonances, slips of the tongue.

Even the breakdown, when it comes, is generally muted, seeming from the outside as much slothfulness as madness, the obligatory junior-year interlude. The break is quantitative: the tones are darker, the world somewhat more distorted and remote, the voice, almost never breezy now, is more than disaffected—it can become nasty, a trifle bitchy, even cruel, streaked with violence. She makes some gestures toward suicide—as much amusing as they are frightening; and then though she very nearly brings it off, we almost can't bring ourselves to believe it, so theatrically staged is the scene. Yet even then, after breakdown and hospitalization, electroshock and insulin, she composes the book's funniest, most charming scene—of her incidental, much-delayed defloration; and in the knowledge of its appalling consequences. The chap, accidentally encountered on the steps of the Widener (where else?) is, she carefully notes, a 26-year-old full professor of Mathematics at Harvard, name of Irwin; and ugly. Him she elects to 'seduce'; and after the fastest such episode in fiction, she isn't even sure it happened at all. Wanting more direct evidence, she can only infer it from her massive hemorrhaging. Concluding now that, no longer a virgin, she has put behind her childish things, she lies down and, bleeding profusely, writes: 'I smiled into the dark. I felt part of a great tradition.' At the end, the tone is ambiguous but not despairing; she has been readmitted to Smith, where out of old habit she will keep getting nothing but A's; the bell jar has descended once, and may again.

She laid out the elements of her life, one after the other, and left to the late poems the necessary work of imagining and creating it: it is for this reason that we feel in the book an absence of weight and complexity sufficient to the subject.

On balance, *The Bell Jar*, good as it is, must be counted part of Sylvia Plath's juvenilia, along with most of the poems of her first volume; though in the novel as in a few of the early poems she foretells the last voice she was ever to command.

41. Mason Harris, '*The Bell Jar,*' *West Coast Review*

October 1973, 54–6

Mason Harris (b. 1931) was born in Boston and grew up in eastern Massachusetts. He is an Associate Professor of English at Simon Fraser University in Canada, specializing in Victorian fiction and science fiction.

There is a general tendency to view Sylvia Plath's only novel as an immature and artistically flawed piece of catharsis, useful as background to the lyrics but not up to par for the author of *Ariel*. This rating of the novel is supported by the author herself, who, as we learn in the 'Biographical Note,' explained to her mother that

What I've done is to throw together events from my own life, fictionalizing to add color—it's a pot boiler really, but I think it will show how isolated a person feels when he is suffering a breakdown.... I've tried to picture my world and the people in it as seen through the distorting lens of a bell jar.... My second book will show the same world as seen through the eyes of health ('Note,' 294–95).

Her mother thought this admission amply justified blocking publication of the novel in the U.S. on the grounds that it contained unkind caricatures of a number of people 'whom Sylvia loved' when she was sane. However, authors' opinions of their own work are notoriously suspect, Sylvia's here in particular. Firstly, it would seem that she is trying to mollify in advance the wounded feelings that her mother would experience when she read the novel and found that she was one of the caricatures. Also the plan for a 'healthy' novel smacks of the brisk, determinedly cheerful, efficient woman Sylvia strove to appear in her everyday life, but fortunately not in her writing. Does any of her best work seem healthy, or even tell us what health is?

Perhaps as a poet Sylvia felt some contempt for the limitations of prose. While the novel seems as morbidly self-obsessed as the final poems it can hardly, as straightforward narrative, score *Ariel*'s extraordinary breakthrough in language and imagery. However, the novel also achieves something that intense confessional lyrics cannot: the poems dredge a private sickness which seems to arise only from the personal past while the novel throws open the social dimension of madness, indicting the culture in which the heroine has grown up, or rather which prevents her from doing so. Nowhere have I found so forceful a depiction of what it was like to be an adolescent in the stifling, hermetically-sealed world of the Eisenhower Fifties. The 'distorted lens' of madness gives an authentic vision of a period which exalted the most oppressive ideal of reason and stability.

Esther Greenwood, narrator and thinly-disguised version of Sylvia, is a brilliant straight-A student at an ivy-league Eastern women's college (Sylvia graduated *summa* from Smith). With the uncertainty attendant on compulsive drives she secretly suspects, despite all evidence to the contrary, that she is really quite stupid and ignorant and will someday be found out. As the novel opens in the summer of her Junior year she is in New York City as prize-winning guest editor of a leading fashion magazine (*Mademoiselle* in real life) experiencing, along with twelve other lucky girls, a publicity-stunt tour of the fashion world at its most superficial (the 'Note' gives a sample of some deliciously awful prose Sylvia turned out for the mag). Esther forlornly reflects that this is a great opportunity for a girl of such limited means, and that she is supposed to be having the time of her life. The witty satire of the first half of the novel acquires darker meaning as the heroine (like Sylvia) lapses into madness and makes a most determined suicide attempt (far more thorough and apparently foolproof than the one which succeeded ten years later).

If this novel goes less deeply into psychotic experience than Hannah Green's *I Never Promised You A Rose Garden* or Janet Frame's *Faces in the Water* it also does a much more complete job of relating the heroine's madness to her social world. Esther's collapse is precipitated by the discovery of an inner deathliness concealed under the glossy surface of New York and her own compulsive drive to achievement. Because they are so personal, many of the poems of *Ariel* seem liable to explanation in classic Freudian formulae, but here something more is demanded. Granted that Esther-Sylvia suffered from fixation on her childhood relation to her parents, we also must ask how failure to find any feasible road to maturity contributed to her illness. Her longing to regress permeates the novel, but might not regression be partly the result of the apparent impossibility of further development?

In New York Esther acknowledges the inadequacy of the compulsive achievement which dominated her childhood and adolescence, yet cannot find a mature identity to replace it: 'The one thing I was good at was winning scholarships and prizes, and that era was coming to an end. I felt like a racehorse in a world without racetracks....' (84). In a significantly mechanical metaphor she sees her life as a no-thoroughfare: 'I saw the years of my life speed along a road in the form of telephone poles, threaded together by wires. I counted one, two, three...nineteen telephone poles, and then the wires dangled into space, and try as I would, I couldn't see a single pole beyond the nineteenth' (137). Erik Erikson has described the transition from childhood to maturity as a daring leap across an abyss; the heroine of the *Bell Jar* finds only a cliff edge with nothing beyond.

The relation between regression and stifled development is particularly evident in the narrator's use of baby-images—central also to the poetry but developed with special clarity here. Pleasant baby-images are associated with the joys of regression but the novel is also haunted by the nightmare image of a fetus in a bottle—to which she was first introduced by her medical-student boyfriend. This aspect of the baby becomes a graphic expression of that sense of strangled development which is the other side of her tendency to regression. When after her recovery her mother says, 'We'll act as if all this were a bad dream;' Esther thinks 'To the person in the bell jar, blank and stopped as a dead baby, the world itself is the bad dream' (267). A particularly striking image links arrested growth to the world of the 'Fifties. From the pages of *Life Magazine* 'The face of Eisenhower beamed up at me, bald and blank as the face of a fetus in a bottle' (98). Esther also hates babies because they represent the ideal of total domesticity, but sometimes longs to become a mother as a form of psychic suicide.

Esther's breakdown comes after a series of unfortunate encounters with sex in New York. The ensuing psychosis could partly be explained on the grounds of sexual repression and morbid attachment to her dead father, but it is also true that all the men she has known manifest variations on a consistently sick attitude toward women and marriage; since no remotely acceptable relationship is available her libido has nowhere to go but backwards.

The novel's sexuality is dominated by the American Mom as represented by her boyfriend's mother, Mrs. Willard 'with her heather-mixture tweeds and her sensible shoes and her wise, maternal maxims. Mr. Willard was her little boy, and his voice was high and clear, like a little boy's' (245). The most oft-repeated of these maxims are '"What a man wants is a mate and what a woman wants is infinite security,' and 'What a man is is an arrow into the future and what a woman is is the place the arrow shoots off from"' (79). Her boyfriend Buddy, a 'nice, clean boy' and a magnificent specimen of the male ideal of the 'Fifties in all his sentimental nobility, is particularly devoted to his mother. (When he sexlessly exhibits himself to Esther he explains that he wears net underpants because '"my mother says they wash easily"' (75).

The Oedipal split between pure love and degraded sexuality is made explicit by a Southern gentleman who laments to Esther that he can't have sex with a woman he truly loves: 'it would be spoiled by thinking this woman too was just an animal like the rest, so if he loved anybody he would never go to bed with her. He'd go to a whore if he had to and keep the woman he loved free of all that dirty business' (87). Esther gives up on him when he writes with incestuous ardor that she has 'such a kind face, surprisingly like his older sister's.'

In their big date at Yale, Buddy treats her 'like a friend or cousin,' kissing her only once gently behind the chem. lab—'"Wow. it makes me feel terrific to kiss you"' (68). Esther has been much impressed with the necessity of remaining pure till her marriage night, and is outraged to find that while dating her the 'clean' Buddy has fornicated at least thirty times with 'some tarty waitress' who seduced him over the summer. Her more experienced friends explain that 'most boys were like that' but Esther can't stand 'the idea of a woman having to have a pure life and a man being able to have a double life, one pure and one not' (90). She also begins to suspect that being the object of his 'pure life' might become a bit oppressive: 'I...remembered Buddy Willard saying in a sinister, knowing way that after I had children, I would feel differently. I wouldn't want to write poems any more' (94). Perhaps 'infinite security' is only a more painful form of suicide.

The most intense form of Oedipal passion is demonstrated by Marco, a Latin woman-hater Esther meets at a party on her last evening in New York. He adores his first cousin—about to enter a nunnery—but can't marry her because of South American ideas about incest. When Esther offers the consolation that someday '"you'll love somebody else"' he responds by throwing her in the mud—'"Your dress is black and the dirt is black as well"'—spitting in her face, and trying to rape her while repeatedly hissing '"Slut!"' in her ear. She virtuously fights him off but he still insists. '"Sluts, all sluts.... Yes or no, it is all the same"' (121). It would seem that some violence also lurks in Buddy's love. He contracts T.B. and when Esther visits him at the sanitorium he resents her relative health and freedom. He forces her to ski down a dangerous slope and when she takes the inevitable spill informs her, smiling with a 'queer, satisfied expression,' that '"Your leg's broken in two places. You'll be stuck in a cast for months"' (109). These episodes seem so apt that one wonders whether they really happened that way, or were structured by the author to represent the inner truth of her experience—but since they are quite convincing this hardly matters.

Thus personal relationships present no alternative to Esther's pursuit of straight A's. Hysterical and sexless devotion to the performance principle is exemplified by her friend Joan Gilling, a local 'big wheel—president of her class and a physics major and the college hockey champion' (65). Joan, who later turns out to be a lesbian, dates Buddy because she so admires his mother. After learning of Esther's suicide attempt Joan becomes inspired to try it herself and winds up at the same asylum, where Esther sees her as 'the beaming double of my old best self' (231). Joan brings along all her school-books, studies Freud, plans to become a psychiatrist, and finally hangs herself. At her funeral Esther finds some consolation in the fact that she herself has escaped this fate, but the reader knows that her apparent recovery is only a reprieve.

This novel is enclosed in many prisons, all expanded forms of the bell jar. The ladies in 'Belsize,' the 'best' ward of Esther's exclusive hospital, put on a good imitation of upper middle class living: 'What was there about us, in Belsize, so different from the girls playing bridge and gossiping and studying in the college to which I would return? Those girls, too, sat under bell jars of a sort' (268). During her summer in New York the Rosenbergs are electrocuted and Esther 'couldn't help wondering what it would be like, being burnt alive along all your nerves' (1). Later in a seedy private mental hospital she is punished for madness by shock therapy incompetently (or sadistically) administered: 'with each flash a great jolt drubbed me till I thought my bones would break and the sap fly out of me like a split plant. I wondered what terrible thing it was that I had done' (161). The parents of Esther's world seem to feel that mental and even physical illness arises from weak moral character. Esther's mother makes her become a volunteer worker in local hospitals because 'the cure for thinking too much about yourself was helping somebody who was worse off than you' (182). Buddy's father 'simply couldn't stand the sight of sickness and especially his own son's sickness, because he thought all sickness was sickness of the will' (101).

In the end Esther's cure seems to consist more of resignation to prison than escape from it. If madness was precipitated by a demand for something better than the compulsive past, recovered sanity seems a depressing return to her 'old best self' because nothing better has been found. Esther's coldly calculated plan to lose her virginity ends in a freak hemorrhage which seems to comment on the fallacy of trying to will an emotional experience. Sylvia once described the *Bell Jar* as 'an autobiographical apprentice work which I had to write in order to free myself from the past' ('Note,' 293). Though better than this the novel did not grant the self understanding that would free her, nor did the even more brilliant *Ariel*. On the other hand if madness is a form of insight and itself a comment on its causes, then effective expression of it may achieve success in art, if not in life. In its forceful linking of private to public madness the *Bell Jar* not only adds a new dimension to the poetry but deserves to be considered a major work in its own right.

42. G(eoffrey) W(olff), *'The Bell Jar,'* Newsweek

19 April 1971, 120

Geoffrey Wolff (b. 1937) is a California-born novelist, critic, and essayist.

Sylvia Plath was a fine poet who killed herself in London eight years ago when she was only 30. Her best poems are her last, collected in *Ariel*, and they collate images of frightening and hopeless despair. They are confessional poems by a writer of orderly intelligence slipping into madness, wittily conscious of every piece of solid ground she gives up. A great mystery, then, the mystery of psychosis: why, if you see so clearly what is going wrong, don't you just *stop*, just will yourself back into balance and purchase?

The Bell Jar, her autobiographical novel published in 1963 in England but never before in the U.S., explains in the clearest possible way the inaccessibility of the psychotic. The heroine leaps from a life of customary troubles to a far world of madness all at once. No reasons are provided because none are available. Suddenly, the heroine does not want to live. She falls apart utterly. There are no clinical words here, just hanging ropes and razor blades and sleeping pills and electric shocks through the brain.

The novel has a special poignance, of course, because it shuts down on the upbeat note of cure, and we know the end of the author's life. It has a special force, a humbling power, because it shows the vulnerability of people of hope and good will. It has a special interest because it was written by a very, very special poet.

43. Margaret L. Shook, 'Sylvia Plath: The Poet and the College,' *Smith Alumnae Quarterly*

April 1972, 4–9

Margaret L. Shook (b. 1929) graduated from Smith College several years before Plath, and now teaches there. Her academic field is British poetry, and her PhD is from the University of California at Berkeley.

I am chiefly interested in the poetry of Sylvia Plath, in the work by which she will outlive the brevity and pain of her experience, and even if this were not the case, I knew her so slightly when we were students at this college, that I can contribute no new facts for the biographers. Nevertheless, in reading her poems, even those of the *Ariel* volume, poems which many critics view as 'confessions,' intimate psychic self-revelations, I am stirred by a sense of shared experience, an awareness of the ways in which she speaks for a particular generation of women. In what follows on Sylvia Plath and Smith College, I emphasize, therefore, certain conflicts and preoccupations which were a portion of the common experience, even while they affected most profoundly the life of the under-graduate poet who was eventually able to transform and transcend them in her art.

I begin with *The Bell Jar*, where the transformation is not wholly successful, because that work provides, under the gossamer veil thrown over persons and places, an authentic autobiographical account of Sylvia Plath's experience at the College, and yet it is an account in several ways misleading, as I shall attempt to show.

There is a certain narrative confusion in *The Bell Jar*, which damages, I think, its structure and threatens the integrity of its meaning. This confusion stems from a failure on the part of its author to solve the problem of point-of-view, a problem which is for the story-teller most pressing, and at the same time most difficult of solution, when the materials of the story to be told are deeply personal, autobiographical, exerting their own compelling pressure to be re-lived in imagination, and recounted with exactitude. The autobiographical impulse may arise from any one of several sources. In the case of Sylvia Plath, I believe, the never-quite acknowledged impulse is guilt and the motive is self-justification, the need to plead this special case before the bar of the unknown judges. Undergoing shock-treatments for the first time, at the hands of the iniquitous Dr. Gordon, her surrogate heroine comments, 'I wondered what terrible thing it was that I had done.' But *The Bell Jar* is not merely disguised autobiography, it is fiction (albeit fractured fiction), and the fictional motive at work in the novel is to tell the story of Sylvia Plath, not because her case is special, but on the contrary, because it is exemplary. Anyone who was a student at Smith College, or at any other East-Coast, Ivy-League women's college in the early fifties, will recognize just how representative she wished to make her case appear.

I speculate that five years' residence in England had led Sylvia Plath by 1961 to recognize what was typical and exemplary in her experiences of the summer and fall of 1953, and of the preceding three years at college. *The Bell Jar* shows, at any rate, in its selections of what to tell, particularly in the first nine chapters, the author's consciousness of addressing an English audience, her consciousness therefore of her public, national and historical identity as that quaint and curious, comic yet tormented, product of a culture, the American college girl of the fifties.

Given the compelling need to recount accurately the history of her madness and her suicide attempt, she wished also to make that madness seem symptomatic, and further, she wished to evince her detachment and maturity by treating her case with irony and humor. To this end, she found a narrative 'voice,' evoked a style, and adopted the persona of Esther Greenwood. But only partially. The result is a flawed novel.

In attempting to simplify her own character into that of Esther Greenwood, Sylvia Plath doubtless wished to demonstrate the psychic fragility and vulnerability of the girl who has assumed a public identity which proves to be for her an empty cliché, and who, when that bubble bursts, cannot find any other identity to take its place, because none of the roles readily available to her, save indeed that of madness, will accommodate the visionary intensity of her private experience. Nevertheless, Esther Greenwood is a novelistic failure.

Here is the way she sometimes speaks:

As I lay there in my white hotel bed feeling lonely and weak, I thought I was up in that sanitorium in the Adirondacks, and I felt like a heel of the worst sort. In his letters Buddy kept telling me how he was reading poems by a poet who was also a doctor and how he'd found out about some famous dead Russian short-story writer who had been a doctor too, so maybe doctors and writers could get along fine, after all. (p. 61)

It is the sort of passage that bears out the view expressed by novelist and critic Charles Newman, and doubtless others, that Sylvia Plath is the first woman to write in the Salinger vein, and that Esther Greenwood is a sort of female Holden Caulfield. She certainly sounds like it. Obviously, her mind is not that of the undergraduate Sylvia Plath, who knew perfectly well the names of Chekhov and William Carlos Williams.

But then again sometimes Esther speaks like this:

The next thing I had a view of was somebody's shoe.

It was a stout shoe of cracked black leather and quite old, with tiny air holes in a scalloped pattern over the toe and a dull polish, and it was pointed at me. It seemed to be placed on a hard green surface that was hurting my right cheekbone.

I kept very still, waiting for a clue that would give me some notion of what to do. A little to the left of the shoe I saw a vague heap of blue cornflowers on a white ground and this made me want to cry. It was the sleeve of my own bathrobe I was looking at, and my left hand lay pale as a cod at the end of it. (p. 149)

Despite the valiant efforts made by Sylvia Plath to bridge the gap, for instance by sticking to simple sentence structures throughout the novel, I still find it impossible to reconcile these divergent voices. The girl who thinks and talks like the speaker in the first passage simply cannot perceive like the narrator in the second, and by the same token, the poet of the second passage, who renders with such vividness, immediacy, and particularity the felt shape of her sensible experience, has surely had thoughts which the first speaker would never dream of. If the first speaker derives from J.D. Salinger (actually I intend to suggest in a moment a different origin), the second derives from Camus. The mixture is not a happy one.

To be sure, the novel as it stands could ill spare the first speaker. Naive, shallow, suggestible, yet shrewd to the point of cunning, greedy for experience, fundamentally selfish—she is redeemed by the candor of her innocence. This is a comic character, and her presence in the novel is responsible for some of its best and funniest scenes, like the one where Buddy Willard is literally and figuratively unveiled. It is she too who furnishes the candid observations which give the novel its satiric punch; as when, having witnessed the excruciating birth of Mrs. Tomolillo's baby, and having been informed by Buddy Willard that Mrs. Tomolillo will remember no pain, she comments: 'I thought it sounded just like the sort of drug a man *would* invent.' (p. 72)

However, as Esther moves towards madness, and the second voice becomes more dominant, the novel turns and rends itself, the comedy now revealing its hollowness, the satire its superficiality.

The first speaker (whom I will now call for the sake of simplicity, Esther Greenwood), is a kind of parody of the undergraduate Sylvia Plath, and her history is a parody of the experience of Sylvia Plath, and just as these experiences were shared to greater or lesser extent by all of us who were students at Smith College in the fifties, so Esther Greenwood is a part of all of us. She is the product of a communal imagination. She is the image we had of what we were, or rather of what we thought we were, in moods of comic awareness. And like other communal images, for instance, the comic Irishman or the Schlemiel, she is perhaps not so funny after all. I had a strong feeling, as I read the opening chapters of *The Bell Jar*, that I had met this character some place before, and not in the pages of J.D. Salinger. So I went in search of her in old college newspapers, humour magazines, and so forth, and presently I ran her to ground. I shall later on approach from another angle the particular implications of Sylvia Plath's attempt to identify herself in real life with this image. In the meantime, let me juxtapose a passage from *The Bell Jar* with a passage which comes from a humorous essay written by an undergraduate in the fifties, so as to illustrate the genealogy of Esther Greenwood.

I was surprised to hear this, because of all the blind dates I'd had that year not one called me up again for a second date. I just didn't have any luck. I hated coming downstairs sweaty-handed and curious every Saturday night and having some senior introduce me to her aunt's best friend's son and finding some pale, mushroomy fellow with protruding ears or buck teeth or a bad leg. I didn't think I deserved it. After all, I wasn't crippled in any way, I just studied too hard, I didn't know when to stop (*Bell Jar*, p. 64)

My date was at the foot of the stairs. 'O God,' he said, 'Phew! Watcha got that on for?' I should have known. My mouton (ever since I got caught in the rain) had smelled like a dead albatross. He was one of those people that they must have invented contact lenses for—you know—only he didn't have them yet. He lisped just a little and was just a little shorter than my younger brother. Right at the beginning I could tell that I wasn't going to be popular.

The second passage comes from the college newspaper *Scan* and was written by some anonymous senior in September of 1951. She is a skilled writer. The fashionable mouton coat which fails to appeal to the myopic young man is appropriately likened to 'a dead albatross,' for it represents her feeling of social and sexual inadequacy. The point she makes is one made repeatedly in *The Bell Jar*. No matter how homely, stupid, and characterless the young man on the blind date may be, he asserts his superiority over the young woman. On the other hand, quite unbeknownst to herself, her attitude toward the young man reflects the prevailing prejudices of the Smith girl of the fifties, with her Ivy-League snobberies. The same is true of Esther in *The Bell Jar*.

Here are more passages:

What I always thought I had in mind was getting some big scholarship to graduate school or a grant to study all over Europe, and then I thought I'd be a professor and write books of poems or write books of poems and be an editor of some sort. Usually I had these plans on the tip of my tongue. (*Bell Jar*, p. 35)

Perhaps you might be wondering what Mother's views on the subject were. Mother was a very intelligent, practical woman and she saw what was going to happen to me right from the start. When I arrived home for my first vacation, I proudly announced to my parents that I had learned how to drink beer and scotch and that Greek was such a fascinating subject that I might go into archaeology.

The first passage comes from the account in *The Bell Jar* of Esther's interview with the successful editor, Jay Cee, an interview which stirs up all fears and misgivings about the real meaning of her academic achievements, and leads into the pages of reminiscence about her life at college. A little later in the novel, she indicts herself as a failure. Her crimes are multiple: she cannot cook, she cannot dance, she cannot sing, she cannot ride horseback or ski, she has ignored her mother's warnings and has learned no shorthand. 'The one thing I was good at was winning scholarships and prizes, and that era was coming to an end.' (p. 84)

The writer of the second passage also has a practical mother. This passage comes from a little humorous supplement which was put out by the editors of the Smith Review (now the Grécourt Review) at exam time. It was got up to look exactly like a Blue Book. The title of the essay in which the passage occurs is as follows: 'The Effective Application of a Liberal Education, or The Illiterate Always Win,'[1] and it is written by one who calls herself 'Harassed.' She pretends to be a recent graduate from Smith College. It is her father who has sent her to college (mother knew better), wanting her to learn how to deal with 'the problems of life.' But it turns out that her education casts no light on her problems, which are, in essence, a gourmet husband and a howling baby.

I am going to quote this little satiric essay further, because, not to make any secret of it, the stylistic resemblances to Esther's speech in The Bell Jar are so strong, and the concatenation of this girl's worries are so like Esther's own, that I think Sylvia Plath was herself the anonymous 'Harassed.' This does not invalidate my claim that Esther Greenwood is a communal image, her voice a common one. On the contrary, if Sylvia Plath, in writing The Bell Jar, did hark back to a style employed by herself earlier, it was in order to evoke with the collegiate style the assumptions and doubts of the college girl. There is a significant difference within the similarities of style and character that I have noted. 'Harassed' is rather more sophisticated than Esther, and rather better educated. She writes,

The baby finally came along, and was I glad! But when we got him home, we didn't know what to do with him. We'd read every baby book we could lay our hands on, but they didn't help; they only served to confuse us. It was then I wished that I'd gone to nursing school instead of college. There are some problems whose explanation cannot be delved out of Kant or Spinoza or even that all-purpose detergent, Freud.

And her conclusion about the general usefulness of a Smith College education is this:

However, I am very glad that I did go to college and shall never regret it. My son will, I think, be a well-rounded individual. He is five weeks old and has been to six cocktail parties and has thoroughly enjoyed them. He was most pleasant and genial at all times even though he did abstain from alcoholic beverages. He is regarded as quite an adult baby. He has had the Smith alma mater crooned to him, (which aggravated him), and his bedtime stories and lectures have embraced such subjects as Willie Mays, the power of positive thinking, correct diction, Joe McCarthy and Peter Rabbit. Peter Rabbit is the best of the lot.

I shall refer later to the idea of the 'well-rounded individual' that is mocked here, for it is an idea of considerable importance to Sylvia Plath. But I wish first to illustrate the prevalence in the minds of Smith students in the fifties of the idea that 'the illiterate always win,' or, to paraphrase in current terms, that college education is irrelevant to life—the life, that is, that most students expected to lead—of hungry husbands and crying babies.

At Smith in the fifties we all sang, some of us not quite like larks, and what we *all* sang (as distinguished from those who sang in the choirs, glee club, and various choruses) were college songs. The Smith College songs often originated in Rally Day shows and were perpetuated from year to year by ritual celebrations in springtime called Stepsings. These songs were often parodies composed to Broadway show tunes, and not coincidentally, we sang Broadway show tunes as well.

Ted Hughes says that Sylvia Plath's 'interest in music was average,' but adds, 'She...could play on the piano any number of popular hits from the early 1950's.' The yearnings for love and domesticity that are so dominant in the musicals of the fifties— *Oklahoma*, *Kiss Me Kate*, *Guys and Dolls*, perhaps most significantly, *South Pacific*—these musical reflections of emotions that were natural in the aftermath of World War II, rang constantly in our ears, and were not, I think, without their influence on our sense of destiny.

Here is a stanza from a very popular Smith song written to a tune from *Annie Get Your Gun*.

> You're sharp as a pen point,
> Your marks are really 10-point,
> You are Dean's List, Sophia Smith,
> But when a man wants a kiss, kid,
> He doesn't want a Quiz Kid,
>
> Oh, you can't get a man with your brains.

Many other humorous songs, stories, and poems adumbrate the theme of this one. There is, for example, a song beginning:

> We're working our way through college,
> To learn a lot of knowledge,
> That we'll probably never ever use again.
> We have a lot invested in our Smith Diploma,
> But will it pay the mortgage on the home sweet home-a?

This song hints at another common concern. How were we to use our education if we had to go to work, for our families, or for ourselves? Esther Greenwood's mother recommended shorthand advisedly.

> We're ready to wow *Life, Time, Fortune* and Luce.
> We've energy, brains, and when we turn on the juice,
> Our style is so subtle it drives men to tears.
> But we're doing the copy for ads of brassieres.

These stories and songs about men, marriage, and jobs reflect actual pressures, expectations, and anxieties. At the same time, they demonstrate what was probably the common attitude toward these pressures and anxieties—a half-humorous, half-stoical acceptance. For the first issue of *Smith Review*, which was revived after a period of oblivion in the fall of 1952, Mary Ellen Chase wrote a prefatory essay, entitled 'Smith College—A Definition.' It reads in part:

I vastly like the relative absence among us of any misconceptions or delusions concerning our incomparable and far-reaching service to the world, not only outside our gates but within them. I think few, if any, of us indulge ourselves in the fantastic notions that we shall reform American society, or develop countless master minds, or turn out many giantesses in the earth. We are, instead, inclined to look upon such presumption as a bit ridiculous, and, on the whole, mistrust taking ourselves too seriously.

I am not mocking Smith College in quoting this definition, much less am I criticizing Mary Ellen Chase. She spoke then from the wisdom of middle age, and she gave a perfectly accurate description of the attitudes toward self and society which would bring peace of mind and sanity to the lives of the girls she was addressing in the fifties. Moreover, these attitudes which she describes as the common ones, *were* common. I suppose from the perspective of many young women today, the college girls of the fifties look like victims of Society, which is true enough, provided society is not viewed as a kind of eternal Monolith. To the extent that we were victims, I should prefer to view us as victims of history, and even here, it must be admitted, most of us were less victims than collaborators.

But what of the ambitious, highly-gifted, sensitive, and extremely, but extremely, intelligent girl like Sylvia Plath, who cherished in secret precisely the absurd fantasy decried by Miss Chase, to be 'a giantess in the earth?' Such a girl was bound to have a double image of self.

William Butler Yeats, who influenced the development of Sylvia Plath's poetry in a way much more profound than might be guessed from the relatively few echoes of Yeatsian images and ideas, wrote that:

> The intellect of man is forced to choose
> Perfection of the life, or of the work,
> And if it take the second must refuse
> A heavenly mansion, raging in the dark.
>
> ('The Choice')

I believe most of you would agree that these words are even truer for a woman. It was a long time after she graduated from college before Sylvia Plath made that choice.

At the time of writing *The Bell Jar*, when she had become extremely critical of her earlier attempts to be at once the perfect all-round American girl and the aspiring poet, she nevertheless envisioned the recurrence of the conflict in new forms. 'I'll be flying back and forth between one mutually exclusive thing and another for the rest of my days.' (*Bell Jar*, p. 104).

In an article published posthumously in *Punch*, but written, it is my guess, around the time she finished *The Bell Jar*, Sylvia Plath criticized on the basis of her own experience the degrading conformity enforced on students in American public high schools in the late 1940's. 'Eccentricities,' she writes, 'the perils of being *too* special, were reasoned and cooed from us like sucked thumbs.' College admissions policies and the girls' guidance counsellor, she says, persuaded her to adopt the arts of Machiavelli, and cultivate those extra-curricular activities which would make her appear to be the ideal 'All-Round' student.[2] This little essay, however just its criticism of American education, is somewhat less than candid. It was certainly no pressure from guidance counsellors which drove her while at Smith College to conform to the 'Okay Image,' and, I firmly believe, it was not Machiavelli either. Her willingness to immerse herself in college activities (she was, among other things, secretary of Honor Board, a member of Studio Club, a Press Board Correspondent, entertainment chairman and decorations committee member for various proms and balls) represents perhaps her own recognition of the dangers of eccentricity, the perils of being too special.

Whether or not this be true, Sylvia Plath (not her mother, or her guidance counsellor) cared very greatly about her college successes, academic and extra-curricular, and cared even more when she returned to college after her breakdown. For now, continued success meant not only social normalcy, but sanity itself. Thus she writes in her journal in June of 1954:

...exams & papers proved I hadn't lost either my repetitive or my creative intellect as I had feared...a semester of reconstruction ends with an infinitely more solid if less flashingly spectacular flourish than last year's.

If *The Bell Jar*, by presenting a satiric portrait of the befuddled Esther Greenwood, obscures the extent to which the real Sylvia Plath sought to become the perfect Smith girl, it obscures also something else of crucial importance in her relation to the college. And that is, to put the matter as truthfully and as simply as I can, the extent to which she loved the study of literature, and correspondingly, the extent to which she was grateful to those who directed and encouraged her in that study.

She had had from childhood the ambition to become a college professor, perhaps partly in emulation, or in placation of her dead father, who was himself a professor. And at Smith College she found this ambition confirmed and reinforced. While she was still a student, her academic work and her writing of poetry were not conflicting, but rather complementary activities. She hoped when she returned to teach here that they might continue to be so. Thus she wrote at the time of her appointment as instructor:

I'll be scared to death the first day, but am really excited about it: if I had a million dollar fellowship to write in Italy next year, I would refuse it: I've gotten sick of living on great grants & feel very much that need...of 'giving out' in some kind of work: my way, apart from writing, I know is teaching.

Under the pressures of seventy papers to mark every other week, she quickly came to recognize a conflict between her desire to teach and the absolute necessity which was upon her to write poetry. Even so, according to the accounts of her husband and all her biographers, her decision to abandon teaching at Smith College cost her great pain. Paradoxical though it may seem, I believe the measure of that pain is revealed in the seemingly casual and cruel treatment in *The Bell Jar* of certain of her old teachers, benefactors, and friends.

NOTES

1 *Smith Review:* Exam Blues Issue, Winter, 1955, pp. 7–8.
2 'Maids From School: The Okay Image,' *Punch*, April 3, 1963.

44. Teresa De Lauretis, 'Rebirth in *The Bell Jar,*' *Women's Studies*

1976, 173–83

Since its publication in 1963, Sylvia Plath's autobiographical novel *The Bell Jar* has rapidly attained the status of feminist manifesto.[1] Plath's is certainly not the first novel whose protagonist is a woman, nor the first account of a heroine's struggle with herself and the world. But it is a statement about the female condition which, filtering a unique emotional and experiential content through the sieve of symbolic discourse, communicates at the highly complex interpersonal, or universal, level of literature. I believe that its success and forcefulness are due in large part to the author's ability to integrate the historical, diachronic self (the heroine in her contemporary world) with a synchronic, timeless, mythical structure, the descent–ascent pattern, in which the heroine mediates the transition from one world to another, or from one state of being to another. The theme of rebirth, underlying the narrative pattern, and witnessing the attainment of her consciousness and self-determination, makes of Esther a true culture-heroine.[2]

The Bell Jar is the account of a journey, of Esther's descent into the hell of self-disintegration, her rebirth, and ascent to self-unity and freedom. Although she actually travels through different physical spaces from one geographical location to another, the journey is mainly an inner one, inward into the self and outward to the world. Thus it follows the pattern of psychoanalytic novels and case histories,[3] but whereas in the latter the main interest lies in the psychological processes described rather than in cultural and existential ones, Esther's story is totally entwined with a specific and fully detailed culture, from which it takes life and meaning. Her 'madness' is presented as a necessary consequence of, indeed as consubstantial with, the world surrounding her. We perceive Esther's alienation not as individual and aberrant (hence, an illness), but as a quality of existence itself, defined in the confines of the book and in terms with which we are familiar. Esther's madness is not 'another country,' it is New York in the 50's, the small Massachusetts town, the United Nations, the private clinic, the state psychiatric ward where she is submitted to shock treatment, the cellar where she hides to die. To us, Esther's words sound as familiar as the echo of our own voices, as Plath's private vision has become today's public awareness. But such precise and keen sociocultural consciousness is not the only distinctive trait of her writing. There is also the qualitative difference between experience and expression which is brought about by the medium of language and its symbolic and semantic functions. The events of her life are presented to us in an order not chronological but emotional, both in flashbacks and in forward linear sequence. We first see her in New York, at the crucial moment of her life, when all the threads of her existence, disillusionment with people, fears, guilt, doubts, frustrated expectations, and vain longing, come to a sharp focus in the false, alienating environment of the city and the ladies' magazine milieu:

Only I wasn't steering anything, not even myself. I just bumped from my hotel to work and to parties and from parties to my hotel and back to work like a numb trolleybus. I guess I should have been excited the way most of the other girls were, but I couldn't get myself to react. I felt very still and very empty, the way the eye of a tornado must feel, moving dully along in the middle of the surrounding hullabaloo (p. 2).

Her first experience in New York is that of being used by her girlfriend Doreen who asks her to go along to a man's apartment where Esther sits alone watching the other two's sexual play, and feeling 'gawky and morbid as somebody in a sideshow' (p. 8). As the man walks across his living room, Esther's perception of him is that he 'grew smaller and smaller until he vanished through a door in the distance' (p. 12). And shortly after the distortion occurs again, this time in herself:

The two of them didn't even stop jitterbugging during the intervals. I felt myself shrinking to a small black dot against all those red and white rugs and that pine paneling. I felt like a hole in the ground (p. 14).

Returning alone to her room in the Amazon Hotel, Esther looks at her mirror: 'The face in it looked like the reflection in a ball of dentist's mercury' (p. 16). She tries in vain to sleep and then decides to take a hot bath.

I don't believe in baptism or the waters of Jordan or anything like that, but I guess I feel about a hot bath the way those religious people feel about holy water.
  I said to myself: 'Doreen is dissolving. Lenny Shepherd is dissolving, Frankie is dissolving, New York is dissolving, they are all dissolving away and none of them matter any more. I don't known them, I have never known them and I am very pure. All that liquor and those sticky kisses I saw and the dirt that settled on my skin on the way back is turning into something pure' (p. 17).

At dawn Doreen is back at the hotel, sick and worn out. Her vomit on the carpet appears to Esther 'an ugly, concrete testimony to my own dirty nature' (p. 19).
  All the major themes and motifs of the novel are contained in the opening two chapters: the guilt of loneliness, desire for purgation, purification by water, the warmth of womb-like enclosures, sleep, death, shrinking, disintegration, dissolution. All of these will reappear throughout the novel's imagery, not at random but following a specific movement, which is the movement of Esther's inner journey. Especially recurrent are the images of fragmenta-tion, disintegration, separatedness, isolatedness, unrelatedness. They recur more and more often until Chapter 13, in a crescendo that culminates with Esther's attempted suicide. The cut-up cadavers and the babies in glass bottles that she once saw in a hospital with her boyfriend Buddy come back to Esther's mind

while lying inert and apathetic in her New York bed. At the UN the simultaneous interpreter sits in her booth mechanically 'rattling off idiom after idiom in her unknowable tongue' (p. 61). Esther admires her accomplishment, and for herself, 'I wanted change and excitement and to shoot off in all directions myself, like the colored arrows from a Fourth of July rocket' (p. 68). Esther sees her life like a fig tree with figs hanging alluringly from its branches, each fig a possible future, a possible direction to take. Yet she is unable to choose even one. And as she sits, empty and dull like the eye of the tornado, the world around her is separating, disintegrating, becoming meaningless: she stands on a snowcovered slope for her first ski lesson, and 'On every side of me the red and blue and white jacketed skiers tore away from the blinding slope like fugitive bits of an American flag' (p. 77). Below her, 'Buddy's arms went on waving feebly as antennae from the other side of a field swarming with tiny moving animalcules like germs, or bent, bright exclamation marks' (p. 79). Then she plunges down 'past the zigzaggers, the students, the experts, through year after year of doubleness and smiles and compromise, into my own past. People and trees receded on either hand like the dark sides of a tunnel as I hurtled on to the still, bright point at the end of it, the pebble at the bottom of the well, the white sweet baby cradled in its mother's belly' (p. 79). And when she comes to, her perception is more partial, fragmented:

Buddy's face hung over me, near and huge, like a distracted planet. Other faces showed themselves up in back of his. Behind him, black dots swarmed on a plane of whiteness. Piece by piece, as at the strokes of a dull godmother's wand, the old world sprang back into position (pp. 79–80).

She lives on in New York. Day by day the world becomes one-dimensional, flat surface, people are automata, mannequins, her own bodily responses are mechanical ('like the mouth of a ventriloquist's dummy, my own mouth started to quirk up,' [p. 83]). During her last night in the city, returning from a double date where she is almost raped and then called a slut, Esther performs a symbolic funeral for herself:

Piece by piece, I fed my wardrobe to the night wind, and flutteringly, like a loved one's ashes, the gray scraps were ferried off, to settle here, there, exactly where I would never know, in the dark heart of New York (p. 91).

127

The next chapter, ten, deals with Esther's return home, when her physical and psychic disintegration begins. Accordingly, the imagery is intensified:

Like a colossal junkyard, the swamps and back lots of Connecticut flashed past, one broken-down fragment bearing no relation to another (p. 92). All through June the writing course stretched before me like a bright, safe bridge over the dull gulf of the summer. Now I saw it totter and dissolve, and a body in a white blouse and green skirt plummet into the gap (p. 93).

Then plan after plan started leaping through my head, like a family of scatty rabbits.

I saw the years of my life spaced along a road in the form of telephone poles, threaded together by wires. I counted one, two, three...nineteen telephone poles, and then the wires dangled into space, and try as I would, I couldn't see a single pole beyond the nineteenth (pp. 100–101).

She tries in vain to write a novel about Elaine (herself). Her limbs do not respond to her will:

My hand advanced a few inches, then retreated and fell limp. I forced it toward the receiver again, but again it stopped short, as if it had collided with a pane of glass (p. 97).

I tried to speak in a cool, calm way, but the zombie rose up in my throat and choked me off (p. 103).

When I took up my pen, my hand made big, jerky letters like those of a child, and the lines sloped down the page from left to right almost diagonally, as if they were loops of string lying on the paper, and someone had come along and blown them askew (p. 106).

She tries to work at her dissertation on *Finnegans Wake* and 'My eyes sank through an alphabet soup of letters to the long word in the middle of the page.'

It sounded like a heavy wooden object falling downstairs, boomp boomp boomp, step after step. Lifting the pages of the book, I let them fan slowly by my eyes. Words, dimly familiar but twisted all awry, like faces in a funhouse mirror, fled past, leaving no impression on the glassy surface of my brain.

I squinted at the page.

The letters grew barbs and rams' horns. I watched them separate, each from the other, and jiggle up and down in a silly way. Then they associated themselves in fantastic, untranslatable shapes, like Arabic or Chinese (p. 102).

At home her anxiety increases, all activity loses meaning. Sleeping, eating, and 'everything people did seemed so silly, because they only died in the end' (p. 105).

I saw the days of the year stretching ahead like a series of bright, white boxes, and separating one box from another was sleep, like a black shade. Only for me, the long perspective of shades that set off one box from the next had suddenly snapped up, and I could see day after day after day glaring ahead of me like a white, broad, infinitely desolate avenue (pp. 104–105).

Death becomes her only production. She identifies herself with suicide victims in the local scandal sheet, or sees her pain as somebody else's. Nothing makes sense:

I brought the newspaper close up to my eyes to get a better view of George Pollucci's face, spotlights like a three-quarter moon against a vague background of bricks and black sky. I felt he had something important to tell me, and whatever it was might just be written on his face. But the smudgy crags of George Pollucci's features melted away as I peered at them, and resolved themselves into a regular pattern of dark and light and medium-gray dots (pp. 111–112).

Her attempts at suicide, in all forms and places, are the same as this effort to objectify herself. She is drawn more and more to places of enclosure and death—the zoo, the prison, the graveyard, the bathtub, the deep sea, and lastly the dark cellar where she takes an overdose of sleeping pills and the final plunge into silence—all of them object-symbols of what she later (after rebirth) describes with the extremely powerful metaphor of the 'bell jar,' which unites the meanings of water, purification, immobility, unrelatedness, birth, and death (the 'pickled' still-born babies).

The silence drew off, baring the pebbles and shells and all the tatty wreckage of my life. Then, at the rim of vision, it gathered itself, and in one sweeping tide, rushed me off to sleep (p. 138).

Until this moment Esther's language is packed with similes and metaphors of automatism (from the 'numb trolleybus' to the 'zombie' in her throat) and disintegration, in a crescendo that reflects the advancement of the 'sweeping tide' over her. Both automatism and disunity are symptoms of an affective deficiency, a lack of meaning, the unrelation between the self and the world.

Esther's coming to, described in the next chapter, is a literary simulation of birth. It represents symbolically the journey of the fetus from the dark womb through the birth canal ('I was being transported at enormous speed down a tunnel into the earth' [p. 139]), to the opening ('a slit of light opened like a mouth or a wound' [p. 139]). Then a voice cries 'Mother!' (we later learn it was her own voice), and Esther becomes aware of the air and the space around her: 'If I opened my eyes, I would see colors and shapes bending in upon me like nurses' (p. 139). With rebirth a new life begins in which Esther, no longer the repressed dutiful daughter and straight-A scholarship winner, expresses herself, her violence and aggression, by openly hostile acts. For one of these, breaking the nurse's thermometers, she is punished by seclusion. But before she is taken to the place of loneliness, she manages to secure an important and magical object,[4] a symbolic safeguard of the self, a little ball of mercury which trembled 'like celestial dew.'

I opened my fingers a crack, like a child with a secret, and smiled at the silver globe cupped in my palm. If I dropped it, *it would break into a million little replicas of itself, and if I pushed them near each other, they would fuse, without a crack, into one whole again.* I smiled and smiled at the small silver ball (p. 150).

This moment, at the close of Chapter 14 marking Esther's rebirth, is the beginning of her journey upward. The imagery of disintegration no longer occurs in the novel, to be replaced by Esther's conscious and intellectual efforts to come to grips with her self. She covers in reverse the path already trod downward, now meeting experience and controlling it to the extent it is possible to her. She faces the Other in her lesbian friend Joan, whom she rejects and yet feels much in common with—her destiny of womanhood, mortality, frustration, defeat. She faces the sexual taboo and buys her freedom from it in the shape of a diaphragm. No longer threatened with the stigma of pregnancy, the nightmar-ish vision of bottle babies disappears, to give way to mature considerations about maternity. And if she is not yet willing nor inclined toward it, we must remember that Esther is still a very young girl, that at the time of the novel's beginning she does have a child (p. 3). She faces sexuality, and her hemorrhage is the counterpart of the vomit caused by food poisoning at the Ladies' Day banquet (both occur in a taxi). Again, the symptom/symbol has become the conceptually accepted reality.

At the end of the novel, Esther is going to her interview with the doctors who will decide on her freedom and sanity. After walking through 'the familiar labyrinth of shoveled asylum paths' (p. 196) she faces the doctors in the examination room and 'guiding myself by them, as by a magical thread, I stepped into the room' (p. 200). The magical thread that holds the self to the world is like the magical ball of Mercury (the guide of travellers, the winged messenger of the Gods)—it may break into a thousand fragments and be put back together. And it may also be shattered again, as we know it came to pass for Sylvia Plath. But Esther is forever safe, and able to share with us her experience and what she has learnt in her journey. For her also, life is no rose garden, but rather a very precarious path on which choices must be made, enemies fought, and false myths demystified.

The episode of the ball of mercury, so cleverly understated that it may pass unnoticed among the wealth of imagery and brief, seemingly unimportant incidents that constitute the fabric of the novel, is a very clear example of the way in which the literary work contains and releases a multiplicity of meanings. I will compare briefly *The Bell Jar* with *Autobiography of a Schizophrenic Girl* which, being non-fictional, supplies what we may consider factual evidence. Esther's anguish over the meaninglessness of words, whose letters separate and reassociate themselves 'in fantastic, untranslatable shapes' (p. 102), or the dissolution of human features into meaningless patterns of dots (p. 112), is the fear of complete loss of meaning. In fact, when Renée is at the farthest point of her regression, 'sunk beyond language, beyond thought,' she utters syllables that have no meaning to herself or to others.[5] For her the symbols of sustenance (the apples representing the nurturing breasts), prenatal unity (the 'green sea,' water), serve as actual substitutes for the objects. Only with recovery will they change to concepts, i.e. become conscious. To Esther the mercury ball is a symbol of unity, or better of the integration of the many (selves) into one (self). It is the emblem of a magical process that Esther accepts, irrationally, as a model of reality. Unlike Renée's apples, the mercury is not a substitute for the object, but the meaningful symbol of a new relation between Esther's self and reality. For us, however, the mercury ball has a further connotation, which we perceive on the basis of a shared cultural substratum. For, at Plath's suggestion, we make the connection between the mercury and the later metaphors 'familiar labyrinth' and 'magical thread,' and assess the significance of Esther's journey as a particular version of the mythology of our Western culture. In its total communicative context formed by the author, the novel, and the readers, the mercury episode is then a sign (in the Saussurian sense) functioning in the system of denotations and connotations which is the novel.

Esther's words show Plath's constant, strenuous effort to express experience by verbal equivalents: the elaborate similes, the images recurring at different moments in slightly different contexts are all carefully chosen to represent fractions of change, minimal shifts in consciousness. (The few pages devoted to Esther's attempt to write an autobiographical novel show beyond doubt both the author's intent and her method of writing, and thus give us a mirror image of Plath herself.) But in addition to imagery and word association, there is another aspect of stylistic elaboration of the personal experience that we must consider, the arrangement of the time sequence. Almost all flashbacks occur within Chapters 1 to 9, during Esther's stay in New York. They tell of Esther's experience up to that time, supplying background and psychological motivation for her present apprehension of reality. The mere position of the flashback constitutes a built-in interpretation of the heroine, her culture, the reasons for her present state. Take the ski accident in Chapter 8, when not knowing how to ski, Esther plunges down a crowded slope, exhilarated by the risk and conscious of her desire for death and purification. This episode is apparently brought to memory by a pain in her ankle (which was broken in the ski fall) Esther feels after her date with Constantin, the UN interpreter.

Then I thought, 'Buddy Willard made me break that leg.' Then I thought, 'No, I broke it myself. I broke it on purpose to pay myself back for being such a heel' (p. 70).

At the bottom of the slope, Esther had seen Buddy's face hanging over her 'near and huge, like a distracted planet.' This distorted perception, joined with that of glossy surfaces and white light, is amazingly similar to what Renée describes as unreality ('illimitable vastness, brilliant light, and the gloss and smoothness of material things.'[6] By juxtaposing the ski slope flashback to the efficient and mechanical life of UN translators (a parallel of Esther's scholastic achievements) and to the frustrating noncommunication of Esther's date with Constantin, Plath suggests connections and causes for

Esther's feeling of unreality in a purely literary form—she is giving us the diagnosis by showing only the symptoms. In her novel, character, narrator, and doctor's interpretation exist all together and at once, in one view of reality which may seem simple and direct, but is actually the result of much literary elaboration of a very complex experience.

The Bell Jar is built on the mythical descent–ascent pattern, with parallel novelistic situations symmetrical to the central symbolic episode of the ball of mercury. Thus it belongs to the subgenre of the quest novel as well as to the autobiographical portrait—it is a novel of the self much in the sense in which Joyce's, Kafka's, Proust's, and Svevo's are. Traditionally men have sought to define themselves and mankind by writing stories. They have succeeded, with varying degrees of awareness and impact on their contemporaries, in shaping the images and myths of their culture. Reading *The Bell Jar*, I became aware of how much of myself there was in it that I never encountered in novels before, and I realized how forcefully our view of the world and of ourselves is shaped by the works of literature we read—written mostly by men. *The Bell Jar* is not a single case history, but rather a synchronic view of womanhood, for once seen from the woman's perspective. In it we do not find archetypes such as the *ewig Weibliche*, the Virgin Mother of God, Eve the Temptress, and other man-made glorifications or condemnations of man's desire, to which women have so long adhered that they have accepted them as their own image. For example, the lesbian heroine of Radclyffe Hall's *The Well of Loneliness* apologizes for her 'perversion,' and we are asked to (and do) sympathize with her. On the contrary, when Esther rejects her lesbian friend Joan, she knows that Joan is her double, a part of her that she must assimilate but not become enslaved to—freedom for Esther is availability, refusal of classifications, growth, diversity. She cannot accept the either–or of culturally defined roles which seem to be the only alternatives open to her. What she is looking for, her own self-development, is not yet visible, but by the end of the novel Esther has learned to keep looking. If the new heroine that Plath has given us does not reach the stages of transfiguration and apotheosis, common in myths and folktales, the story is perhaps all the more powerful, insisting as it does on the essential focus of mythical creation, the dialectics of birth, death, and rebirth.

NOTES

1 (New York: Bantam Books, 1972). All subsequent references will be to this edition.

2 The notions of synchrony and diachrony, originally posed by Ferdinand de Saussure (*Cours de linguistique générale*, Paris, 1965), are used here following Claude Lévi-Strauss' theory of myth in *Structural Anthropology* (New York, 1963) and *The Savage Mind* (Chicago, 1966).

3 The best example of a non-fictional account is *Autobiography of a Schizophrenic Girl* (New York: Signet Books, 1970), the story of Renée's struggle with unreality, the terrifying inner world of her psychosis, and her slow return from 'another country' to 'warm reality' and family. The account is followed by the psychoanalytical interpretation of her analyst, Marguerite Sechehaye. A fictionalized account is Hannah Green's (pseudonym of Joanne Greenberg) *I Never Promised You a Rose Garden* (New York: Signet Books, 1964).

4 For the function of magical agents in narrative plots, see Vladimir Propp, *Morphology of the Folktale* (Austin and London, 1968).

5 '"Icthiou, gao, itivare, giastow, ovede' and the like. In no way did I seek to create them; they came of themselves and by themselves meant nothing. Only the sound, the rhythm of the pronounciation had sense. Through them I lamented, pouring out the gruelling grief and the interminable sadness in my heart. I could not use ordinary words, for my pain and sorrow had no real basis' (*Autobiography*, op. cit., pp. 79–80).

6 These are Renée's words: 'But her smile, instead of reassuring me, only increased the anxiety and confusion for I saw her teeth, white and even in the gleam of the light. Remaining all the while like themselves, soon they monopolized my entire vision as if the whole room were nothing but teeth under a remorseless light' (*Autobiography*, op. cit., p. 22).

CROSSING THE WATER

London and New York, 1971

45. Domenica Paterno, 'Poetry,' *Library Journal*

1 October 1971, 3141

Legend has created an image of Plath as the artist of suicide, mesmerized by her own art, driven to have life imitate art, and so killing herself. But perhaps to this should be added Plath, artist of anomie, feminine in genesis but human in 'gender.'

The Bell Jar is a novel of descent into madness, uniquely female in viewpoint (intimate rather than cosmic) and circumstances (personal rather than societal). Its characters could easily be grist for a Woman's Lib tract: the women self-sacrificing robots to career or family or sex; the men self-hating beasts or self-deluded boors. Heroine Esther Greenwood recoils from the future these stunted models signal, her mind split and cracked by the relentless blast of their empty expectations. But the novel is more. It is the soul-hell of the artist, sensitive to, and brutally expressive of, the brutish abrasion of the world. The dead Father-Guide left no plans to order the disorder. Obscenely pregnant Chaos gives birth to countless acts, gestures, phenomena, all meaningless. Life holds not ripeness but rot. Not an arch of striving and achievement, but a bell jar of stifling suffocation. To stop the assault one must sever the pathway from world to mind. By madness. By suicide. Or by creating, through the craft of the writer, the ordered vision of the artist. This Plath has brilliantly achieved: through clean, clear almost conversational prose, with sparks of imaginal description. Craft controls an orthodox prose to capture the quirky jumps of perception of Esther's disintegrating mind.

The catharsis of craft is also very much a factor of composition in her poems. ('The blood jet is poetry, / There is no stopping it.') The balance between self-revelation and artistic form may shift in each collection of poems: *The Colossus* displays the thick overlay of craft upon content usual in a first collection; *Ariel*, on the other hand, is truly in the poet's own first-person voice, indeed, at times that voice is a family scream: 'Daddy, you can lie back now. / There's a stake in your fat black heart. /...Daddy, daddy, you bastard, I'm through.' The poems in this new collection, *Crossing the Water*, were written in the period between the publication of *The Colossus* (1960) and *Ariel* (1966). They represent a varying mixture of the self-consciousness of *The Colossus* and 'the self-intensification of *Ariel*. There is a theatricality about this collection, a setting up of scenery, a pulling in of actors, a mouthing of set-piece monologues. The brain-scalding intensity of *Ariel* is not here. In its place is the coolness of devices deliberately used, but in this case not always successfully. Plath in *Ariel* is the central internal voice, gasping, screaming, plunging, croaking. In *Crossing the Water*, she is a figure in the landscape, a still point for nature in vortex, the observer who finds a truer voice in her novel. The chilled simplicity of death in *Ariel* ('I do not stir / The frost makes a flower, / The dew makes a star, The deathbell, / The death bell. / Somebody's done for.') contrasts with the comforting thanatopsis in *Crossing the Water*: 'Let me have my copper cooking pots, let my rouge pots / Bloom about me like night flowers, with a good smell. / They will roll me up in bandages, they will store my heart / Under my feet in a neat parcel. / I shall hardly know myself. It will be dark, / And the shine of these small things sweeter than the face of Ishtar.' One thinks that an occasional triteness of phrase, such as the ending to 'Love Letter' ('It's a gift') would not have escaped her poetic acuity had she done the final draft. In all, though, this collection deepens Plath's reputation for the talent to capture, and hold unflinchingly, death's apogean cold.

46. Eileen M. Aird, review, *Critical Quarterly*

Autumn 1971, 286–8

Eileen M. Aird (b. 1945) wrote an early study of Plath's work, *Sylvia Plath: Her Life and Work* (Edinburgh, 1973; New

York, 1975). Born in Yorkshire, she teaches at the University of Newcastle.

The poems in *Crossing the Water* were written after the publication of *The Colossus* and before the earliest poems collected in *Ariel*. Five of the poems are published for the first time; the others have already appeared in journals or in *Uncollected Poems*, the limited edition of 150 copies published by Turret Press in 1966. They arrest and disturb more than the poems in *The Colossus*; the tone is violent, almost frenetic at times; the concern more obviously personal even in poems with a dramatic focus such as 'Insomniac', 'The Baby Sitters' and 'In Plaster'. It is an exciting although uneven collection. There are several very fine poems, particularly 'I Am Vertical', 'Parliament Hill Fields' and 'Last Words', but others forcibly suggest suffering but are too esoteric in reference to be fully successful. This is hardly surprising when we remember that Sylvia Plath herself rejected everything prior to 'Poem for a Birthday' as juvenilia; the poems in *Crossing the Water* are the earlier stages in the development which culminated in *Ariel*. However just as the reader does not accept her rejection of *The Colossus* so her judgement of these poems is too exacting: 'These poems do not live: it's a sad diagnosis'.

By providing a collection of the poems between *The Colossus* and *Ariel* the volume emphasises again the unity of Sylvia Plath's work. A poem like 'Wuthering Heights' has very close affinities with some of the earlier poems, particularly 'Hardcastle Crags'. Both poems are about the same area of West Yorkshire, both reject the Romantic celebration of unity with Nature in favour of an uncompromising delineation of a stony force striving to subdue man into its own bleak pattern:

> If I pay the roots of the heather
> Too close attention, they will invite me
> To whiten my bones among them.

However the poem also has affinities with poems in *Ariel*. As the poet encounters the unrecognising gaze of the sheep her sense of identity seeps away until she feels as if she is 'being mailed into space'. This sense of oneself as inanimate and without identity is a recurrent element in *Ariel*, notably in 'Tulips' where the depression and lethargy which follows illness is conveyed in the poet's description of herself as a 'cut-paper shadow', a phrase which also occurs in the title poem of *Crossing the Water*. Sylvia Plath is usually regarded as the poet of despair but the despair is often highlighted by a bitter, self-mocking humour. In the description of the sheep in 'Wuthering Heights' the sense of personal loneliness is balanced against the analytical apprehension of the sheep as rather foolish human beings. This seems to be the forerunner of the sharp-edged humour of *Ariel* which allows her to say with apparent nonchalance: 'Dying is an art like everything else. I do it exceptionally well'. This self-directed mockery is often her way of avoiding sentimentality or self-indulgence.

Several of the poems in *Crossing the Water* refer to pregnancy and motherhood—Sylvia Plath's daughter was born on April 1st, 1960—and are similar in attitude and tone to the poems about her son in *Ariel*. 'Magi' emphasises the poet's thankfulness that her daughter is unaware of the pain characterising her own experience. In this it anticipates 'Nick and the Candlestick', but it is also reminiscent of 'The Disquieting Muses'. The muses of this earlier poem are an embodiment of the forces which Sylvia Plath saw behind her vision; they are 'Mouthless, eyeless, with stitched bald head' and are opposed to the frivolous world of domestic comfort represented by the mother. The poet, finding the two irreconcilable, rejects the bright gaiety of the mother's experience for the stony blankness offered by her muses. In 'Magi' she reflects much more hopefully on her daughter's destiny, for the dull abstracts hovering around the cradle are powerless against the protected innocence of the child:

> For the heavy notion of Evil
>
> Attending her cot is less than a belly ache,
> And Love, the mother of milk, no theory.
> They mistake their star, these papery god-folk.

In the winter of 1960–61 Sylvia Plath had a miscarriage and one of the most satisfying poems in *Crossing the Water*, 'Parliament Hill Fields', seems to refer to this. It is an excellent example of Sylvia Plath's ability to use personal experience as one element in a poem which is only incidentally autobiographical. The imagery is of bareness, deprivation, infertility; a flock of gulls flying inland reminds her of 'the hands of an invalid'. No-one recognises her loss

although Nature coldly offers the balm of silence and forgetfulness, but at the moment of greatest despair the will to survive
reasserts itself and honesty forces her to accept the transience of
grief: 'I suppose it's pointless to think of you at all. Already your
doll grip lets go'. Temporarily the mind struggles to retain the
departing memory but then turns towards the living daughter safe
in a nursery world of love and fantasy. The final lines crystallise the
mother's ambivalent feelings as she leaves behind the memories of
the dead child and accepts both the failures and securities of her life:

> The old dregs, the old difficulties take me to wife.
> Gulls stiffen to their chill vigil in the draughty half-light;
> I enter the lit house.

The masterly control of disparate elements exhibited in this poem
and the absolute honesty with which it analyses pain is characteristic of the best poetry in the volume. *Crossing the Water* is
undoubtedly a valuable and welcome addition to the body of Sylvia
Plath's work.

47. Douglas Dunn, 'Damaged Instruments,' *Encounter*

August 1971, 68–70

The poems in Sylvia Plath's *The Colossus* are largely flawed by a
rhythmical and lexical vulgarity. However, many of them are very
good poems, there is a powerful sense of them having come from a
single, eccentric imagination, and they are full of strange and
startling expressions. They are also identifiably by the author of
Ariel. For example, there are forecasts of *Ariel's* subject-matter, that
evolution of psychological background, domestic oppression and
public and private pain, into a private and ultimate specialisation. In
order to achieve that unique and powerful poetry it was necessary
to abandon the earlier clotted style. She herself said of the *Ariel*
poems: '...I have found myself having to read them aloud to
myself. Now this is something I didn't do. For example, my first

book *The Colossus*—I can't read any of the poems aloud now, I didn't write them to be read aloud. In fact, they quite quietly bore me. Now these very recent ones—I've got to say them. I speak them to myself. Whatever lucidity they may have comes from the fact that I say them aloud.' I doubt if many people find most of *Ariel* exactly lucid, but there is a quite obvious liberation of tone and freedom of movement in her later verse which is unlike anything in *The Colossus*. It will be reasonable to suggest that the compulsion to dramatise what she had come to see as her identity was so strong, and so artistically felt, that it was necessary to devise a way of writing that would be a literary version of the identity she was obsessed with fulfilling—in other words she had to find her 'own voice', that unriddable cliché.

The poems in *Ariel* were written in 1962 and 1963. Between then and the poems in *The Colossus* (written between 1956 and 1959) Plath was perhaps feeling towards her final style, although it seems more likely, bearing in mind that legendary remark about writing three poems a day seven days a week at four in the morning, that the final style was realised very quickly. In this new collection, *Crossing the Water*, Ted Hughes has collected a number of poems written in this so-called 'transitional' period. Many have already been printed in magazines and in two private press selections by the Turret Press and the Rainbow Press, and another volume, *Winter Trees*, is promised.

Crossing the Water is much freer in style than the first book. There is still something formulaic and precious about her phrase-making: '...a valedictory, pale hand'; or 'Black, admonitory cliffs.' However, there is more of that zany, accurate and unexpected imagery that is so central to the style of *Ariel*, and also the first book. Alert, nervous, and often domestic, it is one of her peculiar strengths:

> Now, in valleys narrow
> And black as purses, the house lights
> Gleam like small change
>
> The city melts like sugar
> Now the pills are worn out and silly as classical gods
>
> All morning, with smoking breath, the handy-man
> Has been draining the goldfish ponds.
> They collapse like lungs....

This demotic kind of simile-making is very feminine. She mocks the masculine world with flurries of domestic detail. The irritation and peevishness of this is profound miles beyond the fashionable nonsense of Women's Lib, and it is an essential strand of what Alvarez has called 'the terrible unforgiveness of her verse...violent resentment that this should have been done to *her*.'

But by quoting disjointed excerpts I don't want to give the impression that the book is a mere happy hunting ground of stray felicities, important only in relation to *Ariel*. Sustained poems of great quality are gathered in this book. 'In Plaster', for example, is a monologue spoken by an invalid about the plaster mould that encases her, and which has become an image of her death. Despite the morbid whimsy on which the poem is founded, it is a remarkable poem objectifying a state of mind, and it leads her to frightening statements:

> She wanted to leave me, she thought she was superior,
> And I'd been keeping her in the dark, and she was resentful,
> Wasting her days waiting on a half-corpse!
> And secretly she began to hope I'd die.

'Blackberrying' is a poem of menacing description. Like many others in the book it is made from direct statements—'The only thing to come now is the sea'—leading into surprising language and imagery—'and a din like silversmiths/Beating and beating at an intractable metal.' Above all, however, the new ingredient in her poetry of this period is an improved sense of drama, a much stronger narrative interest, as well as an accompanying thinning out of the clots that made that kind of writing impossible in *The Colossus*, although she came close to it in 'The Disquieting Muses'.

What struck me most after reading *Crossing the Water* was not just that it was so good, or that none of the poems there had been thought good enough for *Ariel*, but that *Ariel* itself represents such a unified stretch of work, such a strong and tragically magnificent working out of a single complicated theme. Only one poem in the new book might be at home in *Ariel*. 'The Tour', a parable of a confrontation between the safe life and the terrors of endangered existence, set entirely in a female context, has all that harrowing vernacular directness of her best-known poems, 'Daddy' and 'Lady Lazarus'. However, it is the imaginative power of a poem like 'In Plaster' or 'Insomniac' that forecasts what I consider to be her best poem—'The Bee Meeting.' There is something shrill about 'Daddy' and 'Lady Lazarus' which, although understandable as overstatements, seem to attain a theatricality, an interior melodrama, that I find hard to take.

> Nightlong in the granite yard, invisible cats
> Have been howling like women, or damaged instruments.

Crossing the Water is an indispensable book, and Sylvia Plath one of that handful of modern poets whom intelligent readers will feel, more and more, that they have no option but to try and understand.

48. Victor Howes, 'I am Silver and Exact,' *Christian Science Monitor*

30 September 1971, 8

Crossing the Water is Sylvia Plath's second posthumously published collection of poems. Gathered from a variety of printed sources, and billed as 'transitional poems' they help to bridge the gap between the sober, workmanlike verses of *The Colossus* and the wild, expressionistic outcries of *Ariel*, poems which, it has been said, 'impressed themselves on many readers with the force of myth.'

Ariel is the shriek of a mandrake being drawn from its native earth. *Crossing the Water* is calmer, but its transitional nature should not be allowed to obscure its genuine merit. It contains finely realized poems like 'Blackberrying' which demonstrate the poet's gift for visualizing small things exactly: 'Blackberries / Big as the ball of my thumb, and dumb as eyes / Ebon in the hedges, fat / With blood-red juices.'

Even more important, this book reveals Sylvia Plath's growing dramatic ability, her power to project herself into 'personae,' as in 'Mirror,' which begins, 'I am silver and exact. I have no preconceptions. / Whatever I see I swallow immediately / Just as it is, unmisted by love or dislike.'

If it is tempting to read such lines as instances of what Keats called 'negative capability', the mark, he thought, of his own greatness, it is even more tempting to seek out lines that may serve as barometers to the poet's disastrous inner weather. Lines like

> Let me sit in a flowerpot,
> The spiders won't notice.
> My heart is a stopped geranium.

lines that could serve as the epigraph for her recently republished novel, *The Bell Jar.*

As it is, the major portion of *Crossing the Water* recollects a tranquillity of happy occasions, but a handful of poems, notably 'The Beast,' 'Witch Burning,' and 'Insomniac,' kindle with a gleam that points forward to the eerie light of 'Lady Lazarus' and 'Daddy' from the *Ariel* volume. 'The Beast' contains these prophetically ominous sounding statements: 'Down here the sky is always falling. / Hogwallow's at the window. / The starbugs won't save me this month.'

The reader may well find that the more traditional poems in *Crossing the Water* are the most fully satisfying. When she deals with sharply observed images, Sylvia Plath is on solid, nonsurrealistic ground, and she is unbeatable. A goldfish pond has been drained, 'the escaped water / Threading back, filament by filament, to the pure / Platonic table where it lives. The baby carp / Litter the mud like orangepeel. /... They glitter like eyes, and I collect them all. /...the lake / Opens and shuts, accepting them among its reflections.'

We shall probably never know what forces led Sylvia Plath to take her life. But, as the materials accumulate by which we can gauge her stature as a writer, we become increasingly aware that she belongs among the small body of poets, Marlowe, Keats, Chatterton, whose lives ended before their greatest poems were written. We become increasingly aware that we had with us for 30 years a woman who was a major modern poet.

49. Robert Boyers, 'On Sylvia Plath,' *Salmagundi*

Winter 1973, 96–104

Robert Boyers (b. 1942) is a poet and critic who edits the literary quarterly *Salmagundi* from Skidmore College. He is Professor of English there.

It would seem that those possessed by the Sylvia Plath legend will have to do some fancy stepping to accommodate the volume of her poems recently issued here and in England. *Crossing the Water* is an extraordinary book, not promising merely nor dazzling as one might have expected of a poet who was later to write the poems in *Ariel*, but perfectly satisfying in the way that only major poetry can be. That her achievement here may be spoken of in terms more orthodox than one could legitimately apply to *Ariel* is but one of the facts the promoters of the legend will have to deal with—how distressing it must be, for some of them at least, to confront a Plath largely in control even of her most terrible associations, and deliberately fashioning a voice by working through the poetry of Stevens, Frost, Lowell, Roethke, and others. The figure of the demon–lady with red hair eating men, and everything else, 'like air,' is considerably attenuated in the perspective of this new volume. Though one was always grateful for the dozen or so magnificent poems in *Ariel*, one may now be grateful that they can be read in a broader perspective wherein we shall more resolutely attend to the poems themselves rather than to the figure of the poet haunting the margins.

The items included in *Crossing the Water* were written, or so at least the dust-jacket of the volume informs us, 'in the period between the publication of *The Colossus* (1960) and the posthumous book *Ariel* (published in England in 1965).' A number had appeared in periodicals before the poet took her life in 1963, but very few writers and critics had taken notice of them in discussing her career. It was as if, with *Ariel*, one had all one needed to reach some proper estimation of the poet, and the intricacies of idea and language were so great in *Ariel* as to provide hungry critics with all they needed to keep busy on Sylvia Plath.[1] We see clearly now that *Ariel* was by no means enough, that we wanted some assurance of substantiality and permanence in our impression of such poems as 'Tulips,' 'Lady Lazarus,' and 'Daddy.' Already too many of us had come to think of these poems we have so often read aloud and heard recited to us as instances in some peculiar event we had lived through and wondered over, but which seemed more and more remote from conventional poetic experience. In part, of course, it is the propensity of our youth and literary cultures to convert disturbed people into heroes that was responsible, but the *Ariel* poems themselves had no small hand in encouraging us to think of them as extraordinary primal events without antecedent or analogue. *Crossing the Water* may be discussed less feverishly, and one does not hesitate to describe it as a book with a number of great poems, a number of less ambitious but beautifully realized poems, and several immature pieces each of which calls to mind a particular poetic voice imperfectly assimilated.

One need only be familiar with the work of a few poets to speak of Plath's failures in *Crossing the Water*. In poems like 'Who,' 'Dark House,' 'Maenad,' and 'The Beast,' the hand of Roethke is unmistakably heavy on the page. To read the following lines in a Plath poem is to have our attention forcibly turned *from* the intrinsic relations among the poem's constituent elements *to* a mode of comparison that has little to do with Plath, but a great deal to do with Roethke's compelling ingenuity and uniqueness:

> Pebble smells, turnipy chambers.
> Small nostrils are breathing.
> Little humble loves!
> Footlings, boneless as noses,
> It is warm and tolerable
> In the bowel of the root.
> Here's a cuddly mother.
>
> (from 'The Dark House')

Or how is one to avoid the inevitable comparison with such Roethkean lyrics as 'Love's Progress,' 'The Other,' or 'She' as one reads:

> This mouth is fit for little.
> The dead ripen in the grapeleaves.

A red tongue is among us.
Mother, keep out of my barnyard,
I am becoming another.

(from 'Maenad')

The presence of Stevens is ordinarily less obvious in Plath, whether one examines *The Colossus* or the present volume, but how startling it is to come upon these opening stanzas in a poem called 'Black Rook in Rainy Weather':

On the stiff twig up there
Hunches a wet black rook
Arranging and rearranging its feathers in the rain.
I do not expect a miracle
Or an accident

To set the sight on fire
In my eye, nor seek
Any more in the desultory weather some design,
But let spotted leaves fall,
Without ceremony, or portent.

It is as though Plath had sat down to write the poem fresh from an intensely involving session with 'Thirteen Ways of Looking at a Blackbird' and a few shorter lyrics in the *Opus Posthumous*, such as 'The Course of a Particular.' Again, one draws attention to these things not to score points on Sylvia Plath but to suggest emphatically how thorough was her absorption in the poetry of her time and how difficultly she forged what is by all accounts an original voice. In her memorable work one hears that voice practically alone—nothing alien clings to it, nothing interferes with its inwardness and that special resonance which is the imprint of a driven and strangely passionate sensibility.

It is not especially challenging to compile a list of the best poems in *Crossing the Water*, though one can always find disagreements if he tries hard enough. So fine are the best poems that they cannot fail to impress a trained reader with their distinctive authority and linguistic abundance. I speak of the following, in no special order: 'Candles,' 'Widow,' 'Leaving Early,' 'Ouija,' 'Wuthering Heights.' Less wonderful but surely finished and moving poems include 'Parliament Hill Fields,' 'Blackberrying,' 'Insomniac,' 'Magi,' 'Two Campers,' 'Last Words,' and 'A Life.' In these poems the Sylvia Plath whom we have learned to speak of as a case, a clinical

item in a running catalogue of the century's abuses, has transformed her character into a fate, an emblem of the singular
personality gorgeously projecting itself into a universe of alien
things allowed their otherness. Though the project of *Ariel*
involved an insistent appropriation and evisceration of this otherness, this peculiar thinginess in the object and human universe
through which the poet moved like a devouring angel, the project
of the major poems in *Crossing the Water* falls short of so
encompassing an enterprise. What we so admire in the present
volume is the formal verbal apparatus which makes possible the
evocation of a conflict without altogether dissolving the initiating
elements in that conflict. The ardor of immediate perception
co-exists here with the hunger to use that perception and transform
its objects into something that they are not, but the tension is
manageable, and the objects retain their identities. In *Ariel*, a poppy
observed had inevitably to be changed into something it could call
to the mind only of a furious and distracted sensibility, into a
bloody mouth, in fact, or 'little bloody skirts.' A warmly upturned
smile in the concerned face of a loved one would turn to a fish
hook, ominous and seductively sinister. There are conversions of
this sort in a number of poems in the new book, but they are
relatively few, and they seem almost out of place here. Frequently
the poet will play with the far-flung association or the grotesque
extension of an already unpleasant image, but it is the original
image itself she cares for here, its special character and irreducible
resonance. In the poem 'Widow,' to take but one instance of the
poet's resolute cultivation of the tension we have described, the
opening stanza threatens to overwhelm us and to work an unhappy
magic on the ostensible subject:

> Widow. The word consumes itself—
> Body, a sheet of newsprint on the fire
> Levitating a numb minute in the updraft
> Over the scalding, red topography
> That will put her heart out like an only eye.

'The word consumes itself—' immediately we suspect the poet of
contriving an occasion for a display of hysteria such as we have
known in *Ariel*, a display in which a series of wondrous
metamorphoses will tell us a great deal about the processes of an
intelligence conceived almost abstractly, as if it were nothing but

process devoid of determinant content. We see though, in succeeding stanzas, that this is not to be the case in 'Widow,' for it is carefully directed towards the establishment of a vital tension between the reality of the widow, the essence of the condition the word itself traditionally invokes, and the poet's emotional relationship to that condition as dictated by her own needs. What she does here is to imagine what the condition must really be like, to insist upon a mode of imaginative relation, in fact, in which the needs of the self will be deliberately restrained. To speak in such a context of responsible imagination is not at all misguided, nor ought it to invite critical reprisal, as if the merest mention of responsibility were to introduce into a specifically aesthetic domain a moral dimension not at all warranted or conceivably welcome. One may speak of responsible imagination, after all, without any reference to realities external to the poem. The question of propriety here refers exclusively to elements set in motion within the poem itself, and the loyalty to experience one feels moved to comment upon in reading *Crossing the Water* is a loyalty to a particular experience whose dimensions the poem initially describes or suggests. Consider the following lines from the middle of 'Widow':

> The moth-face of her husband, moonwhite and ill,
> Circles her like a prey she'd love to kill
> A second time to have him near again—
> A paper image to lay against her heart
> The way she laid his letters, till they grew warm
> And seemed to give her warmth, like a live skin.
> But it is she who is paper now, warmed by no one.

Or these concluding stanzas:

> A bodiless soul could pass another soul
> In this clear air and never notice it—
> One soul pass through the other, frail as smoke
> And utterly ignorant of the way it took.
>
> That is the fear she has—the fear
> His soul may beat and be beating at her dull sense
> Like blue Mary's angel, dovelike against a pane
> Blinded to all but the grey spiritless room
> It looks in on, and must go on looking in on.

How extraordinary that concluding image, spun out really over two entire stanzas, how substantial the condition it evokes, and yet how general and, one is inclined to say, conventional. How unafraid the poet is to inhabit this almost otherworldly dimension of the widow's loss, to give expression to a grief anachronistic in its single-mindedness. The relative simplicity of the phrasing in no way mitigates the striking clarity and interest of the condition as it is developed.

Often in going through *Ariel* one thought of the late R.P. Blackmur's reflection on Robert Lowell's earliest work, to the effect that in it there is nothing loved unless it be its repellence. Blackmur never really understood what Lowell's first volumes were about, and just so does his observation miss the mark if too rigidly applied to Plath. Still there is some truth in the observation taken in relation to *Ariel* where one necessarily thinks of *Crossing the Water* in other terms. If Sylvia Plath does not love the widow she describes, her compassion for and insight into her condition are at least considerable. Always, of course, the impulse to cry me me me is present, but the determination not to clearly masters any such impulse, and one must be moved by the drama the poet enacts among her warring desires. In the poem 'Two Campers in Cloud Country,' she and a companion camp in the woods, and the poet notices at once what poets have frequently recognized in similar circumstances. Looking up at rocks and clouds, she reflects that 'No gesture of yours or mine could catch their attention,/No word make them carry water or fire the kindling/Like local trolls in the spell of a superior being.' This is all rather familiar, though finely observed in a manner uniquely Plath's. But what one trained in the excesses and hungers of *Ariel* would not expect are lines like these:

> It is comfortable, for a change, to mean so little.
> These rocks offer no purchase to herbage or people:

How restrained the sentiments in such assertions and yet how tense the voice that utters them, how unlike comfort are the attendant emotions. If from nothing else in the poem, a reader would know for sure of the tension that rings just in the background of every utterance by listening to the final words:

> Around our tent the old simplicities sough
> Sleepily as Lethe, trying to get in.
> We'll wake blank-brained as water in the dawn.

For Sylvia Plath it was no easy matter to love what did not openly include her or that did not yield to her will, and she did no doubt court repellence precisely so that she might justify her poetic and personal excesses. The image of her acquiescently pondering a blank-brained awakening is then no emblem of an easy regression, but the expression of a determined wish to be, occasionally, nothing at all, and thereby to inhabit a various universe according to the principle of a negative capability. 'The horizons are too far off to be chummy as uncles,' the poet observes, and the line may stand in a sense for the impression one takes of the entire volume. It measures the poet's capacity to endure limited distance and otherness, to resist the temptation to suffocate everything in her fervent embrace.

That readers coming to the new volume from *Ariel* may find this tension very difficult to appreciate we have already suggested, and the reception it has been given by Helen Vendler in the *N. Y. Times Book Review* demonstrates just how great the problem will be. She writes that 'Plath would like, in distrust of mind, to trust nature, and yet she ends in the volume, by refusing nature any honorable estate of its own.' And later in her review, 'the poet's eye bounds the limits of the world, and all of nature exists only as a vehicle to her sensibility.' To which one wants to reply, go back to the poems themselves, and study them even as the *Ariel* poems resound in the inner ear, and consider again whether the former work upon you exactly as do the latter. That the Plath of the present volume would like to trust nature and cannot, we do not deny, but that she permits it some authentic and uncompelled expression in the dozen best poems is a certainty. As one reads through the *Ariel* poems one is taken not by any sense of mystery but by a sense of inevitability that grips one by the throat, occasionally perhaps by the fingers of the hand, and drags him along to an ending that was never really in question, no matter how dazzlingly circuitous the route. There is an element of mystery in *Crossing the Water* that is very different indeed, and one may locate its source at just that point where the object refuses to yield in its intransigent otherness and insists upon a range of potential meanings or associations that lead not in a straight line but in several directions at once. And this mystery is no mere rhetorical affair, but at least equally an affair of a spirit which can still afford a limited generosity. Suffused as so many poems in this volume are by this genuine current of mystery playing over the surfaces of objects and persons, it is no wonder that even ritualistic enactments incorporated by the poet are touched with a gentleness, a tentativeness one will hardly identify with *Ariel*. One need look no further than the poem 'Candles,' in fact, to see a perfectly glorious manifestation of this gentleness, this tentativeness, an alternation of sombre sentiment and delicate perception that constitutes a fabric as fine as anything Sylvia Plath has given us:

> They are the last romantics, these candles:
> Upside-down hearts of light tipping wax fingers,
> And the fingers, taken in by their own haloes,
> Grown milky, almost clear, like the bodies of saints.
> It is touching, the way they'll ignore
>
> A whole family of prominent objects
> Simply to plumb the deeps of an eye
> In its hollow of shadows, its fringe of reeds,
> And the owner past thirty, no beauty at all.
> Daylight would be more judicious,
>
> Giving everybody a fair hearing.
> They should have gone out with balloon flights and
>   the stereopticon.
> This is no time for the private point of view.
> When I light them, my nostrils prickle.
> Their pale, tentative yellows
>
> Drag up false, Edwardian sentiments,
> And I remember my maternal grandmother from Vienna.
> As a schoolgirl she gave roses to Franz Josef.
> The burghers sweated and wept. The children wore white.
> And my grandfather moped in the Tyrol,
>
> Imagining himself a headwaiter in America,
> Floating in a high-church hush
> Among ice buckets, frosty napkins.
> These little globes of light are sweet as pears.
> Kindly with invalids and mawkish women,
>
> They mollify the bald moon.
> Nun-souled, they burn heavenward and never marry.
> The eyes of the child I nurse are scarcely open.
> In twenty years I shall be retrograde
> As these drafty ephemerids.

I watch their spilt tears cloud and dull to pearls.
How shall I tell anything at all
To this infant still in a birth-drowse?
Tonight, like a shawl, the mild light enfolds her,
The shadows stoop over like guests at a christening.

How pleasant to be able to say of such a poem that the Lowellian echoes are unmistakable, and that they do not matter a bit, that so totally has the poet taken possession of her materials and transformed them that the life and breadth of all she has touched are enlarged and enhanced. And as to the craft that makes such a poem what it is, how just it is to observe that mere quotation is nearly sufficient—analysis of dynamics may well take a back seat to a mode of pleasure we may not have thought possible where Sylvia Plath was concerned.

NOTE

1 As one of those 'hungry critics,' I should know. See my essay 'Sylvia Plath: The Trepanned Veteran' in *Centennial Review*, Spring 1969.

50. Terry Eagleton, 'New Poetry,' *Stand*

1971–2, 76

Terry Eagleton (b. 1943) has a PhD from Cambridge. Of his many critical studies the best-known are *From Culture to Revolution* and *Walter Benjamin*.

The poems in Sylvia Plath's *Crossing the Water* belong to an interim period between the publication of *The Colossus* and the composition of the *Ariel* poems; and as Ted Hughes has suggested, in an otherwise unilluminating article in the *Critical Quarterly*, they have a rich and easy beauty beyond much that is achieved in those other two volumes. The characteristic features of Plath's superb work are immediately evident; the curious fusion of radical disturbance and rigorous control; the derangement of senses and textures, such that organic and mechanical processes become confused and transposed; the ways in which individual images are locked impersonally apart, in their own hermetic space, and yet blended into the tone of a distinctively personal speaking voice, scathing, ironic or deceptively level.

Throughout this volume, as in much of Plath's work, run two uneasily conflicting trends of imagery. On the one hand, the perceived world of the poems is hard, blank and static: a world of round, flat, bald, faceless surfaces without depth or solidity, whose apparent dynamism is merely the glitter of tin, the crinkling of paper or the smooth polish of stone. ('Moon' and 'star' are recurrent images, combining as they do a static sparkle with a flat two-dimensional expressionlessness.) Yet at another level there *is* movement beneath these fixed synthetic surfaces: a movement of draining, flaking, melting and emptying, a sticky, protoplasmic dripping, pumping or oozing, a steady dissolution into blackness and absence. On the one hand

> The night sky is only a sort of carbon paper,
> Blueblack, with the much-poked periods of stars
> Letting in the light, peephole after peephole

—but on the other hand

> His head is a little interior of grey mirror.
> Each gesture flees immediately down an alley
> Of diminishing perspectives, and its significance
> Drains like water out of the hole at the far end.
> He lives without privacy in a lidless room,
> The bald slots of his eyes stiffened wide-open
> On the incessant heat-lightning flicker of situations.

> ('Insomniac')

Reality is at once stiffened into mechanical immobility and dissolved into flickering evanescence: the horizons in 'Wuthering Heights' 'dissolve and dissolve,/Like a series of promises, as I step forward', and the wind 'pours by like destiny', but within this incessant crumbling and haemorrhaging of things, organic life-forms petrify to dolls, commodities, artefacts:

> The sheep...
> stand about in grandmotherly disguise,
> All wig curls and yellow teeth
> And hard marbly baas.

The sea in 'Whitsun' can be seen at once as a cheap, meretricious salesman displaying his wares—

> ...the weed-moustachioed sea
> Exhibits its glaucous silks,
> Bowing and truckling like an old-school oriental

and as a sinister organism:

> The waves pulse and pulse like hearts.

Within this disturbed interchange of organic and mechanical qualities, images of pickling and preserving begin to assume importance: life bottled, boxed and artificially suspended, but still, somehow, life:

> I am left with an arm or a leg,
> A set of teeth, or stones
> To rattle in a bottle and take home,
> And tissue in slices—a pathological salami.
> Tonight the parts will be entombed in an icebox.
> Tomorrow they will swim
> In vinegar like saint's relics.
>
> ('The Surgeon at 2 a.m.')

This reification of natural process to mechanisms or bits of flashy furniture ('...the clouds sit tasselled and fancy/As Victorian cushions') seems to follow in part from the very intensity of Plath's perceptions. The fiercely clarifying light shed on the poem's objects—the white, hygienic light of the operating-theatre—defines them so exactly that what emerges is the ominous mystery of their blank self-sufficiency. This is why the poem's objects seem at once alive with menacing potential and neutrally, disinterestedly alien. The paradox reveals itself at the end of 'Wuthering Heights':

> The sky leans on me, me, the one upright
> Among all horizontals.
> The grass is beating its head distractedly.
> It is too delicate
> For a life in such company;

Darkness terrifies it.
Now, in valleys narrow
And black as purses, the house lights
Gleam like small change.

The images here offer a sense of relatedness between man and
Nature at one level, only to undercut it by deeper implication. The
apparent *dependency* of the sky's leaning is, in fact, the repressive-
ness of an alien force; the frenzy of the grass is rendered with
imaginative sympathy, but the grass is wholly self-absorbed; the
monetary imagery of the final lines, while appearing to domesticate
Nature, in fact transmutes it to a commodity, trivializing and
distancing it in the act of seeming to appropriate it to human
concerns.

51. Peter Porter, 'Collecting Her Strength,' *New Statesman*

4 June 1971, 774–5

Peter Porter (b. 1929) is an Australian poet now living in
England. Among his collections are *A Porter Folio* and *The
Last of England*.

This is the second posthumous collection of poems from Sylvia
Plath's official publisher. The first, *Ariel*, containing poems written
just before her death, was one of the most powerful books since the
war. *Crossing the Water* consists of poems written in 1960 and 1961,
after *The Colossus* was published but before her final intense period
of creation. It's important to stress that they are not *Ariel* left-overs,
but poems of the brief interregnum between her strange precocity
and full maturity. A further volume, *Winter Trees*, will follow
shortly, taking us up to *Ariel* itself. It might have been a good idea
to issue one carefully-edited collected edition rather than bring out
everything piecemeal, but the logistics of the Plath inheritance are
nothing beside the advantages of possessing the poems. *Crossing the
Waters* is full of perfectly realised works. Its most striking

impression is of a front rank artist in the process of discovering her true power. Such is Plath's control that the book possesses a singularity and certainty which should make it as celebrated as *The Colossus* or *Ariel*. Once more death has all the best parts, but his disguises and metamorphoses are doubly audacious. In 'Mirror,' for example, the little, four-cornered god denies it has any preconceptions, but when a woman bends over it she sees not only her own agitation but the fate which awaits her:

> In me she has drowned a young girl, and in me an old woman
> Rises towards her day after day, like a terrible fish.

In this period of Plath's poetry, objects come towards the reader like frightening Greek messengers. The gifts are not even ambiguous; they are seen wearing their proud colours of destruction. The language is that carefully judged half-formal, half-vernacular one she perfected in *Ariel*. It's capable of bearing the full weight of the grand style while staying true to the sharpest observation of reality. As John Frederick Nims pointed out, submerged iambics glisten like reefs under her expressionist surfaces. The 'I' of these poems is usually changing, as often as not reaching full authority only in terror. In 'Love Letter,' she is as fanciful as any metaphysical, but the transformation scene is a matter of life and death:

> I started to bud like a March twig:
> An arm and a leg, an arm, a leg.
> From stone to cloud, so I ascended.
> Now I resemble a sort of god
> Floating through the air in my soul-shift
> Pure as a pane of ice. It's a gift.

So speaks the apprentice 'Lady Lazarus.' The vignette, frequently in three-line stanzas, is a form she is especially successful in. The title poem is one case: the scene is a lake with a boat on it, as normal as if she were writing a barcarolle. But with a few changes of harmony and a straightforward summoning of death, she makes it the lake of Hell:

> Cold worlds shake from the oar.
> The spirit of blackness is in us, it is in the fishes.
> A snag is lifting a valedictory, pale hand;
> Stars open among the lilies.
> Are you not blinded by such expressionless sirens?
> This is the silence of astounded souls.

Only a truly remarkable poet could afford to rely upon so much downright statement and mix it so surely with metaphor. When she sets an elaborate metaphorical machine in motion, as with 'In Plaster,' she pursues it as circumstantially as if she were Poe, but there are no ghostly props and no fustian either. In this poem, the plaster-of-paris cast is not just a convenient device to embody schizophrenic otherness, it becomes one of two persons in a closet drama. It could be *Huis Clos* or Isherwood's Mr. Norris bound to his dreadful satellite, Schmidt. The end becomes tragic wish-fulfillment:

> I'm collecting my strength; one day I shall manage without her
> And she'll perish with emptiness then, and begin to miss me.

In the security of theorising, it makes bad art to find death's chrysalis in every stage of life. But Sylvia Plath runs counter to our schools of 'life-enhancing' critics—she deals in what most people cannot accept. And we, her legatees, profit by her courage. The last poem in the book is from hospital, mankind's alma mater. It's called 'Among the Narcissi,' and is a picture of an old man (an old world perhaps?) recuperating on a garden walk. While there is poetry, there is life:

> There is a dignity to this; there is a formality—
> The flowers vivid as bandages, and the man mending.
> They bow and stand: they suffer such attacks!
> And the octogenarian loves the little flocks.
> He is quite blue; the terrible wind tries his breathing.
> The narcissi look up like children, quickly and whitely.

52. Paul West, '*Crossing the Water*,' Book World (*Chicago Tribune*)

9 January 1972, 8

Paul West (b. 1930) has taught in both England and the States. He is a prolific poet, novelist, and essayist.

Had Sylvia Plath been ugly, and not died in so deliberate a manner, I wonder if she would have the standing she has. Maybe so; she seems an unusually good poet, at her best pithy and stark, with a passion for minute accuracy in recording the physical, and not afraid to be caustic or discordant. Something muscular shows up in her work, as unusual in woman poets as visceral self-pity seems common. And (this perhaps gathered from living among the English) she has a way of putting catastrophe casually, without frills, and you wince at the zombie decorum with which she does it. It's precarious, though, only a bit more decorum than it is a shambles; its tautness might snap and scatter. Reading her is like standing on the San Andreas fault or crawling on a glass roof; she sets up a nervewracking excitement after which, as the poems end, you feel drained and down. She cannot be read aloofly.

On the other hand, there is the cult which finds her a seraphic cosmic victim, a self-elected St. Joan of the post-natal clinic, whose every word is loaded with unimpeachable witness. Male reviewers and critics, in England especially, permitted themselves a breaking of the waters; after years of magistrally rebuking poets whose diction wasn't crisp enough, they gushed out on the occasion of *Ariel* (1966), so much so that a new form of verbal solecism—the Plathitude—came into being. One had never realized that these taskmasters of the London poetry playground had any gush in them, anything but calipers and spirit level. When a Yukio Mishima disembowels himself and has himself beheaded, your English literato finds it a piece of tasteless oriental exhibitionism, not in the well-bred or even the fish-and-chips tradition. When a Sylvia Plath does away with herself, she sets off a chain reaction that has more to do with atavistic, sacrificial rituals—Venus romanticized—than with the excellence or unevenness of her writing (which was evident in *The Colossus*, 1960). The novelist, so-called, will always seem a mercantile figure, whereas the poet, so-called, will always seem a visionary, with one foot in myth and one eye on Orpheus. The poetry is in the pituitary. After which it is almost beside the point to note that Sylvia Plath's recently reissued autobiographical novel, *The Bell Jar*, is hardly as well written as her weakest poems; yet the cult touts it, extols it.

Now comes a book of 'transitional' poems, most of which Sylvia Plath wrote between 1960 and 1963, one of which, the title poem, a dim and flimsy thing, 'reveals just how deeply the poet felt the hardness of life *and* death.' Or so the blurb has it, with that knowing italicization of 'and' to tell us tritely this was a *complete* poet. In fact the book is rich with fastidious irony, with a juicy *Schaden-freude* that doesn't go too deep, something neither histrionic nor simplistic; we read about the insubstantiality of being someone—some *one*—in a world of instant certitudes. Here is Plath on sheep:

> The black slots of their pupils take me in.
> It is like being mailed into space,
> A thin, silly message.
> They stand about in grandmotherly disguise,
> All wig curls and yellow teeth
> And hard, marbly baas.

Observant indeed. Here she is on anaesthesia:

> When I was nine, a lime-green anesthetist
> Fed me banana gas through a frog-mask.

On skin:

> Skin doesn't have roots, it peels away easy as paper.

On blackberries:

> I come to one bush of berries so ripe it is a bush of flies,
> Hanging their blue-green bellies and their wing panes
>   in a Chinese screen.

Chrysanthemums:

> Now I'm stared at
> By chrysanthemums the size
> Of Holofernes' head, dipped in the same
> Magenta as this fubsy sofa.

A drained fish-pond:

> The baby carp
> Litter the mud like orangepeel.

Observation as innovative as this functions as all-round allusiveness, as if to suggest everything has been tested by the sense—counterpart to one poem that ends, 'Everything has happened.' It is homework done on the world of things which, although inseparable from us in the ecological tissue, were not created to return our sentient stare. There is always in Plath a sense that this, right here, is as far as the mind may be able to go; so, instead of hermeneutics, settle for a precise look, a concise delineation, something solid to grip while investigating human emotions (which may be just as enigmatic as sheep, anaesthesia, or skin). Her dense specificity makes her people more present than their emotions do. For example, the crystallization in the fourth line of the following not only points the statement as a whole but almost supplants it:

> And my grandfather moped in the Tyrol,
> Imagining himself a headwaiter in America.
> Floating in a high-church hush
> Among ice buckets, frosty napkins.

In that line grandfather becomes a third entity along with the buckets and the napkins; imagining them into being he exists for us in terms of them only—like the surgeon who calls tissue-slices his 'pathological salami,' an image in which the mind (Plath's transposed into his) has gone as far as it descriptively can and the yield of its effort becomes an emblem too of all the mind wants said but can't find. This is Plath's forte: definitions with an incomplete agnosticism, the stock-in-trade of one she calls 'Fido Littlesoul, the bowel's familiar.' The rationale comes in the poem 'Last Words':

> I do not trust the spirit. It escapes like steam
> In dreams, through mouth-hole or eye-hole. I can't
>   stop it.
> One day it won't come back. Things aren't like that.
> They stay...

And the Zoo Keeper's wife proves it on our pulses:

> Your two-horned rhinoceros opened a mouth
> Dirty as a bootsole and big as a hospital sink
> For my cube of sugar: its bog breath
> Gloved my arm to the elbow.
> The snails blew kisses like black apples.
> Nightly now I flog apes owls bears sheep
> Over their iron stile. And still don't sleep.

In the long haul things aren't enough, are too much: Holding on to them, you become beholden to them, nearly lapse into being one; and the last few poems in this collection, all short, blunt, short-winded lines, emphasize the thingness of lines themselves:

The month of flowering's finished. The fruit's in.
Eaten or rotten. I am all mouth.
October's the month for storage.

This shed's fusty as a mummy's stomach:
Old tools, handles and rusty tusks.
I am at home here among the dead heads.

This is the laconic stasis of Plath's mature manner, with her eye as
retentive as ever but her mind like a child's head banging repeatedly
against a wall. The idiom evokes Shakespeare's Poor Tom and
some Old English riddles; the lines add up to something they don't
wholly propel. They enact the difference between a poem that
unfurls or unfolds and a poem that is all halts. Her span of
confidence is usually only a line's length and she seems glad, after
each completed sortie, to return to the left-hand margin which is
fixed and static. She stabs a period at the line's end to stop it coming
after her into the next. The lines cage her in and she shrinks within
her confines.

Crossing the Water (lame title to be foisted on such a skillful
phrasesmith) is a substantial eyeful from an unflagging sharp
sensibility; a small pageant in insistent vernacular; a book of vivid
austerities in which Plath advances from the release of saying
almost anything, so long as it's with an engraver's precision, to the
containment of saying literally next-to-nothing—a nextness of
which her sense was to become woundedly acute. Her later poems
tell us how close you can go before you fall in.

53. Victor Kramer, 'Life-and-Death Dialectics,' *Modern Poetry Studies*

1972, 40–2

Victor Kramer (b. 1939) holds a PhD from the University of
Texas at Austin, and teaches at Georgia State University in
Atlanta, Georgia.

The mystery of fragile and precarious life demanded chartings of
that inexplicability, and Sylvia Plath accomplished such cartogra-

phy continually. The collection *Crossing the Water*, subtitled 'Transitional Poems,' reflects an assurance that, in the process of perfecting her chartings, significant insights were found. It is clear from this volume that Plath's career does not fall into just two easy categories represented by the two preceding volumes. Many of these poems are announcements, warning, and portents, of a power which has found itself. This is apparent in 'Heavy Women,' which has as theme the smugness of pregnant women who 'listen for the millennium, / The knock of the small, new heart' but whose self-satisfaction is scary. 'Smug / As Venus' arisen from the sea, they are unaware that like a machine winter rolls forward; its axle 'grinds round.' A related mood informs 'Dark House,' one of a group of five poems reprinted here that originally formed part of 'Poem for a Birthday' in the British edition of *The Colossus*. The subject is motherhood, artistry, and neurosis:

> I see by my own light.
> Any day I may litter puppies
> Or mother a horse. My belly moves.
> I must make more maps.

This is a monologue from the underground and it seems prophetic. So is 'Maenad,' one of the same group, which begins 'Once I was ordinary.' This successful book is composed largely of material written between the publication of *The Colossus* and *Ariel*.

There are thirty-eight poems here, and often they hover about the beauty of a moment; almost always such moments are informed by an awareness of death. In a near conversational tone these poems often demonstrate the closeness of life to death. With but three exceptions all these poems received periodical publication between 1957 and 1963, mostly in 1961 and 1962. Twenty have already appeared in book form, but of those, ten were excluded from the American edition of *The Colossus*, and ten others appeared only in the *Uncollected Poems* (1965), a limited edition of 150 copies. So while a devoted reader of Plath is probably familiar with many of these poems, this new volume is necessary because it pulls together many previously scattered pieces.

Of the eighteen poems which did not appear either in the British edition of *The Colossus* or in the *Uncollected Poems*, 'Stillborn' and 'Last Words' are new. 'Stillborn' is weak because of its simple one-to-one use of metaphor. Dead poems are pickled foetuses.

'Last Words' reveals a distrust of the spirit which can escape 'like steam / In dreams'; but also it implies the need for poetry, and a doubt that successful poetry can be constructed. Objects, the 'blue eye' of turquoise, and 'rouge pots,' 'stay, their little particular lusters / Warmed by much handling.' Of course, a poem also provides a luster for the commonplace, and the commonplace is regularly revealing itself for Plath. This fact will startle us into an awareness in later poems like 'Cut'; but in this volume, even in a quiet poem like 'Black Rook in Rainy Weather' (which was quite early in composition), we are reminded that 'minor light may still / Leap incandescent.'

This happens in 'Blackberrying', representative of the best of these poems (published first in 1962 and included in the *Uncollected Poems*). There are pleasure of picking berries is caught as they squander their juice, 'a blood sisterhood'; and a bush is 'so ripe it is a bush of flies.' Then quickly an awareness of a plenitude of berries gives way to the openness and space of the ocean in all its emptiness; and against the intractability of the ocean the nature of dead berries is minor comfort.

Other poems are successful in catching the themes of vulnerability and disease in a world which will not deliver its promises. In 'Wuthering Heights' 'horizons ring...like faggots.' In 'I Am Vertical' it is only with sleep that a wished for resemblance to trees and flowers is possible—then thoughts go dim. Death is a temptation. It is important to observe, however, that there is no morbidity in either of these two poems. It is simply that with the 'horizontal' one might be useful. It has often been remarked that the only subject of Plath's poetry is the dialectic between life and death. Both 'Wuthering Heights' and 'I Am Vertical' (and others of this volume) remind us that she saw the dialectic, that in-between, everywhere in a world where life is terrified by darkness. Domesticity can lull us for a moment perhaps, but seen from a poetic perspective '...valleys narrow / And black as purses, the house lights / Gleam like small change' ('Wuthering Heights'). In 'Insomniac' the stars of the night sky bring light, but 'a bone white light, like death behind all things.' The same threat is apparent in 'Two Campers in Cloud Country' when it is suddenly realized that 'The Pilgrims and Indians might never have happened.' No gesture of man can catch the attention of 'man-shaming clouds.'

From time to time when reading these poems one is reminded

that other poets helped to form Plath. Thus, 'Who,' 'Dark House,' 'Maenad,' 'The Beast,' and 'Witch Burning' must have been influenced by Roethke, and 'Ouija' echoes the rhythms and diction of Wallace Stevens. But what is most striking about the book is how it projects a new voice emerging. In 'A Life,' one of the most successful poems of the collection, life's mystery is probed. In the abstract things are ordered—'Palm-spear and lily distinct as flora in the vast / Windless threadwork of a tapestry.' (Hyphenated words abound. Someone should study these hyphenated constructions throughout Plath.) Reference to 'palm-spear and lily' suggest both the pomp of Palm Sunday, and the promise of resurrection. But the poet wonders if it is possible for poetry to be made of the dreariness of living; then the 'light falls,' and we are reminded that it is done regularly:

> A woman is dragging her shadow in a circle
> About a bald hospital saucer.
> It resembles the moon, or a sheet of blank paper
> And appears to have suffered a sort of private blitzkrieg.

This volume is absolutely essential for anyone interested in the poetry of Sylvia Plath. It helps us to realize that her career is of one piece. The collection contains few poems as tightly executed as in *Ariel*, but there are many successes. The title poem, 'Crossing the Water,' is a jewel of compression. It maps life's voyage bounded by darkness in just twelve lines. These poems demonstrate that she became stronger as poet, while her awareness became more intense.

WINTER TREES

London, 1971; New York, 1972

---

54. Unsigned review, 'A World in Disintegration,' *Times Literary Supplement*

24 December 1971, 1602

The posthumous publication of Sylvia Plath's poems has been an oddly ill-organized affair. Forty poems went into *Ariel*; now with the publication of these two volumes, we have a further fifty-two, plus the radio play, *Three Women*, which appears in *Winter Tress*. Of these, thirty-four—collected in *Crossing the Water*—are said to have been 'written... in the transitional period between *The Colossus* and *Ariel*'. How many poems are yet to come, and from which period, is anybody's guess; but perhaps it's time to forget publishing logistics and produce a definitive, chronologically ordered collection.

In any case we should be grateful for small deliveries. The latest poems, like those in *Ariel*, were written at a time when Sylvia Plath had stepped away from the traceable influences of her first book into a discovery of a style—more specifically, a vocabulary—which, in the earlier work, was always on the verge of being liberated. One of the most noticeable aspects of that vocabulary is the way in which it enables discrete images to assume an internal relevance: never glossed by abstraction, but obviating the narrative shifts which would have left the poems limply polemical:

> The Sunday lamb cracks in its fat.
> The fat
> Sacrifices its opacity...
>
> A window, holy gold.
> The fire makes it precious.
> The same fire
>
> Melting the tallow heretics,
> Ousting the Jews...
>
> ('Mary's Song')

165

The effect there is not one of comparison but of a progression made logical by a metamorphosis which brings the poet to the centre of things:

> It is a heart,
> This holocaust I walk in...

The particular value of this permeable vocabulary, and what made it inevitable—even instinctive—for Plath, is the manner in which it incorporates into a private mythology those external events most likely to serve it. The references to concentration camps, pogroms, Hiroshima and so on (often regarded as common currency in Plath's work, though a good deal less frequent than sometimes supposed) are not conscious attempts at empathy so much as an involuntary garnering of metaphors.

The bare bones of this process can be seen in the way in which similar events produce similar images (in fact, a line from 'The Surgeon at 2 a.m.' is used more or less unchanged in 'Three Women'); but it would be wrong to suggest that the poems were written by some irresistible osmotic force. It is the precise control over language which sustains the idiosyncratic, perfectly balanced tone: a symbiotic relationship between lyricism and a carefully judged version of common speech. The startling thing about the poems is that the control over language scarcely ever falters, though if examples of relative failure were to be looked for, 'The Tour', a poem from *Crossing the Water*, might be indicted as an example of the tone tending to become frantic and dissipative. Most often, though, the poems produce a seemingly effortless, though overwhelmingly powerful, congruity of language and content:

> Over one bed in the ward, a small blue light
> Announces a new soul. The bed is blue.
> Tonight, for this person, blue is a beautiful colour.
> The angels of morphia have borne him up.
> He floats an inch from the ceiling,
> Smelling the dawn draughts.
> I walk among the sleepers in gauze sarcophagi.
> The red night lights are flat moons. They are dull with blood.
> I am the sun, in my white coat,
> Grey faces, shuttered by drugs, follow me like flowers.
>
> ('The Surgeon at 2 a.m.')

A poem like the one just quoted from, coming out of a hospital visit, demonstrates the extent to which Plath's sensitivities worked on an external event. The persona of the surgeon is never twisted by simile or bald statement into a gratuitous system of emotional equivalents; if anything, he is committed to a world of exclusive artifact, a singular vision:

> It is a garden I have to do with—tubers and fruits
> Oozing their jammy substances,
> A mat of roots. My assistants hook them back.
> Stenches and colours assail me.
> This is the lung-tree.
> These orchids are splendid. They spot and coil like snakes.
> The heart is a red bell-bloom, in distress....

But the strength and depth of the poet's perception, together with the persuasive universality of the violent imagery, endow the poem with an importance and a perspective well beyond the limitations of a piece of brilliant, if grotesque, description. In the same way, small quotidian occurrences—a cut, a bruise, a child's restlessness at night—conspire to attract, as a magnet attracts metal filings, a perfectly tuned vocabulary: the perennial external horrors, by some almost casual correlative process, have become indivisible from the most intense internal pressures; and the language, miraculously, encompasses them both.

In a poetry where events and objects relate directly to conditions there is no possibility of constancy. The world constructed by these poems is a mutable one, amorphous almost; a world in which, behind the apparent permanency of natural objects, things are breaking up; what makes it compelling is the shock of surprise which comes with recognition—the way in which deeply personal themes are transmuted into poems which look intuitively outward for their effect. These last poems map out a territory which is unique, harrowing, yet always controllable; and which breeds its own distinctive landscapes: 'The wet dawn inks are doing their blue dissolve.' Fixed temporally, that line could be the product of 'that still blue, almost eternal hour before the baby's cry, before the glassy music of the milkman, settling his bottles'; but it is also an emotional landscape: an inescapable affinity. For Sylvia Plath, discovering that landscape must have been like coming home.

55. Linda Ray Pratt, ' "The Spirit of Blackness is in Us...," ' *Prairie Schooner*

Spring 1973, 87–90

An autobiographical novel, a selection of 'transitional poems,' and the final collection of poems by a brilliant young poet, dead since 1963. They tell us more, perhaps, about Sylvia Plath than we had thought we could know. The venom and the suffering are all here again; and again, much as we long to be the objective lovers of poetry, we find ourselves back in 'the peanut-crunching crowd' shoving in to see. This time, however, no one need remain the voyeur, for with these final three books, Plath drops the 'big strip tease' and give us the woman. It is that rare reversal—the humanization of a myth.

The Bell Jar is her early and unsatisfactory novel which never gets below the surface of its real materials. Some critics have compared it to J.D. Salinger's classic of male adolescence in the fifties, *Catcher in the Rye*. The comparison might more accurately be made to the quasi-clinical pop best seller of a couple of seasons ago, *I Never Promised You a Rose Garden*. Plath's thinly veiled autobiographical account of the summer of her college-aged suicide attempt is a small novel distinguished primarily by those occasional images which find their proper expression in the poems. Many of the images in the poems are elaborated on in useful ways in the prose version. For example, that deceptively obvious question which opens 'Fever 103°,' 'Pure? What does it mean?,' may be answered by 'Esther's' prolonged hot baths in which she finds the world 'dissolving' as 'all that liquor and those sticky kisses I saw and the dirt that settled on my skin...is turning into something pure.' The connections between 'growing pure again,' sexuality, and death are clarified by the prose description, though the force of language and meaning is in the poem.

The novelistic narrative is, ironically, limited by the very psychological problems which afflict the heroine. Esther's sickness manifests itself in a self-involvement so intense that she hates all things which intrude upon her deadly concentration. In terms of novelistic technique, this distortion of vision results in a cast of characters who are merely detestable caricatures. Even this limitation might have been redeemed had Plath offered the reader a genuine insight into the character of Esther. The novel lacks real answers to such questions as why, for example, she hates men. Because she dosen't want to be under their thumbs? Because their sex organs look like turkey necks? But why does she only see them that way? Why does the normal adolescent rejection of her mother become a pathological hatred? It can't be because her mother wants her to learn shorthand. In the visit to her father's grave, Esther makes an oblique criticism of her mother, who had not cried either: 'She had just smiled and said what a merciful thing it was for him he had died, because if he had lived he would have been crippled and an invalid for life, and he couldn't have stood that, he would rather have died than had that happen' (p. 189). Her mother's cliché wisdom no doubt seemed gross insensitivity, perhaps even a betrayal of what the marriage had seemed to the child, but is it sufficient reason for the suicide of the college-aged woman? Her later poem, 'Daddy,' gives us better answers than the whole of *Bell Jar*, which remains a maze of 'lost connections.' Plath describes Esther in this novel, but there is no 'person' at the center of this first person narrative.

At the opposite extreme are the poems of *Winter Trees*, the last collection. The voice is that of a woman and a mother whose special anguish is that it is she who will soon be leaving the child. The volume includes some previously published material, including the 1962 BBC verse drama, *Three Women*. The poetic flatness of *Three Women* is offset by such fine poems as 'Childless Woman,' 'For a Fatherless Son,' and 'Child.' In her emptiness, the Childless Woman says, 'My landscape is a hand with no lines.' The suicidal parent of the soon-to-be fatherless child finds that 'Till then your smiles are found money.' Yet another agonizing parental experience is felt in 'Thalidomide,' where

> All night I carpenter
>
> A space for the thing I am given,
> A love
>
> Of two wet eyes and a screech.

In these poems, Plath's images combine the stunning intensity and

169

originality of her best poems with an occasional grace of tenderness and melancholy that is lacking in the nearly hysterical poems of *Ariel*.

The most satisfying of these volumes is *Crossing the Water*, though it contains a number of poems which disappoint more than anything in *Winter Trees* does. *Crossing the Water* is subtitled 'Transitional Poems,' and the selections are primarily from the period between 1960 and late 1961. Nine of them appeared in the 1960 British edition of *The Colossus*, and the others were written before the period of the *Ariel* poems, which came in the last year of her life. All the best poems in this uneven volume are from the middle period. Unlike the woman of *Ariel* who is in a near-frenzy of hate and insanity, this woman is being pressed down by forces which close on her from all sides. She is the 'delicate' and helpless victim as 'The horizons ring me,' and even 'the roots of the heather ... will invite me/To whiten my bones among them.' In this nightmare of English landscape, 'The sky leans on me,' the mists 'stuff my mouth with cotton,' and 'The wind stops my breath like a bandage.' Here,

> the wind
> Pours by like destiny, bending
> Everything in one direction.
>
> ('Wuthering Heights')

'Trapped,' 'done for,' and 'swallowed,' she is the passive victim whose own soul betrays the living woman with its desire to be 'horizontal':

> It is more natural to me, lying down.
> Then the sky and I are in open conversation,
> And I shall be useful when I lie down finally:
> Then the trees may touch me for once, and the flowers
> have time for me.
>
> ('I Am Vertical')

Indeed, these 'transitional poems' trace the most profound of all transitions. In the title poem, which is the last in the volume and completes all movement, she moves from the overwhelming blackness of a 'black lake, black boat ... black trees' to the cold star-dazzle of death:

> Cold worlds shake from the oar.

The spirit of blackness is in us, it is in the fishes.
A snag is lifting a valedictory, pale hand;

Stars open among the lilies.
Are you not blinded by such expressionless sirens?
This is the silence of astounded souls.

('Crossing the Water')

For many readers of Plath, *Crossing the Water* will offer the answers we miss in *The Bell Jar*. She says, in the isolate loneliness of her imagination, 'Nobody can tell what I lack.' Perhaps not, but from *Crossing the Water* we can begin to feel how she was bent and pressed and finally seduced by 'the spirit of blackness.'

56. Roger Scruton, 'Sylvia Plath and the Savage God,' *Spectator*

18 December 1971, 890

Roger Scruton (b. 1944), educated at Cambridge, is best known for his writings about philosophy, particularly *Art and Imagination*.

It is seldom useful to judge a poet's writing in terms of his character, but Sylvia Plath so forces attention on herself that it is difficult to approach her work on other terms. She is present in almost every line, craving attention. Her almost necromantic commerce with nothingness perhaps licenses the reference, in *Winter Trees*, to 'The Courage of Shutting-up,' but this is certainly not the best description of her prevailing attitude:

The courage of the shut mouth, in spite of artillery!
The line pink and quiet, a worm, basking.
There are black discs behind it, the discs of outrage,
And the outrage of a sky, the lined brain of it.
The discs revolve, they ask to be heard—

Loaded, as they are, with accounts of bastardies.
Bastardies, usages, desertions and doubleness.
The needle journeying in its groove,
Silver beast between two dark canyons,
A great surgeon, now a tattooist,

Tattooing over and over the same 'blue grievances.
The snakes, the babies, the tits
On mermaids and two-legged dreamgirls.
The surgeon is quiet, he does not speak.
He has seen too much death, his hands are full of it.

Why does she dignify her sufferings with this figure of the
patient surgeon? It seems a kind of cheat, an attempt to mask the
obsessive character of her feeling.

But if Sylvia Plath's poetry presents the image of death it is not
with alluring accents. Her verse is brutal, and she speaks in it with
her own bitter and destructive voice. Unlike Hart Crane, she has
no sad protagonist to stand proxy for her; her love of death
produces no mellifluous symbolism, only a cluster of images
fathered into plain and ugly moods. Her tone is seldom far from
that of the famous 'Daddy,' published six years ago in *Ariel*—a
violent ritual exorcism of the father whom she loved and whose
death she deeply resented:

You do not do, you do not do
Any more, black shoe
In which I have lived like a foot
For thirty years, poor and white,
Barely daring to breathe or Achoo.

Daddy, I have had to kill you.
You died before I had time—
Marble-heavy, a bag full of God,
Ghastly statue with one grey toe
Big as a Frisco seal

And a head in the freakish Atlantic
Where it pours bean green over blue
In the waters off beautiful Nauset.
I used to pray to recover you.
Ach, du...

The language of this poem is wholly characteristic of her later
work. Throughout *Ariel* and its newly published companion

volume, *Winter Trees*, one finds the same tense rhythms, startling imagery and beautiful control ('Barely daring to breathe or Achoo...'). One of the finest features of her later style—the use of multiple metaphors—is here seen at its most effective. At first the poet is a foot, poor and white, trapped in the black shoe of her feelings for her father. But there is no time assimilate this image of pained submission before a new aspect is presented: the poet does not dare to breathe or sneeze; therefore she must be hiding in the shell of her grievance, fearing punishment. Immediately we discover that it is not she who must be punished, but the dead father whom she has had to kill for a second time. Her phantom father is re-created, not as a black shoe, but 'marble-heavy, a bag full of God.' Again there is no opportunity to absorb the meaning of these images before the father's next appearance as a 'ghastly statue.' As the similes cohere we see something that resembles the Commendatore of *Don Giovanni*, killed once, but now God-like, simultaneously ghost and statue. When the poet addresses the statue with the two poignant lines that end the third stanza, it has already assumed the form of a Colossus, which seems to cast its shadow, beneath the surface of a 'freakish' sea. This extraordinary sequence of images does not blunt the final impact: on the contrary, the language is so precise that each word adds a further subtlety of evocation.

Later in the same poem Sylvia Plath seems to identify her own grievance against her German father with that of the Jews against the German race, and at first sight this seems like another piece of grotesque self-aggrandisement, an attempt to validate a subjective resentment by borrowing the credentials of objective suffering. But again the language is too careful to let slip any lies about the poet's feelings; their obsessive quality is merely emphasised: 'With my gypsy ancestress and my weird luck/And my Taroc pack and my Taroc pack/I may be a bit of a Jew.' It is almost as though the poet were playing a part, but playing it so well that her mood has become self-sufficient and acceptable.

This remarkable quality is characteristic of all Sylvia Plath's later writing, and *Winter Trees* contains many fine examples of it. Although the book consists mainly of poems taken from the same batch as *Ariel*, it is by no means a collection of leftovers; the extraordinary accomplishment of Sylvia Plath's later style is manifest in every line. The book finishes with a radio play—*Three*

Women—which belongs to the same transitional period as the poems now collected in *Crossing the Water*. Although these poems show a departure towards the freer use of speech-rhythm and a more adventurous juxtaposition of images, they are still written in the careful manner of the early works, with their reminiscences of Eliot and their ruminative style. *Crossing the Water* contains many passages of beautiful verse, and *Three Women*, which is remarkable for its relatively selfless attempt to evoke the moods of three separate personalities, is written in an interesting synthesis of the earlier and later styles.

There are a number of passages approaching closer to the poet's familiar realms of feeling, which adopt the imagery and rhythms of the later work:

> I have had my chances. I have tried and tried.
> I have stitched life into me like a rare organ.
> And walked carefully, precariously, like something rare.

But the verse here, with its measured vowel sounds, is still that of a craftsman. One has the sense of a deliberate striving for effect, a mannered and slightly rhetorical afflatus which is very far from the laconic directness of the poems in *Ariel* and in the rest of *Winter Trees*.

It is difficult to describe the peculiar quality of Sylvia Plath's last poems. Their originality is not simply an originality of mood. Nor does it lie in the brilliance and precision of her language, although in a certain sense Sylvia Plath's descriptive talent was greater than any other she had. Perhaps what is most surprising is the complete avoidance of hysteria. For Sylvia Plath's poetry is never reflective: it contains no sympathy for attitudes that were not her own. Her intelligence sought expression not in judgement but in the lightning clarity of revelation. The poems present a sudden glimpse of things, and, caught in that glimpse, a moment of intense emotion. Her great achievement was to evolve a style that would fit this precarious mode of lyrical expression: the multiple metaphors, the quick rhythms, the mastery of colloquial speech, the extraordinary language, and the direct, unhesitant manner.

In the later poetry we find no attempt to *say* anything. Images enter these later poems as particulars only, without symbolic significance, and however much the poet may borrow the emotional charge from distant and surprising sources (from the imaginary life in ocean depths, from the real and imaginary calamities of modern history) it is never with any hint of an intellectual aim. It is tempting to restore to these poems some vestiges of generality, by interpreting them as Freudian parables, or as complex symbols. But although the poems of *Ariel* and *Winter Trees* invite such an interpretation, they also show how valueless it is. It is not through their coincidence with unconscious wishes that these poems affect us, nor do they have any symbolic force comparable to their overwhelming immediacy of impact. Everything in them is objective, concrete, conscious; we can feel moved by Sylvia Plath's obsessions without feeling any need to share in them.

57. Joyce Carol Oates, '*Winter Trees*,' *Library Journal*

1 November 1972, 3595

Joyce Carol Oates (b. 1938) has published over seventy volumes of poetry, fiction, and criticism. The winner of the National Book Award and various other prizes, this American writer has also written a major essay on Plath, 'The Death Throes of Romanticism.'

The poems in this final volume of Sylvia Plath's work were all written during the last year of her life, and are therefore products of the same anguished, meticulous imagination that created the famous *Ariel*. Though in general this particular collection is not so striking as *Ariel*, a number of the poems and the long radio play, *Three Women*, are unforgettable for their eerie fusion of power and helplessness.

The title poem tells us of the 'blue dissolve' of trees at dawn; Plath, observing the 'effortless' seeding of nature, envies the otherworldliness of the winter trees that know 'neither abortions nor bitchery.' The poet's voice is tentative, uncertain. The dissolving of the ego is a characteristic of Plath's work, as if the poet did not believe sufficiently in her own identity, but imagined that the exterior world—whether of men, other women, animals, or inanimate nature—possessed some strange power to annihilate her.

'Mystic' is a poem of 'questions without answer'—a series of speculations on the probable horror of any confrontation with the divine. For Plath, a mystic communion with anything outside herself seems a nightmare: 'Once one has seen God, what is the remedy?' she asks. The poems build up through an accumulation of sharp, deadly images, to a statement of tension, rather than a resolution of tension; they seek out enemies, define them, dissect them, but ultimately acquiesce even when the surrender involves an annihilation of the self (indeed, the word *annihilation* is used often). Thus Sylvia Plath's poems can be said to be the most lyric, precise, and heartbreaking articulation of a totally passive femininity—pathologically suppressed, except in the violence of the poems themselves.

We know from Ted Hughes' remarks that many of these poems are not completed, and it is evident that the bulk of *Winter Trees* does not constitute so finished a work as *Ariel* or *The Colossus*. Nevertheless, the volume is fascinating in its preoccupation with formlessness, with dissolving, with a kind of premature post-humous disappearance of the poet's personality. Outstanding is the verse play, *Three Women*, which takes place in a maternity ward and explores three differing responses to the experience of childbirth. 'There is no miracle more cruel than this,' one of the women cries. Sylvia Plath's talent was for the depiction of extreme, exhausted states of mind, in which the physical aspects of life—or, in some cases, the terror of the physical—so outweigh the intellect's capacity for survival that the poet's identity cannot be sustained. Though critics have begun to react against the initial awe with which Sylvia Plath's posthumous poems were greeted, it seems incontestable to me that her poems, line by line, image by image, are brilliant. Of her emotional and intellectual maturity it is perhaps best to say little, except to point out that poetic genius has rarely depended upon maturity; it is enough to acknowledge the existential authority of these poems, which, ultimately, go beyond criticism.

58. Damian Grant, '*Winter Trees*,' *Critical Quarterly*

Spring 1972, 92–4

Faber have indicated that we may expect the complete edition of Sylvia Plath's poems early next year. Meanwhile we have here the second of two volumes of poems left unpublished at her death in 1963, and now published by Ted Hughes (who introduced them in the Summer, 1971 edition of *Critical Quarterly*). *Winter Trees* is the slimmest as well as the last of Sylvia Plath's collection; there are nineteen poems here on forty printed pages. But there is ample further evidence of her endless imaginative resource in the restatement of her familiar themes: all proceeding, ultimately, from the 'divided self,' the self which is alienated, oppressed, disembodied, dissolved. We meet again the familiar images, particularly the (characteristically schizoid) image of the mirror, which appears in all but two of these poems and seems to haunt them with its inevitability and its destructiveness:

> Mirrors can kill and talk, they are terrible rooms
> In which a torture goes on one can only watch.

We are dazed again by the complicated use of colours, almost as a symbolism, to signify states of mind, attitudes; the alienating absolutes of black and white, the terrifying violence red almost always means, the uncertainty of blue, which can signify the cold night-blue of the moon ('What blue, moony ray ices their dreams?'), blue angels—'the cold angels, the abstractions,' or the sky-blue of a child's eyes; and the occasional consolation of the organic colours, brown and green.

In these poems a woman is on trial before herself, and spared nothing. A woman who longs for the unconscious life of trees: 'Knowing neither abortions nor bitchery, Truer than women,/ They seed so effortlessly!'; a woman who has sacrificed herself to the will of another person: 'I am his. Even in his Absence, I/Revolve in my Sheath of Impossibles'; a childless woman who sees her menstrual cycle as a reproach to her futility: 'The womb

177

Rattles its pod, the moon/Discharges itself from the tree with nowhere to go'; a woman who is tormented by the simple exacerbation of being, to whom the air is 'a mill of hooks.' A woman recalling the abortion that saved her from having a deformed child: 'The dark fruits revolve and fall./The glass cracks across, The image Flees and aborts like dropped mercury'; a woman imagining to herself the future of her fatherless child:

> You will be aware of an absence, presently,
> Growing beside you, like a tree,
> A death tree, colour gone, an Australian gum tree—
> Balding, gelded by lightning—an illusion.
> And a sky like a pig's backside, an utter lack of attention.

A woman addressing her separated self (in the difficult poem 'Lesbos'), a self full of hatred, on the subject of her schizoid child ('Her face is red and white, a panic'), her impotent husband who is kept as 'An old pole for the lightning' of her moods, and the impossibility of her own reintegration: 'We should meet in another life, we should meet in air./Me and you,' but 'Even in your Zen heaven we won't meet.' She must simply suffer the discord of her 'two venomous opposites' floating in 'The smog of cooking, the smog of hell.'

But the most important poem in this collection is certainly the poem for three voices, *Three Women*, which was broadcast by the BBC in 1962 and published four years ago in a limited edition. In this vividly successful dramatic experiment (which must surely be due for another hearing) three women offer a commentary on their contrasting experiences in a maternity ward 'and round about': one woman who gives birth to a child and is fulfilled, a second who has a miscarriage, and a third who suffers the death of her new-born baby. The violence implicit in female physiology, the violence of the phallic intervention into this, the violence of childbirth (recalling Berryman's *Mistress Bradstreet*) are all detained here in the marvellous focus of Sylvia's Plath's imagination:

> He flew into the room, a shriek at his heel.
> The blue colour pales. He is human after all.
> A red lotus opens in its bowl of blood....

and resolved, finally, in post-natal amnesia and its confirming images of peace and growth:

> Dawn flowers in the great elm outside the house....
> ...The little grasses
> Crack through stone, and they are green with life.

Only a detailed analysis—or, better, an attentive reading of the poem—could possibly provide a sufficient idea of its total poetic effect, unravel the complex triple fugue of its counterpointed themes and images.

59. Raymond Smith, 'Late Harvest,' *Modern Poetry Studies*

1972, 91–3

Raymond Smith (b. 1933) edits *Ontario Review* from his home in Princeton, New Jersey. He was formerly head of the English Department at the University of Windsor, Ontario.

Admirers of Sylvia Plath will be grateful to Ted Hughes for presenting us with another posthumous collection of her work. *Winter Trees* consist of fifteen poems that were among those from which Mr. Hughes selected 'more or less arbitrarily' for *Ariel*, as well as her radio play, *Three Women, A Poem for Three Voices*, first performed on the B.B.C. in 1962. Like the recent *Crossing the Water*, this volume is an extension of the urgent thematic obsessions of *Ariel*, and, indeed, we are told by the editors that all the poems of the three books were written at about the same time. What needs to be stated is the exploratory nature of some of the poems—they are not 'finished', not 'perfected', and if Sylvia Plath had lived to collect them into a book, she would certainly have discarded some, revised others, transformed others into totally new works. The turbulence of the creative imagination could only be stilled—ironically—by death.

Three Women is probably the most interesting item in the new collection. Childbirth is the subject of this poem, and it is approached from three different points of view. There is the wife, who unhesitantly accepts her role as mother; the secretary, who suffers a miscarriage; and the girl who gives up her unwanted child. In a series of interlocking dramatic monologues, the poem moves from the women's initial awareness of their condition, through their terrible agony in the maternity ward, to their attitudes after the event. The poem explores with great sensitivity a wide range of feelings associated with this central factor of womanhood. 'I cannot help smiling at what it is I know,' confesses the happily pregnant woman. 'There is this cessation,' mourns a second woman after a miscarriage. 'There is this cessation of everything.' And this is how the mother's first glimpse of her child is evoked:

> Who is he, this blue, furious boy,
> Shiny and strange, as if he had hurtled from a star?
> He is looking so angrily!
> He flew into the room, a shriek at his heel.

Most of the other poems, written some time after *Three Women*, are related to that work insofar as they focus on the woman in her roles as mother and wife. Closely related to the earlier work is the bitter 'Childless Woman', which could almost have been part of the secretary's monologue. Other aspects of motherhood are evoked in the disturbing 'Thalidomide':

> What leatheriness
> Has protected
>
> Me from that shadow—
> The indelible buds,
>
> Knuckles at shoulder-blades...

and in the mournful 'Child', where the mother's wishes for her baby are so woefully frustrated:

> Your clear eye is the one absolutely beautiful thing.
> I want to fill it with color and ducks...
>
> ★ ★ ★
>
> Not this troublous
> Wringing of hands, this dark
> Ceiling without a star.

The absence of the father is the concern of two of these poems, 'By Candlelight' and 'For a Fatherless Son.'

The father's absence suggests a fatal discord in the relationship between the sexes, which is the subject of several of the other poems in *Winter Trees*. 'The Rabbit Catcher' depicts this relationship as a trap: 'Tight wires between us,/Pegs too deep to uproot, and a mind like a ring/Sliding shut on some quick thing.' In 'Gigolo' and 'Purdah', the male appears as Narcissus, blindly staring into his own image. The former poem ends with this observation by the gigolo: 'All the fall of water an eye/Over whose pool I tenderly/Lean and see me.' In 'Purdah', the veiled bride gleams 'like a mirror':

> ...the bridegroom arrives
> Lord of the Mirrors!
> It is himself he guides
> In among these silk
> Screens...

Plath's treatment of the male is not without its satiric humor, intended to deflate the masculine ego. The whole of 'Gigolo' is in this mode. 'By Candlelight' concludes with a satiric note as the mother sardonically comments to her child on the brass candlestick holder—a kneeling Atlas set off by a pile of cannonballs:

> He is yours, the little brassy Atlas—
> Poor heirloom, all you have,
> At his heels a pile of five brass cannonballs,
> No child, no wife.
> Five balls! Five bright brass balls!
> To juggle with, my love, when the sky falls.

The 'little brassy Atlas' without wife and child represents, of course, the absent husband. Such satiric diminution is reminiscent of Pope. Some of the poems included here—and 'Stopped Dead' comes to mind most immediately—are not as successful as the others. This is not to suggest, though, that *Winter Tress* is a collection of leftovers, the crumbs from the feast of *Ariel*. These poems, on the whole, represent Sylvia Plath at her best. One can only wonder why they have not been collected till now.

60. James Finn Cotter, 'Women Poets; Malign Neglect?' *America*

17 February 1973, 140

James Finn Cotter (b. 1929) holds degrees in English and Philosophy, and writes on both Renaissance and modern and contemporary poetry.

Women who are poets have much more trouble winning recognition than do men. A glance though any anthology of contemporary poetry will show you how the men have cornered the market for themselves; rarely do women make up more than ten percent of the poets represented. While not in the category of Indians and blacks, the sisterhood has long been relegated to the shadowland of literature in America, despite the fact that our first poet was a woman, Anne Bradstreet. Two centuries of darkness loom after that, until Emily Dickinson—and she won recognition only after her death.

Women have fared slightly better in this century, but there still was only one Marianne Moore for the dozen Frosts, Pounds, Sandburgs, Eliots, Cummingses, Cranes, etc. The cause was hardly helped by the uxorious efforts of the anthology kingmakers, Louis Untermeyer and Oscar Williams, who tried to slip their own wives into the company of the immortals.

Of course one could point to Amy Lowell, Edna St. Vincent Millay, H.D. (Hilda Doolittle), Sara Teasdale and Elinor Wylie, but the critical establishment—aloof, academic and male—never took these feminine songbirds too seriously. Even Emily won grudging appreciation for her intellectual coolness, metaphysical ingenuity and independence—qualities men can safely admire. Marianne possessed the same virtues, spiced with her own eccentricity and wit, so she could be comfortably allowed into the pantheon. Then the valves of critical attention closed like stone.

For a long while, only Elizabeth Bishop appeared to be judged worthy of succeeding the longevous Miss Moore. Her qualifications again were the right ones: tough, tense, tightly brilliant—

182

nothing offensively female about her! When token attention to blacks was called for, Gwendolyn Brooks began to emerge from obscurity, but the men poets, from Robert Lowell to Allen Ginsberg, remained the unchallenged chanticleers of the hour.

Enter Sylvia Plath, the vixen poetess!

'You do not do, you do not do / Any more, black shoe,' she declares in 'Daddy,' and with one leap—in her collection, *Ariel*, published posthumously in 1966—she finishes him off: 'Daddy, I have had to kill you.' With the help of her novel, *The Bell Jar* (1971), the shock threatens to be felt around the world, with Sylvia the embattled heroine of the Women's Liberation Movement. She is a powerful prophetess, indeed: 'Herr God, Herr Lucifer, / Beware / Beware. / Out of the ash / I rise with my red hair / And I eat men like air.' Her poems are defiant but intensely personal as well: 'I have suffered the atrocity of sunsets.' She describes her anxieties, motherhood with two babies, the loneliness that led to her suicide in 1963: 'Dying / Is an art, like everything else. / I do it exceptionally well. / I do it so it feels like hell. / I do it so it feels real. / I guess you could say I've a call.' These poems, I find, make painful reading in their sheer defensiveness and honesty. Hers is a voice that demands to be listened to.

Sylvia Plath's reputation will be enhanced by another collection of her unpublished last poems, *Winter Trees* (Harper, $5.95). The spiritual dimension of her suffering is more definitely etched here in poems like 'Mystic,' 'Brasilia' and the title poem. We meet her, surprisingly, as a reflective poet, an aspect of her verse hardly ever mentioned. She asks: 'Is there no great love, only tenderness? / Does the sea / Remember the walker upon it? / Meaning leaks from the molecules.' The search these poems articulate was a sorrowful one, but they are devoid of clichés and easy definitions: they rely on their own weight in struggling for transcendence, that particular quest that has been the mark of American literature. The short play *Three Women*, included in *Winter Trees*, attempts to find the transparent spirit in 'the incalculable malice of the everyday.' It ends on a note of hope: 'The little grasses / Crack through stone, and they are green with life.' Sylvia Plath's break with the past and the dominion of 'Daddy' brought bitterness from which we will be a long time recovering, but with the pain came insight and a new self-awareness for women.

61. Ingrid Melander, review, *Moderna Språk*

1971, 360–3

In the course of this year no less than four collections of Sylvia Plath's poems have been published: *Crystal Gazer* and *Lyonnesse* (London; Rainbow Press); *Crossing the Water* and *Winter Trees* (London: Faber & Faber). In addition, Sylvia Plath's autobiographical novel, *The Bell Jar*, which came out in England in 1963, was finally published in the U.S.A. in the early spring and has been on *Time*'s best-seller list until very recently. This activity on the part of the publishers is without doubt due to the growing interest shown by the reading public in Sylvia Plath's literary output, notably her poetry. The strong impact of, in particular, her later poems can be at least partly accounted for by referring to our spontaneous response to literary works that touch on that crucial problem of our age: how to deal with a world that is becoming increasingly hostile to the demands of the individual.

The two volumes of poems published by Faber & Faber are valuable contributions to a fuller understanding of Sylvia Plath's development as a poet. *Crossing the Water* contains a number of poems written in the so-called transitional period between the publication of *The Colossus* (1960) and the composition of the poems in *Ariel* (published posthumously in 1965), i.e. roughly in the years 1960 and 1961. The themes in *Crossing the Water* are very much the same as in *The Colossus*: apprehensions of some lurking threat are frequently felt in these poems and, as in *Ariel*, various aspects of death is the poet's major preoccupation.

As in *The Colossus* and, to some extent, in *Ariel*, the sea is closest connected both with life's indifference towards its own kind and, ultimately, with death itself. In 'Finisterre' the setting is the black cliffs of 'the land's end': the mists are seen as

> Souls, rolled in the doom-noise of the sea.
> They bruise the rocks out of existence, then resurrect them.
> They go up without hope, like sighs.

In the last stanza, however, a note of human warmth and hope is struck: the necklaces and toy ladies are made up of shells which

> ...do not come from the Bay of the Dead down there,
> But from another place, tropical and blue,
> We have never been to.

In the title poem, 'Crossing the Water', the notion of death is the overall impression. What starts as a description of rowing in a boat on a black Canadian lake turns out to be a drifting towards the realm of death:

> Stars open among the lilies.
> Are you not blinded by such expressionless sirens?
> This is the silence of astounded souls.

In this poem the seemingly effortless simplicity of expression of the *Ariel* poems is anticipated, indeed, already arrived at.

In a few poems in *Crossing the Water* the poet's / the mother's concern is with her children, but, strictly speaking, 'Stillborn' is not one of them. Instead, here Sylvia Plath's remarkable wit is ironically used to convey what was obviously her main preoccupation at the time: her dissatisfaction with herself as a poet:

> These poems do not live: it's a sad diagnosis.
>
> They are not pigs, they are not even fish,
> Though they have a piggy and a fishy air—
> It would be better if they were alive, and that's what they were.
> But they are dead, and their mother near dead with distraction,
> And they stupidly stare, and do not speak of her.

Winter Trees includes Sylvia Plath's only poetic piece written specifically for broadcasting, *Three Women*. In this 'poem for three voices' personal experiences from a maternity ward evidently provide a starting-point for the presentment of the poet's ambivalent attitude towads motherhood and the traditional glorification of maternal bliss. As is pointed out by Ted Hughes in an introductory note, this sequence of monologues by three women may well have played an important part in the development of Sylvia Plath's intensely creative powers towards the colloquial ease of phrasing which is the hallmark of the best of her later poems. As she herself pointed out in an interview shortly before her death, these poems were written to be read aloud, and, in retrospect, the composition of *Three Women* for the BBC may therefore be seen as a step towards the final achievement of style in the *Ariel* poems.

The poems in *Winter Trees* belong to the last nine months of Sylvia Plath's life, i.e., they are 'true' *Ariel* compositions. They are a repertory of her major themes and images which bears further witness to the consistency of her literary work. The poet's tenderness in dealing with a mother's feelings for her child manifests itself in poems such as 'Child', 'By Candlelight', 'For a Fatherless Son', and 'Mary's Song'. The latter poem, set against the horrors of the concentration camps of the Second World War, locates the mother–child relationship in a wide religious and political context which gives a universal application to an otherwise commonplace everyday situation:

> It is a heart,
> This holocaust I walk in.
> O golden child the world will kill and eat.

Sylvia Plath's never-ceasing dialogue with death—'The Other'—is carried on in a variety of moods and turns which seem inexhaustible. One of the most memorable poems in *Winter Trees* is 'Lyonnesse', in which the Arthurian story of the prosperous state of Lyonnesse and its supposed disappearance beneath the surface of the sea is used to display the natural ease with which death can be faced:

> No use whistling for Lyonnesse!
> Sea-cold, sea-cold it certainly is.
> It was not a shock—
>
> The clear, green, quite breathable atmosphere,
> Cold grits underfoot,
> And the spidery water-dazzle on field and street.

The subtle complexity of Sylvia Plath's life-long preoccupation with death is further displayed in 'Mystic', which, in the first place at least, should not be interpreted as a personal credo but rather as yet another variation on her wrestling with death (God?):

> Once one has seen God, what is the remedy?
> Once one has been seized up
>
> Without a part left over.
> Not a toe, not a finger, and used.

Used utterly, in the sun's conflagrations, the stains
That lengthen from ancient cathedrals
What is the remedy?

For Sylvia Plath the remedy was most likely her headstrong
defiance of the human predicament. In 'Purdah' the persona's
self-assertion is such as to make herself a revenger, a collaborator
with death itself—a Lady Lazarus in oriental disguise. This daring
defiance is given a typical Plathian twist of wryness in 'The
Courage of Shutting-Up'—'in spite of artillery!':

Do not worry about the eyes—

They may be white and shy, they are no stool pigeons,
Their death rays folded like flags
Of a country no longer heard of,
An obstinate independency
Insolvent among the mountains.

62. Eric Homberger, 'The Uncollected Plath,' *New Statesman*

22 September 1972, 404–5

Eric Homberger (b. 1942) compiled an early bibliography of
Plath's writings. He is Professor of English at the University
of East Anglia, and author of a major critical study, *The Art of
the Real, Poetry in England and America Since 1939*.

And there is a charge, a very large charge
For a word or a touch
Or a bit of blood

('Lady Lazarus')

Sylvia Plath means big business. Ninety thousand copies of the
American edition of *The Bell Jar* were sold by Harper & Row at
$6.95; the paperback edition sold one million copies betweeen April

and July of this year; and it was chosen by the Literary Guild. Literary editors can expect to pay double the normal rate for her juvenilia, and are glad to do so; and her name sells copies of the *Observer*. Yet there is no collected poems nearly a decade after her death. Her English publishers, Faber, make no firm predictions; they may have the poems to publish by the autumn of 1973 or by the spring of 1974; then again they may not. Harper & Row are waiting for the sale of film rights of *The Bell Jar* before beginning work on the collected poems. We shall probably be offered substantially a reprint of *The Colossus, Ariel, Crossing the Water* and *Winter Trees* as a 'collected' Plath, but perhaps less than half of her poems are in these four volumes. The text of the poems is sometimes problematical ('Steadily the Sea / East at Point Shirley' in *The Colossus* should read 'Eats at Point Shirley'). There are a lot of uncollected poems which have appeared in periodicals, a number of unpublished early poems in the Cambridge manuscript, and an unknown quantity of poems, some very late, still in manuscript.

Plath wrote some 300 poems—about as many as Yeats before the *Last Poems*. She also completed a novel, drafted seven chapters of a second (some sources suggest that only three chapters exist), and published eight short stories. One has only to glance at the many articles on her work, the doctoral dissertations completed and underway, the presence of *Ariel* as a set-text in universities, to realise that she was probably the central poet of the Sixties. But it is difficult to get her achievement into any sort of perspective with at least half of her poems uncollected or unpublished. It only took four or five years to get out the posthumous collected poems of Roethke, Jarrell and MacNeice.

One can only infer Plath's attitude towards the publication of her work. She submitted *Two Lovers and a Beachcomber*, a manuscript of 43 poems, as an 'original composition' for Part Two of the Cambridge English Tripos in 1957. The organisation of the manuscript, the fastidious balancing of theme and mood, suggests unusual care. Her first published book, *The Colossus*, brought out by Heinemann in 1960, represents a culling of the early manuscript, for only six poems were kept. The rest of the book contained work completed between 1957 and 1959, when she and her husband Ted Hughes returned to live permanently in England. *The Colossus* met with a respectful if not enthusiastic reception; a *succès d'estime*, it sold a couple of hundred copies and the publishers were not yet queueing up for her work. Nine poems were dropped from the Heinemann edition when Alfred A. Knopf published *The Colossus* in 1962. Plath was as impatient of her successes as of her failures among the early poems. She had began to write for the ear instead of for the eye; *The Colossus* poems bored her, she said in an interview in 1962, they were unreadable.

'For two or three months, right up to her death,' A. Alvarez remembered, 'she was writing one, or two, sometimes three poems a day, seven days a week.' Highly personal, bitter, written with a great fluency and intensity, there was no market for poetry like this. A literary editor of a weekly returned a batch of them to Sylvia Plath, later remarking that they were 'too extreme for my taste'. Plath's suicide did wonders to reconcile editors to her last poems. Their dramatic appearance in *Encounter* and the *Review* (accompanied by Alvarez's important essay), and the haunting fact of her death, meant that *Ariel* was going to be an important book when it was finally published by Faber in 1965. Long essay–reviews were written by Alvarez, George Steiner, Stephen Spender and Hugh Kenner; the *Tri-Quarterly* devoted a special issue to Plath in 1966; and Robert Lowell contributed an overwrought foreword, which first appeared in the *New York Review of Books*, to the Harper & Row edition of *Ariel* in 1966.

Sylvia Plath's work had already begun to appear in a series of expensive collectors' editions. The market for rare books—more properly, books deliberately made scarce—is the vulgar backside of the 'official' face of literary culture. When Pound published *Hugh Selwyn Mauberley* in an edition of 200 copies in 1920 he did so with ample justification. He was a writer without a public, and therefore of no 'value' to English commercial publishers. But when there is immense interest in a writer, when there is a huge potential readership, the proliferation of collectors' editions begins to look like a bibliographic striptease of uncertain benefit to anyone other than the very wealthy.

The first of the collectors' editions, *Uncollected Poems*, appeared in 1965 from Bernard Stone's Turret Press. Containing 11 poems, it was an edition of 150 copies selling for £1.25. A copy went at Sothebys recently for £50. In 1968 Turret published *Three Women*, a 'poem for three voices', with an introduction by Douglas Cleverdon. There were 180 copies selling at £10.50. *Uncollected Poems* is reprinted entire in *Crossing the Water* and *Three Women* is included in *Winter Trees*. A third title was published by Martin Booth's Sceptre Press, *Wreath for a Bridal*. This poem was included in Plath's Cambridge manuscript, *Two Lovers and a Beachcomber*, and had been published in *Poetry* (January 1957). The Sceptre edition consisted of 100 numbered copies at £10 each, and five copies numbered in Roman numerals (bound in full morocco) at £18. A year later Sceptre published *Million Dollar Month*, a poem which Plath wrote when she was 18, in an edition of 150 copies at £36.10, with five bound in morocco at £18.

The fifth collectors' edition appeared in 1971 from Eric Cleave's Rougemont Press in Exeter. Cleave's first book was by Ted Hughes, who is a director of the press. *A Few Crows*, with illustrations by Reiner Burger, contained ten poems, only one of which was not included in the Faber *Crow* which appeared days after the Rougemont edition. The Plath title, *Fiesta Melons*, was published in 1971 and contained nine poems of which one was previously unpublished. It is profusely illustrated with Plath's Bill Maudlin-like drawings, and was published in an edition of 150 numbered copies, the first 75 signed, for no apparent reason, by Ted Hughes selling for £7. Later in 1971 Rougemont published a facsimile of the holograph manuscript of Sylvia Plath's *Child*, a slight poem which first appeared in the *New Statesman* in 1963, in an edition of 300 copies selling at 75p. *Child* was included in *Winter Trees*, and the holograph manuscript did double duty on the endpaper of *Lyonnesse*, a limited edition of Plath's poems published by the Rainbow Press in 1971.

There were two very welcome 'commercial' collections of Plath's verse in 1971. *Crossing the Water* and *Winter Trees* contain, between the two of them, 53 poems of which three were previously unpublished. While these two volumes were being reviewed, amidst some grumbling at the random and piecemeal way Plath was being published, two further limited editions appeared from the Rainbow Press, run by Ted Hughes's sister, Olwyn, who is also the literary agent for Plath's work. The first of these sumptuous volumes, *Crystal Gazer*, contained 23 uncollected poems. It is described in an advertising leaflet as

A limited edition of 400 numbered copies, in which the text has been hand-set in Centaur type and printed at Daedalus Press... on dampened paper made by J. Barcham Green.... The binding is by Zaehnsdorf Ltd, London. 22 carat gilt top and lettering. Nos 1–20 bound in full vellum in a

Kelmscott style binding in a Solander box £120. Nos 21–100 bound in full Cape goat leather in a slip £50. Nos 101–400 bound in quarter buckram with hand-made Japanese paper slides, in a slip case £21.

The second title, *Lyonnesse*, was published by the Rainbow Press in May 1971 and consists of

A limited edition of 400 copies set in Monotype Ehrhardt and printed by Will and Sebastian Carter at the Rampant Lions Press, Cambridge, on Hodgkinson hand-made paper. All books have 22 carat gold top and lettering on spine. Nos 1–10 bound by Zaehnsdorf... in full vellum sewn on cards in a Solander box. The endpapers bear reproductions of the author's handwritten drafts of the title poem and of the poem entitled *Child* £110. Nos 11–200 bound by Zaehnsdorf... in full calf in a slip case. The endpapers bear a reproduction of the author's handwritten draft of the title poem £40. Nos 101–400 bound by Davis and Hodges, London, in quarter leather with paper sides, in a slip case £12.60.

Future titles by the Rainbow Press include 'thirty of Sylvia Plath's unpublished early poems'.

Scrape together £69.97 and, if you're lucky, you can get the not-quite-complete published poems of Sylvia Plath. The real professionals will spring for the whole £289.27; the poems may not be much improved by the 'Kelmscott style binding' and the deckle on the fore-edge, but it does wonders for an investment.

63. Eileen M. Aird, ' "Poem for a Birthday" to *Three Women*: Development in the Poetry of Sylvia Plath,' *Critical Quarterly*

Winter 1979, 63–74

Critical discussion of Plath's poetry is understandably focussed on the magnificent late poems with occasional forays into the earlier exercises of *The Colossus*—and they were precisely exercises in style and image by a poet identifying her subjects. It therefore seems useful to pay some attention to the question of development, to the nature and timing of the transition from *The Colossus* to *Ariel* and to the poetic and biographical factors affecting this development.

'Poem for a Birthday' initiates the transitional period which ends with *Three Women*. It is significant that these are her two longest poems, 'Berck-Plage' being the only other one which begins to approach their expansiveness of structure and imagery. The theme of pregnancy and birth in *Three Women* is foreshadowed by the opening section of images of hibernation, storage and growth in 'Poem for a Birthday', and in both poems realistic presentation merges into a symbolic opposition between creativity and destructiveness. The individual experience of the woman who conceives, carries and gives birth to a child is emblematic of a world of natural growth and patterned progression in stark contrast to the technological destructiveness of the world of 'bulldozers, guillotines and white chambers of shrieks'.

Ted Hughes's famous account of the development of Sylvia Plath's poetry relates the two major accelerations of quality and command to the birth of her two children. This would date the transitional stage from mid-1960 to early 1962. The chronology of development revealed by the poems themselves does not entirely bear out his analysis. It indicates a longer period lasting from October, 1959 up to June, 1962, and in the work of a poet who developed at the speed of Sylvia Plath months are significant. If we are looking for biographical factors, and I introduce them only to counterbalance the widely held acceptance of Hughes's account, there is a much more precise correlation between the breakdown of their marriage and the writing of the great poems. In a letter to her mother written on 7 November 1962, immediately after moving into the London flat, she said: 'Living apart from Ted is wonderful—I am no longer in his shadow.'[1] The whole letter is over-elated and many of the subsequent heavily edited letters are much gloomier. Her own analysis, however, cannot be disregarded and it does go some way to suggest the much more complex relationship between circumstances and poetic processes that one would expect than the over-simplified and rather sentimental theory of childbirth as *the* stimulus.

'Poem for a Birthday' and *Three Women*, then, mark off a period of rapid change and development in Sylvia Plath's poetry, characterised not only by the movement from written exercises on the page, stylish, crystalline and static, to dramatic poems which need to be spoken aloud—a movement of which she was herself very conscious—but also by an increasing richness of imagery and a confident statement of subject.

The world of *The Colossus* is, for the most part, an external one of landscape and situation into which the personal is rarely allowed to erupt. The emphasis is too firmly on manipulation of both subject and form to make a contained statement; what we are given are neat, aesthetic glimpses of potentially dramatic situations. A case in point is a poem like 'Point Shirley', an elegy for the poet's dead grandmother heavily influenced by Robert Lowell's early style. So self-consciously clever is the language that real grief and loss is ironically excluded from the poem. The simple domestic image at the beginning of the second verse, 'She is dead/Whose laundry snapped and froze here', which does direct us very appropriately to an individual human reality, is immediately negated by the verbally vigorous but emotionless description of the sea. This is academic poetry of a high order, but the emphasis is on structure rather than statement. In the last nine months of her life, craftsmanship becomes the vehicle of expressiveness; there is a complete unity about the poems. Nevertheless there was still a feeling, even in the mature work, that some subjects were not suitable for poetry and this was one of the reasons she gave for turning to the novel: a form which she defined without apparent irony as appropriate for female concerns:

Poetry I feel is such a tyrannical discipline, you've got to go so far, so fast, in such a small space that you've just got to turn away all the peripherals. And I miss them! I'm a woman, I like my little Lares and Penates, and I like trivia, and I find that in a novel I can get more of life, perhaps not such an intense life, but certainly more of life...[2]

This is a revealing statement not just in terms of *The Bell Jar* but also of the late poetry which found a way of including those household details and using them as a stepping-off point for the wider concerns—'A Birthday Present' begins with a woman making pastry, 'Mary's Song' with a woman cooking the Sunday lamb, but in both poems the secure, protected world of kitchen and house very quickly gives way to an inner world of violent and tragic dimensions.

The poems of the last nine months of her life are marked by a complete unity of form and expressiveness and there are hints of this in a few exceptional poems in *The Colossus*, 'The Beekeeper's Daughter' in particular. Ted Hughes has commented very enigmatically on this poem as being 'one of a group of poems that she wrote at this time about her father.... This poem, one of her chilliest, recounts a key event in her Vita Nuova.' Whatever the reason, the poem has an urgent directness and sense of purpose which most of the early poems lack. It also has a very clear progression, a dominant feature of the later work which often rushes towards a conclusion which is also the climax of the poem. The complicated ambivalence of the relationship between father and daughter in the poem is established through the claustrophobic, wantonly erotic imagery of the opening verse:

> A garden of mouthings. Purple, scarlet-speckled, black
> The great corollas dilate, peeling back their silks

but what is initially the abject subjection of the daughter, 'My heart under your foot, sister to a stone' argues itself into an acceptance of that subjection, even a transformation of it into exultant destiny: 'The queen bee marries the winter of your year.' The poem oscillates between the opposed images of the stone and the queen bee, an opposition which Plath was to return to frequently. The stone always represents a reduction to a core, stripped of all pretence and association, the low point from which a gradual ascent is eventually possible; its first important use is in the last section of 'Poem for a Birthday', 'The Stones', where the experience of the suicidal coma is such a reduction to a core, an elemental surviving self:

> The mother of pestles diminished me.
> I became a still pebble.

There are also significant references for this image in *The Bell Jar*, first in the skiing episode where Esther breaks her leg in a wild flight down a slope too difficult for her, which she sees as an attempt to recapture the protective safety of the womb: 'the pebble at the bottom of the well, the white sweet baby cradled in its mother's belly', and secondly at the end of the second section of the novel where having taken a large number of barbiturates—too many in fact, they make her sick—she lies down behind a stack of firewood in the basement expecting to die: 'The silence drew off, baring the pebbles and shells and all the tatty wreckage of my life. Then, at the rim of vision, it gathered itself, and in one sweeping tide, rushed me to sleep'. In opposition to this static defence is the dynamic power of the queen bee. 'The Beekeeper's Daughter' needs to be read in conjunction with the late sequence of bee poems written in the autumn of 1962 where the queen bee is a symbol of female survival soaring triumphantly, if murderously, up:

> Now she is flying
> More terrible than she ever was, red
> Scar in the sky, red comet
> Over the engine that killed her—
> The mausoleum, the wax house.

This vision is in turn one of a series of female images of almost magical power and autonomy beginning with the circus performer of a very early poem 'Circus in Three Rings', written while she was still at Smith; and finding later expression in the avenging Clytemnestra of 'Purdah', 'the pure acetylene virgin' of 'Fever 103°', the vampire killer of 'Daddy', the ascendant phoenix of 'Lady Lazarus' and the majestic 'God's Lioness' of 'Ariel'. 'The Beekeeper's Daughter' is a very significant turning-point from the undirected extravagance of 'Circus in Three Rings' towards the powerful female images of *Ariel*. It finds some similarities in 'The Colossus' and 'Moonrise' and perhaps most importantly in an uncollected poem of the same time, 'Electra on Azalea Path', but like them is still held in the strait-jacket of formalities.

It is in 'Poem for a Birthday', heavily reliant on Roethke's structure and imagery though it is, that she first identifies both her subject and her voice. Roethke was such a fertile influence at this point in her development because she learnt from him that objective reality can serve as a medium to release the inner drama. 'Poem for a Birthday' acknowledges for the first time the supremacy of an inner world which earlier poems, 'Lorelei', 'Full Fathom Five', 'The Ghost's Leavetaking', 'Ouija', only hinted at. The poems which Roethke collected in *Praise to the End* are the most direct influence on Sylvia Plath's poem which has the same structure of short sections connected by theme and imagery. More importantly Plath's subjects—madness, loneliness, sexual identity, family relationships, growth and searching—are very close to

Roethke's in poems such as 'Dark House'. Sylvia Plath acknowledges Roethke as a major influence in a letter to her mother on
2 February 1961: 'Ted and I went to a little party the other night to
meet the American poet I admire next to Robert Lowell—Ted [for
Theodore Roethke]. I've always wanted to meet him as I find he is
my influence.'[3] Her debt to Lowell and Sexton is acknowledged
later in October 1962 and is a much more general recognition of an
exciting mode, a developing convention. For all its raw immediacy, its deliberate assault on the reader's sensibility, *Ariel* has a
dramatic focus and personae which are pared away by Lowell and
Sexton. This becomes very clear if we compare Lowell's own
comment on the intention of *Life Studies* with Sylvia Plath's note on
'Daddy'. Lowell told an interviewer: 'there was always that
standard of truth which you wouldn't ordinarily have in poetry—
the reader was to believe that he was getting the real Robert
Lowell!'[4] whereas Sylvia Plath wrote of 'Daddy': 'The poem is
spoken by a girl with an Electra complex. Her father died while she
thought he was God. Her case is complicated by the fact that her
father was also a Nazi and her mother very possibly part-Jewish. In
the daughter the two strains marry and paralyse each other—she
has to act out the awful little allegory before she is free of it.'[5]
Sylvia Plath's comment is not an evasion of the confessional aspect
of the poem, but an indication of the extent to which the personal is
subordinated to a much more inclusive dramatic structure. Unlike
Lowell, Sylvia Plath was not writing a poetic autobiography but
using personal experience as a way into the poem—this is further
reflected in the reading response to Sylvia Plath which frequently
begins at the level of autobiographical fact and then deepens into an
awareness of the intellectual and tonal complexities of the poem.
The real Sylvia Plath is far from present in the poetry, and there is
clear evidence of this in the comparison of the diary extract in
Johnny Panic and the Bible of Dreams in which she describes the
meeting of bee-hive owners, on which the poem 'The Bee
Meeting' is based, with the poem itself. Although the poem uses
exactly the observed details of the diary—and Ted Hughes has
explained that Sylvia Plath found it a useful discipline to describe
people and places minutely in her diary—the whole mood and
reference of the poem is transformed, the situation is changed from
the humorous precision of the diary to a metaphor of alienation.
Although her later work diverges from Roethkean structure and

imagery, he was seminal in showing her how to balance the personal and the general so that the poem is public rather than bafflingly private.

The purely literary influence of Roethke initiates the development towards poetic maturity, but the biographical factors are also important. The whole of Sylvia Plath's life up to 1959 was one of academic distinction and ambition—she won prizes, gained A grades, conquered one goal after another—but after the year's successful but demanding teaching at Smith, with two degrees behind her and thoughts of graduate work to the fore of her mind, she relinquished academic life in favour of full-time writing. The decision was obviously made under Ted Hughes's influence—he had given up the academic world much earlier—and it was an immensely courageous step for her to take, involving as it did the rejection of one of her most deepseated values. Any one reading her *Letters Home* of the mid-fifties cannot help but be impressed by her sheer tenacity and desire for success. Ted Hughes and Sylvia Plath had decided that they would settle permanently in Europe, so she was also turning her back on her family and cultural heritage as well as on the obvious career towards which all her efforts were previously directed. At this point in the autumn of 1959, she was pregnant for the first time and 'The Manor Garden', which like 'Poem for a Birthday' was written at Yaddo, indicates some of the ambivalence of fear and excitement which this generated in her; its final, very satisfying, image is a brilliant rendering of this ambivalence:

> The small birds converge, converge
> With their gifts to a difficult borning.

The period at Yaddo with its time for concentration and writing is a further factor: to be invited to Yaddo represented society's recognition of artistic merit and for Sylvia Plath such recognition always seems to have been more important than it is to Ted Hughes. Writing to her mother on 16 October 1962 she described her *Ariel* poems with tragic irony as: 'the best poems of my life: they will make my name'.[6] The notion of success was one which she could not relinquish easily, as a scholar, a mother, a wife or a poet.

'Poem for a Birthday' was completed during the time at Yaddo and the title is richly significant reminding us as it does of her own

October birthday, the coming birth of her child, and the metaphorical deaths and births which modulate into the final qualified recovery of 'The Stones'. For the first time in this poem she directly faced the task of relating individual to general experience. That individual experience is female, defined both biologically and experientially; the poem is a dialogue between the dislocated girl who is maenad and witch and 'the mother of otherness'. To be female in 'Poem for a Birthday' is to be protective and procreative: 'The month of flowering's finished. The fruit's in', 'Here's a cuddly mother' but it is also to be demanding and possessive: 'Mother of beetles only unclench your hand:/I'll fly through the candle's mouth like a singeless moth'. This counter-points the major theme of the poem which is the need to rationalise the disparity of childhood and adulthood. The tensions are resolved finally in a rebirth after suffering: 'We grow./It hurts at first. The red tongues will teach the truth.'

Sylvia Plath said of her artistic method: 'I think that personal experience shouldn't be a kind of shut-box and mirror-looking narcissistic experience. I believe it should be generally relevant to such things as Hiroshima and Dachau and so on.'[7] The relevance of this to the late poetry is abundantly clear, but the process begins with 'Poem for a Birthday' where private experience—breakdown and the reasons for it, clinical treatment, pregnancy—is extended through the images which accumulate layer upon layer until it becomes a metaphor for suffering throughout the natural and the human world. The attempt to communicate the 'real Robert Lowell' emerges in *Life Studies* as a painfully accurate analysis of one man's dilemmas which gains universal significance through the depth and detail of its treatment. Sylvia Plath's method is essentially different. Rather than delineating the individual in a recognisable cultural context, she uses the private to gain access to the universal by ruthlessly mythologising her own experience and, in doing this, moves a long way from autobiography—'Lady Lazarus' is not Sylvia Plath but a mythical character of suffering and rebirth, ultimately a type of the tragic poet of Yeats's 'Lapis Lazuli'.

If both the themes and the images of Sylvia Plath's poem are closely influenced by Roethke's, the ending is markedly different. Typically Roethke's poems end in a moment of revelation even if his mood quickly falls back into the old state of waiting: the end of the quest is an organic awareness of wholeness, of the full recovery of identity. Although the image of the vase reconstructed at the end of 'Poem for a Birthday' recalls Roethke, Plath's mood is far from elated or affirmative:

> Ten fingers shape a bowl for shadows.
> My mendings itch. There is nothing to do.
> I shall be as good as new.

To be 'as good as new' is to have lost the tragic intensity which characterised the earlier sections of the poem and is very close to the ending of Lowell's 'Home after Three Months Away': 'Cured, I am frizzled, stale and small'.[8]

The sense of reduction and nullity points forward to the fear of the static in *Ariel*, the constant search for the dynamic: 'What I love is / the piston in motion— / My soul dies before it.'

'Poem for a Birthday' explores the metaphoric complexities of a series of balanced opposites—fertility / sterility, child / adult, day / night, death / life, animal / human, illness / recovery—and the poems in *Crossing the Water* continue this exploration. Sylvia Plath's own analysis of some of the poems in this volume is penetrating: bewailing their lack of dynamic accuracy with the self-mocking irony she employs with such brilliance in *Ariel*, she indicates the gulf between poetry as craft, the period of *The Colossus*, and poetry as necessity, the period of *Ariel*. The poems, she says, are like those pickled foetuses of *The Bell Jar*, specimens for learning, not the real living being, and yet:

> It wasn't for any lack of mother-love
> O I cannot understand what happened to them!
> They are proper in shape and number and every part

But to be 'proper in shape and number and every part' is no longer the keynote of authenticity. The period of villanelles, of elaborate rhyme schemes and regular stanzas, is over but the absolute confidence and daring of *Ariel* has to be worked for, and many of the poems in *Crossing the Water* elaborate a world which is no more than gothic. The title-poem for instance is little more than a playing with images of darkness and silence relieved by characteristically lyrical moments: 'A little light is filtering from the water flowers', 'Stars open among the lilies'. To take her own criteria of judgement this poem is not relevant to Hiroshima or Dachau; it remains in a private fantasy world although it is visually and verbally attractive. A much more accomplished poem is 'Insomniac' but this still lacks the fusion of elements which distinguishes the great poetry; it is never more than descriptive of a hollow world, it fails to evoke it despite the deliberate metaphorical violence:

> Night long in the granite yard, invisible cats
> Have been howling like women, or damaged instruments.

What she did achieve for the first time in *Crossing the Water*, however, was the wry, mocking humour which in *Ariel* frequently allows her to maintain the balance between public and private by deflecting interest from 'the needle or the knife'.[9] 'In Plaster', which owes something to Sylvia Plath's observations of a fellow-patient when she was recovering from her appendectomy, is wry, brilliant, humorous in its portrait of the relationship between cast and patient. The persona of the poem is mocking but by the end of the poem we see that there is a complex balance between command and dependence in the relationship, and in the last verse that mockery merges into a defiance which is the flimsiest of disguises for the sense of helpless dependency which lies beneath it:

> She may be a saint, and I may be ugly and hairy,
> But she'll soon find out that doesn't matter a bit.
> I'm collecting my strength; one day I shall manage without her,
> And she'll perish with emptiness and begin to miss me.

In the end the mocker himself is mocked and his earlier contemptuously pragmatic acceptance of the cast gives way to an awareness of the superior consistency of his partner. The word-play in the last line indicates that an uneasier intellectual wit has replaced the confident laughter of the beginning—humour as a mode of experiencing has become wit as an attempt to control.

Many of the poems of *Crossing the Water* are precise forerunners in subject, tone and imagery of the achievements of *Ariel*; the obvious companion poem of 'In Plaster' is 'The Applicant'. Both are poems about marriage—'The Applicant' more obviously so than 'In Plaster' which suggests it only through the final identification of the patient as male and the cast as female; but the tone of 'The Applicant' has a ferocious humour which makes 'In Plaster' seem almost whimsical by contrast. It is clear that Sylvia Plath's description of 'Daddy' and 'Lady Lazarus' as 'light verse'[10] is descriptive of a mode which contrives a highly sophisticated blend of the ironic and the violent. The tentative beginnings of this mode are present as early as 'Poem for a Birthday' in the constant perception of self in animal or doll-like images. There is a deliberate pretence at belittling the enormity of experience which makes it more accessible. When the poetry fails, it is sometimes because the ironic perspective is missing. This is very rarely the case in *Ariel* or *Winter Trees* but it happens more frequently in *Crossing the Water*. In the poem 'A Life', for instance, there is too sharp a contrast between the amused affectionate description of an idealised, even deliberately sentimentalised, Victorian past and the rigours of the present:

> This family
> Of valentine-faces might please a collector:
> They ring true, like good china.
>
> Elsewhere the landscape is more frank.
> The light falls without let-up, blindingly.
>
> A woman is dragging her shadow in a circle
> About a bald hospital saucer.
> It resembles the moon, or a sheet of blank paper.
>
> And appears to have suffered a sort of private blitzkrieg.

Although the poetry of *Ariel* constantly presses forward into extremes, they are contrived, not confessional, extremes. The much discussed ending of 'Lady Lazarus' is perhaps the best illustration of this, with its images of transcending suffering both personally and aesthetically. Out of the ashes of the concentration camps and the emotional ruins of the suicidal patient rises the mythical phoenix affirming her identity as both female and poet. As in 'Fever 103°' the very experience of pain is the means by which the persona grows to a new power: the first statement of this is in 'Poem for a Birthday': 'We grow / It hurts at first. The red tongues will reach the truth.' The skill of 'Lady Lazarus' is exhibited by the tone of this ending which is ironic but without bitterness—we are out of the human world either of the voyeuristic onlooker or the concentration camp doctors and rising into the half-delirious visionary Paradise to which the 'pure acetylene virgin' of 'Fever 103°' aspires. It is a Paradise of autonomy and recognised identity, an image of completeness; and completeness is one of the central subjects of *Ariel*. *Crossing the Water* achieves the ironic perspective but it fails to organise the opposites of Plath's vision into the drive towards perfection of *Ariel*.

A final demonstration of the distinction between the assurance and imagistic richness of the late poetry and the valuable experiments of the transitional period lies in a comparison of 'Candles' with 'Nick and the Candlestick'. Both poems start from the imaginative associations of a mother nursing her child by candlelight, but whereas 'Candles' goes no further than a consideration of the passage of time which links the Edwardian grandparents with the new baby, 'Nick and the Candlestick' encompasses the painful world of the creative imagination and the potential dangers of the man-made world but is able to move beyond both in the affirmation of the mother's love for the child:

> You are the one
> Solid the spaces lean on envious.
> You are the baby in the barn.

The last verse is an elliptical comment on the poem's structure for the baby is realised with detail and humanity at the heart of a poem which deals in abstractions. 'Nick and the Candlestick' is a very densely structured poem where each image, almost each word of the first half, finds its echo in the second half and the joy of the ending does not evade the pain of the first half—baby and mother have not escaped from the subterranean cave, only hung it with soft roses; and the mercuric atoms still drip into the terrible well. The structure of 'Candles' in comparison is merely linear.

Sylvia Plath's greatness lies not in the extremity of her subjects, although it is this extremity which may initially draw the reader into the poem, but in her handling of richly allusive images. This is the point of 'Stillborn' which recognises that formal structure must give way to the organic unity of associative imagery. The more one reads the poetry, the less possible it is not to seek echoes in other poems. The poet who composed slowly and cerebrally with frequent recourse to the thesaurus and dictionary, and who delighted in the esoteric and archaic, was involved in the intellectual discipline of analogy and alternative which paved the way for the apparently effortless flow of association and image. 'Nick and the Candlestick' is an extraordinary, complex and intellectually difficult poem but that difficulty is not a high gloss imposed on the poem by a mind still confined by an academic tradition; it is the natural attribute of what Sylvia Plath called 'that unicorn thing—a real poem'.[11]

NOTES

1 *Letters Home by Sylvia Plath, Correspondence 1950–1963*, ed. Aurelia Schober Plath (London and New York, 1975), 477–9.
2 *The Poet Speaks*, ed. Peter Orr (London, 1966), 171.
3 *Letters Home*, 407–8.
4 'Interview with Robert Lowell', *Paris Review* (spring 1961), 70.
5 Quoted in a poetry broadsheet issued by the *Critical Quarterly* society in 1964.
6 *Letters Home*, 468–9.
7 *The Poet Speaks*, 169.
8 Robert Lowell, *Life Studies* (1960).
9 *The Poet Speaks*, 169.
10 A. Alvarez, 'Sylvia Plath', in *The Art of Sylvia Plath*, ed. Charles Newman (London, 1970), 60.
11 'Context', *Johnny Panic and the Bible of Dreams* (London, 1977), 98.

LETTERS HOME BY SYLVIA PLATH, CORRESPONDENCE 1950-1963

Edited with commentary by Aurelia Schober Plath

New York, 1975

---

64. Erica Jong, 'Letters Focus Exquisite Rage of Sylvia Plath,' *Los Angeles Times Book Review*

23 November 1975, 1, 10

Erica Jong (b. 1942), poet and novelist, is best known for her novels *Fear of Flying, Fanny*, and *How to Save Your Own Life*.

Sylvia Plath's poetry meant an enormous amount to a whole generation of readers and poets, not only because it was the first poetry by a woman to fully explore female rage—but because it did so with exquisite artistry. These were no feminist rantings by a newly-awakened member of a consciousness-raising group, now ready to throw off the shackles of woman's lot and writing poetry as 'therapy.' These were the deeply felt perceptions of a consummate artist who had made a journey into her own personal psychological hell and was bringing back the truths that only a voyager of genius into the nether regions of the communal unconscious can retrieve. But Plath's message was muddied by the feminist political currents of the time and also by the myth that sprang up out of her suicide. It was further muddied (and muddled) by the relatives of hers who remained on earth and were anxious (for their own reasons) to suppress the truth:

Her husband, Ted Hughes, from whom she was unamicably separated when she died; her two children—in whose name Hughes sought to suppress her work and the facts of her life and death; her mother, Aurelia Schober Plath, who must have felt the grief and frustration of a loving parent who cannot save her child from self-destruction; her sister-in-law, Olwyn Hughes, who became the agent for her literary estate; and all the friends, ex-friends and hangers-on with axes to grind and reputations to make who now saw a free ride into print on a dead woman's back.

Everyone wanted a piece of Sylvia. The feminist movement wanted a martyr. The suicide-theorists wanted someone to theorize about. The estranged husband (also a poet) wanted a relief from his guilt, a chance to raise two motherless children as well as he could, a chance to somehow continue his own creative work. The poet's mother also wanted self-justification, a respite from grief and the best possible future for her grandchildren. And all the literary jackals wanted something to write about, a subject, a cause, a potential best-seller.

What would Sylvia want? What does the work demand? The history of art and literature are strewn with examples of 'well-meaning' relatives and friends suppressing great works for their own seemingly altruistic motives.

Ruskin burned Turner's paintings of brothels because he did not believe a great painter like Turner should be associated with 'smut.' Boswell's Victorian grandchildren obliterated parts of his randy 18th-century diaries in the interests of Victorian morality. Times change, tastes change, and often relatives and friends are profoundly embarrassed by the presence of a genius in their family tree. Proud of the association, yes, but ashamed of the work— particularly when it is truth-telling in a not very flattering way.

Sylvia Plath's lifework fell prey to all these problems. In addition, it fell prey to the misunderstanding that exists in our culture concerning autobiographical art. We tend to confuse the artist who mythologizes his or her own life (among whom the major writers Colette, Proust, Henry Miller and Anne Sexton must be counted) with the exhibitionist who simply and inartistically spills his guts. We do not understand that even an artist who draws heavily on the material of his or her own life is not always telling the literal truth, that there are many versions of the same story and that a major artist will tell the story over and over in different ways throughout the course of his or her life.

Just as Fellini mythologizes his life one way in *8½*, another way in *Amarcord*, each time learning new things about himself and his craft, so Sylvia Plath, had she lived, would have presented many different versions of her own life in poems, novels, letters. Unfortunately she did not have that chance, and still more unfortunately, the work she did write has been left to be culled over by others—others with various psychological scores to settle.

Apparently one of the reasons Aurelia Schober Plath wanted to publish these *Letters Home* by Sylvia Plath was because the picture of the mother and the mother–daughter relationship in *The Bell Jar* was so grim, and these letters largely depict her own relationship with Sylvia as warm and loving (the letters are so cheery and upbeat, in fact, that one tends at times to wonder whether Sylvia's need to always show her mother how happy she was wasn't perhaps part of her problem). Of course one sympathizes with Aurelia Plath in human terms; it is never easy for a mother to see a hostile depiction of what she assumes to be herself in a novel that is read by millions of people. But, in literary terms, it is naive to worry about counteracting such an image, and here is where our misconceptions of the autobiographical artist are so important.

It is perfectly possible for a versatile and gifted writer to write about a hostile mother–daughter relationship in one early novel and yet love her own mother a great deal. Human relations are complex. We love and hate at the same time. Young writers often rebel against their families to establish their independence. Young poets often rage first, celebrate joy later. Anger is cleansing—but it is not all there is to know. Surely, had Sylvia Plath lived, she would have created many mothers and many daughters in many books. She would not be known only from the raging adolescent voice that comes through in *The Bell Jar* or from the intense and passionate despair that comes through in so many of the poems in *Ariel*, *Winter Trees* and *Crossing the Water*.

Letters Home is a fascinating and essential document for many reasons—but first because it adds another voice to the voices of Sylvia Plath we already know. Here is the rapturous high school girl ('Somehow I have to keep and hold the rapture of being 17 ... Now, now is the perfect time of my life ...'); the poetic college freshman ('Music drifted out from the houses; fog blurred the lights, and from the hill, it looked as if we could step over the edge into nothingness ...'); the triumphant college senior ('Handed in my thesis today! ... I was so excited that I cut classes to proofread it.'); the ambitious young poet ('Best of all was a eulogistic letter from John Ciardi, my favorite of the judges, who

called me 'a real discovery,' saying: "She's a poet…"'); the
passionate tourist ('We docked at Cherbourg and Carl and I went
ashore for the most enchanting afternoon of my life…'); the
woman who has just fallen madly in love with the man who is fated
to change her life ('I met the strongest man in the world… a
singer, story-teller, lion and world-wanderer… this man, this
poet, this Ted Hughes…'); the lover in love with life ('I have never
before had so much to give…'); the passionate poet ('… a woman
poet like the world will gape at…'); the man-loving feminist ('I
shall be one of the few women poets in the world who is fully a
rejoicing woman, not a bitter or frustrated or warped man-
imitator, which ruins most of them in the end. I am a woman and
glad of it, and my songs will be of fertility and of the earth…'); the
new bride ('… I was so happy with my dear, lovely Ted. Oh you
will love him, too…'); the delighted new mother ('Our life seems
to have broadened and deepened wonderfully with her…'); the
jealous wife ('I simply cannot go on living the degraded and
agonized life…').

But here the story oddly breaks off or is interrupted—and the
end of the life is pruned so severely that the reader is left with many
more suspicions than would be present if the book were forthright
and frank in its inclusions. There are too many ellipses in this
book—especially during the period of Plath's astonishing poetic
creativity, the last months of her life.

The secrecy is appalling, especially in the light of the myth of the
morbid suicidal poet that has grown up around Plath. These letters
show her to be prone to the wild swings of mood that characterize
the psychic lives of most artists. When she was happy, she was
manic, ebullient, madly in love with herself and the world, and
when she was miserable, she was utterly self-deprecating, self-
despising, misanthropic, suicidal. In the face of 50 major triumphs
a minor rejection could plunge her into utter gloom. She had that
curious sensitivity which, in addition to great talent, is one of the
tools of the poet's trade. She had the capacity to be a lighting rod
for the world around her. This made for explosiveness and
intensity in her art, but it also made for great vulnerability in her
life.

At the end of her life, this volatile, talented, incredibly
hard-working and hard-living writer was subjected to stresses that
even the strongest person would flinch at. She was living alone in a

foreign country with two small children, practically no money, no central heating, no mother's helper. She was going through the ignominous hassles of a divorce, trips to lawyers, pleas for support, the sudden astonished discovery that the law was not on her side at all.

Her husband was off with another woman—and all their friends saw her as having been ditched. She was jealous, embattled, torn, weary, tied down. Her new poems (which she knew were breakthrough works that would make her name immortal) had been rejected by the prissy literary quarterlies in prissy literary England. (These were the poems which later became famous in *Ariel*.) Her novel, *The Bell Jar*, had just been published under a pseudonym, true; but nevertheless to the sort of reviews that American writers and particularly American women writers are so familiar with in misogynistic, anti-American England.

She was ill, lonely, and determined not to show her desperate need of help to her family and friends for fear of seeming weak. If, under these circumstances, a person with no history of suicide attempts broke down and made a suicide gesture, we would not say about him the things we have said about Sylvia Plath. We would not say things about his dark longing for death, his suicide compulsion, and thereby implicitly deny his great courage in the face of repeated rejections. Surely Sylvia Plath was the author of her own despair in that she was constantly drawn toward impossible challenges, but she was also immensely brave.

She was rising at dawn to write before the children woke. She was consumed with writing astonishingly brilliant poems which very few people (until after she was safely dead) would appreciate. It is in the nature of female psychology (inculcated and reinforced by our culture) that men turn their rage against women while women turn their rage against themselves, and it is a supreme irony that, having died under these circumstances, Plath's work should now be edited and pruned by the very man who pruned her life.

Nevertheless, *Letters Home* is an immensely valuable work and I am grateful that Mrs. Plath and Ted Hughes let it be published. It adds so much that is invaluable to our understanding of Plath. One wishes it were even fuller. One wishes it were not as interesting for what it excludes as for what it includes. By all means, read it. You will understand Sylvia Plath better and her work better. You will have read the best biography of her available to date—written by herself, with annotations by a mother who is both loving and probing (if at times a bit aggrieved and self-justifying).

But if you read between the lines, between the ellipses, you will see another story. The story of what it means to be a woman of genius in a world in which most of the nurturing is reserved for men of genius. Admittedly, Sylvia Plath must have been difficult, explosive, suicidal as well as passionately loving, manically happy—but then so are most poets. So probably is the husband she left behind, who, remarried and still writing book after book, now edits her oeuvre as he sees fit. The saddest thing of all is that Sylvia Plath should now be known as the antithesis of what she wished for herself and for a new generation of women poets. She adored being pregnant, having babies, adored her husband and saw no conflict at all between robust womanhood and strong poetry. In 1956 she wrote to her mother:

... I need no sorrow to write; I have had, and, no doubt, will have enough. My poems and stories I want to be the strongest female paean yet for the creative forces of nature, the joy of being a loved and loving woman; that is my song. I believe it is destructive to try to be an abstractionist man-imitator, or a bitter, sarcastic Dorothy Parker or Teasdale ...

What happened? Is the myth of the bitter man-hating woman poet so strong that it has overshadowed the reality of Plath's work? Or is she known only for poems and fiction written during the blackest period of her life, a period when she was feeling utterly rejected and desperate? Or has her work been deliberately presented to the public in a way that accords with popular myths of what a woman poet is?

The best thing about *Letters Home* is that it raises all these questions.

65. Anne Tyler, '"The Voice Hangs On, Gay, Tremulous,"' *National Observer*

10 January 1976, 19

Anne Tyler (b. 1941) is an important American novelist and short fiction writer. Her most recent novels include *Dinner at the Homesick Restaurant* and *The Accidental Tourist*.

In 1970, shortly before *The Bell Jar* appeared in America, Sylvia Plath's mother wrote Harper and Row to register her protest against its posthumous publication. According to her, *The Bell Jar* was merely a pot-boiler—something her daughter would never have wanted published under her own name. Its purpose, said Mrs. Plath, was to show how the world looks 'as seen through the distorting lens of a bell jar.' A sequel was supposed to depict 'the same world as seen through the eyes of health.'

'Practically every character in *The Bell Jar* represents someone— often in caricature—whom Sylvia loved,' wrote Mrs. Plath. 'As the book stands by itself, it represents the basest ingratitude. That was not the basis of Sylvia's personality.'

Apparently her words had no effect on Harper and Row; *The Bell Jar* did come out on schedule. But what has always struck me about Mrs. Plath's letter (which is quoted in the biographical note at the end of the novel) is that it seems unnecessary. Almost as unnecessary as 'Victoria Lucas,' the pseudonym under which Sylvia Plath first published the book in England.

The Bell Jar is not of typical pot-boiler quality, after all; nor is it venomous, and none of its recognizable characters are given more than a gentle poke. It is plain, from beginning to end, that we are merely looking at people through the eyes of utter, numb misery. 'To the person in the bell jar, black and stopped as a dead baby,' says Sylvia Plath, 'the world itself is the bad dream.' Why should she want such a book suppressed, or concealed behind a pseudonym?

Well, I think we may have the answer now. For Mrs. Plath has assembled *Letters Home*—Sylvia Plath's correspondence, mostly with her mother, for the years from 1950 until her death. The book was intended, I believe, as an antidote to *The Bell Jar:* a view of Sylvia Plath's brighter side. But what it gives us far more clearly is a view of a system of values in which happiness is a virtue, success is the only outcome possible, and perfection is the very least one can expect of oneself or anyone else.

The person who emerges from *Letters Home* is so elated and so feverishly gay that it makes the reader anxious for her. To Sylvia Plath, apparently, an admission of sorrow was an admission of defeat. No wonder *The Bell Jar* was written by Victoria Lucas.

'I love everybody ... I'm *so* happy ... you are the most wonderful mummy that a girl ever had ...' is interspersed with endless lists of prizes won, compliments gathered, young men captivated. Not much different from the average college-girl letters, I suppose, except that these don't change as she grows older.

Through the years, her few lapses into despair are retracted, apologized for, brushed over almost in the next mail. When she marries, her husband is 'the handsomest, most brilliant, creative, dear man in the world,' and 'wherever Ted and I go people seem to love us.' At the time when the marriage was encountering its first serious difficulties, she writes, 'I don't know when I've been so happy or so well.' And finally—separated from her husband, ill and exhausted, coping with two babies through a London winter: 'I have never been so happy in my life.'

In moderation, I suppose, this quality is called 'courage in adversity,' and I do believe she had a great deal of courage. But too much of this sort of courage can do you in. Over and over again, throughout her poetry, Sylvia Plath gives almost passionate attention to the discrepancy between the white, clean outer self and the dark inner self—'the old yellow one,' and 'this dark thing that sleeps in me.'

> ... I inhabit
> The wax image of myself, a doll body.
> Sickness begins here.

Letters Home is a picture of Sylvia Plath's wax image, her outer self. It is chatty, affectionate, filled with photographs like 'Sylvia

Going Off to Smith' and 'Sylvia's Graduation Photo'—a typical family scrapbook, in other words.

But do we need a family scrapbook for Sylvia Plath?

It is ironic that, like Diane Arbus, Anne Sexton, and a good many others, Sylvia Plath has come to the public attention less for her art than for her manner of dying: I don't know, and I don't think I *want* to know, why this is the way things work nowadays, but the fact is that Sylvia Plath the poet is overshadowed by Sylvia Plath the suicide. It was no doubt partly as a defense against this situation that Mrs. Plath published her letters. But a picture of Sylvia Plath the daughter is even less relevant than one of Sylvia Plath the suicide. What matters is her work.

In none of the letters does Sylvia discuss her work in any real depth. At most, she will announce the completion of a poem, or its acceptance or rejection by a magazine. Occasionally she will include the poem itself. She does not go into the whys and hows of writing it. In fact, what little information we do glean comes less from the letters than from Mrs. Plath's comments. (Her description of her husband's death, for instance—the result of his steady refusal to consult a doctor—casts some light on Sylvia Plath's insistence, in her poems, that her father was a suicide.)

I would especially like to know how it came about that Sylvia Plath finally 'found her voice'—emerging from her early stiffness to the pure and unforced style of her later prose. Or how she viewed the fact that these poems seemed to come from her darkest self, as if it were gradually taking over. But the letters from this period are concerned with the very real problems of finances, illness, house-hunting, and baby sitters. I don't suppose my questions will ever be answered.

What we have, in the end, is the selected correspondence of a college and postcollege girl of the '50s—some 700 letters assembled by a mother who obviously loved her daughter very much and was proud of her achievements. The letters are not going to be much help to scholars, and in content they are not very unusual. But they do convey a certain spirit that is surprisingly hard to forget. Long after you close this book, Sylvia Plath's voice hangs on in your mind: gay, tremulous, and fragile, forever balancing on a fine, thin, delicate edge.

212

66. Jo Brans, 'The Girl Who Wanted to be God,' *Southwest Review*

Summer 1976, 325–8, 330

Jo Brans, formerly at Southern Methodist University, now lives in New York. Her book, *Mother, I Have Something to Tell You*, appeared in 1987.

'The girl who wanted to be God,' Sylvia Plath called herself in her diary at seventeen, and somehow the poignant past tense of the phrase lays the burden of her death at thirty on us once again. Of all our American literary suicides, hers is the heaviest to bear. Young, smart, pretty, talented, enterprising, and disciplined, the best product of America, she had, as we say, everything going for her. Our Puritan roots tingle indignantly at the waste of it all. What went wrong? we ask, and, It had better be good, we mutter angrily. Here are two books which seek to answer that question, but which probably only add to the confusion.

Letters Home consists of a portion of the 696 letters Sylvia Plath wrote to her family, especially to her mother, from the fall of 1950 when she began her freshman year at Smith to the week of her death in February 1963. Selected and edited with commentary by her mother, the letters included might mostly have been composed by Dame Kindness, who is the object of her ironic observer's bitter scorn in a poem written just before Plath died: 'Sugar can cure everything, so Kindness says.' From the schoolgirl beginnings, the most consistent tone of the letters is bright insincerity, indicated by all kinds of giveaways to anyone conscious of style, especially of the clarity and certainty of Sylvia Plath's style in poetry. Here they flock in numbers, those triple exclamation marks, those parenthetical asides ('What a life!'), those bromides ('Dearest-Mother-whom-I-love-better-than-anybody'), those cute closings ('xxx Sivvy'), all the devices mercilessly banished from the poetry, if indeed they ever had the temerity to venture into that stark territory.

One has no wish to hurt Mrs. Plath, who has suffered enough, and who doubtless believed these letters, as mothers will. My point is simply that we can learn very little of the Sylvia of the poetry, the only Sylvia in whom we can take a legitimate interest, from these letters. The attitudes taken by the poetry and by the letters toward any specific incident of Plath's life are so disparate as to lend complete credibility to the theory of the divided self of the artist. For example, the letters in March, 1961, describing an emergency appendectomy focus on the usual aspects of a hospital stay, the food, the other patients, the good-natured nurses. Yet 'Tulips,' the poem which came from the same experience, shows a patient 'learning peacefulness,' falling in easily with nothingness and death:

> I didn't want flowers, I only wanted
> To lie with my hands turned up and be utterly empty.
> How free it is, you have no idea how free—
> The peacefulness is so big it dazes you,
> And it asks nothing, a name tag, a few trinkets.
> It is what the dead close on, finally; I imagine them
> Shutting their mouths on it, like a Communion tablet.

The tulips of the title are a strident burst of pure color, of involuntary life, 'like dangerous animals' driving the persona away from the 'white,' 'quiet,' 'snowed-in' world she craves.

One other instance. In 1956 Sylvia Plath married the British poet Ted Hughes. In the late summer of 1962, in the last year of her life, she broke with him, ending what she had insisted throughout the letters to be an idyll of poetic and personal fulfilment for them both. In June of that same summer, just before the fatal break, Mrs. Plath visited the young couple in their home in Devon. Of that visit she writes:

The welcome I received when I arrived ... was heartwarming. The threshold to the guest room ... had an enameled pink heart and a garland of flowers painted on it ... Sylvia said proudly, 'I have everything in life I've ever wanted: a wonderful husband, two adorable children, a lovely home, and my writing.' Yet the marriage was seriously troubled, and there was a great deal of anxiety in the air.... When I left on August 4 ... it was the last time I saw Sylvia.

The daughter's efforts at saving face evidently failed, and from that time forth she resisted all her mother's attempts to get her and the children to come to America, or Mrs. Plath's offers to return to her. To her brother Warren Sylvia writes: 'I hope you can tactfully convey to mother...that we should not meet for at least a year.... After this summer, I just could not bear to see her; it would be too painful and recall too much.' She obviously regretted the break in composure, the genuine exposure of feeling, to her mother. Though the weekly letters and the forms of feeling persist ('I was so glad to have your letter saying you got *my* letter'), the poems tell a different tale, even find the mother responsible for the end of the marriage, as in 'Medusa':

> I didn't call you.
> I didn't call you at all.
> Nevertheless, nevertheless
> You steamed to me over the sea,
> Fat and red, a placenta
> Paralyzing the kicking lovers...
>
> Who do you think you are?...
>
> Off, off, eely tentacle!
>
> There is nothing between us.

In addition to questions raised by this discrepancy between poetry and letters, we rightfully question the reliability of the letters because of their editing. Hardly a letter of those already 'selected' is without its ellipsis, and most letters have many. The answer to our original query, What went wrong?, gradually falls in these cautiously written, selected, and edited letters into the following pattern: Sylvia Plath was martyred, ironically enough, by the American success saga that she lived, from all-A student to Fulbright fellow to financially independent poet at twenty-five or so. Such success is created by and carries with it a continuing and obsessive drive for perfection. Any failure, however small, can lead to a response 'magnifying a situation all out of proportion,' as Mrs. Plath says. Thus Plath's first suicide attempt in 1953 between her junior and senior years at Smith was in her mother's mind clearly triggered by a series of 'failures'—to get into Frank O'Connor's writing class, to make progress on her honors thesis, even, absurdly, to learn shorthand. Her second, successful attempt Mrs. Plath also explains rationally and reductively: 'Her physical energies had been depleted by illness, anxiety and overwork, and although she had for so long managed to be gallant and equal to the life-experience, some darker day than usual made it seem impossible to pursue.' A mere indisposition, a mother's perfect rationale. The beauty of it is, it blames no one, not even Plath herself....

To 'know' Sylvia Plath, finally, we must return to the poems, where she created her most singular self. To comprehend her art we must submit to her myth, a myth of a life governed by 'fixed stars,' but of a genius often triumphant. She called the bitterest of her poems 'comic,' and they are, blackly so, in the frequency and energy with which the persona escapes her sex and kills off her own destroyers. The poems in *Ariel*, written at the height of her poetic powers, show the creator while working to be androgynous. In 'Ariel,' the persona is metaphorically somehow both sperm and womb, the creation autogenetic. In 'Stings,' the persona definitively separates herself from 'unmiraculous women, / Honey-drudgers. / I am no drudge / Though for years I have eaten dust / And dried plates with my dense hair' and reveals herself to be the most creative member of the hive, the queen bee emergent:

> They thought death was worth it, but I
> Have a self to recover, a queen,
> Is she dead, is she sleeping?
> Where has she been,
> With her lion-red body, her wings of glass?
>
> Now she is flying
> More terrible than she ever was, red
> Scar in the sky, red comet
> Over the engine that killed her—
> The mausoleum, the wax house.

67. Martha Duffy, 'Two Lives,' *Time*

24 November 1975, 101–2

When Aurelia Plath told her eight-year-old daughter Sylvia that her father was dead, the child said, 'I am never going to speak to God again.' When she came home from school that day she presented her mother with an oath to be signed: 'I promise never to marry again.'

Sylvia took all of life with terrifying seriousness; the words 'never again' came only too quickly to her. She was capable of emotional fixity that makes the poems written just before her suicide in 1963 nearly unbearable: pictures of rage and despair drawn virtually in words of one syllable. Her novel *The Bell Jar*, while written in quasi-Salinger style, is a remorseless account of adolescent breakdown.

Little Bayonets. The book was also a painful blow to Aurelia Plath. Like all the other characters in *The Bell Jar*, the narrow-minded, hard-working mother is ferociously cartooned. Shortly before trying to kill herself, the heroine watches her sleeping, 'the pin curls on her head glittering like a row of little bayonets.'

Partly to adjust the image that the novel created of both mother and daughter, Mrs. Plath is publishing an edited edition of Sylvia's copious letters home, from the time she entered Smith College in 1950 until her death. The correspondence will not erase *The Bell Jar*—those caricatures are indelible. But they do give a different, lively, poignant picture of Sylvia.

The Smith letters are the frankest. Sylvia arrived trailing three scholarships and several writing prizes. The Plaths had no money, and she worried continually about it. She owed her 'charmed Plathian existence' to her schoolteacher mother's efforts, and she was driven by gratitude. 'You are the most wonderful mummy that a girl ever had,' she wrote, 'and I only hope I can continue to lay more laurels at your feet.'

It also appears that Sylvia took to heart every bit of propaganda ever put out by the Protestant ethic, college deans of admission and the slick fashion magazines of the '50s. In addition to grinding out straight A's and submitting potboilers to *True*, 'to keep our pot of caviar boiling,' she wanted desperately to be 'well-rounded.' Thus during weekends at Yale or Princeton Sylvia undertook her blind-date excursions cheerfully, and tried to include them in her mother's vicarious life. 'Picture me then,' she gloats, 'in my navy-blue bolero suit and versatile brown coat, snuggled in the back seat of an open car.'

With her blonde good looks and long legs (which she considered her best feature) Sylvia was popular, but none of the dates measured up. She wanted a 'colossus.' She thought such a man might be found in England and applied for a Fulbright grant ('If only I get accepted at Cambridge! My whole life would explode in a rainbow!').

Mental Agony. Sylvia was accepted, and in 1956 found her colossus in the young British poet Ted Hughes. Even in her first ecstasies, there are forecasts of trouble: 'I have fallen terribly in love, which can only lead to great hurt. I met the strongest man in the world, a large, hulking, healthy Adam with a voice like the thunder of God.'

The next two years were probably her happiest. She sent bulletins of social success ('Your daughter shook hands with Bulganin'; 'We rode up in the elevator with Lionel and Diana Trilling'), and accounts of travel in France and Spain, which show a capacity for wonder and joy unreflected in her work. After marrying, she and Hughes came back to the U.S. to teach. Life was never easy. They lived in tiny apartments and worked ceaselessly to clear a little time to write.

Restless, they moved back to England where two children, Frieda and Nicholas, were born. Shortly afterward the marriage collapsed. Hughes' formidable powers to charm were turned on other women and Sylvia was consumed by jealousy. Sensing a return of the earlier breakdown, Aurelia begged her daughter to come home. Though sick, broke, alone and in mental agony, she refused. 'If I start running now,' she predicted, 'I will never stop, I shall hear of Ted all my life, his success, his genius,' At times in the last months of her life she dreamed of 'a salon in London. I am a famous poetess here.' But there was another reason for not seeking shelter. 'I haven't the strength to see you for some time,' she informed her mother. 'I cannot face you again until I have a new life.'

Household Despot. Sylvia never did face Aurelia. It was one more blow to someone who had never had much of a life. Aurelia's husband, a Boston University entomologist, was a household despot who died from complications of diabetes because he refused for years to consult a doctor (he considered his own diagnosis of lung cancer sufficient). At 34, Aurelia was a widow with two small children and a chronic ulcer. Years later she was driven to the Smith commencement—where her daughter graduated summa cum laude—lying on a mattress in a friend's station wagon. The time of Sylvia's death must have been hell. The posthumous publication of *The Bell Jar* can only have added to the pain.

Now 68, Mrs. Plath has retired and spent the past two years working on this essential volume. Her preface and connecting notes—plainspoken, styleless and intelligent—give the outlines of the bleaker, less event-ridden life that Sylvia's letters tried to fill. Though different in temperament, mother and child recognized that they were very close. Before her first suicide attempt when she was 20 Sylvia had grasped Aurelia's hand and cried, 'Oh Mother, the world is so rotten! I want to die! Let's die together!' It is now clear that the end came for Sylvia not only because she lost Hughes but because she could no longer grasp that hand.

68. Carol Bere, '*Letters Home*: *Correspondence 1950–1963*,' *Ariel*

October 1977, 99–103

Since her premature death in 1963, the Sylvia Plath cult has proliferated, and she seems to have become the martyred high priestess of contemporary poetry. To a great extent the myth has been fed by feminist fuel and reams have been written about Plath, the super-achiever who fell victim to both the repressions of the woman's role and society's willingness to constrain female artists. Her brief career has generated a surge of psychological studies that explore the relationship of female creativity to madness and suicide. Over-analyzed poems such as 'Daddy,' 'Lady Lazarus,' and 'Lesbos,' have been cited as testimony while the very real development of Sylvia Plath, the poet, has been largely ignored.

Letters Home, the recently published letters of Plath to her mother, while compulsively interesting reading, will do little to dispel the myth. True, the collection does reveal Plath's indefatigable discipline and ambition, yet the portrait that emerges is finally unreal. Plath strove relentlessly to create a singular image; ironically, the Plath who emerges in this collection seems to be a persona fused by relatives and editors.

Over 600 letters were written during the period of 1950–1963, yet less than 400 have been included in this volume. The majority of these letters appear to have been selected to stress 'Sivvy's' love of life', 'gay philosophy,' and continued resourcefulness. Rarely does she rail at circumstances, and the stilted, romanticized superlatives that proclaim her ability to cope are often embarrassing. The letters of the crucial last six months of Plath's life are marred by obvious gaps in information and disconcerting ellipses. Separated from her husband, alone with two infants, ill, yet at the height of poetic creativity—the period of *Ariel* and *Winter Trees*—Plath is finally permitted (or permits herself) to drop the stoic mask: 'I just need someone to cheer me up by saying I've done all right so far.'

Perhaps the person who emerges with most clarity in *Letters Home* is Mrs. Plath herself. Largely in an effort to correct the damaging portrait of the mother in the autobiographical novel, *The Bell Jar*, Mrs. Plath has attempted to show how Sylvia 'manipulated experience' and 'fused parts of my life with hers.' Yet from beneath the outlines of Mrs. Plath's personal history, which is narrated with aggravating restraint, a life of self-sacrifice—and one lived mostly vicariously—surfaces.

Unfortunately, Mrs. Plath has exposed a minefield for psychological exegetes as she relates a story of childhood loneliness, denied academic opportunities and resentment of her husband. Otto Plath, the poet's father and a noted biologist and professor at Boston University, was a demanding, authoritarian figure. In order to circumvent potential marital problems, Mrs. Plath, in her words, became more 'submissive,' gave up a teaching position that she enjoyed and devoted herself entirely to her family. Her irritation is barely veiled as she recounts a life revolving around her husband's work, THE BOOK and of evenings spent editing and typing THE CHAPTER. The resentment was compounded when Otto Plath, who would not listen to the advice of physicians, died leaving Mrs. Plath a young widow, with two children and no life-insurance policies.

Thereafter, Mrs. Plath moved to Wellesley, Massachusetts, with her parents, worked tirelessly teaching medical-secretarial techniques at Boston University and gave herself totally to her children. The pressures that Sylvia Plath must have felt to excel, to both repay and justify her mother's efforts, must have been excessive. In a letter written to her mother while she was on scholarship at Smith College, Plath conveys a permeating theme of the collection, that of filial gratitude: 'You are the most wonderful mummy that a girl ever had, and I only hope that I can continue to lay more laurels at your feet. Warren and I both love and admire you more than anybody in the world for all you have done for us all our lives. For it is you who has given us the heredity and the incentive to be mentally ambitious.'

Curiously, Plath seems to have felt a recurrent need to explain herself to her mother, which she does in inordinately formal syntax: 'My main concern in the next year or two is to grow as much as possible, to find out, essentially, what my real capabilities are, especially in writing and studying, and then to plan my future life in consistency with my abilities and capabilities.' Or, more tellingly, there is the letter in which she recapitulates the year's haul of prizes and awards. Finally, with the collapse of her marriage to the British poet Ted Hughes, and with what must have been a tragic sense of having failed her mother, Plath writes:' ... as you can see, I haven't the strength to see you for some time. The horror of what you saw and what I saw you see last summer is between us and I cannot face you again until I have a new life: it would be too great a strain.'

Outwardly, the Smith College letters replay the typical studies–dates–clothes syndrome of many college campuses of the 1950's and the jargon frequently is a distillation of English novels and ladies' magazines. But there are disturbing elements in the correspondence. Underlying the buoyant, artificial accounts of weekends at Yale or studies with renowned authors is a compulsive determination to perfect the self—to avoid mediocrity, to build a 'strong inner life,' to prepare oneself for the 'big moments.' To compromise at less than the full life—the honors, the publications, the great love, the family—is to fail. Thus, the letters convey a sense of deferred expectations and a romanticized craving for experience.

Later, at Cambridge, she writes of her love for Ted Hughes: 'I feel that all my life, all my pain and work has been for this one thing. All the blood spilt, the words written, the people loved, have been a work to fit me for loving ... I see the power and voice in him that will shake the world alive. Even as he sees into my poems and will work with me to make me a woman poet like the world will gape at; even as he sees into my character and will tolerate no fallings away from my best right self.' The psychological weight of this commitment to the marriage must have been enormous.

The importance of *Letters Home* as a key to understanding Plath, the poet, must ultimately be confronted. On a surface level, the collection will be an invaluable source for many of the early poems. The influence of Emily Dickinson, Theodore Roethke and the primitive painters can be tagged easily from comments and inserted poems. The admitted influence of the powerful Hughes, both on the subject matter and technique of *The Colossus,* is evident, yet Plath did retain her individuality. Hughes attacks all of creation in words that appear to erupt spontaneously from some natural, untapped source. Plath, conversely, is a more willed poet who explores her themes in direct, economical language. But her early poems, as Plath herself acknowledged, were 'exercises,' and it is on the late poems of *Ariel* and *Winter Trees* that she will be judged.

To resolve the obvious discrepancies between the Sivvy of the letters 'singing' her 'native joy of life' and the violent, destructive poet of *Ariel*, some critics have asserted that Plath suffered from a divided self. This assessment is too facile. Many of Plath's letters to her mother, while undeniably egocentric, were still assurances that she was succeeding at what must have been a mutually accepted blueprint for her 'life experience.' It would be unlikely that she would deliver less to a woman who asserts that '... my motherhood was the most important thing in my life. It was what my whole life went to.'

It was in the last period, however, when the poetic sensibility and the life merged incontrovertibly that Plath assumed her own voice. Although she realized that 'I am writing the best poems of my life: they will make my name,' little is advanced about the incredible depth and marked technical assurance of these poems. Sadly, we are left with Mrs. Plath's words which can only perpetuate what is already an overworked Plath literary machine: 'She began at 4 a.m. each morning to pour forth magnificently structured poems renouncing the subservient female role, yet holding to the triumphant note of maternal creativity in her scorn of "barrenness".' Surely, Plath's poetry deserves more.

69. Rose Kamel, '"Reach Hag Hands and Haul Me In": Matrophobia in the Letters of Sylvia Plath,' Northwest Review

1981, 198–208

Between 1950 when she entered Smith College and 1963, the year she committed suicide, Sylvia Plath wrote her mother nearly a thousand letters many of which Aurelia Plath published in *Letters Home*. Ostensibly meant for her mother's ears alone, Plath's letters throb with an almost daily account of her growth and development as a writer. Their cumulative effect is that of an autobiography with a beginning, a middle, and an implied end. It can be read as an attempt, at times desperate, to delimit where Aurelia ends and Sylvia begins.

We have little evidence of how Aurelia Plath responded to the letters. A self-supporting widow, she consistently supported her daughter's ambitions to write, teach, marry, bear children— ambitions reflecting not only the compartmentalization of women's lives in the 1950's, but the way Aurelia had structured her own life. Furthermore, Plath's letters project little of the hate she vented against her father and Ted Hughes in her brilliant final poems. Her statement that the root of her childhood trauma lay in her father's death invites a Freudian interpretation of her writing that is distortive because it minimizes Aurelia's role in their relationship:

And this is how it stiffens, my vision of that seaside childhood. My father died, we moved inland. Whereon those nine first years of my life sealed themselves off like a ship in a bottle—beautiful, inaccessible, obsolete, a fine white flying myth.[1]

Understandably, critics are reluctant to delve more deeply into Plath's relationship with her mother, who in the aftermath of her daughter's suicide has certainly suffered enough. We cannot, however, overlook Plath's perception of her mother as an anti-self she feared, yet deeply loved and identified with.[2] An anxious tone permeates the exuberance of most of the letters signed 'Sivvy,' and

223

their careful reading suggests that Plath perceived her mother as a Doppelgänger, a double, undermining her sense of herself as a separate being. It is this perception that charges the epistolary I–You dialectic with ontological tension rooted in matrophobia, defined by Adrienne Rich in another context as:

the fear not of one's mother or of motherhood but of *becoming one's mother*. ... Matrophobia can be seen as a womanly splitting of the self, in the desire to become purged once and for all of our mother's bondage, become individuated and free. The mother stands for the victim in ourselves, the unfree woman, the martyr. Our personalities seem dangerously to blur and overlap with our mothers'. ...[3]

Although Plath needed to believe herself an 'inaccessible' ... 'white flying myth,' the narrative progression of her letters indicates that she internalized her mother's experiences, made of them analogues for a mythic dramatization of herself as Horatio Alger's virtuous novice starting humbly and obscurely, moving steadily upward to achieve fortune and fame. Plath's mythologizing of her childhood experiences have their counterparts in her mother's reminiscences of her own early life.

Aurelia recalls that growing up near the sea in a household where her parents spoke German, she often felt isolated from her playmates. A highly intelligent child, she was doubly promoted in school and moved from the first to the third grade, 'a great boon for me, for I left behind those who had made such sport of my early mispronunciations.' Nonetheless, she was again ostracized during World War One when, because of her German-Austrian back-round, the other children called her 'spy-face'.[4] Aurelia turned to books. She became an avid reader and her fare included 'every one of Horatio Alger's stories.' She read as if in a dream world. 'Fortunately, my mother was most sympathetic and when I was in college read my literature books too, saying cheerily, "More than one person can get a college education on one tuition." (I remembered that vividly when my daughter went to Smith and I, through her, broadened my horizons further in modern literature and art)' (*LH*, p. 5).

In high school an 'inspirational English teacher' improved her taste and probably fostered her hopes of some day teaching in a liberal arts college. Her father, however, insisted that she go to business school and her first job was relentlessly dull—'a grim experience I vowed no child of mine would ever have to endure.' She managed to persuade him to let her study two additional years at the Boston University College of Practical Arts and Letters so that she could teach English and German at the high school level. Then a secretarial job with an M.I.T. professor, 'a true genius in both the arts and the sciences', motivated her to prepare lists of reading material to improve her mind: 'Greek drama, Russian literature, Hesse, Rilke.' 'It was the beginning of my dream for the ideal education of the children I hoped someday to have' (*LH*, p. 6).

At Boston University Aurelia Schober met Otto Plath, a scientist who became her instructor in Middle High German. The son of a skilled worker, he had emigrated from Germany and was twenty years older than she. Aurelia got her master's degree: they married. Adhering to his wish that she stop working and become a faculty wife, she typed his dissertation and bore his children in accordance with his schedule.[5] Together they read manuals on infant development and decided that their babies would be 'rocked, cuddled, sung to, recited to, and picked up when they cried.' 'At the end of my first year of marriage, I realized that if I wanted a peaceful home—and I did—I would simply have to become more submissive, *although it was not in my nature to be so*' (*LH*, pp. 12–13, italics, mine).

She subdued her nature throughout Otto Plath's long illness until he died of diabetes milletus. Her stoicism exacted its price: a duodenal ulcer plagued her for years. Sylvia, who was not allowed to attend her father's funeral, felt betrayed.[6] Sylvia's grief and rage were to remain unvoiced for years, as did her perception of what Aurelia's silence probably concealed: *her* rage that Otto, for whom she had denied herself, had left her and his two small children to struggle against economic and emotional penury.

Necessity forced Aurelia to find a teaching job. It paid well but her focus was no longer on self-advancement. Wellesley offered more for her children, so she decided to move there, selling the house in Winthrop by the sea mythologized years later by her poet-daughter. In Wellesley she undertook an innovative, but poorly paid job developing a course in medical secretarial procedures at Boston University: 'I vowed that I would make the course interesting, yes fascinating by presenting the stenographic skills as only the first step up the ladder.'[7] To step up the ladder entailed her working hard on a tight budget in order to secure the social advantages that living in Wellesley offered her children. Edward Butscher's biography of Plath records that Aurelia sent Sylvia and her brother Warren to 'summer camps, scouting, sailing, piano and violin lessons, dance "assemblies".... She cannot be faulted for neglecting any activity which she felt would emotionally and intellectually enhance the best future prospects of her offspring. They seemed destined to have everything the mother lacked as a child.'[8]

Outwardly, they accepted her ambition for them to make good. Aurelia writes:

Throughout her high school years, Sylvia was very uncritical of me. The remark I treasured most and wrote in my journal was made by Sylvia when she was fifteen. 'When I am a mother I want to bring up my children just as you have us.' (*LH*, p. 37).

Aurelia Schober Plath was no waif passively awaiting a prince to make her dreams come true. Energy and hard work made her, like a Horatio Alger protagonist, pull herself up by the boots-straps, not for self-actualization, but to vindicate through the achievements of her golden children, her own loss of the American Dream. Nevertheless, despite the Alger-like components of her prose style—cliché-ridden, aphoristic, sentimental—she is deeply responsive to language, at times excited by its power enough to affect Sylvia profoundly.[9] Her capitulation to *kitsch*, then, is not the Alger-like stance of a man secure in the aggressive energy that propels *him* up the ladder. It is the defeat of the woman taught by her father and inadvertently, perhaps, by her hausfrau mother to be agreeable at all costs, even though 'Grammy' Schober genuinely encouraged Aurelia's intellectual proclivity; it is the renunciation of a woman conditioned by the genteel milieu in which she was raised to conceal her competitive drives, to disguise the underside of her creativity by adopting a rigid perfectionism. Thus, she could only assume the virtuous posture of an Alger hero without availing herself of the unbridled energy that makes of this posture a palatable game.

Sylvia's aggressiveness likewise lay dormant. Her rage self-centered, its manifestation self-punitive, her letters project the persona of a Barbie Doll with brains. Her early letters reveal that the pain surfacing occasionally from the welter of Dale Carnegie declaratives was infused with fear. To brother she writes:

One thing I hope is that you will make your own breakfasts in the a.m. so mother won't have to lift a finger. That is the main thing that seems to bother her. You know, as I do, and it is a frightening thing, that mother would actually kill herself for us. She is an abnormally altruistic person, and I have realized lately that we have to fight against her selflessness as we would fight against a deadly disease. (*LH*, p. 112).

Seldom did she fight her mother openly. The narrative flow of the letters reflects the internalization of her mother's concerns. Obsessed with the dollar value of every prize and scholarship she won, like Aurelia she worked at menial part-time and summer jobs to supplement the family income. Often fatigued to the point of exhaustion, prone to sinus and flu attacks, occasionally needing surgery, she armed herself with the will to overcome these vicissitudes and, like a Horatio Alger hero, push on. Even her resolve to be more playful is undermined by the uneasy purposefulness she brings to this effort:

I am really regrettably unoriginal, conventional, and puritanical basically, but I needed to practice a certain healthy bohemianism for a while to swing away from the gray-clad, basically dressed, brown-haired, clock regulated, responsible, salad-eating, water-drinking, bed-going, economical, practical girl I had become—and that's why I needed to associate with people who were very different from myself.... I know how to have happy gay times when I really want to (*LH*, p. 144).

Letters Home delineates obvious mother–daughter parallels. Somewhat lonely as a child, Sylvia was exceptionally studious. She read and overread the right books and was good about winning prizes for her stories and poems even before she entered Smith. Like Aurelia she appeared overawed by a prestigious campus 'resplendent with colors, medals, emblems... I can't believe I'm a SMITH GIRL!' (*LH*, p. 46), and about being in the presence of celebrities. Although time modified this freshman euphoria, she was later as overwhelmed about being a Cambridge girl in the presence of David Daiches, John Lehmann and C.P. Snow as she had been studying in the 'Illustrious' presence of Alfred Kazin during her undergraduate years.

Tailoring her studies to conform to the expectations of successful women patrons such as Olive Higgins Prouty and Mary Ellen Chase obliged Plath to monitor her behavior and inhibit her hostility. For the most part the glossy, superficial poems and stories she wrote as an undergraduate masked an undercurrent of anger that would be revealed in *The Bell Jar*. Occasionally, an awareness that her conformity was depleting her poetic creativity made her pause in her relentless drive to perfect every aspect of her life. For instance, during her instructorship at Smith after her marriage to Ted Hughes, she recoiled from the demands made on her time and energy and even more from the anemic and alienating quality of campus life, fearing that it would mean 'death to writing.'[10] Despite the prestigious rewards—the Glascock, Cheltenham, Fulbright and Saxton prizes, despite the encouragement of gifted women scholars like Chase and Dorothea Krook at Cambridge, Plath became increasingly aware that writing and having babies tapped a deeper drive to become reborn as a poet. Eventually she gave up the security of teaching to live with Hughes in England.

Ironically, however, this departure from the Alger format also paralleled Aurelia's career. Like her mother, Sylvia had married a foreigner, the son of a Yorkshire working man. Impressed with his physical strength, height, intellectual precocity, she married someone she believed she could serve. Like her mother, she subordinated her own ambition to further Hughes' fame though it was 'not her nature to do so.'[11] In part through Plath's publishing contacts Hughes' poems were printed in *The Atlantic Monthly* and *Harper's*. After they moved to England she typed revisions of his manuscripts, organized them painstakingly, sent them out unfailingly. Ecstatic when *Hawk in the Rain* was accepted for publication, she wrote:

I am more happy than if it was my book *The Colossus* published! I have worked so closely on these poems of Ted's and typed them so many countless times through revision after revision.... I am so happy *his* book is accepted *first*. It will make it so much easier for me when mine is accepted.... I can rejoice much more, knowing Ted is ahead of me.[12]

Contrary to her doubt that she 'could never be either a complete scholar or a complete housewife or a complete writer,' but 'must combine a little of all, and thereby be imperfect in all,' she kept house efficiently and cooked gourmet meals (*LH*, p. 219). Like her mother she first bore a daughter, Frieda (whom she shakily described on a transatlantic phone call to Aurelia an hour after the baby was born as 'Ein Wunderkind' (*LH*, p. 373); and within two years she bore a son. The Hughes moved to Devon where Plath alternated intense periods of writing with housework, gardening, beekeeping—combining the domestic rituals of her mother and her grandmother with her father's work with bees.

At this time her letters express a desire for closeness with Aurelia based on their common experiences as mothers who also write. She anticipates her children's creativity and wants to provide them with cultural advantages. She asks about recipes and wants all the back issues of *The Ladies' Home Journal* (*LH*, p. 433). She even urges her mother to write, as she herself has done, for the slicks:

You could do it.... You might start with someone resembling yourself .... What do you think? Make use of the old adage you taught me: 'Get your hero/heroine up a tree, fling stones at him/her, then have him extricate himself.' People 'identify' with people in trouble, people wrestling with problems! Get to it mummy! (*LH*, p. 393).

Revelling in 'newsy pink letters from home,' hers abound in domestic images: crackling fires, red curtains, rabbit stews, 'the daily ration of soup plates of hot oatmeal (something you and Grammy taught me).' Even the landscape has become housebound: 'the merest dusting of snow on everything, china-blue skies, rosy hilltops, new lambs in the fields' (*LH*, pp. 440–441). Somewhere in this pastoral background, Hughes is affably adjunctive, gardening, helping with the babies.

In allying herself to and identifying with her mother as a purveyor of the *Ladies' Home Journal* mystique, Plath probably increased her deep-seated fear of artistic mediocrity personified not only by Aurelia but by her lifelong mentor, Olive Higgins Prouty, whose *Stella Dallas* resonated with the kind of sacrifice Aurelia had made on her daughter's behalf.[13] More than that: Plath's compulsion to get published in slicks from *Mademoiselle* to *Vogue* warred with her apprehension that the 'plushy air-conditioned offices' of these journals peopled with stenographers like her mother whose skills she could never master, oppressed women writers. By remote control, men ran those offices eroding women's creative vitality, turning them into consumers. This apprehension had helped foster her earlier suicidal breakdown in 1953.

Mediocrity is linked to a stenographer's life experiences. Of *The Bell Jar* Marjorie Perloff observes: 'Typing and shorthand; her mother's domain become the symbols of male oppression: she rejects her mother's practical notion that "an English major who knew shorthand... would be in demand among all the up-and-coming young men and she would transcribe letter after thrilling letter."[14] For Plath, mediocrity was that which abstracted the poet from the wellspring of her creativity, which is why she had found her science courses at Smith repellant:

I really am in a state of complete and horrible panic.... I can't reconcile the memory and rote with my philosophy of a creative education. Science is to me, useless drudgery for *no purpose*. A vague superficial understanding of molecules and atoms...(*LH*, pp. 98–99).

It is not imaginative science she fears, but applied technology, second hand abstraction, formulaic solutions, the world of Otto Plath translated by Aurelia Plath.

The excerpt from *The Bell Jar* quoted above links mediocrity to rote skills, unproductive work, conventional courtship, packaged relationships. And it terrified Plath that even while repudiating *The Ladies' Home Journal* 'blither about birdies going tweet tweet and happy marriages,' even after Hughes had left her, she was still attracted to these conventions (*LH*, p. 473). Her last letters reveal her ambivalence about becoming a successful poet no longer in Hughes' shadow, yet unable to overcome the puritanical rigidity that did not allow her to envision intimacies other than those found in marriage and motherhood. Husbandless, with two young children to support, she ironically recapitulates her mother's former predicament. Helpless, ill, in desperate need of Aurelia's financial and emotional support, she fears its price—the incorporating of her mother's values which made of the failed marriage a failed self:

I am writing with my old fever of 101 alternating with chills back. I must have someone with me for the next two months to mind the babies while I get my health back and try to write... I need help very much just now. Home is impossible. I can go nowhere with the children, and I am ill, and it would be psychologically the worst thing to see you now or to go home... (*LH*, p. 468).

Letters Home suggests that 'with his vast fund of knowledge and understanding: not facts or quotes of second hand knowledge, but an organic, digested comprehension which enhances his every word,' Hughes strongly influenced Plath's growing strategies that drew upon the animistic forces 'inherent in the world of nature' in her *Ariel* poems (*LH*, p. 256). While there is little overlap between the demonic persona embodied in 'Lady Lazarus' and the dutiful daughter sending cheery messages to New England, a tonal shift near the close of her epistolary narrative expresses, perhaps, Aurelia's creative influence on Sylvia's poetic powers:

I shall be one of the few women poets in the world who is a fully rejoicing woman... I am a woman and glad of it, and my songs will be of fertility of the earth... (*LH*, p. 450).

I think having babies is really the happiest experience of my life.... I am enjoying my slender foothold in my study in the morning again... the feeling that nothing else but writing and thinking is done there... I have the queerest feeling of having been reborn with Frieda—it's as if my real, rich happy life started just about then... I hope I shall always be a 'young' mother like you... (*LH*, p. 450).

Despite Plath's tendency to mimic her mother's ladylike prose, rendering people and landscapes as if she were painting teacups, overusing intensifiers and adjectives, e.g., 'beautiful,' 'nice,' 'charming,' 'dear,' the excerpts above indicate more than a response to Aurelia's gifts of pewter and copperware. They demonstrate Plath's awe of the engendering powers of language linked to childbirth[15]—her perception that a symbiotic bond existed between biological and literary motherhood during the time when she was writing 'at about four in the morning—that still blue, almost eternal hour before the baby's cry, before the glassy music of the milkman, settling his bottles.'[16]

Unfortunately, these epistolary fragments fail to shed light on the final explosive poems, that distanced her sufficiently from her mother. Instead, *Letters Home* tells us that while Plath feared the Doppelgänger staring back 'from the mercury-backed glass' with 'hag hands waiting to haul [her] in,'[17] she was drawn to those hands as she was to the great mother ocean in which she 'could swim forever straight into the sea and sun and never be able to swallow more than a gulp or two of the water and swim on' (*LH*, p. 130). This attraction, reenforced when Hughes' abandonment of her recapitulated the death of her father, could not help but make Plath acutely conscious of Aurelia's self-negation. Fearing the risk individuation would impose on her, the poet chose in 1963 the self-extinction she had evaded in 1953 when 'only by returning to the womb in the shape of the basement crawl space at her mother's house... does she hope to find the "dark... thick as velvet" which is the dark of death.'[18]

NOTES

1 Sylvia Plath, 'Ocean 1212-W,' in *The Art of Sylvia Plath: A Symposium*, ed. Charles Newman (Bloomington: Indiana University Press, 1970), p. 272.

2 Plath's most savage caricature of Aurelia appears in *The Bell Jar*. Some poems also reflect her hostlity. In an analysis of Plath's poems on motherhood, Margaret Uroff observes that in 'The Disquieting Muses' the mother's middle-class platitudes cannot protect her daughter from physical and psychological danger. See Margaret Uroff, 'Sylvia Plath on Motherhood,' in *The Midwest Quarterly*, 15 (October, 1973), p. 73.

3 Adrienne Rich, *Of Woman Born: Motherhood as Experience and Institution* (New York: W.W. Norton, 1976), pp. 235–236.

4 *Letters Home by Sylvia Plath: Correspondence 1950–1963*, ed. Aurelia Schober Plath (New York: Harper and Row, 1975), pp. 3, 32. All further references will be cited as *LH* and appear in the text.

5 Otto Plath planned his son's arrival two and a half years after Sylvia's birth and so it came to pass.

6 Aurelia writes: 'What I intended as an exercise in courage for the sake of my children was interpreted years later by my daughter as indifference. "My mother never had time to mourn my father's death." I ... remembered a time when I was a little child, seeing my mother weep in my presence and feeling my whole personal world was collapsing. *Mother*, the tower of strength, my one refuge *crying*! It was this recollection that compelled me to withhold my tears until I was alone in bed at night' (*LH*, pp. 25, 28).

7 To the projected course outline she also added 'a brief history of the evolution of medicine itself as it emerged from witchcraft, superstition and religious practices' (*LH*, p. 29). Sylvia also compiled and added to her reading lists during her terms at Smith and at Cambridge.

8 Edward Butscher, *Sylvia Plath, Method and Madness* (New York: The Seabury Press, 1976), p. 21. Butscher's Freudian bias expressed too often in sexist terms tends to contradict the evidence he has amassed from interviews, tapes, and letters that 'Sylvia knew with a kind of instinctive wisdom and dread that Mrs. Plath was essential, the great mother-sea without whom she could not survive, but with whom she could never achieve independent sanity' (Butscher, p. 121).

9 Reading Arnold's 'The Forsaken Merman' aloud to Sylvia, Aurelia inflamed *her* as well: 'A spark flew off Arnold and shook me, like a child I wanted to cry; I felt very odd. I had fallen into a new way of being happy.' Quoted by Mrs. Plath, *LH*, p. 32.

10 Interestingly, the possibility of an instructorship for Plath occurred

about the time her mother was appointed Associate Professor at Boston University (See *LH*, p. 313).

11 Cf. Introduction to *Letters Home*, p. 13.

12 Aurelia comments: 'From the time Sylvia was a very little girl, she catered to the male of any age so as to bolster his sense of superiority' (*LH*, p. 297).

13 The novel deals with a mother who sacrifices her relationship with her daughter in order to secure for her a prestigious marriage to a wealthy man. Plath probably saw thematic parallels in her own mother's life.

14 Quoted by Majorie Perloff in 'A Ritual for Being Born Twice. Sylvia Plath's *The Bell Jar*,' *Contemporary Literature*, 13 (1972), p. 517.

15 Hughes' encouraging Plath to delve deeper into herself renewed her interest in German, the language of her parents.

16 Quoted by A. Alvarez in *The Art of Sylvia Plath*, pp. 58, 59.

17 Sylvia Plath, 'All the Dead Dears,' in *The Colossus and Other Poems* (New York: Alfred A. Knopf, 1967), p. 30. Adrienne Rich, writing of Plath's effort to let Aurelia know that 'her struggles and sacrifices to rear her daughter had been vindicated,' indicates the psychic pain of that osmosis. See *Of Woman Born*, p. 230.

18 Marjorie Perloff, 'A Ritual For Being Born Twice,' *CL*, p. 511.

JOHNNY PANIC AND THE BIBLE OF DREAMS: SHORT STORIES, PROSE AND DIARY EXCERPTS

Edited by Ted Hughes

London, 1977; New York, 1979

70. Douglas Hill, 'Living and Dying,' *Canadian Forum*

June 1978, 323–4

Those who would deal in the legend of Sylvia Plath, who would buy and sell the myths and mystifications surrounding the image of a woman propelled by psychosis into a fury of poetic creation and a compulsion to destroy herself, do her actual career—her dedication to craft and her precocious artistic commitment—something of a disservice. After all, over a ten-year span she published 170 poems, a novel, a verse play, and a considerable number of shorter prose pieces. Such an achievement suggests that she hardly needs to be rescued from anybody, even if the cultists, quite understandably and often persuasively, have overemphasized the apocalyptic nature of the end of her life and art. This volume should help correct distortions; it also will remind us how much more there is to be learned, and indicates how frustrating that search is going to be.

The best of the stories collected here (there are non-fiction pieces and journal excerpts as well) are as indelibly distinctive as *The Bell Jar* and the finest poems. In flowing perceptions of terror—in the title story, for instance—Plath exposes the world as a refraction of consciousness, consciousness as a version of the world. Into this split—other/self, real/surreal, phenomenal/intuitive—her imagination dives, her dream descends. The dream *is* often destructive—of the narrator 'Johnny Panic' and 'The Wishing Box,' of the hero in 'The 59th Bear'; it's the dream of a moment, one commentator has said, both girlish and deadly. Plath's special talent is not merely the creation of that moment but the naming of its shattered pieces. Even the weaker stories share this power; they have flashes of intense vision, but lack the consistent pressure.

Plath's truest voice is the most painful, the one closest to the nerve. 'I must write about the things of the world with no glazing.' Her best prose has an aggressive innocence, a jumping eagerness to see and spell experience in her own alphabet. Like Hemingway in his early stories, she often appears to want to strip down rhetoric to a point where object and self everywhere meet but never touch. The form and rhythm of the stories, too, can be brilliantly open—chopped, jerky, elliptical, but always clear and focussed however erratic.

Among the bits of non-fiction prose, the autobiographical 'Ocean 1212-W' is essential ('I sometimes think my vision of the sea is the clearest thing I own'). So is 'Context,' a five-paragraph assessment of her poetry for London Magazine ('The poets I delight in are possessed by their poems as by the rhythms of their own breathing'). The real stunner, though, is the first of the four journal passages, printed here, from the time of her Fulbright studies at Cambridge. Parts of it are naive and self-conscious, if not trite, but even when Plath strikes a conventional pose for herself, it's a totally engrossing and often revealing one. There's not enough of it, however; the selection gives only the barest sampling of the range and quantity of her unpublished material.

Literary judgments aside, the question of when, how, and by whom Plath's works are to be edited and presented is now—as it has been for fifteen years—absolutely crucial. Even granted an inhuman amount of tact, taste, and impartiality, Sylvia Plath's mother and husband—Aurelia Plath and Ted Hughes—ought not to have the exclusive responsibility of deciding what the world is to know of her. No wonder we have a legend on our hands.

Hughes's editorial decisions in this volume may raise some eyebrows, but I'm basically in sympathy with most of them. To divide the public prose into 'more successful' and 'other' is of course arbitrary, but considering what he had to work with, I see no other course he could have followed that would have given as useful a picture, tantalizingly partial though it is, of Plath's development and continuity. (He's had limitations: a postscript to his Introduction, added when the book was in proof, reports the emergence, in the States, of 'a large number' of manuscripts formerly belonging to Mrs. Plath.)

Where Hughes is less convincing, as was Mrs. Plath in her selection of the letters, is in his argument—essentially with himself—for restricting publication of the most personal and potentially defamatory journals. It's best to quote him:

I am more and more inclined to think that any bit of evidence which corrects and clarifies our idea of what she really was is important, insofar as her writings persuade us of her importance. But living people figure everywhere even in her most private discussions with herself, and—an editor has to face it—some things are more important than revelations about writers.

It's a tough choice: since I can hardly expect to play a large part in Plath's diaries, I'd opt for complete publication and hope for understanding or thick skins on the parts of those who do. At least that way I might be spared such speculations and ambiguities as arise from the knowledge that the single Cambridge entry Hughes prints in this book—the single 'personal' as opposed to 'literary' entry—was written less than a week before Plath met him for the first time, a meeting sufficiently impressive that she described him in a letter to her mother a few days later as 'the only man I've met who'd be strong enough to be equal with.'

There's another sort of inference to be drawn—tentatively, to be sure—from Hughes's editorial control, this from the Introduction itself. On his own evidence, I'd support his implicit claim that he both understood and helped Sylvia Plath, fully and honourably, at the extremes of their relation—in the spiritual business of connecting poetically with an artist and in the practical business of getting through the days and dirty dishes with one. He was good with her images and with her sinus trouble; he understood her terribly and trivially. What he seems to have missed was the necessary middle, the kind of support, the quality of love or understanding, that might have made it possible for her to live. So she, too, may have been unable to find this middleground: Plath killed herself that morning, we know, in the grip of an iron winter's desperation, but not before setting out bread and butter and two mugs of milk for her children.

To be fair, I'd say Hughes is sensitive to his lack. He calls the work of Plath's last year 'liberation.' If the term applies, surely it includes her attempt at liberation from him. Hughes's introductory remarks quietly imply a recognition of this.

The acolytes of Confessional or Extremist poetry have emphasized, over and over, the tremendous risks involved in Plath's 'murderous art.' This basically admiring view finds the source of her creative energy in self-destructiveness (A. Alvarez), and the imagination of dying as the climactic experience of living (Charles Newman). The cultivation of derangement, dying as *the* mode of life—enticing and fashionable as these attitudes are, they ignore, or try to overwhelm by rhetorical force, the moral aspects of the relation between aesthetic value and suicidal madness. Such an approach may ultimately be unfair to Plath.

I don't know if this question can be settled. Certainly we need to look at more evidence; even if we get it all, the secrets may stay hidden and the answers remain suppositions. The publication of *Johnny Panic* is important in part because it can make these issues live once more, can put the hard crystals of Plath's reputation into solution again for another generation to analyze. The book also adds a good fifty ineradicable pages to the anthology of contemporary consciousness.

71. Lorna Sage, 'Death and Marriage,' *Times Literary Supplement*

21 October 1977, 1235

This selection, made by Ted Hughes, of Sylvia Plath's miscellaneous prose—published stories, articles, a few passages from the notebook–journals—is probably the best that can at present be done to pad out the record. A lot more early stories have recently surfaced in America, but given the whimsicality and drabness of the lesser pieces here, they are hardly likely to alter the cranky profile of either her work or her public image. Ted Hughes's remark in his introduction that 'her dogged, year-in-year-out effort to write conventional fiction . . . was like a persistent refusal of her genius' seems entirely accurate. The stories that work manage to cheat their way past her banal ambition to be conventionally 'sensitive' and successful; the ones that do not are nastily eager-to-please concoctions, doubtless a continuation of the kind of writing that got her A grades for creativity at school.

Where Ted Hughes's editorial intervention does matter is with the scanty material from the notebooks. She seems often to have used them for characteristically compromising practice in the art of memory, treacherously reconstructing friends' and neighbours' houses, clothes, personalities, lampshades and so on for future reference. The passages printed here, 'three of the most harmless pieces—by no means the best,' Hughes says, reveal how extensively she mined this sort of 'record' for the poetry, so that sooner or later much more of it should doubtless be published. There does not seem to be an issue of principle here. Mad housewives and literary critics are all going to want to know as much about the processes behind the poems as they can, because that is exactly what her public work invites. Yet only mortality or forgetfulness (presumably) will make that possible, since we are all inclined (despite talk of confessional *art*) to take private performances in letters and journals as somehow truthful. And that, in Sylvia Plath's case (witness *Letters Home*), would be very rash. Bad enough to pay a call and be transmogrified into the obscene duo of 'Death & Co,' or to let Sylvia Plath into one's kitchen only to be stewed in the cabbage water of 'Lesbos,' but at least in the poems the distortions are formally obvious. The journals, judging from these extracts, look 'authentic'—that is, are only about a third created—so would do damage.

Anyway, of the relatively 'harmless' pieces, the notes from Cambridge (1956) are the most remote, not just in time. They reek of closet-theatre, and are full of self-disliking yet somehow cosy parentheses—'as I have so often boasted cleverly,' 'see, how dangerous,' 'always patching masks.' She sounds bored with the gothic contents of her consciousness; the motifs are all there (Lazarus, the cold moon, father/lovers, birth-damaged babies, stillborn poems) but devoid of passion or even interest, as though she had grown weary of rehearsing them. It was perhaps a defensive pose; however, it seems to have stuck, and obviously had to be unstuck—'My God, I would love to cook and make a house, and surge force into a man's dreams, and write'—before these gruesome relics could work their miracles in the later poems. Odd, now, to see them lying around in limbo waiting on her marriage, especially since she seems to have thought the right man might banish them for good.

More interesting, if less paraphrasable, are the pieces from 1961–62 which record some of the events that went into 'The Bee Meeting' and 'Berck Plage.' The tone is very different, though how far it's representative is impossible to tell. It would be cheering to think that it was since these were professional notes, ready-tailored to be used for poetry, shorn of self-analysis. She hardly needed to make notes about herself—what she did need was visual recall, the 'soap-coloured oak' and 'raw date' on Percy B.'s coffin; the different veils, the cow parsley and angry bees zinging 'as at the end of long elastics.' There are some interesting contrasts between her private tone and her bardic finalities: 'The end, even of so marginal a man, a horror,' says the journal of her dead neighbour. 'This is what it is to be complete. It is horrible,' says the poem, placing him centre stage, but at the same time merging him with all the dead, especially Daddy. Or again, there is the prosaic grave as a 'narrrow red earth opening,' compared with the 'naked mouth, red and awkward' that gapes in the verse. The poetry and the prose seem at last to have sorted themselves out—as though now that she was writing poems that pleased her, she no longer needed to compose sub-lyrics in her journals. The closer she got to simply gathering material, the better her prose.

'Fifteen-Dollar Eagle' (about watching a heroic sailor bloodily tattooed) and 'Mothers' (a Devon Mothers' Union tea) likewise pick on opportune experiences, and their claim to being in the story section rests on the exoticism of the events in question. She is surprisingly inept at inventing structures, even ordinary plots, taking refuge instead in archaic, would-be wry, O. Henry 'twists' to rescue directionless narratives. Only four or five of the stories take on a full fictional identity, and then it's done through large-scale mythic patterns rather than the discreet adjustments that usually belong to the form. For example, the only endings she can make work seem to be death or waking out of a hallucination, or both at once as in the title story, 'Johnny Panic.' There, and in a companion piece, 'The Daughters of Blossom Street,' she manages something like the metamorphosed autobiography of The Bell Jar, turning a brief job she had in 1958 as secretary to a psychiatrist at

Massachusetts General Hospital into a cold, gleeful vision of the sharable nightmare:

It's into the lake people's minds run at night, brooks and gutter-trickles to one borderless common reservoir. It bears no resemblance to those pure sparkling-blue sources of drinking water the suburbs guard more jealously than the Hope diamond in the middle of pine woods and barbed fences.

It's the sewage farm of the ages, transparence aside. Even here, though, there are signs of self-consciousness and the worry about pastiche, since the heroine arrives at her 'bible,' her collection of dreams, by stealing them out of people's files.

Indeed, in so far as the stories have—or suggest—a theme, this is it. Perhaps because they are so often hesitant, dependent, ill at ease, they reveal even more clearly than her poems her fear that for all her isolation, she was a psychic parasite. 'Day of Success,' which tries to disclaim any such parasitism, must be one of the creepiest instances: an attempt at a woman's magazine story (unpublished until last year) about a young wife and mother coping with her writer-husband's sudden breakthrough into realms of money and fame. It is saccharine-sweet, and entirely (deliberately?) fails to hide its bitterness. The first paragraph buries the heroine under a pile of 'freshly folded nappies,' and has her proudly contemplate 'the forest-green cord drapes she's hemmed by hand' as the phone rings for him, a 'small, black instrument of doom.' A brisk lady producer making a lunch date sets her fantasizing about 'author and producer collaborating on the birth of something wonderful,' luring him away from herself and their baby daughter. It's terrible stuff, with the feeblest of happy endings, a parody of the zest with which she threw herself into the role of housewife and insisted on an exaggerated separation of roles in the earliest part of her marriage. (Here, when the hopeful husband sells a story and tries to buy her a present, the heroine asks for a pram big enough for twins.)

Along the same lines is 'Sunday at the Mintons',' a story dating back to 1952, about a mutually destructive brother–sister relationship, where he is a creature of rigid rationality obsessed with maps and clocks, and she a ludicrously fey spinster in lavender skirts:

Hers was a twilight world, where the moon floated up over the trees at night like a tremulous balloon of silver light and the bluish rays wavered through the leaves outside her window.... The wind blew in gentle, capricious gusts.

This time it ends with a dreamy, seaweedy double death, the heroine (with obvious help from the author) has subtly, vaguely arranged.

The most explicit version of the theme is 'The Wishing Box,' published in 1957 at a time when, according to her biographers, she was playing the self-effacing wife with almost ostentatious modesty (for example, at a reading of her own poems, 'Ted, what do you think?'). Here, she treats Agnes and Harold's marriage as a dreaming contest; he 'spending one third of his life among celebrities and fabulous legendary creatures' while her mind empties of even the usual banal nightmares, 'without a single image of its own to ward off the crushing assault of smug autonomous tables and chairs,' let alone his gratifying technicolour visions. She soon gives up the competition, the implication being that they have only one identity, one store-box of wishes, between them, despite the surface distinctness of their lives. Agnes tries to populate her mind from elsewhere with novels, television, drink, but her only way of restoring a balance of imaginative power is to set up an unanswerable final tableau:

on the sofa ... dressed in her favourite princess-style emerald taffeta evening gown, pale and lovely as a blown lily, eyes shut, an empty pillbox and an over-turned water tumbler on the rug at her side. Her tranquil features were set in a slight, secret smile of triumph, as if, in some far country unattainable to mortal men, she were, at last, waltzing with the dark, red-caped prince of her early dreams.

At best, it is an ending out of a perverse fairy tale; writing it may have offered some unsavoury satisfactions, but, like so many other pieces of prose, it must have confirmed her fear that she was short on 'shaping imaginative powers.'

It also suggests that Ted Hughes was accurate when he said in a *Guardian* interview (1963) that 'There was no rivalry between us ... in these circumstances you begin to write out of one brain.' The absence of 'rivalry' was not due to her cloying attempts at making a separate 'wifely' persona, but to something much more interesting, with much more potentiality for better or worse—the ideal of the creative marriage. This involves not so much relationship as identity, man and wife one angel, as Swedenborg said, and Lawrence made Tom Brangwen repeat in *The Rainbow*. The aspiration is suggested by Aristophanes's cruel picture in the *Symposium* of those four-armed, four-legged hermaphrodites ('we were like two feet of one body,' Hughes said in the same interview) who were split down the middle by envious gods, and doomed for ever to seek their other halves. In the nature of things, men were the main beneficiaries and casualties of this myth until fairly recently, poets expecting a mental marriage to remedy 'penury and loneliness of soul.' The phrase is Milton's, in one of the divorce pamphlets, where he argues that just as the ideal marriage is enriching, so its failures are poisonous. If you gamble on being augmented by a 'fit conversing soul,' you risk diminishment. Milton produced too an image that may serve as a context for some of Sylvia Plath's necrophiliac versions of father/husband: 'instead of being one flesh, they will rather be two carcases, chained unnaturally together, or, as it may happen, a living soul bound to a dead corpse.' Then the trick is, as in Plath's late poems, to decide which is the dead one.

The first literary marriages I can think of in which the myth applied both ways are the Romantics', Shelley's and Byron's. Shelley certainly happened on the same horrible image as Milton (before his first wife drowned herself in the Serpentine, and made it real), and Mary Shelley dallied with it in *Frankenstein* (less sensible in this than Mary Wollstonecraft who said you should stop making 'an absurd unit' of man and wife). *Frankenstein* is probably the most suggestive analogy (I don't suppose it would have been an influence) for the personal myths about assembling a creative identity out of bits and pieces of the dead in Plath's hate-poems. Both women seem to have drawn on pitiful and grotesque pictures of dead babies as images of their *own* struggles to come into existence. The use of exploring such far-flung analogies would be to remove some of the burden of having to represent a particular (female) generation from Sylvia Plath's work. No doubt much of her difficulty in making or appropriating a style is due to her sex, but the basic wretchedness and triumph of the best poems allies her with insecure, greedy poetic egos of both genders. At worst, her unfairness is merely, childishly, vengeful. Again, the degree to which she contrived to confuse art and life is perhaps new, but not the confusion itself, which has always been sinisterly fertile. This collection of prose belongs to the semi-created level of her work, but even here she has the power to set off like firecrackers problems that go way beyond the often dull or scrappy style.

72. G.S. Fraser, 'Pass to the Centre,' *Listener*

27 October 1977, 541–2

G(eorge) S(utherland) Fraser (1915–80) was a poet and critic as well as a journalist and editor. Born in Scotland, he taught at the University of Leicester.

Much of the writing in this collection has the peculiar kind of glossiness which marks fiction in even very good American magazines (the brilliant title-story made the high middlebrow *Atlantic Monthly*, and a grippingly gruesome story about tattooing, 'The Fifteen-Dollar Eagle', was published in the oldest and most prestigious of American periodicals, the *Sewanee Review*).

At the same time, Sylvia Plath was quite content to be accepted by the homely *McCall's* or the smart *Mademoiselle*. With the American desire to 'make it', her ideal, till her poetic genius took over, was through stories and journalism to be rich, famous, and travel, while remaining a wholesome and nice American girl. The daydream is spelt out in embarrassing fullness in 'Day of Success', the last of the second selection of stories here, those which Ted Hughes rightly considers inferior to the first batch. There the wholesome girl is the wife, the genius is the husband, and it ends happily when the husband, having sold a play for acting and publishing on the same day, decides to buy the country cottage that she has always longed for.

Ted Hughes is certainly right when he says she must have known this was sentimental *pastiche* aimed at a popular market, just as in 'The Fifty-Ninth Bear' she knew what was wrong: '...a stiff, artificial piece about a man killed by a bear, ostensibly because his wife willed it to happen, but none of the deep emotional undercurrents gone into or developed . . . I just can't get out of myself.'

But getting in, painfully deep, was part of her genius. She was, as Ted Hughes notes, a much better journalist than short-story writer. I think a naturally pleasant personality and ease of conversation, for which she had no room in the stories, got out in journalism easily.

The fragments from her journal are something else again. The Cambridge passages are embarrassingly egotistic. In passages containing detailed observation of outer behaviour and visible surroundings, 'Widow Mangada' and 'Rose and Percy B', she is wonderful but also frightening. The Widow Mangada was devious and on the edge of madness. Percy B was no doubt all the more disgusting in his prolonged dying because of his false teeth, and his wife Rose was shallow and a bit of a scrounger. But, though the impression must be wrong, since one feels the pity and involvement oneself, there is the sense of someone who sees things almost indecently clearly.

The frightening and powerful title-story springs from a job in the records office for mental patients in the Massachusetts General Hospital in Boston; and in its heroine's growing obsession with the recording of horrific dreams for their own sake, and her final confinement in the ECT room, it shows that humanly the job was the worst she could have taken, imaginatively the best.

She could only escape from what Ted Hughes, in his introduction, calls 'the limitation to actual circumstances . . . the prison of so much of her prose' by getting to the centre of the prison, the terrified self with the candy-sweet surface, and exploring all its horrors. At the centre, too, there were little glimpses of heaven as well as hell: 'the purple "lucky stones" I used to collect with a white ring all the way round, or the shell of a blue mussel with its rainbowy angel's fingernail interior' that she speaks of in a lovely broadcast, 'Ocean 1212-W'.

Ted Hughes shows himself in his introduction a critic of the first order. He shows how she fought doggedly against the special nature of her own genius:

But mainly what she wanted in her stories was the presence of the objective world. 'I must write about the things of the world with no glazing.' She fought doggedly against the great suction of her own subjectivity: 'I shall perish if I can write about no one but myself.'

In a sense, she did in the end write about that and perished of doing so. 'She had,' as Ted Hughes says, 'an instant special pass to the centre....' But one could add that the work in the stories was not wasted because in the wildest death-dance she is also coolly observing herself, the images are from real life rearranged, and 'the centre', though so few of us have a pass to it, is also the centre from which we shape 'the objective world.'

73. Melody Zajdel, 'Apprenticed in a Bible of Dreams: Sylvia Plath's Short Stories,' *Critical Essays on Sylvia Plath*

1984, 182–93

Melody Zajdel (b. 1949) is Assistant Professor of English at Montana State University at Bozeman. She writes on H. D., Dorothy Richardson, and contemporary women writers.

Although Sylvia Plath wrote approximately 70 short stories, only 10 were published in her lifetime. Since her death, three appeared in popular magazines and an additional seven stories were printed in the recently published volume *Johnny Panic and the Bible of Dreams*. What is interesting to the reader of these twenty stories is the consistency with which Plath dealt with the same materials and themes throughout her fiction. Although her prose works span over ten years, much of that time seems spent in writing and rewriting the same story, the story which reaches its fruition in *The Bell Jar*. This is particularly obvious in several of the short stories published after her death ('Tongues of Stone,' 'Sweetie Pie and the Gutter Men,' and 'Johnny Panic and the Bible of Dreams'). These stories, along with 'In the Mountains,' (published in the *Smith Review*, 1954), serve almost as apprentice pieces for key scenes in

The Bell Jar, containing episodes with the same actions, characters, images, sometimes even the same words. Beyond these apprentice pieces, however, a reader discovers that not only do Plath's stories stylistically show her direct movement into the writing of *The Bell Jar*, but they also mirror her continued thematic concern with two interrelated ideas: first, the idea of living and sustaining a life of the imagination, and second, the socio-mythic form of this theme, what Joephine Donovan has called 'the sexual politics of Sylvia Plath.'[1] Although Plath's short stories will probably not change her reputation from poet to proficient popular fiction writer (an epithet that Hughes suggests she desired[2]), they are markers to understanding Plath's skill in her finished fictional effort, *The Bell Jar*, just as *The Colossus* stands as a necessary apprenticeship to the final poems of *Ariel*.

Hughes indicates that Plath 'launched herself into *The Bell Jar* in 1960.'[3] But at least the four stories mentioned above, written between 1954 and 1959, deal with some of the same material. One in particular, 'Tongues of Stone' (1955), uses the experience of a young girl's nervous breakdown much as Plath uses it in *The Bell Jar*. At least six key incidents appear first in this story, before being transformed and interpolated into the novel. The start of the breakdown is the same in both pieces. The main character is suffering from extreme apathy, anxiety and insomnia. In *The Bell Jar*, Esther enters the first clinic, Walton, after three weeks of not sleeping; in 'Tongues of Stone,' the character is at the end of two months of sleeplessness. In setting the scene, the 'Tongues of Stone' narrator explains 'It was sometime in October; she had long ago lost track of all the days and it really didn't matter because one was like another and there were no nights to separate them because she never slept anymore.'[4] Both young women try to forestall their depression by looking for intellectual occupations to, literally, kill time. Each tries particularly hard to read, only to find the print on the pages of their books indecipherable, 'dead black hieroglyphs' (JP, 263) and 'fantastic untranslatable shapes, like Arabic and Chinese'.[5] Both are denied solace by their alienation from the dead intellectual world represented by the printed books. But more obvious in their similarities than these parallels of general circumstances are the active steps in their attempted suicides and their subsequent treatments. Looking at these steps, the reader can see Plath's movement from a rather flat narrative to the evocative and powerful personal voice of the novel. The apprentice piece has all the isolated units but doesn't have the developed style, theme or political focus of *The Bell Jar*.

First, in both 'Tongues of Stone' and *The Bell Jar*, each of the girls visits her sleeping mother and comes to an important realization: there is neither parental security nor any meaningful reason to continue being in either the present or the future. In 'Tongues of Stone,' the main character slips into her mother's bed and, lying beside her, 'Listen [s] to the thin thread of her mother's breathing, wanting to get up and twist the life out of the fragile throat, to end at once the process of slow disintegration which grinned at her like a death's head everywhere she turned' (JP, 265). The girl (who remains nameless throughout the story), has sought out her mother. By getting close to her, the girl hopes to stave off the fears and despair she feels. But the mother can neither solace nor protect her daughter. Asleep, she is even unaware of the girl's presence. She is perceived by her daughter as fragile and disintegrating, not a possible haven or shelter against the death her daughter sees everywhere, even in her. This same incident occurs in *The Bell Jar*, but some of the narrator's feelings have changed. In the novel, the mother is less mutual victim, another fragile throat which can be stopped, and more a despised perpetrator of circumstances, a guardian of the world's values and actions. The main character, Esther, looks at her sleeping mother, listens to her piggish snores, and explains '...for a while it seemed to me that the only way to stop it [the sound in her mother's throat] would be to take the column of skin and sinew from which it rose and twist it to silence between my hands' (BJ, 101). Not only is the mother more unattractive in this version (being piggish and irritating), but the action of strangling her is not done to stop a mutual disintegration, a slow and painful change, but more to assuage Esther's aggressive dislike of what her mother represents. She and her mother are struggling against one another, tussling between them expectations for Esther's future and Esther's own inchoate desires. Neither is totally passive. Esther views the strangling not as euthanasia, but as a means of effectively changing her own world. Where in 'Tongues of Stone' the girl creeps into her mother's bed for solace, in *The Bell Jar* Esther merely looks at her mother from the bedroom door, not seeking communion with a source of safety so much as observing the enemy.

After this scene, both stories show the female protagonist trying to escape the world around her by hiding under the mattress of her bed. In each case, she hopes to be crushed, to never reawaken to the oppressive world of sleepless, meaningless, comfortless living. In 'Tongues of Stone,' the girl leaves her mother's bed, 'Creeping back to her own bed, then, she had lifted up the mattress, wedging herself in the crevices between mattress and bed-springs, longing to be crushed beneath the heavy slab' (JP, 265). More immediately, the same scene is enacted in *The Bell Jar*: 'I crawled between the mattress and the padded bedstead and let the mattress fall across me like a tombstone. It felt dark and safe under there, but the mattress was not heavy enough. It needed about a ton more weight to make me sleep' (BJ, 101). In the second scene, the tone is sharper. The slab has been defined as a tombstone, the oppression and death imagery are more overt. Plath's character recognizes consciously what she is seeking (the safe dark of death) and what it would take to achieve it (about a ton more.)

Both girls then attempt suicide (actually reach out to take hold of the darkness), but are discovered at the last moment and saved. Upon first awakening from their drugged state, each believes herself blind. In 'Tongues of Stone,' the narrator explains that

At first they thought she would be blind in that eye. She had lain awake the night of her second birth into the world of flesh, talking to a nurse who was sitting up with her, turning her sightless face toward the gentle voice and saying over and over again, 'But I can't see, I can't see.'

The nurse, who had also believed that she was blind, tried to comfort her, saying, 'There are a lot of other blind people in the world. You'll meet a nice blind man and marry him someday.' (JP, 266)

In this scene the nurse is an acknowledged presence, someone known and staying *with* the girl, not just beside her. She is described as gentle and comforting, albeit not well-informed. This same scene is recreated in *The Bell Jar*, only this time the nurse's presence is not so immediately felt as sympathetic.

I opened my eyes.
It was completely dark.
Somebody was breathing beside me.
'I can't see,' I said.
A cheery voice spoke out of the dark. 'There are lots of blind people in the world. You'll marry a nice blind man someday.' (BJ 140)

Although the changes are slight, they do match up with the more sinister and detached feelings of Esther in the novel. The nurse in the second presentation is not known immediately, she is somebody. She is not with the girl, she is beside her. Although she is cheery, unlike the original image of comforting presence, we have no reason to assume her intentions are personal; rather, they smack of habitual, professional cheeriness.

Each girl also tries to strangle herself, although the timing of the attempt varies. In 'Tongues of Stone,' the girl is in the sanatorium, frustrated and depressed that the insulin treatment is not working. She considers strangulation as a means to end the continuing depression and self-disgust.

One night she hid the pink cotton scarf from her raincoat in the pillowcase when the nurse came around to lock up her drawers and closet for the night. In the dark she had made a loop and tried to pull it tight around her throat. But always just as the air stopped coming and she felt the rushing grow louder in her ears, her hands would slacken and let go, and she would lie there panting for breath, cursing the dumb instinct in her body that fought to go on living. (JP, 266)

In *The Bell Jar*, Esther considers and experiments with strangulation as one possible form of suicide, trying a number before the final attempt with sleeping pills. At first, in her version of the scene, she hopes to hang herself, but finding no adequate beam in the house, she explains,

... I sat on the edge of my mother's bed and tried pulling the cord tight.
   But each time I would get the cord so tight I could feel a rushing in my ears and a flush of blood in my face, my hands would weaken and let go, and I would be all right again.
   Then I saw that my body had all sorts of little tricks, such as making my hands go limp at the crucial second, which would save it, time and again, whereas if I had the whole say, I would be dead in a flash. (BJ, 130)

In this revised scene, the body's instinctual response is more malevolent; it is not simply 'dumb,' but it has 'all sorts of little tricks.' In *The Bell Jar* the character's paranoia and mind–body split is strongly felt. The world is active in its oppression, the body active in its rebellion to the will.

Finally, both stories describe the insulin treatment used to combat the character's suicidal depressions. Each story starts with the appearance of a nurse to administer the insulin injection. In 'Tongues of Stone,'

At seven the nurse came in to give the evening insulin shot. 'What side?'
she asked, as the girl bent mechanically over the bed and bared her flank.

'It doesn't matter,' the girl said. 'I can't feel them any more.'

The nurse gave an expert jab. 'My, you certainly *are* black and blue,' she
said. (JP, 267)

In *The Bell Jar*, the characters are both detached as well. The section
is a little less calm, however, since we are at least aware of what
Esther sees when she views herself.

The nurse gave a little clucking noise. Then she said, 'Which side?' It was
an old joke.

I raised my head and glanced back at my bare buttocks. They were
bruised purple and green and blue from past injections. The left side looked
darker than the right.

'The right.'

'You name it.' The nurse jabbed the needle in, and I winced, savoring
the tiny hurt. (BJ. 157)

It is also useful to note that Esther does feel something in this
episode: Pain. And that is welcomed, for it is something instead of
the dull apathy of the first scene.

The final movement in each story is the breakthrough caused by
the girls' reactions to the insulin treatment. In each case, the
reaction signals the momentary lifting of the oppressive atmosphere, the depression, and bell jar which each of the characters is
laboring under. After what has seemed a fruitless waiting in
'Tongues of Stone,' a period where even the sun's warmth is
absent from the day, the girl's reaction occurs, accompanied
by a proliferation of growth and light images.

In the blackness that was stupor, that was sleep, a voice spoke to her,
sprouting like a green plant in the dark.

'Mrs. *Patterson*, Mrs. *Patterson*, Mrs. *Patterson*!' the voice said more
and more loudly, rising, shouting. Light broke on seas of blindness. Air
thinned.

The nurse Mrs. Patterson came running out from behind the girl's eyes.
'Fine,' she was saying, 'fine, let me just take off your watch so you won't
bang it on the bed.'

. . . .

The dark air had thinned and now it lived. There had been the knocking at
the gate, the banging on the bed, and now she was saying to Mrs.
Patterson words that could begin a world: 'I feel different. I feel quite
different.'

'We have been waiting for this a long time,' Mrs. Patterson said, leaning over the bed to take the cup, and her words were warm and round, like apples in the sun. 'Will you have some hot milk? I think you'll sleep tonight.'

And in the dark the girl lay listening to the voice of dawn and felt flare through every fiber of her mind and body the everlasting rising of the sun. (JP, 267–68)

As the ending of the short story, this scene optimistically portends a healing conclusion. The sun has returned; in fact, it is speaking directly to the girl. Both the blackness she emerges from and the real world (represented by the nurse) are positive; the first is a plant; the second, warm and round as an apple. The air is clear, the light quite literally and figuratively dawns. The girl herself speaks words and listens to a voice which apparently signals the start of a new world. In *The Bell Jar*, the parallel scene follows the same progression, but has a slightly different tone.

I had fallen asleep after the evening meal.

I was awakened by a loud voice, *Mrs. Bannister, Mrs. Bannister, Mrs. Bannister, Mrs. Bannister*. As I pulled out of sleep, I found I was beating on the bedpost with my hands and calling. The sharp, wry figure of Mrs. Bannister, the night nurse, scurried into view.

'Here, we don't want you to break this.'

She unfastened the band of my watch.

'What's the matter? What happened?'

Mrs. Bannister's face twisted into a quick smile. 'You've had a reaction.'

'A reaction?'

'Yes, how do you feel?'

'Funny. Sort of light and airy.'

Mrs. Bannister helped me sit up.

'You'll be better now. You'll be better in no time. Would you like some hot milk?'

'Yes.'

And when Mrs. Bannister held the cup to my lips, I fanned the hot milk out on my tongue as it went down, tasting it luxuriously, the way a baby tastes its mother. (BJ, 164)

In this version of the scene, several things have changed. In 'Tongues of Stone,' the girl is the first one to focus on the change in both herself and her surroundings. She feels 'different' and it is not just her, but the atmosphere, the world, which is light and airy. In *The Bell Jar*, Esther feels 'funny,' 'light and airy.' But we have no sense of whether the external world is in accord. In 'Tongues of Stone,' the girl seems to have become attuned again to the physical, natural world. In *The Bell Jar*, the natural world referred to is that of mother and child, not the most hopeful image when taken in the context of the heavily negative connotations given to that relationship throughout the rest of the novel, both before and after this scene. (Consider, in particular, Esther's own relationship with her mother, her sense of all mothers—hers and Buddy's—as circumscribing her opportunities, the notion that becoming a mother herself would kill her chances to be writer, a complete person in her own right.)

Obviously, Plath is using the same material, even some of the same phrases and images, in this early story and *The Bell Jar*. Equally obviously, there are some significant differences in her presentations, many of which seem caused by an increased thematic awareness on Plath's part in the novel. In 'Tongues of Stone,' we have a description more than a clearly delineated conflict. The causes of the breakdown, the fears for the future, the active resistance of the girl to both medical help and her surroundings, are never presented. It seems doubtful that the girl herself is aware of all the factors surrounding her previous actions. We are given a third-person, limited view of the events. All conflicts and conditions leading to the suicide attempt are cloaked. In the expanded scope of *The Bell Jar*, on the other hand, the older Esther, the narrator, has moved to a recognition, frequently frustrated and angry, of the social and familial forces which lead to her breakdown. Her mother is seen in sharply critical relief. Her male doctor is at best indifferent to Esther's struggle; at worst he denies its value. It is a world of stultified options and intellectual sterility which places Esther under the bell jar. It is this thematic awareness even more than a stylistic change which gives *The Bell Jar* a power lacking in the earlier story. This same factor accounts for much of the difference between the other apprentice pieces and the novel.

'In the Mountains' also rehearses a scene for *The Bell Jar*. Isobel, a young college woman, goes to visit her boyfriend, Austin, who has been in a TB sanatorium for six months. (This parallels Esther Greenwood's later visit to Buddy Willard under the same constraints.) Isobel comes to visit, to find an unchanged Austin, 'Still strong, she thought, and sure of himself...' (JP, 277). But she comes also with the awareness that 'everything was changed for her,' (JP, 277), and it is this awareness that she needs to articulate to Austin. In a discussion about marriage in general, their differences are highlighted. Austin implies his desire for a commitment, a marriage, while Isobel, in her newly changed persona, explains that she is not ready to consider such a step. '"Affairs are one thing," she said. "But signing your life away because you're lonely, because you're afraid of being lonely, that's something else again.... That's the way I figure it now anyway."' (JP, 278). For the first time in their relationship, Austin is vulnerable and expresses his need for Isobel. But part of his attraction to her is still the result of seeing her as appropriate to be his wife. Austin notes she is attractive, just as his doctor's wife is attractive, just as a doctor's wife should be. He sees her as fitting a role, a role which he needs filled, not necessarily one she *wants* to fill. He recalls all the things they've 'been through together,' but where they serve to be fond memories for him, Isobel recalls 'how it was all so lovely and hurting then. How everything he said had hurt her' (JP, 282). Where he is now able to proclaim his need for her, she is no longer as needing of him, nor does he offer her anything beyond his need. In the end, when he reaches out for her, thinking to claim her, she is stricken, immobilized and feels them surrounded by a landscape 'hushed and still' (JP, 284), frozen and deathlike. In the story, the reader is made aware of the change in Isobel, as we are similarly made aware in *The Bell Jar* of the change in Esther. However, in 'In the Mountains,' there is less overt understanding of the cause of Isobel's change. The novel form allows Plath to finally put all the isolated scenarios together, to juxtapose them until the common conflicts become clear. Esther's rejection of Buddy is more clearly a rejection of not just the individual, but also the prescribed role which her relationship to Buddy (as his future wife) threatens to lock her into. Likewise, the almost malicious pleasure that Buddy feels when Esther breaks her leg (and thus becomes less threatening, less independent) is missing from the short story. In the story, the reader can still pity Austin, if only slightly; in the novel, Plath gives us little option to disliking Buddy almost as much as Esther does because we see the large issues capitulation to his vulnerability and vision would represent.

In 'Sweetie Pie and the Gutter Men,' Myra Wardle, a young, childless, married woman who has lately 'started wondering about babies,' (and simultaneously has taken to 'tearing off low-hanging leaves or tall grass heads with a kind of wanton energy') (JP, 140), tells of viewing a birth with her medical school boyfriend while she was in college. The details she remembers and the horror she feels at the process are reiterated almost word for word by Esther Greenwood. Myra remembers walking in the hospital, past 'blind, mushroom-colored embryos in the jars' and 'four leather-skinned cadavers, black as burnt turkey...' (JP, 138). Esther, too, sees four cadavers with 'leathery, purple-black skin,' and big glass jars of fetuses (BJ, 51). But what lingers with both women most strongly is the memory of the drugging of the patient and her subsequent forgetfulness of the pain of childbirth. Both blame the invention of the drug, which doesn't stop the pain, just induces later forgetfulness, a 'twilight sleep' (JP, 139; BJ, 53), on the sinister intents of men. Both view men as acting for their own good without a concern for women's experience. Myra first describes her horror at the false security induced by the drug.

Although erased from the mind's surface, the pain was there, somewhere, cut indelibly into one's quick—an empty, doorless, windowless corridor of pain. And then to be deceived by the waters of Lethe into coming back again, in all innocence, to conceive child after child! It was barbarous. It was a fraud dreamed up by men to continue the human race; reason enough for a woman to refuse childbearing altogether. (JP, 139)

Esther later recalls the same scene, using even the image of 'that long, blind, doorless and windowless corridor of pain' (BJ, 53) and noting that if women knew or remembered the pain they would forget about having children altogether (BJ, 53). More than 'Tongues of Stone,' written in 1955, 'Sweetie Pie and the Gutter Men,' written in May of 1959, shows not just the same incident but Plath's increased thematic awareness. Myra has begun to focus on her discontent—more importantly, finding its source in the negative implications of her role as wife/mother. She finds herself having to bite back her views concerning being 'just' a mother. She is depressed at the thought of joining the rest of women in this reproductive role and blames men for devising means to keep women unconscious of the pain involved. For Myra, this pain extends beyond the labor process and stretches into the rest of her potential lifetime as a mother. Myra's depression is presented less as a result of a personality defect and more as an understandable disgust with an undesired, unfulfilling expectation. She has begun to move into a clearer awareness of gender delineation and the politics of sexuality.

The fourth short story, 'Johnny Panic and the Bible of Dreams,' contains two shorter images rather than major events that move into *The Bell Jar*. The first is simply the description of a woman who enters the psychiatric clinic and whose dream the narrator seeks to record. The woman was brought to the Emergency Room because her tongue was stuck out and she couldn't return it to her mouth. This occurred during a party for her French-Canadian mother-in-law, whom she hated 'worse than pigs' (JP, 156). This same character appears equally briefly in the novel, in the state psychiatric ward, as Mrs. Tomolillo. Again, she has a hated French-Canadian mother-in-law, and again her symptom is the uncontrollable tongue which sticks out until it's swollen. The second image is more powerful, for it is crucial to both the story and the novel: the narrator's experience of electroshock treatment. In 'Johnny Panic and the Bible of Dreams,' the final scene is the administration of the shock treatment. In the misapplied shock, the narrator sees her first direct sight of Johnny Panic himself. He comes into view as she is 'shaken like a leaf in the teeth of glory,' while 'the air crackled with blue-tongued lightning-haloed angels' (JP, 166). The treatment is likewise described in *The Bell Jar*, when Dr. Gordon fails to properly administer the shock. 'Then something bent down and took hold of me and shook me like the end of the world. Whee-ee-ee-ee-ee-ee, it shrilled, through an air crackling with blue light' (BJ, 117).

What distinguishes this story from the three previously discussed is that for the first time the story is as strong a narrative as the novel. In part, this is because of the stylistic change to first-person. For the first time we have a conscious persona dealing with the experience of the breakdown. There is no additional narrator-filter to feeling and understanding the character. Further, 'Johnny Panic and the Bible of Dreams' is a short story which contains a very central theme of Plath's, one which she is building up to in *The Bell Jar* and one which has appeared in other stories throughout the '50's not related to the breakdown: the need to validate the realm of imagination and possibility against the 'real world,' the world of limited and stereotyped roles. In 'Johnny Panic,' for the first time in the stories relating the story of her breakdown, Plath's narrator is not becoming aware of the conflict, she already understands it and has begun to act in·response to it. She has taken up a battle that the other three narrators are just discovering might exist. It is this recognition and choice of action which thematically is the focus to almost all of Plath's fiction, even those stories which stand apart from the drafting of *The Bell Jar*.

Given the centrality of this theme, it is not totally coincidental that the two strongest characters in Plath's fiction, Esther Green-wood and the narrator of 'Johnny Panic,' are writers. Plath's major fictional characters, from Elizabeth Minton (in 'Sunday at the Mintons',' 1952) forward, are all incipient artists. That is not to say that all, or most, are professional artists. Rather, they are, as so many characters in feminist fictions, engaged in creating them-selves, reshaping the world around them to give significance to the actions and places in which they spiritually and actually reside. They come to see themselves as the creation of an imagination at odds with the culture and people around them. They are constantly striving to keep at bay the deadening, self-invalidating, oppressive sterility of the 'real world,' a world which devalues their experience and prohibits new patterns of thought and self awareness. Their true world is the realm of imagination, even if this imagination leads to socially defined madness. When not so extremely labeled, the characters are at least alienated from the technical, coldly rational world they exist in. They escape from this real world to the one of imagination, for none can accept a world which denies the power of fantasy, denies the right of each individual—regardless of gender—to be fully developed and fulfilled, denies (then electrical-ly and chemically obliterates) the fears and thoughts of adults without replacing them with stronger beliefs and dreams.

Thematically, the feared death of the imagination runs through-out all of Plath's fiction in the decade preceding publication of *The Bell Jar*. Plath's characters reverse Hamlet's cry: they wish to dream, not sleep, much less just exist. As Plath explains in the 'Cambridge Notes' excerpt from her journals:

What I fear most, I think, is the death of the imagination. When the sky outside is merely pink, and the rooftops merely black; that photographic mind which paradoxically tells the truth, but the worthless truth, about the world. It is that synthesizing spirit, that 'shaping' force, which prolifically sprouts and makes up its own worlds with more inventiveness than God which I desire. If I sit still and don't do anything, the world goes on beating like a slack drum, without meaning. We must be moving, working, making dreams to run toward; the poverty of life without dreams is too horrible to imagine; it is that kind of madness which is worst: the kind with fancies and hallucinations would be a Bosch-ish relief. (JP, 260)

The main characters in 'Sunday at the Mintons,' (1952), 'Superman and Paula Brown's New Snowsuit' (1955), 'The Wishing Box' (1956), 'All the Dead Dears' (1956/57), 'Stone Boy with Dolphin' (1957/58), and 'Johnny Panic and the Bible of Dreams' (1958) all express a need and determination to foster and live in a world governed more by that 'synthesizing spirit,' that God-like personal inventiveness, than the social strictures of the people around them. For example, Elizabeth Minton's fanciful daydreams are continually interrupted by her brother Henry, a demanding but practical man. Elizabeth's image for their differences is summed in her imagined view of the interior of their minds. Henry's mind would be 'flat and level, laid out with measured instruments in the broad, even-sunlight.... The air would be thick with their accurate ticking.' (JP, 301). Conversely, her mind would be 'a dark, warm room, with colored lights swinging and wavering ... and pictures ... [and] from somewhere sweetly coming, the sound of violins and bells' (JP, 301). Clearly her preference (and the author's) is for the vague impressionist world of her mind.

Likewise, in 'The Wishing Box,' Agnes Higgins despairs of her loss of dreams. She can remember 'her infinitely more creative childhood days' (JP, 206), but she seems doomed to be unable to recapture them in the adult world in which she now lives. Suicide finally releases her from her empty reality to another world, 'some far country unattainable to mortal men ... [where she is] waltzing with the dark, red-caped prince of her early dreams,' (JP, 210). More importantly, Agnes' death is a triumph, not a defeat, for she *does* reenter the world of the imagination.

Similarly, in 'Stone Boy with Dolphin' Dody Ventura longs for something to happen, for something to match the intensity of her dreams. Her dreams are peopled by visionaries:

In her third-floor attic room she listened, catching the pitch of last shrieks: listened: to witches on the rack, to Joan of Arc crackling at the stake, to anonymous ladies flaring like torches in the rending metal of Rivera roadsters, to Zelda enlightened, burning behind the bars of her madness. What visions were to be had come under thumbscrews, not in the mortal

257

comfort of a hot-water-bottle-cozy cot. Unwincing, in her mind's eye, she bared her flesh. (JP, 175)

Although all the characters mentioned (witches, Joan of Arc, Zelda) are 'mad,' their madness is the 'Bosch-ish relief' that Dody (and her creator) craves. This same craving is most graphically presented in 'Johnny Panic and the Bible of Dreams,' where the narrator's entire life's goal is to be the recorder of dreams, the treasurer of the imaginative world which both underlies and runs counter to the pragmatic world we recognize as 'reality.'

Plath's short stories show her development as a fiction writer. Stylistically and thematically they prefigure and serve as her apprenticeship for *The Bell Jar*. Without them as test grounds, *The Bell Jar* could not have been so rapidly produced, so strongly presented. After all the pre-tellings and thinking, in *The Bell Jar* Plath is able to move into her own narrative voice and pace. Her well-wrought and hard wrung apprenticeship yielded to a haunting powerful craftsmanship.

NOTES

1 Josephine Donovan, 'Sexual Politics in Sylvia Plath's Short Stories,' *Minnesota Review* (Spring, 1973), pp. 150–57.
2 Ted Hughes, 'Introduction,' in *Johnny Panic and the Bible of Dreams* by Sylvia Plath (New York: Harper Colophon, 1980), p. 3.
3 Ibid., p. 6.
4 Sylvia Plath, 'Tongues of Stone,' in *Johnny Panic and the Bible of Dreams* (New York: Harper Colophon. 1980), p. 262. Hereafter, all page references to short stories are from this edition and noted in the text (JP).
5 Sylvia Plath, *The Bell Jar* (New York: Bantam Books, 1972), p. 102. Hereafter all references to the novel refer to this edition and are noted in the text (BJ).

THE COLLECTED POEMS OF SYLVIA PLATH

Edited by Ted Hughes

New York and London, 1981

74. Laurence Lerner, 'Sylvia Plath,' *Encounter*

January 1982, 53–4

The most important book of poetry published this year is Sylvia Plath's *Collected Poems*. 'About time too' might be one's first, understandable reaction. It is 19 years since she died, and ten years since the last of the posthumous volumes: now at last everything has been gathered together, and edited with care and tact by Ted Hughes. All good things are worth waiting for, and reading through the volume makes it clear that she was one of the most remarkable poets of her time.

Let us take not one of the really well-known *Ariel* poems, but, to start with, a lesser-known piece that is short enough to be quoted in full. 'Mirror' was written in 1961, and published in *Crossing the Water*:

I am silver and exact. I have no preconceptions.
Whatever I see I swallow immediately
Just as it is, unmisted by love or dislike.
I am not cruel, only truthful—
The eye of a little god, four-cornered.
Most of the time I meditate on the opposite wall.
It is pink, with speckles. I have looked at it so long
I think it is a part of my heart. But it flickers.
Faces and darkness separate us over and over.
Now I am a lake. A woman bends over me.
Searching my reaches for what she really is.
Then she turns to those liars, the candles or the moon.
I see her back, and reflect it faithfully.
She rewards me with tears and an agitation of hands.

> I am important to her. She comes and goes.
> Each morning it is her face that replaces the darkness.
> In me she has drowned a young girl, and in me an old woman
> Rises toward her day after day, like a terrible fish.

This is a witty poem in the best sense, not only in the precision of the details, and the verbal sprightliness, but in the amusing self-importance given to the mirror. It is not as wild as, say, 'Lady Lazarus' or 'Fever 103°': its inventiveness shows no sign of spilling over into free association or surrealism. Yet it implies those other, more disturbing poems, and satisfying as it is in itself, it takes on a deeper resonance in the context of Sylvia Plath's work. Is the woman who bends over the mirror, for instance, to be seen as the author? We cannot say, but if she is, there is an extra irony in knowing that she is not yet 30 when she sees an old woman rising towards her; and the obsessive concern with itself given to the mirror takes on an extra resonance if it echoes the similar obsession in the author of the poem. This poem steps back from the terrible intensity of the experiences of *Ariel* while inviting us to remain aware of them. I find it an almost perfect poem, stronger for its limitations.

It undercuts at least one popular view of Sylvia Plath, that her early work is controlled, formal, even superficial, and the later poems make true contact with her anxieties, and so are imbued with a new power. There is some truth in this, but it should not be taken too rigidly. Here we have a late poem that gains force from its ability to stand back. True, it does not stand back in quite the same way as the poems of *The Colossus* do. Take 'Spinster,' written five years earlier:

> Now this particular girl
> During a ceremonious April walk
> With her latest suitor
> Found herself, of a sudden, intolerably struck
> By the birds' irregular babel
> And the leaves' litter....

What is the difference? Is it just the greater formality· of this poem in half-rhymes and regular stanzas? Is it the echo of Auden in the way the half-rhymes are used for sinister effect? There seems to be the same disturbing experience behind it as behind 'Mirror': both, in their different ways, keep a superb distance from hysteria.

Yet it is not difficult to find poems in *The Colossus* that would seem at home in *Ariel*—the marvellous 'Lorelei', for instance. The fatal lure of a siren's song provides the perfect subject for Sylvia Plath, obsessed as she was with the horrible beauty of dying, and this poem blends its death-wish with a cool awareness of its folly:

> Sisters, your song
> Bears a burden too weighty
> For the whorled ear's listening
>
> Here, in a well-steered country,
> Under a balanced ruler....

The impudent assurance of the pun ('well-steered') reminds us of detachment while mocking it slightly: like all her best poetry, it neither surrenders to hysteria nor escapes from it. And the haunting last line ('Stone, stone, ferry me down there') is enriched by the stone-like qualities of the underwater shapes of which we have glimpsed a vision.

Of course in a poetic career that lasted only seven years we would expect continuity. In stressing this, and in praising the control of the early poems, am I suggesting that the great frenetic outbursts which have become so famous are artistically inferior? Some enthusiasts for 'confessional poetry' would say at this point, So much the worse for art; but that is a very superficial conception of the relation of art to experience. Artistic success that destroys the living nerve for the sake of an elegant pattern produces only literary exercises, but there is a deeper and more necessary art that seizes the experience and brings it to life in language, involving the reader's emotions, where artlessness might leave him cold and even resentful. It is the miracle of a poem like 'Lady Lazarus' that though it seems a wild and incoherent outpouring of terror and self-hatred, it also has the true control of art. Not, this time, through the imposition of any formal metrical pattern, but through the use of repetitions that capture the frenzy of the speaking voice and find a pattern in it, and above all through the deliberate self-dramatisation that presents suicide as a form of role-playing, almost of comedy:

> Dying
> Is an art like everything else.
> I do it exceptionally well.
>
> I do it so it feels like hell.

I do it so it feels real.
I guess you could say I've a call.

The last line can be said with a giggle, as a boast, or as wry
self-deprecation, and each implies the possibilities of the other.
The poem has deservedly become one of the best-known of our
time.

75. William H. Pritchard, 'An Interesting Minor Poet?' *New Republic*

30 December 1981, 32–5

William H. Pritchard (b. 1932) is Professor of English at
Amherst. He is widely regarded for his work on modern and
contemporary poets.

During Sylvia Plath's short life of just over 30 years, she saw only
one book of her poems published: *The Colossus* (1960). She had
prepared a second one, even worked out the order of its poems, and
that appeared as *Ariel* in 1965 after her death, with a number of
poems added which were written in her final months. Two further
volumes were published posthumously: *Crossing the Water* (1971),
containing mainly earlier poems, and *Winter Trees*, in the same
year, containing 18 late ones plus *Three Women*, a lugubrious 'poem
for three voices' written for the BBC. The result of such piecemeal,
though perhaps advisable, publication was to create confusion in
our minds about those remarkable seven years (1956–1963) in
which 224 poems were written and finished. Now, 18 years after
her death by suicide in February 1963, we are at last given a
thoroughly responsible presentation of the poems in chronological
order, more than a third of them not previously published in book
form. The old volume titles have been dropped, and poems are
simply grouped under their appropriate year, dated by month and
day whenever possible. The result is to make her appear an

altogether larger and more satisfying poet than this reader had taken her to be.

Reading these poems through in chronological order calls into question the received idea of the clever craftswoman producing beautifully shaped objects, almost too beautifully shaped, who suddenly achieved a 'breakthrough' into—in the phrase of one of that book's reviewers—the 'raw genius' of the later *Ariel* poems. You could even read it as a lesson in liberation, with the early volume coming at the end of those evil 1950s (and she went to Smith too!) and the later one heralding, along with Robert Lowell and Anne Sexton and lesser talents, a confessional freedom from the repressive, whether prosodic or personal:

> What a thrill—
> My thumb instead of an onion.
>
> —'Cut'
>
> Dying
> Is an art, like everything else.
> I do it exceptionally well.
>
> I do it so it feels like hell.
>
> —'Lady Lazarus'

Never mind that in both poems, as in so many of her other late ones, there was not only a bitter but a mockingly self-lacerating and playful wit, a pure revel in felicities of language ('My thumb instead of an onion'—some fun there after you get through wincing) which the desperateness of her running-out life somehow gave birth to. Too many readers, younger ones especially, approached these later poems with religious awe as if 'Sylvia' (or as they would now say, 'Plath') were to be treated in a manner befiting Jesus Christ; it was she who had died for our sins—so the distressed young student might feel, especially if female. Of course the backlash wasn't long in coming. One college newspaper in the early 1970s printed 24 Sylvia Plath jokes, grisly riddles the mildest of which by far went 'Why did SP cross the road?' 'To be struck by an oncoming vehicle.'

Ted Hughes has done an exemplary job in editing these poems, writing notes to them year by year (one only wishes for more notes, since they are so interesting), and giving us a generous selection of the juvenile pre-1956 poems. And he strikes the right note in his introduction when he remarks that 'her attitude to her verse was artisan-like: if she couldn't get a table out of the material, she was quite happy to get a chair, or even a toy. The end product for her was not so much a successful poem, as something that had temporarily exhausted her ingenuity.' The right note, for surely she was one of the most ingenious poets in this latter half of our century; and to speak of her in terms of artisan and chair-maker, rather than transmitter of pure inspiration from heaven upstairs or downstairs hell, does justice to her resourcefulness and skill as a maker.

She did not always do justice to herself in this respect; or rather, she sometimes spoke as if formal ingenuity and true feeling might not be compatible. For example, this remark made about 'Point Shirley,' a poem she completed in January of 1959: 'Oddly powerful and moving to me in spite of rigid formal structure.' 'Point Shirley' was written at the time she had begun to attend (along with Anne Sexton and George Starbuck) Robert Lowell's writing seminar at Boston University, and the poem's debt to Lowell's work is evident. But consider its opening two stanzas, in which her grandmother's house is evoked:

> From Water-Tower Hill to the brick prison
> The shingle booms, bickering under
> The sea's collapse.
> Snowcakes break and welter. This year
> The gritted wave leaps
> The seawall and drops onto a bier
> Of quahog chips,
> Leaving a salty mash of ice to whiten
>
> In my grandmother's sand yard. She is dead,
> Whose laundry snapped and froze here, who
> Kept house against
> What the sluttish, rutted sea could do.
> Squall waves once danced
> Ship timbers in through the cellar window;
> A thresh-tailed, lanced
> Shark glittered in the geranium bed—
>
> Such collusion of mulish elements
> She wore her broom straws to the nub.

This may have been, as her biographer Edward Butscher says it was, a deliberate attempt to capture Lowell's seaside grays; but the strict stanza, the rhymes and half-rhymes, above all the careful syntax and enjambed lines—even running over from one stanza to the next—show an attention to (in Frost's words) 'the sound of sense' that is compelling and demanding of any reader's agility. The continuations and suspensions which the speaking voice must make to navigate these lines are surely central to the poem's power. If we may correct Sylvia Plath, it moves us not in spite of but partly because of its 'rigid formal structure.' And it is quite different from anything Lowell had done in *Lord Weary's Castle*—where the blank verse proceeds in a breathless, hurtling way—or was doing in *Life Studies*, which appeared in 1959.

During the preceding two years, Plath had grown extremely skilled at rendering sentence sounds in poems which this volume allows us to read for the first time. Here is the opening of 'The Great Carbuncle' (1957):

> We came over the moor-top
> Through air streaming and green-lit,
> Stone farms foundering in it,
> Valleys of grass altering
> In a light neither of dawn
> Nor nightfall, our hands, faces
> Lucent as porcelain, the earth's
> Claim and weight gone out of them.

And it continues just as expertly. Imagine deciding, as evidently she did, that such a poem was not quite good enough to be included in her first book! When she spoke (in another remark quoted by Hughes) with respect to the admirable 'Mushrooms' (which did make *The Colossus*) of 'my absolute lack of judgment when I've written something: whether it's trash or genius,' she spoke with her characteristic either/or absoluteness. But 'The Great Carbuncle,' or 'Above the Oxbow' (here my Connecticut River sentimentality may be intruding), or 'In Midas' Country,' or 'Child's Park Stones' (a first rate poem), or 'Green Rock, Winthrop Bay' are not trash— perhaps not genius either, but something else, less sensational: assured performances, with a technical control wholly adequate to sustain the observant, grave, responsive presence that makes itself felt audibly over the carefully tracked course of stanza and whole poem. John Frederick Nims said it succinctly when he suggested that young writers should be advised to 'forget *Ariel* for a while;

study *The Colossus.*' With the new volume, this study can more intelligently take place.

If she could only 'let things slip a bit,' said a reviewer in admiration of her earlier poems, she will do something really special. What happened in fact was that she let them slip with a vengeance into the 'stream of repulsions' (the phrase is Hugh Kenner's) that inform the poems from the last months of her life. Ted Hughes left her in October of 1962. During that month she wrote or finished 25 poems, including the ones for which she is best known. Beginning with one new to me, 'The Detective,' we read on through, among others, the bee poems, 'The Applicant,' 'Daddy,' 'Medusa,' 'Lesbos,' 'Fever 103°,' 'Cut,' and 'Lady Lazarus.' Much adjectival overkill has been employed by reviewers attempting in desperation of vocabulary to outdo the poems themselves, and George Steiner, never at a loss on such occasions, has referred to 'Daddy' as the 'Guernica of modern poetry.' But really it is nothing of the sort, reading now like a very clever, very nasty, very hopeless horror song which holds up partly by its resourceful way of exploiting our reticence and embarrassment at what we are hearing:

> I have always been scared of *you,*
> With your Luftwaffe, your gobbledygoo.
> And your neat mustache
> And your Aryan eye, bright blue.
> Panzer-man, panzer-man, O You—

Poor Otto Plath, a diabetic professor of biology at Boston University who had the misfortune to combine the diabetes with gangrene and broncho-pneumonia, so double-crossed his daughter by dying too soon, scarcely deserved such a tribute (I know, it's really a myth). And the stanza, indeed the whole poem, contains much that is repellent about Plath's poetry: the clever 'gobbledygoo,' a word like the one English teachers used to write on freshman themes; the relentless caricaturing of another, in tough baby-talk, all done in the interests of 'art.' And the panzer-man repetition. Earlier in 'Daddy' we hear that 'The tongue stuck in my jaw': 'It stuck in a barb wire snare / Ich, ich, ich, ich,' and the poet's tongue sticks also in 'Elm' ('These are the isolate slow faults / That kill, that kill, that kill'), in 'The Bee Meeting' ('They will not smell my fear, my fear, my fear'), in 'The Applicant,' and elsewhere.

There are many more questions now, fired off by an 'Ich' whose tongue really isn't stuck at all, but extraordinarily adept and daring in its leaps and spins; like the one done around the first line of 'Lady Lazarus,' 'Dying is an art':

> I do it so it feels like hell.
> I do it so it feels real.
> I guess you could say I've a call.
>
> It's easy enough to do it in a cell.
> It's easy enough to do it and stay put.
> It's the theatrical
>
> Comeback in broad day
> To the same place, the same face, the same brute
> Amused shout:
>
> 'A miracle!'
> That knocks me out.

A brilliant show, but there may be a problem about how many times one wants to watch it again. That is why encountering it here, as poem no. 198 in a chronological sequence, is a very good thing for its continued life. She had done, could do so much with words; now she had to do this, *would* do this new turn.

But as 'Lady Lazarus' goes on to say, 'There is a charge...a very large charge/For a word or a touch/Or a bit of blood.' The sad joke is that the reader—surrounded by all those other poets in the imaginary museum who can be summoned up in a twinkling for a performance—really doesn't have to pay very much to watch the show. It was Sylvia Plath who paid the charge in full, and one feels in reading the final 12 poems in this collection, those written in the month and the days of 1963 which preceded her death, form a sort of coda, or perhaps a rehearsal for a new part to be played somewhere else.

The mood is set by the bleakly wonderful 'Sheep in Fog' ('My bones hold a stillness, the far / Fields melt my heart') and holds largely through until the last poem, 'Edge,' in which 'The woman is perfected. / Her dead / Body wears the smile of accomplishment.' But just before the finality of 'Edge' comes 'The Balloons,' a touching surprise after the histrionic agonies of more sensational Plath-poems. For four stanzas, composed with that fluidity of motion she had grown so expert at achieving years before, these

'Guileless and clear/Oval soul-animals' are celebrated for being themselves, for living with the mother and her children since Christmas, for keeping them company. Two last stanzas address the daughter:

> Your small
>
> Brother is making
> His balloon squeak like a cat.
> Seeming to see
> A funny pink world he might eat on the other side of it,
> He bites,
>
> Then sits
> Back, fat jug
> Contemplating a world clear as water.
> A red
> Shred in his little fist.

This was finished a week before she died, and unlike the balloons it remains with us, in its own words

> Delighting
> The heart like wishes or free
> Peacocks blessing
> Old ground with a feather
> Beaten in starry metals.

For years I have endorsed Irving Howe's limiting judgment of Sylvia Plath as an 'interesting minor poet'. But I don't think anyone who submits to this collection is likely to be comfortable with that judgment. She was rather, was indeed—as the expression goes—something else.

76. Dave Smith, 'Sylvia Plath, the Electric Horse,' *American Poetry Review*

January 1982, 43–46

Dave Smith (b. 1942) is a poet and critic who teaches at Virginia Commonwealth University.

This extract is a part of Smith's essay on women poets, 'Some Recent American Poetry: Come All Ye Fair and Tender Ladies.'

We know her. How odd it is to say that of a poet dead nearly two decades. It is certainly not the Truth, yet we feel we know her and in important ways it is the truth to say we know her. For many readers Sylvia Plath is still the phosphorescent ingenue of contemporary American poetry, not a woman who would be now on the edge of fifty, a woman whose children are nearing their majority ages. She is, almost, *the* American woman poet, yet she is featured in British anthologies of their poetry. No one knew Sylvia Plath less than she knew herself but *The Collected Poems* is, I think, beyond anything else the record of her struggle to know herself, which was the struggle finally to accept the self she was, beyond all choosing and posturing. That is why we know her. If we do not really *know* her poetry, her prose, her letters—in the sense that one means when one has immersed oneself in another's written life, or even in the sense of the scholar who has 'mastered the canon'—we continue to speak of her as if we do know her. At parties, in lectures, in conversations we invoke her name to describe a kind of poetry. Sometimes it is in derogation, sometimes in admiration, and lately as the name of places, mostly unpleasant, we had to pass through. No one who invokes her name feels compelled to explain who she is. Or was. Can we really say *was* about Sylvia Plath? None of the women I have reviewed here could have written as they have, not quite, without the example of Sylvia Plath. If they breathe poetry, they breathe that which has Plath in it. They may not know this, may not actually know her poems, are unlikely to know her. Because these days her absence is more pronounced than her presence, they may know her glancingly but not wholly. Still Sylvia Plath's presence abides in the ways any contemporary poem gets written; in what is possible, what is assumed, and most especially in the conviction that the self and its myths—their constructions and sources, evidences, spoors—are the only true and inevitable subject for the poet.

Reading *The Collected Poems* straight through on a gray fall day, after a week of dipping in and out of it, I am astonished to discover this poet is not the Plath I have vaguely remembered, the Plath I have called *interesting*, that epithet, when students jittery with their fresh discoveries of her, have asked what I think. So caught up in this cranky, beautiful, maudlin, neurotic, soaring book am I that I have rummaged the shelves to read those critical assessments of contemporary poetry which I have casually acquired out of a mild intention to read them someday. I discovered what I did know: she has become a critical industry, the subject of all manner of intense speculation. There is even a book whose purpose is to set at rest the burning question of whether she is the creator of her ex-husband Ted Hughes or the creation of that poet. Everyone, it appears, has had to have a say about her. No index is complete without her name. There is much talk of the Plath myth, many sincere assertions that this essay and that study will penetrate the myth and lay bare the real Sylvia Plath: here she is obsessed with love, there she is a hate-monger, her trouble is men, in spades; she is schizophrenic or depressed. Robert Phillips, in *The Confessional Poets,* says 'In the act of committing her confession to paper, she was committing her life to death.' I bet Robert Phillips wishes he hadn't said that. I think it is balderdash. Doubtless there is good and even sufficient passion in all the speculative muttering her poetry has engendered but most of it seems little more than a snipe hunt. She can't be explained away. Maybe we feel if we can't explain her we can't explain ourselves. We all feel we know her.

Yet if we know her, clearly we haven't a clue. Rummaging through my books, I keep returning to her *Johnny Panic and the Bible of Dreams* and to her *Letters Home.* But my hand will not stay long from *The Collected Poems*—and not because I make any attempt to correlate the poems with the prose and the letters—because the poems are just there like members of our family, the suspicious members. This book is the record of a life. That is an ordinary thing to say but not less true for saying it. Her life in most respects is ordinary, even typically American. Yet it is like the life of a crowd all at once, only a special, enormously talented, complicated, hyper-hungry crowd. In that crowd the real Sylvia Plath will not stand up, quite. Perhaps we may be self-generous enough to say we are that crowd and through her poems we almost see ourselves. This is why we know her and don't know her.

Flip Wilson, the black comedian, has told us 'What you see is what you get.' But is it what we want? How do we know what we ͜ ͞id Sylvia Plath know? There are as many answers to that as there are dissections of her poetry. Her selves wanted different things, with varying intensity, and maybe her great struggle was the attempt to manage those selves. At any rate we shall see, no one can doubt, a surf of reviews, views, studies, and reappraisals, and if the smugness is not too thick we may learn something valuable. But we can learn better from the poems. They have stung me as never before and they compel me to talk, too, about who Sylvia Plath is, who I knew so little until *The Collected Poems*.

Many of us spend, and have spent, our literal and literary lives well outside the New York–Cambridge corridor and we just can't fully understand the young woman Sylvia Plath was, the woman who seems so desperately to have wanted the coinage and spoils of the eastern life. Smith and Wellesley colleges, the starlet writer for *Mademoiselle*, meetings with famous writers and teachers, a Fulbright to England's Cambridge University, publication not merely of a first collection of poems at age twenty-eight but a truly significant book, publication before that of poems in magazines which would bring her eastern certification—this was some of what she wanted and got. Where the roads diverged she took the intellectual one, the well-traveled one. But it wasn't enough. She wanted to be perfect, a new Keats. She says in 'Cambridge Notes,' written at twenty-four, 'I too want to be important.' And she adds, 'By being different.' Even in the boonies we understand that. Only she by god did it.

Yet, I think, Sylvia Plath also wanted another eastern road, one that she denigrated as the scribbling young intellectual. She wanted to be very pretty, charming, well-dressed, well-heeled, well-loved, well-married, the kind of young woman who shimmers early on and goes sadly, painfully soft in John Updike's fiction. She wanted to be an intellectual junior leaguer. That, too, is a kind of perfection. And it is hardly different from the dreams of most young Americans, excepting eastern idiosyncrasies. Out here we may not seek exactly the objects of her desires, but the desire is something we know all too well. We recognize that desire in her physical ache to achieve the 'perfection' of status she would attach to publishing in the 'right' magazines. She says, '*New Yorker* rejection of poems may smack me in the stomach any morning. God, it is pretty poor when a life depends on such ridiculous sitting ducks as those poems, ready for editors' grapeshot.' Sylvia Plath, too, could be 'shot down.' She wanted the perfect life, fame,

fortune, glory, love. To what shall the heart be given? Her wanting
turns so scary at times that in 'Cambridge Notes' she writes herself
an homiletic reminder:

PS: Winning or losing an argument, receiving an acceptance or rejection, is
no proof of the validity or value of personal identity. One may be wrong,
mistaken, a poor craftsman, or just ignorant—but this is no indication of
the true worth of one's total human identity: past, present, and future!

She wanted to be a good girl, a good woman. That sort of corn
pone was something Plath had to chuck out to be the poet she was
destined to be. Maybe she never had a choice; maybe her only
choice was to learn to ignore the self that was a good, conscientious
soldier. By now I may have fabricated entirely some words I *think* I
heard the writer Shelby Foote say twenty years ago. I think he told
my class that he would stick into the oven the head of any wife who
got in the way of his book. I was young, appalled, angered, and
confused. Weren't writers noble citizens? Perhaps Foote meant that
metaphorically, if he said it. But there is Faulkner saying that any
number of old ladies might be sacrificed for Keats's 'Ode on a
Grecian Urn.' All the necessary do-gooders in society, including
those inside us, may very well *understand* what Faulkner and Foote
mean, but they do not know it as the obsessive writer does. This
writer is bound to the relentless pursuit of perfection, and
perfection changes so that the pursuit is both endless and
increasingly insular. The perfectionist ceases to care about the
conventional world and then the stakes go up. Failure often
becomes the poet's fear and a looming companion. This is why
when Sylvia Plath has six years of incredibly intense writing behind
her at the age of twenty-nine she says in 'Context' that 'The poets I
delight in are possessed by their poems as by the rhythms of their
own breathing.' Ted Hughes talks about this in the fine introduction to *Johnny Panic and the Bible of Dreams:*

It was only when she gave up that effort to 'get outside' herself, and finally
accepted the fact that her painful subjectivity was her real theme, and that
the plunge into herself was her only real direction, and that poetic
strategies were her only real means, that she suddenly found herself in full
possession of her genius—with all the special skills that had developed as if
by biological necessity, to deal with those unique inner conditions.

This change of life sounds easy enough. It sounds as if Plath
matured enough to select the life of the artist and abandon all other

dreams of perfection. But it was not so. In *Letters Home* there is ample evidence of the girl who wanted to belong back home even as she panted to live in Yeats's old London flat. She is sincerely devoted to seeing Mr. Hughes has the wifely support which will make him a great man even as she notes, dazzled, all the great men and women she is meeting. Her letters show you a young wife and mother in curlers, surrounded by diapers, frenetic trying to be a perfect maiden, trying to control the insurgent writer in her. I keep thinking that had she lived she would be sporting L.L. Bean finery and Sperry Topsiders. No, it wasn't an easy change which would allow her to isolate the self that wrote the poems at the expense of those others. Sylvia Plath had given her heart to nothing but the *idea* of perfection, not the practice of perfection. But she had no choice about that. She was a writer, however she might make poems that were stages upon which her other selves kept trying out. The maiden she wanted to be was constantly losing to the poet she was and she knew it. She says it in 'Spinster':

> And round her house she set
> Such a barricade of barb and check
> Against such mutinous weather
> As no mere insurgent man could hope to break
> With curse, fist, threat
> Or love, either

Though we might think so, she would not find it ironic that six years after 'Spinster' she is writing about *kindness* when she says abruptly 'The blood jet is poetry, / There is no stopping it.'

During those six years Plath had learned to write what would be her poem, the poem which was unlike any other, the poem Ted Hughes and others call the Ariel poem. I like it that this poem takes the name of her horse, the horse she is hell-bent on in a pre dawn ride that is all fluid feeling: 'Stasis in darkness. / Then the substanceless blue / Pour of tor and distances.' Nobody ever rode a horse exactly like that, then she did. She not only rode it, but as the physical meld of the images shows she became it in blood and hoof and stride and foam. When she calls what this comes to 'The dew that flies / Suicidal, at one with the drive / Into the red / Eye, cauldron of morning…,' it is not suicide that interests her but the ebb and surge of passion. It has to be sexual and has to feel total. Plath did not, of course, come to the Ariel poem without labour.

The Collected Poems shows as none of her single volumes do the chorus of voices she had been hearing. Stevens, Ransom, Roethke, Eliot, Hardy, Hopkins, some Frost and Robinson, of course Shakespeare, even a little William Carlos Williams and not a little Emily Dickinson. They were mostly the hard chargers, the stress makers with swift, clattering boots. Ted Hughes may have been responsible for reinforcing this direction but Plath's pre-Hughes juvenilia proves she was no sweet singer ever. Evanescence wasn't enough for her; she had to be the flame and the radiance, the electrical horse. She came close as early as 1956 with 'Street Song' and 'Black Rook in Rainy Weather.' She failed often and often had partial successes but on such an ambitious scale that it seems unfair to compare her with most younger poets. In time she wrote more than her share of poems which altered ordinary reality for the rest of us, 'Lady Lazarus,' 'Cut,' 'Death & Co.,' 'The Moon and the Yew Tree,' 'Daddy,' 'Blackberrying,' and one of my favorites 'Among the Narcissi.' There was that brief tour de force 'The Munich Mannequins' where she wrote 'Perfection is terrible, it cannot have children.' She meant that perfection is barren because it is absolute. She also meant the perfectionist should not be allowed to have children because they will be neglected. One of the most finely terrible poems was the last one she wrote, 'Edge,' which begins 'The woman is perfected.' Ted Hughes has spoken of the true poet's need to lay hold to the power circuit of the universe, a metaphor for the life that is in poetry as well as the life that poetry is. There are not many willing to pay the toll for that power. Sylvia Plath's *The Collected Poems* is a record of how she learned to ride that electric horse sitting, then trotting, then galloping, finally becoming the current, the motion itself. *The Collected Poems* is that shimmering change, a gothic fairy tale with the properties of dry ice: it keeps, it burns, it lives.

Poetry became Sylvia Plath's life. It did not kill her except where it failed her. The record of these poems, 224 written after 1956—many in jets that amazingly come one after another on the same day—and 50 written before 1956 (selected from 220 plus, Hughes says in his introduction), is the drive toward fusion of herself and poetry, a life she meant to perfect as deliberately and single-mindedly as Yeats had. There will be many arguments down the road about what, if anything, Plath perfected and a lot of talk about poets killing themselves. They don't have to kill themselves for art, but they won't amount to much without a killing drive. Moreover what does it matter how she died? I don't know why she killed herself. I don't care. And I don't think it helps us to know the value of her poetry when we hear the sort of gibberish that is in 'Ariel's Flight: The Death of Sylvia Plath,' by N.J.C. Andreason, who says:

The death of Sylvia Plath seems to have resulted from a complex interaction between personal conflicts, the strain of her creative drive, and recurrent psychiatric illness—three factors that hovered over her life and struck with vicious energy during its last months. The role of each of these must be examined and weighed. The weight of the evidence suggests that psychiatric illness must be implicated as the primary factor.

Suppose we knew without a doubt what caused her death? What does that change? It will not explain nor can it alter the poems. It is perverse logic which begins with the fact of Plath's suicide and works back to find the poems as scripts of illness. Poetry kept Sylvia Plath alive; her poems are ectoplasmic with the will to live, to be as right as poetry can be, to be unequivocally, seriously, perfectly the voice of the poem as magical as a heartbeat. That is a burden no poet can bear forever, and it surprises any poet who bears it at all. Plath knew this in the end of 'Poppies in October':

> O my God, what am I
> That these late mouths should cry open
> In a forest of frost, in a dawn of cornflowers.

Maybe Sylvia Plath wanted too much life. We shall be likely to think that is something peculiarly and sinisterly American. We have lots of psychiatrists and psycho-critics to tell us what happens when you want too much, too fast, and how you can get into corners where even the walls accuse you. But the Faust myth tells us how little new there is under the sun. And it breaks our hearts every time. It will be a hard heart that doesn't break at Sylvia Plath's story. I do not mean that we ought not, as we will anyway, sit before this book as before the open casket of one we loved and swap the prickly, picky stories and assays and conjectures and lies—good and bad—by which we keep alive the dead. I mean she tried to stay alive. And she did keep alive. The poems, famous and unknown, brilliant and blurred, show us that. They have made it possible for others to know and to enter the poem's struggle for life. Sylvia Plath cannot be blamed for all the weird, silly, decadent poems that followed her anymore than the Beatles can be blamed for Wendy and the Spasmodics. Or whatever. Her dying may have been a failure greater than ours but is not her life somehow also greater than ours? More intense, closer to the heat? We know her because the shape of her words contains the shape of our lives. In a poem written during her thirtieth year, during the month of her death, she calls words 'Axes/After whose stroke the wood rings,/And the echoes!' She was letting us know, as she had known for some time, that the chips could fall where they might. Perfect or not, she was a poet. She would be nothing else so long as the lightning kept striking, as Jarrell might have said. That is what I feel in *The Collected Poems*, the crack and sizzle of lightning that Mrs. Shelley invited down to create life. We can no more turn away from Sylvia Plath than we have been able to escape the unnamed creature we, not Mrs. Shelley, dubbed Frankenstein's Monster, the monster we persist in regarding as Death. If you think you know Sylvia Plath, read her again. For the first time.

77. Michael Kirkham, 'Sylvia Plath,' *Queen's Quarterly*

Spring 1984, 153–66

Michael Kirkham (b. 1934) grew up in England and was educated at Oxford and the University of London. Author of books on Robert Graves and Edward Thomas, he is Professor of English at the University of Toronto, Canada.

Ted Hughes has provided an annotated, chronological arrangement of Sylvia Plath's poetry. The editorial matter is admirably succinct and to the point. The notes consist mainly of explanatory biographical details and quotations from Plath's own descriptions of the poems. The edition includes a brief introduction, a generous selection and a complete list of uncollected juvenilia, and a concordance with the published volumes. Hughes has established for the poems written before 1960, a selection of which comprised the contents of *The Colossus* (1960), an approximate order and for those written after, almost all in typescripts dated by the poet, an exact order. It is satisfying to have at last a clear view of the emergence, elaboration and interweaving of her themes; frequently a sequence of thought—images varied or extended—can be traced from poem to poem. Even more satisfying for those disposed to resist the critical consensus, the evidence of continuous development strengthens their case against the evaluative assumptions that seemed to underly the original division of Plath's later work, in the three posthumous volumes, into poems written between 1960 and April–May 1962 (*Crossing the Water*), and poems written in the last nine or ten months of her life (most of *Ariel* and *Winter Trees*). Whether an accident of publishing or not, the same assumptions are implicit in Hughes's description of the poems collected in *Crossing the Water*: 'In retrospect one can see that these are little safe planets floating near the solar conflagration of *Ariel*.' 'Safe' suggests that courting danger is not only courageous but also poetically more rewarding.

The appearance of this important collection of the work of an outstanding contemporary poet calls for a new way of looking at her craft. In what follows I shall attempt to offer a fresh perspective on Plath's writing.

The decisive event in Sylvia Plath's life, inflicting an emotional wound that never healed, was, it seems, the death of her father when she was eight. The facts are only too familiar. The traumatic effect and the meaning it came to have for her are suggested by her comment on 'Daddy': 'Here is a poem spoken by a girl with an Electra complex. Her father died while she thought he was God.' For her, it re-enacted the myth of the Fall. A journal entry reads: 'My father died, we moved inland. Whereon those nine years of my life sealed themselves off like a ship in a bottle—beautiful, inaccessible, obsolete, a fine, white flying myth.' This has the ingredients of a poem. 'Obsolete,' a word that returns in the poetry, hints at ambivalent feelings: is it a myth, a state of being, to be re-entered or disowned? The absent father casts a shadow over much of her work. A disabling agent in her emotions, it is not only a recurrent theme; it is there also in the pervasive sense of fragmentation and alienation. That, however, is only half the story.

Ted Hughes has described 'the central experience' of her poetry as the 'shattering of the self, and the labour of fitting it together again or finding a new one.' Rebuilding and fitting together are what, for example, 'The Colossus' and 'The Stones' (the last piece in the sequence 'Poem for a Birthday') are about. Only, in the former it is the reassembling of the statue of her father; in the latter it is the remaking of herself. The first always, by implication, includes the second, but self-renewal is not always figured as depending on restoration of the father. Plath came to feel that the need of the lost father, the identification of herself with him, rather than the loss itself, was her prison, and 'Daddy,' notably, in an ambiguous gesture of repudiation, proclaims her release from the tyranny of his image.

Plath has been praised and criticized for being either a confessional or an extremist poet. The labels no longer matter. Extremism, at least, identifies a partial truth: that her poetry favours extreme situations and emotions, and that, in the painful last months of her life after her separation from Hughes, when she wrote of 'going through and facing the worst, not hiding from it,' this reflected a deliberate choice; these are facts, which say something about the character though not the value of her poetry. But 'confessional' has proved an unhelpful and frequently a misleading epithet. Certainly it does not describe Plath's intentions as she explained them to Peter Orr: 'I cannot sympathize with these cries from the heart....I believe that one should be able to control and manipulate experience, even the most terrifying, like madness, being tortured...and one should be able to manipulate these experiences with an informed and an intelligent mind.' The poetry itself, critics now agree, is the antithesis of anything that 'confessional' might suggest: controlled, manipulative, dramatic—as in her decision to face the worst, she is a peculiarly *deliberate* poet. She makes her poems, it is true, out of subjective experience; many of them are, in her own words, 'psychic landscapes'; but the autobiographical details are absorbed into what has been called 'mythicized biography.' The states of mind most frequently expressed are the result of mental sickness or mental suffering; some poems draw on her experience in hospitals; but Thom Gunn's gibe, in an essay recently reprinted, at poets who '*boast* about experience in hospitals or mental institutions,' if it is meant for her, misses the target by a mile.

These are no longer the critical issues. The poems show not lack of control but sometimes too much or the wrong kind of control. It is her method of dramatizing and distancing personal emotion that must be reassessed. Poems that, in dramatizing sick or extreme states of feeling, exhibit a fierce, witty, sardonic resilience should be distinguished from those that inflate subjective suffering by identifying it too readily with objective horrors or, in a greed for significance, by prematurely giving universal, archetypal status to private experience. A simple phrase in 'Pheasant,' an attractive poem uncharacteristically focused on the external world, identifies the quality that, for me, marks Plath's best writing. The poem celebrates the vivid intrusion one winter of a pheasant (visiting or trespassing upon man's domain?); it is a Frostian commonsensical, understated replaying of Lawrence's 'Snake': 'It is simply in its element./That gives it a kingliness, a right.' It comes immediately after, and takes up a thread of thought from, a poem written two days earlier, 'Among the Narcissi'; for Plath, always vigilant against the seductions of narcissism, the closing lines of 'Pheasant' bear a secret message: 'It was sunning in the narcissi. / I trespass stupidly. *Let be, let be.*' Taking our cue, then, from this injunction, we may say that the distinction is between a poetry that, however forcefully, 'lets be,' and a poetry that seeks to dominate, its contents—between, shall we say, a poetry of the will and a willful poetry. It may be framed in terms of the following oppositions: the dramatic and the theatrical, statement (or understatement) and overstatement, implicit and imposed analogical thinking.

The terse power and concentrated thought of Plath's art is best examined in a brief, undemonstrative poem, such as 'Event.' Here are the first three stanzas and the fifth:

> How the elements solidify!—
> The moonlight, that chalk cliff
> In whose rift we lie
>
> Back to back. I hear an owl cry
> From its cold indigo.
> Intolerable vowels enter my heart.
>
> The child in the white crib revolves and sighs,
> Opens its mouth now, demanding.
> His little face is carved in pained, red wood....

> Where apple bloom ices the night
> I walk in a ring,
> A groove of old faults, deep and bitter....

The verse imitates the inexorable rigidity of fact: it seems to sculpt in words the wordless pain (an inarticulate cry of vowels) of the poet's estrangement from her husband. They lie in bed as if petrified in their posture of apartness. It is evident from the images of petrifaction and division and how the one entails the other that Blake's *Book of Urizen* had settled into a substratum of her mind. In Blake's myth the fall, the void opened by Urizen's abstraction of himself from the society of eternals, is simultaneous and identical with the creation; the solidity of creation, which is the division and constriction of unbounded immensity and eternal change into fixed, separate forms. 'A wide world of solid obstructions' is the ultimate consequence of Urizen's self-withdrawal and self-enclosure. It is doubtless a simplification, but one that shows how Plath is using Blake's imagery, to say that the creation of solidity signifies the destruction of love.

The banishment of love is realized, almost palpably, as an 'intolerable' physical ache, but also from the first line the meaning of that ache *grows*, organically, out of the physical and mental reality of the situation. The solidification of the event into immutable forms produces the chalk cliff and rift of moonlight. The white coldness of the light is linked to the 'cold indigo' infinity of the sky and the bleak cry of the owl. Parts of the outer scene have their own existence but their primary reason for being in the poem, and the connections they have with each other, belong to the inner life at the moment of the speaker. Thus the *open* mouth of the child, 'demanding,' in a carved gesture of pain, extends the metaphorical range of the rift image. The 'faults,' another variation of it, are geological and moral; along with 'groove' they link 'deep' to (in the next stanza) the 'black gap' dividing man and wife. White as a color symbol—dry, bloodless, cold, disembodied, obscene—grows, too, from stanza to stanza: chalk cliff, white crib, stars ('ineradicable, hard'), apple bloom, culminating in 'A small white soul is waving, a small white maggot.' Words are hard-edged, definite, separate; yet the pattern of connections between them, the isolations and accentuations devised by sound, movement and lineation pack them with significance. 'I cannot see your eyes,' in this situation and within the gravitational field of the central metaphor, becomes a statement dense with latent implications: further into the meaning of the estrangement. When, in the penultimate line, the poet asks 'Who has dismembered us?', the bare verb, at this stage, brilliantly focuses the wide spread of the poem's meaning with a triple pun: Who (or what, since some fatality is suggested by the imagery) has separated us; who, or what, has disintegrated our separate personalities; who, or what, has de-sexed us?

In any positive account of Plath's work its sanity and moral maturity should be emphasized: the poet's control of difficult material, the lean toughness of her best poems, her flexible command of a range of voices, a quality of poise. For her the making of psychic landscapes is not a euphemism for neo-romantic posturings. 'The Moon and the Yew Tree,' for example, was written as an 'exercise' in interpreting a moonlit pre-dawn scene, churchyard and yew, visible from her window, and is grounded in the external world; moreover it is notable that, in constructing its subjective significance, the poet makes *deliberate* play with its properties—we are, so to speak, invited to watch her manipulating them. It is, then, a deliberate exercise in self-exploration, as it were a problem to be solved. Each image is a clue, picked up, scrutinized, twined with the others, and followed to final revelation: the poem starts with moonlight and trees, winds through four stanzas, and ends with the moon as a cruel Muse, 'bald and wild,' and 'the message of the yew tree'—'blackness and silence.' In its self-aware artistry its affinities are with Metaphysical poetry: 'This is the light of the mind, cold and planetary. / The trees of the mind are black. The light is blue.' The voice is that of tough, unanswerable truth-telling—uncovering the bleak geometry of truth. The light mockery of the next lines at the same time questions the attitude of heroic stoicism projected by the voice (as if it were self-deifying) and parodies its antithesis, a Christian style of sentimentality: 'The grasses unload their griefs on my feet, as if I were God, / Prickling my ankles and murmuring of their humility.' The ironic treatment of Christian spirituality is developed in the following lines: 'Fumy, spiritous mists inhabit this place / Separated from my house by a row of headstones—' 'Fumy, spiritous mists' (in the image, in the faintly absurd sibilance and in the redefinition of 'spiritous' that results from its association with 'fumy') brilliantly imposes the wrong kind of insubstantialness on the spirituality of the place. The attitudes change; each one, occupying a pair of lines, is in turn put on and taken off. After these sophisticated maneuvrings for a position of detachment, the colloquial flatness of the stanza's closing line, 'I *simply* cannot see where there is to get to,' reads like a *simple* understatement of numb helplessness. The changes of voice maintain a delicate equilibrium between neutrality, irony and pain. The next stanza begins:

> The moon is no door. It is a face in its own right,
> White as a knuckle and terribly upset.
> It drags the sea after it like a dark crime; it is quiet
> With the O-gape of complete despair. I live here.

A style like this, unadorned, colloquial, supple enough to slip almost imperceptibly from baldness to fanciful wit and back again, can domesticate these portentous figures and give them apparent equality with a matter-of-fact statement like 'I live here'. In the second line the opposite voices of Dylan Thomas and W.H. Auden balance and, as it were, neutralize each other: 'white as a knuckle,' a spare reminiscence of 'Her fist of a face died clenched on a round pain' ('After a Funeral') which like that line mimes the pain, is checked by an Audenesque use of flat social language, debarred from entering into the experience it observes, as a form of understatement.

> Twice on Sunday, the bells startle the sky
> Eight great tongues affirming the Resurrection.
> At the end, they soberly bong out their names.

After the witty transformation of the moonlit churchard scene, the pleasure of these lines, ending the second stanza, lies in the impression created by the contrast with the previous bold internalizing of the scene that here symbol and reality are identical—reality sealing the emotional truth of the preceding lines with the plain factual truth of the bells, first the peal of triumph and then the single chimes dourly forswearing extravagance of feeling.

'Event' and 'Moon and Yew Tree' represent one norm of Plath's poetry at its best: a verse that exercises a hard, taut restraint, practices a bald, curt truth-telling. 'Insomniac' represents another norm, not absolutely distinct from the first. Though this kind of poem is no less tough-minded, it allows itself a greater extravagance of image; it is brought under control, however, by the device of dramatic distancing. We are made to perceive the world through the distorting medium of the protagonist's consciousness, but in imagery that draws attention to the distortion: we are at once prisoners and observers of the mind we occupy (first-person speaker or third-person point of view). I must not leave the impression that this is the equivalent in a dramatic mode of the balance of pain and detachment exemplified by the line 'Moon and Yew Tree' recalling Thomas and Auden; dramatization—our awareness that the speaker or consciousness of the poem is not identical with the poet—is, by intention, only sufficient to remove the observing intelligence to a very short distance. We are more aware of what the tormented insomniac's special perception of things has to say about the common experience of life than of the limits to his insight, though it is clear that it has narrow limits. It must be emphasized, however, that we are not pressed to sympathize but to see with his eyes what his suffering has privileged him to see—we are made to share not his feelings but his vision. Dramatization does not *place* that mind's distortion of vision, by comparison for example with a standard of 'normal' vision: it puts a subjective view in ambiguous tension with not an identifiable counterview but an unfocused, unspecific objective consciousness. We know the insomniac's view is insufficient—we see how it is conditioned by his ailment—but we do not know what would complete it or correct it.

Perceptual distortion draws attention to itself in the opening lines:

> The night sky is only a sort of carbon paper,
> Blueblack, with the much-poked periods of stars
> Letting in the light, peephole after peephole—
> A bonewhite light, like death, behind all things.

The last line contains the illuminating insight, but the reductive irreverence of the first three lines ('only...much-poked...peephole'), the poet's contemptuous substitutions, on the insomniac's behalf, for metaphors expressing more 'suitable' responses to night and stars, even as it prepares for the serious reversal of the fourth line, at the same time mimics a petulant skepticism eager to deprive the scene of any glory it may hold for other eyes ('*only* a sort of carbon paper'). The lines do not offer or imply a specific objective counterview; they say, rather, that the view expressed is one subjectivity among others, with its limitations and its rewarding intensities of vision. The third-person perspective allows Plath also to practice a method of balance consistently used by her—we have seen it at work in the Thomas–Auden line of 'Moon and Yew Tree'—in the closing lines of this stanza:

> Under the eyes of the stars and the moon's rictus
> He suffers his desert pillow, sleeplessness
> Stretching its fine, irritating sand in all directions.

Language that magnifies the pain ('desert') is combined with the language that diminishes it ('irritating'). The method displays something of the quality of mind commended by Eliot and the Metaphysical poets; some of his terms ('tough-minded,' 'internal equilibrium') are applicable. The fine poise of tone here is refined to the point of ambiguity in the third stanza, which describes the insomniac's former search for relief in sedatives and his present immunity to them:

> Those sugary planets whose influence won for him
> A life baptized in no-life for a while...
> Now the pills are worn-out and silly, like classical gods.
> Their poppy-sleepy colors do him no good.

It combines mockery of the world's superstitious faith in drugs (and the wit includes a devaluation of religions) with the insomniac's self-contempt for having sought a cure for reality—the only reality he knows, the truth of night sky and starlight. It is characteristic of Plath's intelligence and discipline that 'sugary planets,' the fantasy of some benevolent power, takes up and defines itself in contradistinction to the image of starlight that lets through the 'bonewhite' truth 'behind all things.' It is also characteristic that the thread of connection is tenuous, uninsistent. Her poetic strategy is, by submerging the analogical sequence, to isolate the individual shock of each sudden metaphorical conjunction and to give image-thinking the appearance of being an uncontrived, spontaneous, immediate response to the living particularities of an experience.

This way of structuring a poem was the realization of an ambition clearly envisaged before she had developed the means of accomplishing it, and was the subject of some remarks made during an interview in 1958: 'To be able to speak straight out, you know, the way you talk, is terrifically hard, while getting all the richess and allusions in that you get in rhetoric.' The ability to do it is evident everywhere in her mature poetry. In the first stanza of 'Parliament Hill Fields,' for example, there is the same skillful management of halfburied connections between one image and the next:

> On this bald hill the new year hones its edge.
> Faceless and pale as China
> The round sky goes on minding its business.
> Your absence is inconspicuous;
> Nobody can tell what I lack.

This is surely what Plath meant by speaking straight out. The lines have a cumulative but not a flowing 'music.' Statements are short and curt, the syntax is basic. Each line is either discrete or a distinct rhythmic unit parading its self-sufficiency. If the reader compares this stanza with the opening stanzas of 'Crossing the Water' and 'Winter Trees' (title poems of their respective volumes), he will find the same short-breathed, spasmodic quality, as though the poet had given us only the bare bones of poetry, jottings, notes for a poem rather than the poem itself; as though the associations between the separate observations and images had not been fully worked out. In fact, they grow together by a process of accretion and, as a contesseration of pieces building up into a mosaic pattern, accumulate an extraordinary power and expansion of meaning. 'Bald,' an obsessive word with Plath, indicates not merely mid-winter bareness, an absence, but the repellant hardness of something inimical to life; in conjunction with the knife-edge of winter, it becomes the butcher's steel or knife-grinder's stone, an inorganic, pitiless substance, 'Faceless' links it with the (sinisterly) featureless surface (bloodless, unnatural) of china and the pale, porcelain-like circle of the enclosing, indifferent sky. Anonymous, impersonal, irresponsive—a nothing landscape becomes nobody, not showing becomes not telling; absence (a dead child) becomes solid grief. This is compact, assured writing; yet it is not cryptic and, though it reproduces, seemingly without reworking or re-arrangement, the rapid associations of concentrated thinking, it has the colloquial ease and openness of narrative.

Later, in keeping dormant an analogy that, whenever her private sufferings were the theme, sprang too readily to mind, she displays an exemplary tact. Encountering in her walk 'a crocodile of small girls...in blue uniforms' which, obliviously, 'opens to swallow' her, flowing round and on, she feels the terror of being a thing, 'a stone, a stick,' a nothing.

> Now silence after silence offers itself.
> The wind stops my breath like a bandage.
>
> Southward, over Kentish Town, an ashen smudge
> Swaddles roof and tree.
> It could be a snowfield or a cloudbank.
> I suppose it's pointless to think of you at all.

Without the prelude of uniforms and a crocodile formation that threatens to engorge the poet, and perhaps, too, without the confirmation of other poems, the whispering intimation of the Holocaust and the crematoria might go unheard. But the poem is a lament for a death, and the details add up. We have a wind that kills and the ashen smoke of a grey industrial sky, and this is the numbness of aftermath, the terrible comfort of knowing that at least it is over: a silence that ignores you yet 'offers' a bandage; the ugly smudge of dead fires that (to capture only some of the connotations) dissolves and disguises the evidence and, swaddling roof and tree, keeps the world safe from the horror of immediate knowledge; that seems to make memory and the memorial of a poem 'pointless.' The association is not willful. 'Tact'—not interfering with the imagery, letting the fusion of the personal and the general, the suffering of one victim and of many, take place with natural inevitability—is necessary not as an observance of literary good manners but to guarantee the authenticity of the impulse that joins the experiences.

'Tact' in this sense, not coherence, is what many otherwise impressive poems lack, a failing more common perhaps in the late poetry of *Ariel* and *Winter Trees* than in the so-called 'transitional' phase represented by the other posthumous volume, *Crossing the Water*. Some of the finest poems were written in the last nine months of Sylvia Plath's life—'Ariel' is certainly one of them—but the reputation of those poems is such that few attempts have been made to distinguish the successful from the imperfect work. 'Fever 103°' belongs to this period. Introducing the poem for a BBC radio reading, Plath said that it 'is about two kinds of fire—the fires of hell, which merely agonize, and the fires of heaven, which purify. During the poem, the first sort of fire suffers itself into the second.' She does not mention that at the level of literal meaning it is about fever. The poem has the elliptical compression typical of her later style; it is not obscurity, however, but the disparity between the literal heat and suffering of the body and the fires of hell and heaven that makes it difficult to accept the poem. The transmutation of fever into destructive personal suffering ('low smokes roll/From me like Isadora's scarves') and then into moral anguish ('Incapable/of licking clear/The aguey tendon, the sin, the sin') and the rapid enlargement of the circle of sin and destruction to include Hiroshima and perhaps the Holocaust, fail to combine the disparate experiences into one. In the interview with Peter Orr quoted above Plath also contends that personal experience 'should be relevant, and relevant to the larger things, the bigger things such as Hiroshima and Dachau, and so on'; the progression in this poem from the personal to 'the larger things' would seem to be an almost pedantically faithful translation of prescriptive theory into poetic practice. Insomuch as the statement applies to her own work, the tense expresses ambition—her resolve that personal experience *should be* made relevant—rather than a necessity of poetic meaning: she does not explain by what process or under what conditions the personal becomes the general meaning—or, for that matter, why it is so important it should do so. The motive for her ambition is clear: 'relevance' was for her an antidote to narcissism; the more exclusively private and eccentric is the generative impulse of a poem, the more urgently and imperiously does she seek to command a large, inclusive and universally central meaning. The analogical progression displays virtuosity—'heterogeneous ideas... yoked by violence together'—and the will to transform the personal occasion into an image of what she has decided would make it relevant—to get a 'moral' out of it at all costs. The warp in the poem results from the poet's need to transcend rather than acknowledge her experience and to magnify rather than explore its significance.

Examples could be multiplied of an arbitrariness in the linking of images. The ending of 'For a Fatherless Son' is a conveniently simple example of an arbitrary leap from a particular to a general situation. Now her infant son is ignorant of what he lacks, a father, but one day the mother will cease to be all in all to him and he 'will be aware of an absence, presently…an utter lack of attention'; 'One day you may touch what's wrong/The small skulls, the smashed blue hills, the godawful hush.' If there is any preparation at all for that 'godawful' scene, it is in the phrase 'utter lack of attention,' and that is not enough to justify the sudden lunge after a larger meaning. The willfulness in the surreal logic of 'Brasilia' is no less apparent but not so easily demonstrated. Working with motifs that occur again and again in the late poems—torture, sacrifice, redemption, concentrated here in one phrase, 'the star,/The old story'—the poet imagines the giant steel sculptures of that drawing-board city as 'super-people' and asks anxiously, 'Will they occur?' Super-people, Nietzsche, Nazism—the implicit associations produce a fear for her child: 'And my baby a nail/Driven, driven in./He shrieks in his grease….' The mental process that makes such connections is intelligible, but the casting of her child in the role of sacrificial victim eternally at the mercy of an imagined collective savagery overstates the agony and, being so inclusive and so absolute, misrepresents the true character of her fear; the unstated assumption that what happened to the prisoners of Belsen, Dachau, Auschwitz exemplifies a law of the universe, therefore, has no justification in the poem.

'Brasilia' and 'For a Fatherless Child,' like 'Fever 103°,' belong to the last months of the poet's life. Failures of 'tact' are not, however, confined to that period. 'The Surgeon at 2 a.m.,' written in 1961, in some ways a brilliantly successful poem, is yet flawed by the attempt to insinuate an interpretation of its contents that they will not sustain. That the 'artificial' perfection of the hospital, 'hygienic as heaven,' should be ruled by the godlike power and impersonal professionalism of the surgeon-healer is acceptable (Plath is remembering her experiences of mental illness and therapy), but the power and the impersonality become signs of an incipient fascism, in the third stanza, only by a species of legerdemain. I cite this poem, however, to raise another question. The poem is the surgeon's monologue—a reminder, if one is needed, that, though it uses autobiographical material, this is not confessional poetry. Plath's poems are mostly, as Hardy said of his own, 'dramatic or personative.' Not infrequently, in the effort to enlarge the relevance of the poet's private obsessions, they extend personal experience, as we have seen, into contemporary history. The aspiration to a universal meaning also expresses itself, as some critics have noted, in more or less explicit references to myth and fable. It has been assumed by these critics, taking the will for the deed, that the incorporation of a mythic dimension guarantees the conversion of personal facts and fantasies into universal truths. In 'Surgeon at 2 a.m.' the opposite happens. When, in stanza four, the idea of a broken statue combines perhaps with the myth of the dismembered Osiris, we may say the same of its appearance here as in the earlier poem 'The Colossus,' that the imagery detaches itself from the experience it is supposed to interpret:

> It is a statue the orderlies are wheeling off.
> I have perfected it.
> I am left with an arm or a leg,
> A set of teeth, or stones
> To rattle in a bottle and take home,
> And tissue in slices—a pathological salami.

In 'The Colossus' Plath associates the piecing together of the fragments with the restoration of her father and therefore of her own disintegrated personality. There are lines that give us the 'feel' and substance of this experience: 'Thirty years now I have labored / To dredge the silt from your throat,' 'My hours are married to a shadow.' Compared with these, the detailed description of the ruined colossus seems no more than picturesque or fanciful:

> I open my lunch on a hill of black cypress.
> Your fluted bones and acanthine hair are littered
> In their old anarchy to the horizon line....
> Nights, I squat in the cornucopia
> Of your left ear, out of the wind,
> Counting the red stars and those of plum-color.

The images distract us from the psychic reality. The same is true of 'The Stones':

> This is the city where men are mended....
> A workman walks by carrying a pink torso.
> The storerooms are full of hearts.
> This is the city of spare parts.

Apparently quarried from an African folk tale called 'The City Where Men Are Mended,' these metaphors for mental breakdown and recovery have the liveliness but also the separate existence of a game.

Another aspect of 'Fever 103°' needs examining. Part of what I was saying is that the moral element, cardinal to a poem that contrasts hell and heaven, is in the event willfully imported into it. The whole moral intention of the poem is further tainted by contrary impulses. A sequence of images joins the destructive fires of personal anguish to the fires of hell, which 'will not rise' but, trapped in the world's atmosphere, kill by physical and moral contamination, and finally to the atomic radiation that kills the 'Hothouse baby in its crib,' at the same time 'greasing the bodies of adulterers / Like Hiroshima ash and eating in. / The sin. The sin. The choice and association of victims, the baby and the adulterers, as it were the just and the unjust—the line about the adulterers hisses with vindictiveness—is evidently in retaliation against her husband for his infidelity and for exposing by his act of betrayal children and mother to the cruelty of the universe. The same revulsion connects fever heat with sexual heat: 'Darling, all night/I have been flickering, off, on, off, on / The sheets grow heavy as a lecher's kiss.' (This moral distortion affects many of the late poems. In 'Lady Lazarus' the liberation–resurrection imagery of the last lines in which the poet impersonates a phoenix Muse, is gloatingly punitive:

> Herr God, Herr Lucifer
> Beware
> Beware.
>
> Out of the ash
> I rise with my red hair
> And I eat men like air.

The man-hating gesture gains an added viciousness from the tacit presence of Coleridge's inspired poet—'Beware! Beware! His flashing eyes, his floating hair!' It is hard to understand a criticism that commends the venom of such poems, declaring its admiration of an art, however coherent and powerful, that serves the emotions of hatred and revenge.) When in 'Fever 103°' hell-fire 'suffers itself' into the fires of heaven and the speaker claims (she is addressing her child) to be purified—'I am too pure for you or anyone/Your body / Hurts me as the world hurts God'—we can be conscious only of the extravagance, the enormity, of the claim (freedom from sin) and the comparison, the obverse of the egoistic morality in the previous stanzas (hell is other people?). The comparison is half-repeated and augmented with a pun on God's name:

> I think I am going up,
> I think I may rise—
> The beads of hot metal fly, and I, love, *I*
>
> *Am* a pure acetylene
> Virgin....   (my italics)

This is of course playful, but neither the jokes ('rise' suggesting resurrection) nor the mime of delirium, *dramatizing* the speaker's metaphorical excesses, can diminish the effect of moral arrogance. No less offensive that her (however playful) self-elevation to sainthood and deity is her assumption, as so often, of the role of Jewish victim, here improved to her spiritual advantage: 'my gold beaten skin / Infinitely delicate and infinitely expensive.'

A strong case could be developed, with the support of many more examples from the contents of *Ariel* and *Winter Trees*, that by and large the wrong poems have been praised or the right poems have been commended for the wrong reasons. Hughes, perhaps inadvertently, is partly responsible for the prevalent misjudgment of her work; with this edition of her poems he has made ample amends. Sylvia Plath's poetry is better—more accomplished, assured, original—than its current reputation; it stands with the best American poetry of the fifties and sixties. Misconceived, it has exercised a baleful influence; a partial exception is Hughes's own *Crow*. Re-read chronologically, it should give a new life to contemporary poetry.

78. Michael Hulse, 'Formal Bleeding,' *Spectator*

14, November 1981, 20

Michael Hulse (b. 1955) is a poet and critic who was educated at the University of St Andrews.

'I am writing the best poems of my life,' wrote Sylvia Plath on 16 October, 1962, four months before her death. She knew what her standards were and knew when she had reached what she was aiming at, and only in that October do her letters betray so full a satisfaction with the poems she was writing. In the *Collected Poems* that month's astonishing achievement becomes apparent: 25 poems, nearly half the year's output, were written in that October alone, including nearly all the now classic Plath—'Daddy', 'Lesbos', 'Lady Lazarus', 'Fever 103°', 'The Arrival of the Bee Box' and the other bee poems. 'Daddy, daddy, you bastard, I'm through': the anguished Plath clinch that strangles her most finely crafted poems at their conclusions clips tightly on all of these poems.

In such statements the authority that is in pain found an expression at once simple and complex. It is simple because Plath had by then gone far beyond those early influences (Marianne Moore, the Wilbur generation of the Forties and Fifties) that had introduced the baroque tone into her voice; but it is also complex because other influences—the abiding presence of Emily Dickinson and the more recent revelation of Lowell's *Life Studies*—had come together with the personal experiences of marriage and childbirth to produce a rich texture in Plath's perception of inner being. Simplicity of language wedded to complexity of emotional perception: it is this that constitutes the origin of everything that is typical of Plath, from the shredded syntax to the startling, beautiful images.

And it is this synthesis that has proved Plath's most inimitable asset. Hundreds of magazine poets have been ruined by too shallow an understanding of Plath, and the reason why so much post-Confessional poetry is bad is that probing of personal problems seems to so many the easy way to write an instant poem. Plath knew better. Her distinctive authority derives from her stern, almost harsh insistence on submitting the responses of the emotions to the scrutiny of the intellect, on wedding the result of this scrutiny to images and ideas distilled by acts of indefatigable will and active curiosity from the life around her. Robert Lowell, who also knew the strength that is in a poem which unites inner experience and public fact, praised those October poems highly; John Bayley, recently dismissing them as 'factitious' and 'embarrassing reading', fails to understand that power.

The *Collected Poems*, with indispensable notes and introduction by Plath's husband, Ted Hughes, contains 224 poems written between 1956 and February 1963, as well as a selection of 50 earlier poems which are frequently interesting because they demonstrate the secure formal base from which Plath proceeded. Those who see Plath as a daemonically-inspired explorer of anguish will see more clearly now than in any of the individual volumes how earnestly and passionately she grappled with the technical problems of the stanza—how, for example, late tercet poems like 'Lady Lazarus', 'Purdah' or 'Ariel' come at the end of a long development which begins with *terza rima* variants like 'Sow' or 'Lorelei', written in 1957 and included in *The Colossus*, the only one of her collections to appear in her lifetime.

Those who see Plath as obsessed with the landscape of the self can now see more clearly than before how high a proportion of her poems are quite literally topographical—her sense of place was keen. *Collected Poems* is not only the most important collected volume of the last 20 years, it is also a corrective to many myths and misunderstandings.

79. Marjorie Perloff, 'Sylvia Plath's *Collected Poems,' Resources for American Literary Study*

Autumn 1981, 304–13

Marjorie Perloff (b. 1931) is Professor of English at Stanford University. She has written widely on modern and contemporary poets.

At last, almost twenty years after her death on February 11, 1963, here are the *Collected Poems* of Sylvia Plath. It is a book that should have appeared much sooner. By 1982, its publication seems somehow anti-climactic: witness the rather cool response it has received from newspaper reviewers. To reread Sylvia Plath today is to realize, somewhat ruefully, how different the early 1980s are from the early 1960s. Schizophrenia, of consuming interest to a generation brought up on R.D. Laing's *The Divided Self*, is now regarded either as a disease to be controlled biochemically or as part of a larger cultural phenomenon: Lacanian criticism, for instance, is more interested in unmasking the verbal strategies of 'sane' discourse than in dealing with individual psychosis. Again, the feminist revolution—the only *real* revolution of our time—has put the 'marriage plus career' problem at the center of Plath's writing in a rather different perspective; it is not that the problem has been solved, but Plath's stated desire to have 'millions of babies' and her scorn for the 'spinster bluestockings' of Cambridge and Smith is not likely to strike a sympathetic chord in women undergraduates today. Most important: Plath's rhetoric, at least the rhetoric of the poems she wrote prior to *Ariel*, now seems anything but revolutionary. Her controlled stanzas, heavy with assonance and consonance, her elaborate syntax with its inversions and subordinate clauses, her ingenious metaphors—all these now look almost genteel, almost Victorian.

Nevertheless, Plath remains an extraordinary poet and the *Collected Poems* reveals a side of her we have not really seen before. In his brief introduction, Ted Hughes remarks: 'Some time around Christmas 1962, she gathered most of what are now known as the "Ariel" poems in a black spring binder, and arranged them in a careful sequence. (At the time, she pointed out that it began with the word "Love" and ended with the word "Spring". The exact order of her text is given in the Notes, p. 295)' (p. 15). The list on page 295 contains the following poems not included in *Ariel* (1965): 'The Rabbit Catcher,' 'Thalidomide,' 'Barren Woman,' 'A Secret,' 'The Jailer,' 'The Detective,' 'The Other,' 'Magi,' 'Stopped Dead,' 'The Courage of Shutting-Up,' 'Purdah,' and 'Amnesiac.' Why did Hughes omit twelve of the forty-one poems that Plath had so carefully chosen for inclusion just a month before her suicide? Here is his explanation:

The *Ariel* eventually published in 1965 was a somewhat different volume from the one she had planned. It incorporated most of the dozen or so poems she had gone on to write in 1963, though she herself, recognizing the different inspiration of these new pieces, regarded them as the beginnings of a third book. It omitted some of the more personally aggressive poems from 1962, and might have omitted one or two more if she had not already published them herself in magazines—so that by 1965 they were widely known. The collection that appeared was my eventual compromise between publishing a large bulk of her work—including much of the post-*Colossus* and pre-*Ariel* verse—and introducing her late work more cautiously, printing perhaps only twenty poems to begin with. (p. 15)

What Ted Hughes doesn't say is that the 'more personally aggressive poems from 1962' he chose to omit were those that expressed, most directly and brutally, Plath's anger, bitterness, and despair over his desertion of her for another woman. Five of the poems on Plath's list ('The Rabbit Catcher,' 'Thalidomide,' 'The Other,' 'The Courage of Shutting-Up,' and 'Purdah') eventually made their way into the collection *Winter Trees* (1971), but the rest are published here for the first time along with a number of other previously unpublished poems of 1962. As a group, these 'Terrible Lyrics,' as we might call them by analogy to Hopkins' 'Terrible Sonnets,' are powerful works in which Plath the passive sufferer of 'I Am Vertical' or 'Last Words' (both 1961) becomes Plath the avenger—Medea as well as Dido. I want to look at these poems in some detail, but first a few comments about the Hughes edition.

The control that Ted Hughes has exerted over the publication (or non-publication) of Plath's work ever since her death is, to say the least, problematic. It is Hughes who was responsible for the excisions in *Letters Home* (see my discussion of this text in *Resources for American Literary Study*, 7 [Spring 1977], 77–85), Hughes who controlled what poems went into the posthumous volumes *Crossing the Water* and *Winter Trees*. Because some of the 'more personally aggressive poems'—for example, 'The Other' and 'Stopped Dead'—had been submitted to various journals by Plath herself in the winter of 1962–63, Hughes could not prevent their publication, but the reader should take note that it has taken sixteen years since the publication of *Ariel* to get a poem as important as 'Burning the Letters' (pp. 204–05) into print. And even now, when we finally have the whole poetic oeuvre before us, it appears in an edition that is curiously inadequate.

True, all the poems written since 1956 are now included, and there is an appendix of fifty poems chosen from approximately 220 written prior to 1956. These juvenilia are, Hughes admits, 'of interest mainly to specialists' and Plath 'would certainly never have republished them herself' (pp. 15–16). 'Nevertheless,' Hughes hopes, 'quite a few seem worth preserving for the general reader. At their best, they are as distinctive and finished as anything she wrote later' (p. 16). I take this to be a rather lame excuse for padding the volume with another forty-three pages; the fact is that the juvenilia are almost invariably exercises, many written for creative writing courses, so imitative (of Donne, Yeats, Dickinson, Eliot, Auden—what have you) that it is difficult to identify them as belonging to Plath at all. Certainly they belong in a scholarly edition of Plath's poems, but then this is hardly a scholarly edition. Indeed, the notes (pp. 275–96) are of little use. Certain things are annotated: we learn that 'Hardcastle Crags' is a valley of the Hebden River in West Yorkshire, that Plath composed 'Full Fathom Five' 'while reading one of Cousteau's books about the submarine world,' that 'Azalea Path was the name of the cemetery path beside which SP's father's grave lies.' But when we come to poems that concern, not Plath's father but her mother, husband, children, friends, or 'the other woman,' there are no annotations at all beyond citations from Plath's own BBC commentaries, which have been available for years. What, for example, was the situation described so vividly and viciously in 'Lesbos'? Who is the 'you' of this poem? Is 'Dame Kindness' (p. 269) Aurelia Plath or someone else? Who is the 'Sister-bitch! Sweet neighbor!' of 'Eavesdropper'? Perhaps Hughes considered it indelicate to reveal the identity of living persons, but in that case, why annotate the text at all? On the other hand, the edition purports to furnish us with scholarly apparatus: a schoolroom translation, and a poor one at that, of a Rilke poem is unaccountably reprinted, and there is a 'Concordance with Published Volumes' (p. 296). The latter contains numerous errors: poems 44, 72, and 87 are listed as appearing in *The Colossus* (London, 1960; New York, 1962); in fact, they do not appear in the New York (Alfred A. Knopf) edition. Poem 44 ('Black Rook in Rainy Weather') did, however, appear in *Crossing the Water*, as did four of the lyrics from the sequence 'Poem for a Birthday' (Poem 119): 'Who,' 'Maenad,' 'Dark House,' and 'Witch Burning,' yet the Concordance merely lists No. 119 under *The Colossus*. 'Event' (Poem 165) is listed as appearing in *Crossing the Water*, but it is not, in fact, in that volume, at least not in the American edition. These are errors that should be corrected when the *Collected Poems* goes into a second edition; that edition should also include a list of first publications, something very important in the case of a poet like

Plath, whose magazine publication was so substantial. As it stands, there is no way of telling where and whether a poem has been published before.

A sloppy edition, then, for which we must blame both Ted Hughes and the publisher, especially in the case of something as simple as the short concordance. Still, it is good to have all of Plath's work in front of us, presented year by year from 1956 to 1963. Faced with so many early poems (more than half the volume covers the poetry written prior to 1960, the year *The Colossus* was published in Britain), many reviewers of the *Collected Poems* have declared that too much attention has been paid to the *Ariel* poems, that the early work is just as important and as accomplished. I find this now-fashionable judgment wholly frivolous, for, as I have argued elsewhere,[1] Plath's carefully constructed persona, the mask she presented to her adoring mother as well as to editors, professors, and friends, governed not only her domestic life but her poetry as well: until the summer of 1962, when Aurelia Plath became an inadvertent witness to the dissolution of the Plath–Hughes marriage, Sylvia Plath—or 'Sivvy' as she called herself in her letters home—never quite abandoned the carefully constructed voice that won her prizes and awards in all the right quarters, a voice her mother could and did approve of. Indeed, the early poems display a bewildering hodge-podge of influences: Hopkins and Yeats, Auden and Wilbur, Stevens and Thomas, and, a little later, first Lowell and then Roethke and Hughes himself. Influence is not quite the word here, for most of the early poems are merely imitative: here, for example, is the first stanza of 'Wreath for a Bridal,' written in 1956 on the occasion of her marriage:

> What though green leaves only witness
> Such pact as is made once only; what matter
> That owl voice sole 'yes', while cows utter
> Low moos of approve; let sun surpliced in brightness
> Stand stock still to laud these mated ones
> Whose stark act all coming double luck joins.

> (p. 44)

The omission of articles and linking verbs, the packed monosyllabic lines with inverted word order—these recall the early Auden just as the mannered sound structure and archaic diction and phrasing ('let sun surpliced in brightness / Stand stock still to laud these mated ones') echo Dylan Thomas. 'Low moos of approve,' incidentally, is vintage *Mademoiselle*—Plath's early work is full of such phrases.

It is hard to imagine a follower of Dylan Thomas writing like Wallace Stevens, but here, written in the same year, is Plath's version of 'Thirteen Ways of Looking at a Blackbird':

> Among orange-tile rooftops
>   and chimney pots
> the fen fog slips
>   grey as rats,
>
> while on spotted branch
>   of the sycamore
> two black rooks hunch
>   and darkly glare,
>
> watching for night,
>   with absinthe eye
> cocked on the lone, late,
>   passer-by.
>
> (p. 28)

By 1958, Plath is trying out the witty metaphoric mode of Richard Wilbur:

> Enter the chilly no-man's land of about
> Five o'clock in the morning, the no-color void
> Where the waking head rubbishes out the draggled lot
> Of sulfurous dreamscapes and obscure lunar conundrums
> Which seemed, when dreamed, to mean so profoundly much.
>
> ('The Ghost's Leavetaking,' p. 73)

Or again, she fuses Boston landscape and Catholic imagery in what is almost a pastiche of early Lowell:

> On Boston Common a red star
> Gleams, wired to a tall Ulmus
> Americana. Magi near
> The domed State House.
>
> Old Joseph holds an alpenstock.
> Two waxen oxen flank the Child.
> A black sheep leads the shepherds' flock.
> Mary looks mild.
>
> ('A Winter's Tale,' p. 86)

By the following year, during what Ted Hughes calls her 'breakthrough' period at Yaddo, Wilbur and Lowell have been replaced by Roethke:

> Pebble smells, turnipy chambers.
> Small nostrils are breathing.
> Little humble loves!
> Footlings, boneless as noses,
> It is warm and tolerable
> In the bowel of the root
> Here's a cuddly mother.
>
> ('Dark House,' p. 133)

It is curious how impervious Plath was to what Harold Bloom has called the anxiety of influence. Hers was not the struggle with the great precursor so as to clear a space for herself. Rather, when, in the last two years of her life, she finally came into her own, the adopted voices merely evaporated, and a new harsh, demonic, devastating self, only partially prefigured in such poems as 'The Thin People' (1957) and 'The Stones' (1959), came into being.

The transformation of the 'Sivvy' who wrote 'The Ghost's Leavetaking' and 'A Winter's Tale' into the Sylvia of 'Tulips' or 'Cut' or 'Medusa' has been discussed often enough,[2] and I won't dwell on it here. Rather, I want to take a closer look at the poems of anger and outrage written in 1962 when Plath discovered that Hughes was having an affair with someone else. The first of these poems, 'The Rabbit Catcher,' is dated May 21, 1962, and evidently refers to the brief interval when Plath and Hughes were still living together despite her discovery of his infidelity. 'The Rabbit Catcher' oddly inverts the imagery of Lawrence's 'Love on the Farm': in both poems, the woman who speaks identifies with the rabbit her husband has killed, but whereas in Lawrence, the caress of 'his fingers that still smell grim / Of the rabbit's fur' produces instant sexual arousal, in Plath, the same incident, as viewed by a female poet, not just a female speaker, spells only death; indeed, here the husband's hands caress an inanimate object:

> I felt hands round a tea mug, dull, blunt,
> Ringing the white china.
> How they awaited him, those little deaths!
> They waited like sweethearts. They excited him.
>
> And we, too, had a relationship—

Tight wires between us,
Pegs too deep to uproot, and a mind like a ring
Sliding shut on some quick thing,
The constriction killing me also.

(p. 194)

In the next poem, 'Event,' the woman who cannot sleep in the hours before dawn perceives the marriage bed as a kind of tomb: 'The moonlight, that chalk cliff/In whose rift we lie/Back to back.' In this landscape, everything is frozen, petrified: 'the stars—ineradicable, hard,' the 'apple bloom [that] ices the night'— even 'The child in the white crib' who 'Opens its mouth now, demanding,' has a 'little face ... carved in pained, red wood.' The loved baby is an intolerable reminder of its unloving father:

Love cannot come here.
A black gap discloses itself
On the opposite lip.

A small white soul is waving, a small white maggot.
My limbs, also, have left me.
Who has dismembered us?

The dark is melting. We touch like cripples.

(p. 195)

The poem avoids self-pity by focusing so sharply on effect rather than cause; there is no circumstantial detail here, no rehashing of the events and bitter words that precipitated the current crisis. The poem's very reticence, coupled with its explosive anger, has a painful effect on the reader: Hughes becomes a kind of shadow ('Who has dismembered us?') and since one can't fight shadows there is only a 'black gap,' a gap measured by Plath's new staccato lines and straightforward syntax.

'Burning the Letters,' dated August 13, 1962, takes us to a further stage of anger and despair. It might have been an embarrassing poem: what, on the face of it, is more maudlin than the image of a woman burning the love letters of the man who no longer wants her? But Plath renews this tired theme by treating the letters as if they had a life of their own even as their author and recipient are transformed into objects. Thus the letters have 'white fists' (they can strike and hurt); they rattle in the wastebasket; inside their 'cardboard cartons the color of cement' they become 'a dog pack/Holding in its hate/Dully.' The dog pack, moreover, brings

300

to mind the image of hunters ('a pack of men in red jackets'), and the very postmarks have 'eyes,' eyes that burn like wounds inflicted by the hunters.

As the letters 'melt and sag' in the fire, the poet remarks: 'here is an end to the writing, / The spry hooks that bend and cringe, and the smiles, the smiles.' But she knows very well that there is really no end to it. As she 'flake[s] up papers that breathe like people . . . fan [ning] them out / Between the yellow lettuces and the German cabbage' of her garden, they appallingly come back to life: 'a name with black edges / Wilts at my foot.' A condolence card of sorts—condolence for her loss, for her lover's 'death,' but also the name of the other woman, the 'Sinuous orchis / In a nest of root-hairs and boredom—/ Pale Eyes, patent-leather gutturals!' (Assia, the other woman, was part German, part Russian). When the rain begins to fall, it brings no relief; on the contrary, it 'greases my hair, extinguishes nothing.' There cannot, in fact, be any relief for the pain:

> My veins glow like trees.
> The dogs are tearing a fox. This is what it is like—
> A red burst and a cry
> That splits from its ripped bag and does not stop
> With the dead eye
> And the stuffed expression, but goes on
> Dyeing the air,
> Telling the particles of the clouds, the leaves, the water
> What immortality is. That it is immortal.

The weary, self-correcting repetition in the last line tells us that burning the letters has changed nothing. The eyes of the postmarks, like the dead eye of the fox, cannot be erased from consciousness. Indeed, the image reappears in a Blakean parable poem called 'The Fearful,' written three months later:

> This man makes a pseudonym
> And crawls behind it like a worm.
>
> This woman on the telephone
> Says she is a man, not a woman.
>
> The mask increases, eats the worm,
> Stripes for mouth and eyes and nose,
>
> The voice of the woman hollows—
> More and more like a dead one,

Worms in the glottal stops.
She hates

The thought of a baby—
Stealer of cells, stealer of beauty—

She would rather be dead than fat,
Dead and perfect like Nefertit,

Hearing the fierce mask magnify
The silver limbo of each eye

Where the child can never swim,
Where there is only him and him.

Here the jangling tetrameter couplets (some quite regular like 'And cráwls behind it like a wórm,' some purposely dissonant like 'Sáys she is a mán,//not a wóman') culminate in the implacable drum-beat of the closing lines: 'Whére the child can néver swim, / Where thére is ónly him and him.' The drama of infidelity is played out with classic simplicity—'This man,' 'this woman,' the worm, the mask. Gone are the trappings of 'Wreath for a Bridal,' where husband and wife, 'pure paragons of constance,' lie in the 'cut-grass assaulting each separate sense.' The poet is twice betrayed, for the rival wants not only her man; she also wants to remove him from his children, from Plath's own children. The eye of the former beloved thus becomes a 'silver limbo ... Where the child can never swim.'

In 'The Fearful,' the surrender to death that becomes prominent in slightly later poems like 'Paralytic,' 'Sheep in Fog,' and 'Contusion' is still held in abeyance. For the speaker of this poem still cares; she is still a fighter, protecting her own from the 'Stealer of cells.' She is the avenger of 'Purdah' (October 29, 1962), who declares:

And at his next step
I shall unloose

I shall unloose—
From the small jeweled
Doll he guards like a heart—

The lioness,
The shriek in the bath,
The cloak of holes.   (p. 244)

As a group, these 'Terrible Lyrics' of 1962 thus extend Sylvia

Plath's range and heighten the pathos of her work. We see her as more than the schizophrenic whose earlier suicide attempts prefigure her final successful one, the Lady Lazarus who has 'done it again' ('Dying / Is an art, like everything else. / I do it exceptionally well'). Rather, she becomes the outraged wife, a modern Medea who gave everything and was nevertheless betrayed. What an irony that the publication of these poems has depended precisely on the man who is their subject.[3] What an irony that in 'burning the letters,' Sylvia Plath really could not destroy them or their legacy. Even as carbon, scattered around the cabbage patch of the poetry world, they continue to punish the dead poet.

NOTES

1 'Sylvia Plath's "Sivvy" Poems: A Portrait of the Poet as Daughter,' *Sylvia Plath: New Views of the Poetry*, ed. Gary Lane (Baltimore: Johns Hopkins Univ. Press, 1979), pp. 155–78.

2 Robert Lowell (Foreword to *Ariel* [New York: Harper & Row, 1966]) was the first to see that before the 'triumphant fulfillment' of her late poems, 'Her humility and willingness to accept what was admired seemed at times to give her an air of maddening docility that hid her unfashionable patience and boldness' (p.xi). See also my '*Angst* and Animism in the Poetry of Sylvia Plath,' *Journal of Modern Literature*, 2 (First Issue 1970), 57–74.

3 Critic after critic has downplayed Hughes's role in Plath's suicide. Even in their otherwise excellent psychoanalytic study, 'The absence at the center; Sylvia Plath and Suicide,' Murray M. Schwartz and Christopher Bollas tell it like this:

> The crisis of motherhood seems gradually to have overwhelmed Plath's resources. Her daughter was born in April 1960. By April 1961, she was in the midst of writing *The Bell Jar*. In 1961 she suffered a miscarriage, an appendectomy and became pregnant again. ... In January 1962, her son was born, and like her own mother she now had a daughter and a son. The birth of her son seems to have provided her both with new confidence and new access to her own rage. In the summer of 1962 she suffered flu and high fevers, and in June she was involved in a driving accident that she described to A. Alvarez as a suicide attempt. In the fall of 1962 she moved herself and her children from Devon to London, where she rented a house once occupied by Yeats. The move was probably a response to a triangular situation in which she felt abandoned by Ted Hughes. (*Sylvia Plath*, ed. Gary Lane, p. 198)

> The word 'probably' in the last sentence is remarkable. One would think that the 'triangular situation' of 1962 was just one more upsetting event. The poems of the period tell a different story.

THE JOURNALS OF SYLVIA PLATH, 1950–1962

Edited by Frances McCullough
Consulting Editor, Ted Hughes

New York, 1982

80. Marni Jackson, 'In Search of the Shape Within,' *Maclean's Magazine*

17 May 1982, 57

Sylvia Plath killed herself at the age of 30, and regardless of what she meant, if anything, by her death, readers will forever regard her novel, *The Bell Jar*, and her fierce, time-hungry poetry in the light of that fact. That's not how the literary archivists like it, but it seems to be human nature. Plath's death is such a cryptic signature to her work that we look for clues in her life to understand who she was.

So, despite the good scholarly reasons for poring through *The Journals of Sylvia Plath*, covering the years 1950 to 1962 (a year before she died), most of us are looking for what only diaries can deliver: secrets. In a poet as devoted as Plath was to unearthing her own secrets, this is no morbid preoccupation, and she comes across in her notebooks with wondrous clarity.

In her formal writing Plath struggled constantly with self-consciousness and her desire to please a certain audience (she sometimes dreamed in *New Yorker* typeface). But in her journals she is all vulnerability: not only is the writer's love of the world here, but so is the fearful '50s woman driven to be everything to everyone. Plath's delighted vision of her future self, as she swooned into marriage with poet Ted Hughes, was 'Books & Babies & Beef stews.' She managed all three, but in her own mind she was always falling short. Her private writing is one long ache of self-recrimination between bursts of radiant well-being and paralysing depressions. Plath always felt on the threshold of her own 'deep

304

self,' the one she longed to write from, and her inability to either shut the door or enter that room, at least during these years, stamps everything she writes with the suspense of yearning. It's a hard book to put down for this reason.

What are really annoying are the long editorial shadows that fall over these pages. First, Hughes tells us how he destroyed her last notebook because he didn't want their children to read it. Then, Plath's mother steps in at midbook with a signed release as a preface to a section that is hostile toward her. And the general editor, Frances McCullough, has spared us certain 'intimacies' that 'have the effect of diminishing Plath's eroticism, which was quite strong.' We'll have to take her word for it, because what she gives us instead are passages interrupted by the word 'omission.' But apart from protecting real people from damaging remarks, there is no need to protect the reader from Plath herself. The decision to publish her journals should respect her contradictory selves; instead, the editing makes us feel that Plath's husband, mother and editor are peering over our shoulders as we read, much the way Plath hallucinated them peering over hers as she wrote.

Plath was her own stern editor, who saw her problems clearly: 'I have a good self that loves skies, hills, ideas, tasty meals, bright colors. My demon would murder this self by demanding that it be a paragon.' Her urge to be perfect was boxed in by an equally strong fear of failure: 'My worst habit is my fear and my destructive rationalizing.' Elsewhere she strikes a different, more confused note (although no less revealing): 'I love too much, too wholly, too simply for any cleverness. Use imagination. Write and work to please. No criticism or nagging. [Omission] He is a genius. I his wife.' She could be unhinged by seeing her husband walk with another woman and plunged into despair by the success of a peer. Despite all this, her journals radiate a huge health, an energy that she kept taming into the sort of writer and woman she felt, and the times suggested, that she ought to be.

The one factor she overlooks in her ruthless self-scrutiny is her isolation. She had no close women friends, no group of people who cared whether or not she made it into print. Nevertheless, it puzzled her that she led such a charmed life, writing with 'the magic and hourly company of a husband so magnificent,' and wondering at the same time, 'where is my old bawdy vigor and interest in the world around me?' The period of her life between her early college success and the arrival of both her book and first baby is full of plaintive stoicism, as she chisels away in search of the shape within. In some ways these journals give a voice to feelings many women must have had, undergoing the sea change of marriage in the '50s. Part of Plath's gift is her loyalty to something in her that was normal, concrete, female, and yet original. She hammered that self to a fineness in her poems, but in her journals she is her whole self, a large-boned girl, rather indistinct.

Plath once had a dream about Marilyn Monroe, who gave her an 'expert manicure.' It's easy to associate these two women, who in their vastly different ways pursued love and recognition with an intensity greater than the roles they assumed. Both projected a desire to become someone else, except that Monroe accumulated layers of imagery and lost herself in the icon, the blond outline, and Plath kept trying to shed those layers—to get from the 'golden girl' down to the 'deep self,' and back again.

81. Linda W. Wagner, '*The Journals of Sylvia Plath,*' *Contemporary Literature*

Winter 1983, 521–3

Linda W. Wagner (b. 1936) has published a variety of books on American modern and contemporary writers. Professor of English at Michigan State University, she edits the *Centennial Review*, and has recently published a biography of Syliva Plath.

Few people will read *The Journals of Sylvia Plath* without pain. All the promise of the talented, exuberant, and strangely candid college student erupts on the page. That spirit tries to survive Plath's breakdown in 1953, though there are no journal entries for the two years following, 1953 to 1955. When her journals resume, during her first year abroad in Cambridge as a Fulbright student, Plath's tone is more wary. Entries are sometimes strained, and obsessively announce the cultural pressure on an unmarried, bright, attractive women: 'Suddenly everyone else is very married and happy, and one is very alone, and bitter about eating a boiled tasteless egg by oneself every morning and painting on a red mouth to smile oh-so-sweetly at the world with.'

The either–or mentality of the 1940s and 1950s plagues Plath obsessively. She does not want to marry and never have a career; neither does she want to be an unfulfilled spinster. One of her primary concerns is her ignorance, her lack of role models: 'Why did Virginia Woolf commit suicide? Or Sara Teasdale.... Neurotic? Was their writing sublimation (oh, horrible word). If only I knew. If only I knew how high I could set my goals, my requirements for my life!'

By 1957, married to Ted Hughes, teaching at Smith while they both wrote poems and worked at becoming known, Plath's journal is euphoric: 'All joy for me: love, fame, life work, and, I assume, children, depends on the central need of my nature: to be articulate, to hammer out the great surges of experience jammed, dammed, crammed in me over the last five years.' She can see how the dual lives—marriage and writing—can be accomplished; she feels she has won over the previously forbidding odds.

Plath's joy in her marriage with Hughes seems genuine—in the *Journals* as well as in her letters to her mother (*Letters Home*). Balanced with dissatisfaction in her own work is happiness because Hughes is writing well. An example is this entry from 1959:

> Ted's good story on the caning. Very fine, very difficult. He advances, unencumbered by any fake image of what the world expects of him. Last night, consoling, holding me.... I have experienced love, sorrow, madness, and if I cannot make these experiences meaningful, no new experience can help me.

But there is also a steady stream of entries that show the rivalry Plath felt, the inferiority, as she tried to keep her work secret from him. The external pressures on her to do well—for her mother, for her sponsors, for Smith—had not changed ('telling Ted nothing'; 'will not tell Ted of rejection'; 'DO NOT SHOW ANY TO TED. I sometimes feel a paralysis come over me: his opinion is so important to me').

That sense of competition is coupled with a pervasive dissatisfaction with herself and her responses to life: 'A misery.' 'Lousy dreams.' 'I make up problems, all unnecessary.' 'First time I've had the heart to write in here for weeks. A lousy green depressing cold. Cried with the old stone-deep gloom yesterday.' 'Very depressed today.' 'Yesterday very bad oppressed.' The moments of brightness in Plath's litany of sorrow come as she records her insights after meetings with Dr. B., her psychiatrist. As readers, we are grateful for those moments. They help us to feel that Plath might have rescued herself, might have shrugged off those layers of guilt that kept her buried in dissatisfaction. One can only wish there had been more of those good moments.

The published journal excerpts, dating from 1950 through 1959, represent one-third of the material now housed at Smith College. Scattered prose pieces from 1960 to 1962 are also included, although these are not in any sense journal entries. In fact, their inclusion may have been a mistake because they call attention to the absence of journals from these important last years. Sylvia Plath's suicide occurred February 11, 1963; the last journal entry is dated November 15, 1959. As Hughes explains in his Foreword, there were two other journals. He destroyed the last journal, containing entries from the last several months of Plath's life. The other volume, which can be assumed to cover from late 1959 to mid-1962, has—in Hughes's words—'disappeared.' For most readers, the value of such a book as this lies in its ability to reveal the reciprocity between Plath's journal writings and the more formal work she was doing simultaneously. To see valuable literary material purposely destroyed saddens us all.

82. Miriam Levine, 'The Journals of Sylvia Plath,' American Book Review

May–June 1983, 3–4

Miriam Levine is a Massachusetts poet whose most recent collection is *The Graves of Delawanna*.

This journal— written between the summer of 1950, just before Plath entered Smith College, and 1962—is first of all a writer's diary in which the writer's work-life and search for identity are almost indistinguishable. There were two other notebooks. Ted Hughes destroyed the one she kept from late 1959 to within three days of her suicide. The other has been lost, although some descriptions of neighbors in Devon written in 1962 have survived, and appear in this volume. Despite the terrible omissions and deletions, we have the record of a poet's vocation and fate.

Comparing herself to Adrienne Rich, Plath judged herself as a poet of sensation and lamented her lack of philosophy, of ideas. Yet her journals embody a central philosophy and idea of reality, and her relation to it, from the earliest pages (when she was still living at home in Wellesley just before her freshman year at Smith) to this passage written shortly after her return to Smith as a teacher in 1958:

My face I know not. One day ugly as a frog the mirror blurts it back: thick-pored skin, coarse as a sieve, exuding soft spots of pus, points of dirt, hard kernels of impurity—a coarse grating. No milk-drawn silk.... Hair blued with oil-slick, nose crusted with hair and green or brown crusts. Eye-whites yellowed, corners crusted, ears a whorl of soft wax. We exude. Spotted bodies. Yet days in a dim or distant light we burn clear of our shackles and stand burning and speaking like gods.

Her wish is 'To be god: to be every life before we die: a dream to drive men mad.' The philosophy embodied in this passage is an extreme statement of dualism, the split between mind and body. After reading these extraordinary words, two questions came to mind: what caused this revulsion and hatred for the body, her own woman's face, and what god did she mean?

The bodies of women, the houses of women, were traps separating her from the truth she wanted to reach. At eighteen she felt locked into the 'warm, feminine atmosphere of the house' which closed her into a 'thick, feathery smothering embrace.' Locked in, she cannot reach the square of night seen from the small window. Going to bed in this house she was sickened by the 'warm feline odor like musk' which threatened to 'assimilate' her. She sees life ricocheting between glory and disgust, the same poles as the body of pus and the body of fire which she returns to in the long passage I have quoted above.

In her teens she saw life circumscribed by biology; she was angered by nature's determinism: the earth as life-giver was female and women were 'engines of ecstacy' who must 'mimic' the earth. Since she saw women only as mother-feeders of children and husbands, she believed her entire sphere of action would be narrowed in marriage and child-bearing. Lesbians escaped the problem, but according to Plath had to give up a large share of life.

Like many of us Plath could not see beyond the enshrined ideas of her time. And because of her particular relationship with her mother, she could not find or rely on the nurturing principle in nature. Much of her life Plath felt she would die engulfed by her mother. She described the frightening symbiosis: 'And you were frightened when you heard yourself stop talking and felt the echo of her voice, as if she had spoken in you, as if you weren't quite you, but were growing and continuing in her wake, and as if her expressions were growing and emanating from your face.' She believed she had not been loved for herself, but for her achievements, and that her mother had enacted her unfulfilled desires through her daughter who complied, so afraid was she of abandonment after her father's death when she was eight.

When she could separate from her mother as she began to do in therapy in Boston in 1958, she was freed from the 'Panic Bird' which sat on her heart; then she understood that she could not write to please her mother and that prizes were no substitute for love. She was brave enough to go after the truth. At this time Plath also felt she had to separate her life from her husband's and not rely on him as much as she had.

Both Plath and Hughes had created a marriage in which they were hardly ever apart for more than a few hours: two introverted writers writing at home every day. She had to promise herself not to discuss her ideas; in separation she worked toward her true material; the journals show the exhilaration of her release.

Her writing became the record of her search for identity, a field of action where in understanding her own story, an idea with the body of myth, she could burn through like a god.

Now we are at my second question. What sort of god is this? First of all: not a goddess, neither Demeter nor Artemis. Plath's mode was masculine-heroic, and brings to mind the story of Heracles, and of Charon who drove his chariot too close to the sun and was destroyed. Heracles becomes immortal because he can pit his strength against nature, and up to a point, win the battle. He cleans the filth of the Augean Stables; he kills the many-headed

Hydra, who with fecund power is able to regenerate until Heracles instructs his nephew to sear the stumps with fire. The Hydra's blood is poisonous. Later his death and apotheosis will come from *female* blood. Unknowingly he will put on a shirt which has been dipped in the Hydra's blood and in pain ask to be burned alive. His mortal parts are consumed in the funeral pyre and he becomes a god.

Plath felt herself impelled to burn through the filth of existence to reach a pure reality and to speak like a god naming reality. She labored out of will. Life was 'single-chancish.' Without will, without propelling herself to see and to create, she was afraid the phenomenal world would fold up and leave nothing, only 'rags' and dirt. 'If I sit still and don't do anything, the world goes on beating like a slack drum, without meaning.' This was the stasis of passivity she breaks out of in the poem 'Ariel' where she like Charon rides her horse into the sun, 'the red / Eye, the cauldron of morning.'

The geography of her days was divided between masculine and feminine. The mornings were 'god's time' in which most things were possible. Night was the grave, the engulfing realm of the mothers, rank with dreams of deformities.

She also saw her marriage in mythic terms. Planning a novel, *Falcon Yard*, based on her meeting Hughes, she says this love is 'a falcon, striking once and for all: blood sacrifice.' Her actual first meeting with Hughes was marked by blood: 'And when he kissed my neck I bit him long and hard on the cheek, and when we came out of the room, blood was running down his face.'

When I read Hughes' introduction to the journals, I was not convinced by his statement of Plath's true birth into herself. I found instead her brilliant mastery, her heroic burning through to describe the landscape of desolation, destruction, rage and spiritual abandonment, her fall from grace, her incomplete self. Like Virginia Woolf Plath did not have a secure sense of who she was apart from either the praise or criticism of other people. Rage is not an identity, nor is the poem—no matter how good—an equivalent of identity.

Plath said she wanted to be anchored to the maternal world of things which she thought might save her. Why wasn't the world good enough for her? Although the freedom to hate her mother allowed her to discover herself, it also carried with it her enormous feeling of guilt for her rejection of a woman who had done so much for her. Separating from Hughes she not only reenacted the feeling of her father's abandonment, but also the anger against her mother. This anger would have been clarifying and purging and would have brought her into her own identity if she had not turned so much of this rage against herself, if the female body had not sickened her.

Plath's parents had the power of gods, her father a buried colossus over which she crawled like a fly, her mother a devouring Medusa, the absolute negative-mother, 'fat and red, a placenta.' To overcome gods one must become a god, a hero. Only the heroic will transfigure the world into glory. The journals show how she prepared herself for *Ariel*. In that final book she is the hero with the raised sword, exorcising in the poems 'Daddy' and 'Medusa' the linked gods of her childhood. But after the rage of separation she is not able to begin her human life. In her journals at the time of a severe depression she said she talked to God but the sky was empty. Her great poem of spiritual desolation, 'The Moon and the Yew Tree,' presents with more detail the death-haunted world where she was wedded to the death-monster; the sweet mother Mary was lost to her. When she fell from the exhilaration of rage, her power left her and exacted its price. Like the hero she must pay for killing with her own death.

It has become customary in discussions of self-destructive writers to point out how they could have saved themselves if they had only: made political connections, made feminist connections, forgiven their mothers, joined A.A., etc. As Americans we believe in self-improvement and change. Our mode is comedy or black comedy, not tragedy. In tragedy certain stars are fixed; freedom is limited. When we read Plath's brilliant and lucid journals we must understand her fixed stars and the distance she was able to travel without the beneficent grace of love and forgiveness which she believed was lost to her.

83. Steven Gould Axelrod, 'The Second Destruction of Sylvia Plath,' *American Poetry Review*

March–April 1985, 17–18

Steven Gould Axelrod (b. 1944) has written widely on Robert Lowell. He teaches at the University of California, Riverside.

What the person out of Belsen—physical or psychological—wants is nobody saying the birdies still go tweet-tweet, but the full knowledge that somebody else has been there and knows the worst.

—Sylvia Plath

Plath... and her... struggle for survival.

—Adrienne Rich

Some time after her death, Ted Hughes destroyed one of Sylvia Plath's surviving manuscripts, and a second one somehow vanished. In the 'Foreword' to Plath's published *Journals* he writes: 'Two more notebooks survived for a while... and continued the record from late '59 to within three days of her death. The last of these contained entries for several months, and I destroyed it because I did not want her children to have to read it (in those days I regarded forgetfulness as an essential part of survival). The other disappeared' (xiii).

What was in those manuscripts, the one destroyed like a Jew in Nazi Germany, the other lost like a *desaparecido*? Hughes tells us that together they contained the last three years of Plath's journal. I need not belabor the value of the manuscripts as historical record, since it is obvious. What may be less obvious is the literary worth of those lost and destroyed pages. Frances McCullough, co-editor with Hughes of the journal, convincingly claims that, next to Plath's poems, the journal is 'her most important work' (ix). Yet its climactic last section, comprising perhaps a third or more of the entire work, is now gone.

These were the years when Plath fully found her literary voice.

313

In her last six months, she was finally free of Ted Hughes's oppressive 'shadow,' and she felt blessed by Yeats's spirit (she moved with her children to a London flat where he had once lived) (*Letters* 566–67, 577). Trying to write herself out of the 'hole' she was in, fighting for 'air and freedom,' she produced 'terrific stuff, as if domesticity had choked me' (*Letters* 549–51). She believed that she had discovered her true gift 'in time to make something of it' (*Letters* 568). 'I am a genius of a writer,' she wrote exultantly, 'I have it in me' (*Letters* 553). Out of these last months of her life came the great poems upon which her reputation principally rests today: 'Daddy,' 'Lady Lazarus,' 'Ariel,' and most of the other poems published in *Ariel*. At the same time she continued to work on another major text, her journal. One can reasonably surmise that in quality, the later journal entries were to earlier ones as the poems of *Ariel* are to Plath's earlier poems. Even without its climaxing segment, McCullough can call the journal comparable in value to *Ariel*. It seems likely that if the journal had been allowed to survive in its entirety, it would have taken its place as a masterwork, Plath's *Walden*, her *Writer's Diary*, her *Education*.

Even the sections of the journal that have been preserved have been heavily, and to some extent misleadingly, edited for publication. The editorial commentary is not altogether trustworthy, but more importantly, the text is a trace of omission marks and ellipses. Frances McCullough explains in her 'Editor's Note' that 'There are quite a few nasty bits missing—Plath had a very sharp tongue and tended to use it on nearly everybody...' (ix). Given the democratic generosity of this motive, it is perhaps churlish to observe that many of the deletions occur when Plath is poised to use her 'sharp tongue' on Ted Hughes. For example:

Grumpy with Ted, who sometimes strikes my finicky nerves [omission].... (212)

No criticism or nagging. [Omission.] He is a genius. I his wife. (259)

I picked a hard way which has to be all self-mapped out and *not* nag [omission]... (anything Ted doesn't like: this is nagging); he, of course, can nag me. (259)

Some of the suppressed material is available for inspection in the Neilson Library of Smith College, but the majority of it has been sealed until well into the twenty-first century. Mary Lynn Broe (author of *Protean Poetic: The Poetry of Sylvia Plath*) is presently engaged in an intensive study of the editing of *The Journals* that should shed further light on this topic. But even at this point, we can agree with Marjorie Perloff that the editing of Plath's work is a 'scandal' ('Extremist Poetry' 585), and one whose dimensions are likely to increase the more we learn about it.

Although the omissions may someday be restored, the destroyed portions can never be. Of the twenty-seven disappointing pages of work sheets that have been printed as *The Journals'* conclusion, McCullough remarks: 'Because only work notes survive from this last section of the journal, it almost gives the impression that Plath died long before she actually did end her life' (357). It is important to insist that this impression is wholly misleading, a result of Hughes's disposition of the manuscripts rather than of Plath's mind and art. The surviving poems and letters demonstrate that, for all her torment, Plath had never been more alive than in her final three years and especially the miraculous last six months. Her journal, in the state she left it, undoubtedly exposed and exfoliated that vibrancy, concluded on its note.

Of course one desires to see every word of Plath that survived the flames, but one wishes that McCullough had thought to print those fragmentary 'work notes' as an appendix to the journal rather than as an ersatz conclusion. A blank page testifying to all that Plath wrote and Hughes lost and destroyed would have been more eloquent than the notes that have been printed, which were clearly not journal entries at all but drafts destined for the waste basket. The essential ending of Plath's extant journal occurs in December 1959, when Plath and Hughes returned from the United States to England. The rest is silence, requiring a starkness to represent it, not a lingering on of irrelevant words to disguise it.

Plath's journal will always be a great work with its greatest part cut out of it—a presence pointing toward an implicitly richer absence. And so the published journal assumes a different character than it would have had, if the whole had survived. At its moment of peak intensity it is a void, a negative capability only, words ripped away from their pages. Instead of a monumental creation, the journal becomes at the end a monument to night and fog, to the holes in history and in unlucky human lives. And it remains our responsibility to recognize and remember those holes, to seek to populate them in our imaginations and daily lives. They stand for our lost, our disappeared ones; and they remind us of the nothingness curled like a worm at the heart of being.

In addition to the lost and destroyed portions of the journal, there was also a novel that 'disappeared' about 1970. Hughes reports that this manuscript, which Plath planned to entitle *Double Exposure*, contained only 130 pages (*Johnny Panic* 1), but months before her death Plath strongly implied that the book was nearly finished (*Letters* 552, 559, 577). Since her suicide closely followed the ebbing of her literary inspiration, it is quite probable that she had essentially completed the draft.

What was the novel about? She began writing it after discovering her husband's infidelity in July 1962, a discovery evoked in 'Words heard, by accident, over the phone' and 'The Fearful' (*Poems* 202–203, 256). Its title, *Double Exposure*, suggests that it provided a dual perspective on a marriage that seemed ideal on the surface but which was in reality riven by deceit and discord. On October 18, 1962, Plath wrote home about the degradations she had suffered during her last years of marriage and added: 'I shall never forget and shall commemorate in my next novel' (*Letters* 557). Judith Kroll, who was allowed to see the outline of the novel, reports that its principal characters were a 'heroine,' a 'rival,' a 'husband,' and the 'rival's husband' (66). Pretty clearly, Plath's lost novel was inspired by the painful dissolution of her marriage.

If we may judge by the general quality of Plath's writing in her last six months, and by her particular enthusiasm for the novel as she worked on it—she wanted to dedicate it to her 'literary mother' Olive Higgins Prouty (*Letters* 578)—*Double Exposure* would appear to have been another important work, perhaps surpassing even *The Bell Jar*. Writing to her mother, who she knew would resent any exposure of privacies (however transformed), Plath termed both novels 'potboilers' (*Letters* 577), and casually promised to publish the second pseudonymously, as she had the first. But her firm intention to dedicate the new book to Olive Prouty indicated that this work would not in fact appear pseudonymously. She valued her 'terrific second novel' too highly to omit her name from the cover (*Letters* 559). In her last months Plath described herself interchangeably as a 'novelist' and a 'poet,' and spoke of her new novel in the same breath that she used to describe the poems of *Ariel*. It is reasonable to ascribe to the fiction and the poetry an equivalent level of artistry. We may presume, then, that a major novel has been lost.

The accidental loss, if that is what it was, of the novel calls forth only lamentation, but the intentional destruction of the journal raises questions. Hughes claims that he destroyed the last portion of Plath's journal because 'I did not want her children to have to read it....' Without knowing precisely what those journal entries contained, one can still suspect Hughes of being disingenuous on this point. Hughes had reasons of his own for not wanting those pages of the journal ever to see print. In her last year, and especially in the last six months of her life, Plath must have focused her journal entries on Hughes himself, his character, his actions. We know that Plath 'had a very sharp tongue' in her journal. The portrait of Hughes in the destroyed sections of the journal must have been devastating.

At the time of her death, Plath was in the early stages of what promised to be an ugly and protracted legal suit over child support and maintenance. After the 'shock' of Hughes's infidelity, after a period of 'degraded and agonized' life with a man who no longer loved her, after the 'final blows' of his desertion and temporary disappearance, after the 'humiliation and begging money from deaf ears,' Plath felt that she had been through 'the most incredible hell' (*Letters* 549, 542, 545, 546, 551). Her way of recovering herself was through her writing: 'I love and live for letters' (*Letters* 557). Her existence centered around her creative productions—her poems, many of which were published in *Ariel* and subsequent volumes, but some of which may conceivably have been lost; her novel *Double Exposure*; and her journal. The journal (like the novel) must have expressed her feelings about the husband she was divorcing. Yet Hughes found that 'her description of neighbors and friends and daily happenings is mostly too personal, her criticisms frequently unjust' (*Johnny Panic* 8). And he found himself in a position to prevent those unjust criticisms from ever seeing light.

What he really did with the last years of the journal, and when he did it, remains unclear. We have seen his statement in the foreword to *The Journals* (1982) about 'those days' when he sought forgetfulness, presumably a time in the distant past. But just four years earlier, in the introduction to *Johnny Panic and the Bible of Dreams* (1978), he wrote; 'How much of it'—apparently the journal in its entirety—'ought to be published is not easy to decide' (7–8).

He then proceeded to publish three excerpts of the journal from the years he subsequently claimed were lost or destroyed. None of the excerpts, of course, touches on Hughes himself. There is also an unresolved question concerning the number of manuscripts that disappeared. In one account, Hughes speaks of a novel manuscript that 'disappeared somewhere around 1970' (*Johnny Panic* 1). In another, he speaks of a journal notebook that 'disappeared' at some unspecified time (*Journals* xiii). Were there two mysterious disappearances or were these items one and the same? The point for us in all this is that there is a certain ambiguity in Hughes's accounts of the manuscripts. It is just barely possible that they have not been lost or destroyed at all, but secreted away.

Hughes in his critical comments about Plath's writing constantly returns to a dominant theme, 'that all her writings appear like notes and jottings directing attention towards that central problem—herself' (*Johnny Panic* 8). But his careful editing of her manuscripts, his efforts to exert control over the work of Plath scholars, his apparent destruction of a manuscript, even his misplacement of manuscripts—all these may be designed to make this generalization seem truer than it in fact is. For it is quite possible that the writings that we have been prevented from seeing have directed attention toward other central problems—for example, the problem of Ted Hughes himself.

Adrienne Rich has written that the male 'culture of manipulated passivity, nourishing violence at its core, has every stake in opposing women actively laying claim to our own lives' (14). Tillie Olsen movingly made much the same point in *Silences*, and Joanna Russ has exhaustively expounded it in her recent *How to Suppress Women's Writing*. Plath's fate may provide just another late and brutal instance of Rich's charge that 'the entire history of women's struggle for self-determination has been muffled in silence' (11).

Yet we must ultimately ask ourselves why Sylvia Plath left herself open to this silencing. Why did she leave her masterworks in the possession and control of a man she considered an enemy, her erstwhile 'jailer,' the 'vampire' who drank her blood for seven years (*Poems* 226, 224)? One answer might be that she wished to continue to play his prisoner and victim even after death, that she wished her work to share in her suicide. I would want to reject such an explanation because it dishonors the struggle for survival, for 'air and freedom,' so evident in her last days and works. 'I feel only a lust to study, write, get my brain back and practice my craft,' she wrote. 'I must not go back to the womb or retreat. I must make steps *out*' (*Letters* 554).

An alternative answer, one initially suggested by A. Alvarez, would be that Plath did not expect to die at all, and thus did not concern herself with the disposition of her literary remains. She planned the suicide attempt at a time when she was expecting a visitor, she left the telephone number of her doctor prominently on her table—she did not expect to have literary remains.

Yet certainly she must have known that there was a *chance* she would die. A game without risk would not have interested her. In her interior conflict between self-assertion and self-abnegation, had abnegation won a final victory, over the art as well as the life? Or was Plath simply enacting the fate of women's words in a patriarchal culture? Was she demonstrating yet again that she 'could hardly speak' (*Poems* 223)? In making her precious words vulnerable to dismemberment by male hands, was she making her final ironic protest, delivering her final proof, writing her final poem, the most bitter yet?

Select Bibliography

A BIBLIOGRAPHIES

HOMBERGER, ERIC, *A Chronological Checklist of the Periodical Publications of Sylvia Plath*. Exeter: Exeter University Press, 1970 (American Arts Pamphlet No. 1).

LANE, GARY, and STEVENS, MARIA, *Sylvia Plath: A Bibliography*. Metuchen, NJ: Scarecrow Press, 1978.

B REFERENCE GUIDE

WALSH, THOMAS P., and NORTHOUSE, CAMERON, *Sylvia Plath and Anne Sexton: A Reference Guide*. Boston, Mass.: G.K. Hall, 1974

C BIOGRAPHIES

BUTSCHER, EDWARD, *Sylvia Plath: Method and Madness*. New York: Seabury Press, 1976.

WAGNER-MARTIN, LINDA, *Sylvia Plath, A Biography*. New York: Simon & Schuster, 1987.

D COLLECTIONS OF ESSAYS ABOUT PLATH

ALEXANDER, PAUL, ed., *Ariel Ascending, Writing about Sylvia Plath*. New York: Harper & Row, 1984.

BUTSCHER, EDWARD, ed., *Sylvia Plath: The Woman and the Work*. New York: Dodd, Mead, 1977.

LANE, GARY, ed., *Sylvia Plath, New Views on the Poetry*. Baltimore, Md.: Johns Hopkins University Press, 1979.

NEWMAN, CHARLES, ed., *The Art of Sylvia Plath, A Symposium*. Bloomington: Indiana University Press, 1970.

WAGNER, LINDA W., ed., *Critical Essays on Sylvia Plath*. Boston, Mass.: G.K. Hall, 1984.

E INDIVIDUAL ESSAYS ABOUT PLATH

For relatively complete listings, see the Lane and Stevens bibliography, the Wagner-Martin biography, and the Lane collection of essays. The quantity of material has now grown to such proportions that a new bibliography is needed, and is being compiled by Sheryl Meyering.

F BOOKS ABOUT PLATH

AIRD, EILEEN, *Sylvia Plath: Her Life and Work*. Edinburgh: Oliver & Boyd, 1973.

BASNETT, SUSAN, *Sylvia Plath*. Towota, NJ: Barnes & Noble, 1987.

BROE, MARY LYNN, *Protean Poetic, The Poetry of Sylvia Plath*. Columbia: University of Missouri Press, 1980.

BUNDTZEN, LYNDA K., *Plath's Incarnations: Woman and the Creative Process*. Ann Arbor: University of Michigan Press, 1983.

HAWTHORN, JEREMY, *Multiple Personality and the Disintegration of Literary Character, From Oliver Goldsmith to Sylvia Plath*. New York: St Martin's Press, 1983.

HOLBROOK, DAVID, *Sylvia Plath: Poetry and Existence*. London: Athlone Press, 1976.

HOMBERGER, ERIC, *The Art of the Real, Poetry in England and America Since 1939*. Totowa, NJ: Rowman & Littlefield, 1977.

HUF, LINDA, *A Portrait of the Artist as a Young Woman: The Writer as Heroine in American Literature*. New York: Ungar, 1983.

JUHASZ, SUZANNE, *Naked and Fiery Forms, Modern American Poetry by Women: A New Tradition*. New York: Harper Colophon, 1976.

KROLL, JUDITH, *Chapters in a Mythology, The Poetry of Sylvia Plath*. New York: Harper & Row, 1976.

LIBBY, ANTHONY, *Mythologies of Nothing, Mystical Death in American Poetry, 1940–70*. Chicago: University of Chicago Press, 1984.

MALMSHEIMER, LONNA M., 'Sylvia Plath.' In *American Writers*, ed. Leonard Unger, Supp. I, Pt. 2. New York: Charles Scribner's Sons, 1979, pp. 526–49.

MELANDER, INGRID, *The Poetry of Sylvia Plath: A Study of Themes*. Stockholm: Almqvist & Wiksell, 1972.

OBERG, ARTHUR, *Modern American Lyric—Lowell, Berryman, Creeley, and Plath*. New Brunswick, NJ: Rutgers University Press, 1978.

RIES, LAWRENCE R., *Wolf Masks, Violence in Contemporary Poetry*. Port Washington, NY: Kennikat, 1979.

ROSENBLATT, JON, *Sylvia Plath, The Poetry of Initiation*. Chapel Hill: University of North Carolina Press, 1979.

ROSENTHAL, M.L., and GALL, SALLY, *The Modern Poetic Sequence: The Genius of Modern Poetry*. New York: Oxford University Press, 1983.

SANAZARO, LEONARD, *Sylvia Plath: The Dark Repose* (radio play). University of Nevada, 1984.

SIMPSON, LOUIS, *A Revolution in Taste: Studies of Dylan Thomas, Allen Ginsberg, Sylvia Plath, and Robert Lowell*. New York: Macmillan, 1978.

STEINER, NANCY HUNTER, *A Closer Look at Ariel: A Memory of Sylvia Plath*. New York: Harper's Magazine Press, 1973.

STEWART, GRACE, *A New Mythos, The Novel of the Artist as Heroine 1877–1977*. Montreal, Canada: Eden Press Women's Publications, 1981.

UROFF, MARGARET DICKIE, *Sylvia Plath and Ted Hughes*. Urbana: University of Illinois Press, 1979.

WILLIAMSON, ALAN, *Introspection and Contemporary Poetry*. Cambridge: Harvard University Press, 1984.

YALOM, MARILYN, *Maternity, Mortality, and the Literature of Madness*. University Park, Pa.: Pennsylvania State University Press, 1985.

Index

Accidental Tourist, The, 210
Agenda, 62–8
Aird, Eileen, M., 16, 136–9, 191–203
Alger, Horatio, 224, 226–8
All My Pretty Ones, 30
Alvarez, A., 2–3, 10, 12, 14, 34–5, 50–1, 55–7, 63, 141, 189, 237, 319
Amarcord, 205
America, 14, 182–3
American Book Review, 308–12
American Poetry Review, 19, 268–76, 313–19
Andreason, N. J. C., 275
Annie Get Your Gun, 120–1
Antioch Review, 3, 44–5
Arbus, Diane, 212
Ariel, 7–8
Aristophanes, 242
Art of the Real, Poetry in England and America Since 1939, The, 187
Atlantic Monthly, The, 3, 80–4, 228, 243
Atwood, Margaret, 18
Auden, W. H., 9, 59, 260, 282–4, 296–7
Auschwitz, 11, 49, 61, 288
Autobiography of a Schizophrenic Girl, The, 131–2
Axelrod, Steven Gould, 313–19

Baldwin, James, 11
Baskin, Leonard, 96
Baudelaire, Charles, 78, 88–9
Bayley, John, 292
Becker, Ernst, 16
Beckett, Samuel, 10
Belsen, 11, 288, 313
Bere, Carol, 219–22
Bergman, Ingmar, 74
Bergonzi, Bernard, 2, 32–3

Berryman, John, 12, 70, 178
Bishop, Elizabeth, 182
'Bitter Pills for the Dark Ladies,' 12
Blackmur, R. P., 149
Blake, William, 9, 38, 78, 280, 301
Bloom, Harold, 299
Bly, Robert, 44
Bobbsey Twins, 6
Book of Urizen, 280
Book Week, 84–8
Book World, 157–61
Booth, Martin, 190
Bosch, Hieronymus, 80, 258
Boswell, James, 205
Boyers, Robert, 144–52
Bradstreet, Anne, 182
Brans, Jo, 15, 213–16
Brautigan, Richard, 16
'Bride in the Thirties, A,' 59
'Bright Star,' 63–4
Brinnin, John Malcolm, 7, 78–9
Broe, Mary Lynn, 16, 314–15
Brooks, Gwendolyn, 183
Brueghel, 93–4
Bundtzen, Lynda, 16
Burger, Reiner, 190
Butler, Rupert, 5
Butscher, Edward, 16, 226, 264
Byron, George Gordon, Lord, 242

Cambridge, 4, 9, 29, 35, 37–8, 42, 188, 217, 227–8, 235–6, 238, 244, 256, 271
Camus, Albert, 10, 116
Canadian Forum, 234–7
Carceri D'Invenzione, 80
Carnegie, Dale, 226
Catcher in the Rye, The, 168
Caulfield, Holden, 101, 116
Chase, Mary Ellen, 121–2, 227–8
Chatterton, Thomas, 143
Chelsea, 3
Christ, Carol, 16

Christian Science Monitor, 3, 142–3
Ciardi, John, 206–7
*City of Words, American Fiction
    1950–1970*, 6
'City Where Men Are Mended,
    The,' 289
Cleave, Eric, 190
Clemons, Walter, 20
Cleverdon, Douglas, 189
Cluysenaar, Anne, 17
Clytemnestra, 72, 195
Coleridge, Samuel Taylor, 290
Colette, 205
Confessional Poets, The, 270
Contemporary Literature, 7, 306–08
Cotter, James Finn, 14, 182–3
'Course of a Particular, The,' 146
Cox, C. B., 5, 11, 99–100
Crabbe, George, 46
Critical Essays on Sylvia Plath,
    245–58
Critical Quarterly, 3, 5, 11, 36–41,
    99–100, 136–9, 152, 177–8,
    191–203
Crow, 190, 219
Cummings, E. E., 9, 182

Dachau, 11, 198–9, 287–8
Daiches, David, 227
Dale, Peter, 62–8
Davison, Peter, 80–4
De Lauretis, Teresa, 124–34
Dean, James, 81
Delta, 29
Dickey, William, 3
Dickinson, Emily, 78, 182, 222,
    274, 292, 296
Dickinson Peter, 2
Didion, Joan, 6
Dido, 295
Dinner at the Homesick Restaurant,
    210
Divided Self, The, 294
Donne, John, 9, 91, 296
Donovan, Josephine, 246
Doolittle, Hilda (H.D.), 182
Dostoevsky, Fyodor, 27, 85
Dowie, William, 17

Duffy, Martha, 6, 15, 216–19
Dunn, Douglas, 139–42
Dyson, Anthony, 11, 36–41

Eagleton, Terry, 152–5
Eberhart, Richard, 1, 2
    8 1/2, 205
Eisenhower, Dwight, D., 106, 108,
    110
electroconvulsive shock, 4
Eliot, T. S., 11, 75, 182, 274, 284,
    296
Encounter, 3, 139–42, 189, 259–62

Faber & Faber, 92, 99, 101, 188
Faces in the Water, 109
Fanny, 204
Fascism, 11, 59
Faulkner, William, 272
Faust, 275
Fear of Flying, 204
Feldman, Irving, 84–8
Fellini, Federico, 205
Few Crows, A, 190
Finnegans Wake, 128
Fitzgerald, Zelda, 257–8
Foote, Shelby, 272
For the Union Dead, 10
Frame, Janet, 109
Frankenstein, 242, 276
Fraser, G. S., 243–5
From Culture to Revolution, 152
Frost, Robert, 144, 182, 265, 274,
    279
Fuller, Roy, 2, 35–6
Furbank, P. N., 73–4

Gall, Sally M., 60
gallows humor, 10; (*see* 'humor'
    under Plath, Sylvia)
Gilbert, Sandra M., 16
Ginsberg, Allen, 12, 17, 183
Goya, Francisco de, 78
Grant, Damian, 177–9
Granta, 3
Greek drama, 225
Green, Hannah, 102, 109
Grimm, the brothers, 3, 35

Gubar, Susan, 16
Guernica, 266
Gunn, Thom, 278
Guys and Dolls, 120

Half-Remembered, 80
Hall, Radclyffe, 113
Hamilton, Ian, 48–51
Hardy, Thomas, 274, 288
Harmonium, 3
Harper & Row, 14, 101, 104, 187ff, 210
Harper's, 3, 288
Harris, Mason, 107 13
Hawk in the Rain, The, 228
Hebben Bridge, 296
Heinemann, William, Ltd., 2, 92, 188
Hemingway, Ernest, 235
Hesse, Hermann, 225
Hill, Douglas, 17–18, 234–7
Hiroshima, 38, 61, 166, 198–9, 287
Holbrook, David, 16
Homage to Mistress Bradstreet, 178
Homberger, Eric, 14, 187–91
'Home after Three Months Away,' 199
Homemade World, A, 74
Hopkins, Gerard Manley, 9, 274, 295, 297
How to Save Your Own Life, 204
How to Supprees Women's Writing, 318
Howard, Richard, 45–7
Howe, Irving, 19, 268
Howes, Victor, 142–3
Hudson Review, 3, 6
Hugh Selwyn Mauberley, 189
Hughes, Frieda Rebecca, 218, 228, 231
Hughes, Nicholas Farrar, 218, 228
Hughes, Olwyn, 12, 15, 190, 205
Hughes, Ted (Edward James), 3, 4, 6–8, 10, 12, 13, 15–18, 20, 36, 40–1, 44, 55, 70, 89, 94, 120, 140, 152, 176–7, 179, 185, 190, 192, 196–7, 204–5, 207–9, 211, 214, 218–19, 221–3, 228–39,

234–8, 241–6, 259, 265–6, 270, 272–3, 276–8, 291, 294–7, 299–300, 304–5, 307–18
Hulse, Michael, 291–3

I Never Promised You a Rose Garden, 102, 109, 168
Indiana University Press, 12–13
Ionesco, Eugene, 10

Jackson, Marni, 20, 304–6
Jarrell, Randall, 1, 70, 188, 276
Jerome, Judson, 44–5
Joan of Arc, 258
Jones, A.R., 11
Jones, James, 5
Jong, Erica, 12, 204–9
Joyce, James, 75, 133
Juhasz, Suzanne, 16

Kafka, Franz, 133
Kamel, Rose, 223–33
Kazin, Alfred, 227
Keats, John, 63–4, 68–9, 77, 89, 143, 271–2
Kenner, Hugh, 74–8, 189, 266
Kenyon Review, 3
Kermode, Frank, 49
King, Nicholas, 48
Kinnell, Galway, 78
Kipling, Rudyard, 59
Kirkham, Michael, 276–91
Kiss Me Kate, 120
Klein, Elinor, 27
Knopf, Alfred A., 3, 81, 92, 189
Kopit, Arthur, 9
Kopp, Jane Baltzell, 28
Kramer, Victor, 14, 161–4
Kroll, Judith, 316
Krook, Dorothea, 228

Ladies' Home Journal, 229–30
Laing, R. D., 294
'Lapis Lazuli,' 198
Larkin, Philip, 94
Last of England, The, 155
Last Poems, 188
Lawrence, D. H. 9, 20, 71, 242, 279, 299

Le Testament, 75
Lehmann, John, 19, 227
Lerner, Laurence, 5, 53–4, 259–62
Letters Home by Sylvia Plath,
  Correspondence 1950–1963, 15–16,
  197, 204–33, 238, 270, 273, 295,
  307
Levenson, Christopher, 29–30
Levine, Miriam, 308–12
Library Journal, 135–6, 175–6
Life Studies, 57, 95, 196, 198, 265,
  292
'light verse,' 200
Linenthal, Mark, 47
Listener, The, 3, 53–4, 73–4, 243–5
Literary Guild, 41, 188
London Magazine, The, 2, 13, 35–6,
  48–51, 235
Lorca, Garcia, 68
Lord Weary's Castle, 265
Los Angeles Times Book Review,
  204–9
Love-Hate Relations: A Study of
  Anglo-American Sensibilities, 69
'Love on the Farm,' 299
Lowell, Amy, 182
Lowell, Robert, 4, 10–12, 30–1,
  55, 57, 60, 70, 73, 76, 79, 80–1,
  89, 91, 95–7, 144–149, 152, 183,
  189, 194, 196–9, 263–5, 292,
  297–9
Lucas, Victoria, 1, 4, 52, 79, 101,
  103, 210

McCall's, 243
Maclean's Magazine, 304–6
McCullough, Frances, 304–5,
  313–15
MacNiece, Louis, 188
Machiavelli, Nicolo, 122–3
Maddocks, Melvin, 6
Mademoiselle, 3, 4, 101, 105, 108,
  229, 243, 271, 298
Maloff, Saul, 103–7
Manchester Guardian, 2, 32–3
Marlowe, Christopher, 143
Massachusetts Review, 90–1
matrophobia, 223–33

Maudlin, Bill, 190
Medea, 295, 303
Melander, Ingrid, 184–7
Milford, Nancy, 20
Millay, Edna St. Vincent, 182
Miller, Henry, 205
Milton, John, 242
Mishima, Yukio, 158
Modern Poetic Sequence, The, 60
Modern Poetry Studies, 161–4,
  179–81
Moderna Språk, 184–7
Moers, Ellen, 16
Monroe, Marilyn, 306
Moore, Marianne, 36, 98, 182, 292
Morris, Irene V., 28–9
Morse, Samuel F., 7
Mother, I Have Something to Tell
  You, 213
Myers, E. Lucas, 3, 4

Nation, The, 3
National Observer, 210–13
Neptune, 40
Newman, Charles, 12–13, 116, 237
Newnham College, 4, 29
New Poets, The, 12
New Republic, The, 69–73, 103–7,
  262–8
New Statesman, The, 3, 14, 155–7,
  187–91
Newsweek, 88–90, 113
New Yorker, The, 3, 271, 304
New York Herald-Tribune Book
  Review, 48
New York Review of Books, 189
New York Times Book Review, 13,
  18, 150
Nims, John Frederick, 156, 265–6
Northwest Review, 223–33

Oates, Joyce Carol, 14, 175–6
Oberg, Arthur, 16–17
Observer, The, 2–3, 34–5, 55–7,
  100, 188
O'Connor, Frank, 215
'Ode on a Grecian Urn,' 272
O'Hara, J.D., 101–2

Oklahoma, 120
Olsen, Tillie, 16, 318
Opus Posthumous, 146
Orr, Peter, 278, 287
Owen, Wilfred, 72

Parker, Derek, 7
Parker, Dorothy, 209
Partisan Review, The, 3, 78–9
Paterno, Domenica, 135–6
Perloff, Marjorie, 15,
  229–30, 293–304, 305
Phillips, Robert, 270
Pigeon Feathers, 5
Pinturas Nigras, 80
Piransi, Giambattista, 80
Plath, Aurelia Schober, 4, 15–16,
  21, 104, 107–8, 204–33, 235,
  296, 305
Plath, Otto, 4, 8, 40–1, 59–60, 70,
  123, 212, 216, 218, 220, 225,
  229–30, 266
Plath, Sylvia: achievement-
  oriented, 4, 28, 30–1; as
  American poet, 34–5, 47–8, 101,
  114–15, 208, 269; children, 4, 70,
  138, 184, 186, 192, 207, 218; as
  college student, 30, 122–3; as
  confessional poet, 11–13, 56, 63,
  90–1, 95–8, 204–5, 237, 270,
  278; critical response to work,
  1–24 and individual essays; craft
  in work, 2–4, 8–9, 11–13,
  18–19, 32–41, 42–78, 100–234,
  289; depression, 4; father, 8, 40–
  1, 59–60, 70, 123, 194–5; as
  feminist, 16–17, 72, 124–34,
  140–1, 183, 204–9, 219; the
  fifties, 4, 20, 30, 42–4, 101–2,
  104, 108, 110, 114–34; as friend,
  27–29; humor in work and life,
  1–2, 9, 27, 35, 44–5, 52–9, 83,
  138, 181, 200, 260; legendary
  qualities, 1–13, 15–16, 55–7,
  77–8, 80–4, 89, 135–6, 144,
  204–9, 219, 234, 270; mother,
  15–16, 104, 110, 112, 203–34; as
  reflexive poet, 14; religious

belief, 76–7, 84–5; suicide of, 1,
  4, 7, 12–13, 19, 48, 64, 70,
  80–91, 102–3, 158, 189, 194–5,
  208, 213, 217, 219; as woman
  writer, 1–2, 12, 16–17, 20, 32,
  34, 37, 47, 158, 182–3, 192–3,
  195, 204–9, 212
Plath, Sylvia, works mentioned:
  'Above the Oxbow,' 265
  'All the Dead Dears,' 38–9, 257
  American Poetry Now, 99
  'Amnesiac,' 294
  'Among the Narcissi,' 157, 274,
    279
  'Applicant, The,' 7, 9, 83, 200,
    266
  'Ariel,' 7, 61, 65, 86–7, 97, 195,
    216, 273, 286, 293, 311, 314
  Ariel (magazine), 219–22
  Ariel (poem collection), 5–14,
    19, 55–91, 93, 95, 97–8,
    99–101, 103, 107, 109, 112–13,
    136–7, 139–42, 144–5, 147,
    149–52, 155–6, 158, 162,
    164–5, 170, 172–3, 175–6, 179,
    181, 183, 184–6, 188–9, 192,
    195–7, 199–202, 206, 208, 216,
    220, 222, 230, 246, 259, 262–3,
    265, 277, 286, 291, 294–5, 297,
    312, 314, 316–17
  'Arrival of the Bee Box, The,'
    56–7, 292
  'Baby Sitters, The,' 137
  'Balloons,' 90, 267–8
  'Barren Woman,' 294
  'Beast, The,' 143, 145, 164
  bee poems, 7–9, 16, 67, 88, 195,
    266, 292
  'Bee Meeting, The,' 64, 142, 196,
    239, 266
  'Beekeeper's Daughter, The,' 8,
    194–5
  'Beggars, The,' 39
  Bell Jar, The, 1, 4–6, 14–15,
    52–4, 79, 93, 95, 99–134,
    142, 158, 168–9, 171, 183–4,
    187–8, 193–5, 199, 206, 208,
    210–11, 217, 228–30, 234,

239, 245–58, 304, 316
'Berck-Plage,' 58–9, 63, 74, 192, 239
'Birthday Present, A,' 7, 66–7, 76, 193
'Black Rook in Rainy Weather,' 40, 146, 163, 274, 296
'Blackberrying,' 141–2, 146, 159, 163, 274
'Blue Moles,' 39, 43
'Brasilia,' 14, 228
'Burning the Letters,' 295, 300–1
'By Candlelight,' 180–1, 186
'Candles,' 146, 151–2, 160, 202
'Child,' 169, 180, 186
Child, 190
'Childless Woman,' 169, 180
'Child's Park Stones,' 265
'Circus in Three Rings,' 195
Collected Poems, The, 10, 14, 18–19, 21, 259–303
'Colossus, The,' 8–9, 37, 44, 47, 195, 278, 289
Colossus and Other Poems, The, 1–4, 8, 14, 19, 32–51, 56, 60, 79, 81, 92–8, 101, 135–7, 139–42, 144, 146, 152, 155–6, 158, 162, 165, 170 176, 184, 188–9, 191–4, 199, 222, 228, 246, 260–2, 265–6, 277, 293, 295–7
'Context,' 235, 272
'Contusion,' 68, 302
'Courage of Shutting-Up, The,' 7, 171–2, 187, 294–5
'Couriers, The,' 67
'Crossing the Water,' 156, 158, 164, 166, 170–1, 185, 199–200, 285
Crossing the Water, 13–14, 35–65, 170, 174, 179, 184, 188–90, 199–202, 206, 259, 262, 277, 286, 295, 296
Crystal Gazer, 184, 190–1
'Cut,' 68, 75, 163, 263, 266, 274, 299
'Daddy,' 7–9, 11, 13, 59–61, 67, 90, 93, 105, 136, 141–3, 145,

169, 172–3, 183, 195–6, 200, 219, 266, 274, 277–8, 292
Daddy, 7
'Dark House,' 145, 162, 164, 196, 296, 299, 312, 314
'Daughters of Blossom Street, The,' 239
'Day of Success,' 240, 243
'Death & Co.,' 58, 61, 68, 82, 91, 136, 238, 274
'Departure,' 44
'Detective, The,' 7, 9, 266, 294
'Disquieting Muses, The,' 92, 94, 138, 141
Double Exposure, 21, 316–17
'Eavesdropper,' 296
'Edge,' 67–8, 267, 274
'Electra on the Azalea Path,' 8, 195, 296
'Elm,' 7, 80–3, 266
'Event,' 279–80, 282, 296, 300
'Eye-Mote, The,' 94
'Face Lift,' 159
Falcon Yard, 311
'Fearful, The,' 50, 301–2, 316
'Fever 103°,' 9, 61, 67, 72, 76, 91, 168, 195, 201, 260, 266, 286, 288, 290–2
Fiesta Melons, 190
'Fifteen-Dollar Eagle,' 239, 243
'59th Bear, The,' 234, 243–4
'Finisterre,' 184–5
'Flute Notes from a Reedy Pond,' 3, 94
'For a Fatherless Son,' 169, 178, 180, 186, 287–8
'Frog Autumn,' 33, 38
'Full Fathom Five,' 8, 195, 296
'Getting There,' 58, 66, 76, 86–7
'Ghost's Leavetaking, The,' 36, 49, 195, 298–9
'Gigolo,' 181
'Great Carbuncle, The,' 265
'Green Rock, Winthrop Bay,' 265
'Hanging Man, The,' 65
'Hardcastle Crags,' 37, 45, 94, 137, 296

'Heavy Women,' 162
'Hermit at Outermost House, The,' 37
'I Am Vertical,' 137, 163, 170, 295
'In Midas' Country,' 265
'In the Mountains,' 245, 252–3
'In Plaster,' 137, 141–2, 157, 200, 211,
'Insomniac,' 137, 141–3, 146, 153, 163, 200, 282–3
'Jailer, The,' 7, 294
'Johnny Panic and the Bible of Dreams,' 234, 239, 243, 245, 255–8
Johnny Panic and the Bible of Dreams and Other Prose Writings, 17–18, 196, 234–58, 270, 272, 317–18
Journals of Sylvia Plath, The, 20–1, 304–19
'Kindness,' 50–1, 65, 75, 135, 213, 273, 296
'Lady Lazarus,' 7, 9, 13, 56, 59, 64, 67, 73–4, 82, 89, 93, 138, 141–3, 145, 156, 195, 198, 200–1, 219, 231, 260–3, 266–7, 274, 290, 292–3, 303, 314
'Last Words,' 136–7, 146, 160, 162–3, 295
'Leaving Early,' 146, 159
'Lesbos,' 82, 178, 219, 238, 266, 292, 296
'Letter in November,' 66, 71
'Life, A,' 146, 164, 201
'Little Fugue,' 67
'Lorelei,' 40, 44, 46, 195, 261, 293
'Love Letter,' 136, 156
'Lyonnesse,' 186
Lyonnesse, 184, 190–1
'Maenad,' 145–6, 162, 164, 296
'Magi,' 138, 146, 294
'Manor Garden, The,' 197
'Mary's Song,' 73, 165–6, 186, 193
'Medusa,' 67, 215, 266, 299, 312

'Metaphors,' 43
Million Dollar Month, 190
'Mirror,' 142–3, 156, 177, 259–60
'Moon and the Yew Tree, The,' 74, 274, 281–4, 312
'Moonrise,' 195
'Morning Song,' 8, 64
'Mothers,' 239
'Munich Mannequins,' 274
'Mushrooms,' 9, 33, 35, 38–9, 49, 92, 265
'Mussel Hunter at Rock Harbour,' 38
'Mystic,' 14, 176, 178, 186–7
'Nick and the Candlestick,' 138, 202–3
'Night Shift,' 49
'Ocean 1212-W,' 235, 244, 277
'October poems, 9
'Other, The,' 186, 294–5
'Ouija,' 38–9, 146, 164, 195
'Paralytic,' 75–6, 302
'Parliament Hill Fields,' 137–9, 146, 285–6
'Pheasant,' 279
'Poem for a Birthday,' 3, 8–9, 33, 43, 74, 137, 143, 145–6, 162, 191–2, 194–9, 201, 278, 296
'Point Shirley,' 37, 193, 264–5
'Poppies in October,' 61, 65, 87, 275
'Private Ground,' 143, 149
'Prospect,' 298
'Purdah,' 7, 9, 177, 181, 187, 195, 293–5, 302
'Rabbit Catcher, The,' 7, 181, 294–5, 299–300
Rabbit Catcher, The, 7
Rival, The, 7
'Sculptor,' 38, 96–7
'Secret, A,' 7, 294
'Sheep in Fog,' 65–6, 267, 302
'Snakecharmer,' 33, 41
'Sow,' 49, 293
'Spinster,' 32, 92, 260, 276
'Stillborn,' 162, 185, 199, 202

'Stings,' 64, 195, 216
'Stone Boy with Dolphin,' 257
'Stones, The,' 3, 46, 94–5, 194, 198, 278, 289, 299
'Stopped Dead,' 181, 294–5
'Street Song,' 274
'Suicide off Egg Rock,' 94
'Sunday at the Mintons',' 240–1, 256–7
'Superman and Paula Brown's New Snowsuit,' 257
'Surgeon at 2 A.M., The,' 154, 166–7, 288–9
'Sweetie Pie and the Gutter Man,' 245, 253–55
'Terrible Lyrics,' 295–302
'Thalidomide,' 169, 180, 294–5
'Thin People, The,' 38, 299
'Three Women,' 9, 14, 16, 165–6, 169, 173–6, 178–80, 183, 185–6, 189, 191–2, 262
'Tongues of Stone,' 245–52, 254
'Totem,' 76
'Tour, The,' 166
'Tulips,' 66–7, 137–8, 145, 214, 299
'Two Campers in Cloud Country,' 146, 149, 163
Two Lovers and a Beachcomber by the Real Sea, 188, 190
'Two Views of a Cadaver Room,' 93
Uncollected Poems, 137, 162–3, 189–90
'Watercolor of Grantchester Meadows,' 34, 37–8
'Whitsun,' 154
'Who,' 143, 145, 161, 164, 296
'Widow,' 63, 147–9
'Winter Ship, A,' 50
'Winter Trees,' 14, 175–6, 285
Winter Trees, 13–14, 140, 155, 165–203, 206, 222, 262, 277, 286, 291, 295
'Wintering,' 8
'Winter's Tale, A,' 298–9
'Wishing Box, The,' 234, 241, 275–8

'Witch Burning,' 143, 164, 296
'Words,' 276
'Wreath for a Bridal,' 190, 297–8, 302
'Wuthering Heights,' 137–8, 146, 153–5, 159, 163, 170
'Hears,' 67, 199
'Zoo Keeper's Wife,' 160
Plath, Warren, 21, 104, 215, 221, 226
Plathitude, 158
Play It as It Lays, 6
Poetry, 3, 45–6, 190
Poetry Australia, 95–8
Poetry Review, 7, 63, 189
Pollitt, Katha, 18
Pope, Alexander, 181
Porter, Peter, 155–7
Porter Folio, A, 155
Pound, Ezra, 75, 182
Pound Era, The, 75, 189
Prairie Schooner, 168–71
Praise to the End, 195
Pratt, Linda Ray, 14, 168–71
Pritchard, William H., 18–19, 262–8
Protean Poetic: The Poetry of Sylvia Plath, 315
Proust, Mareeh, 133, 205
Prouty, Olive Higgins, 227, 229, 316
'Prufrock,' 93
Pulitzer Prize for Poetry, 18, 20
Punch, 2, 122

Queen's Quarterly, 276–91

Rainbow, The, 242
Ransom, John Crowe, 2, 32, 36, 92, 274
Resources for American Literary Study, 293–204
Rich, Adrienne, 224, 309, 313, 318
Rilke, Rainer, Maria, 225, 296
Rimbaud, Arthur, 70
Robinson, Edwin Arlington, 274
Roethke, Theodore, 2–3, 9, 12, 20, 32–3, 36, 48, 66, 70, 89, 91–2,

144–5, 164, 188, 195–99, 222, 274, 297, 299
Rosenberg, Ethel and Julius, 99, 105–6, 112
Rosenblatt, Jon, 16
Rosenthal, Lucy, 6
Rosenthal, M.L., 4–6, 12, 60–2, 92–5
Ruskin, John, 205
Russ, Joanna, 318

Sage, Lorna, 17, 237–43
Salinger, J.D., 1, 5, 104, 116–17, 168, 217
Salmagundi, 144–52
Sandburg, Carl, 182
San Francisco Sunday Chronicle, This World, 47
Saturday Review of Literature, 6
Saussure, Ferdinand de, 132
Savage God, The: A Study in Suicide, 12, 34
Saxton grant, 103, 228
Scan, 118–20
Sceptre, 190
Schober, Aurelia ('Grammy'), 226, 229
Schreiber, Le Anne, 20
Scruton, Roger, 14, 171–5
Seventeen, 3
Sewanee Review, 3, 42–4, 243
Sexton, Anne, 9, 12, 30–1, 91, 95, 196, 205, 212, 263–4
Shakespeare William, 8–9, 274
Shapiro, Karl, 1
Shelley, Percy Bysshe, 242
Shelley, Mary, 242, 276
Shook, Margaret L., 114–24
Showalter, Elaine, 16
Silences, 318
Skelton, Robin, 13, 90–1
Smith, Dave, 19, 268–76
Smith, Raymond, 14, 179–81
Smith, Stevie, 9
Smith College, 4, 15, 102, 114–24
Smith College, Rare Book Room, 21, 308
Smith Alumnae Quarterly, 114–24

Smith Review, 119–21, 245
'Snake,' 279
Snodgrass, W.D., 12
Snow, C.P., 227
South Pacific, 120
Southern Review, 79–80
Southwest Review, 213–16
Spacks, Patricia Meyer, 6, 16
Spectator, The, 2, 3, 5–6, 33–4, 60–2, 92–5, 171–5, 291–3
Spender, Stephen, 39–73, 189
St. John of the Cross, 72
Stand, 152–5
Starbuck, George, 264
Steiner, George, 189, 266
Stella Dallas, 229
Stevens, Wallace, 3, 9, 33, 48–9, 144, 146, 164, 274, 297–8
Stone, Bernard, 189
Swedenborg, Emanuel, 241
Sylvia Plath: Her Life and Work, 136
Symposium, 242

Tanner, Tony, 6
Taubman, Robert, 5
Teasdale, Sara, 182, 209, 307
Tempest, The, 8
'Thirteen Ways of Looking at a Blackbird,' 146, 298
Thirties and After, The, 69
Thin Red Line, The, 5
Thomas, Dylan, 9, 20, 78, 89, 282–4, 297–8
Tillinghast, Richard, 7, 79–80
Time, 6, 77, 216–19
Times, The, 62
Times Literary Supplement, The, 3, 5, 41, 52, 58–60, 92, 165–7, 237–43
Trilling, Diane and Lionel, 218
Tri-Quarterly, 12, 189
Triumph, 74–8
True, 217
Tulip, James, 95–8
Turner, Joseph, 205
Tyler, Anne, 210–13

Untermeyer, Louis, 182

Updike, John, 5, 271

Valéry, Paul, 49–50
Vendler, Helen, 13, 150
Villon, François, 75, 78
Vogue, 229

Wagner, Linda W., 306–8
Wain, Louis, 80
Wain, John, 2, 33–4
Walden, 314
Wall, Stephen, 100
Walter Benjamin, 152
Washington Post Book World, 101–2
Waste Land, The, 11
Well of Loneliness, The, 133
West, Paul, 157–61
West Coast Review, 107–13
Whitman, Walt, 61
Whitstead, 29
Whittemore, Reed, 3

Wilbur, Richard, 1, 292, 297–9
Williams, Oscar, 182
Williams, William Carlos, 78, 116, 274
Wilson, Flip, 270,
Wolff, Geoffrey, 113
Wollstonecraft, Mary, 242
Women's Studies, 124–34
Woolf, Virginia, 307–11
Wordsworth, William, 94
Wylie, Elinor, 182

Yaddo, 4, 197, 299
Yale Younger Poets competition, 3
Yeats, William Butler, 4, 9, 10, 85, 122, 188, 198, 274, 296–7, 314
Yorkshire, 35, 137, 228, 296

Zajdel, Melody, 245–58
Zen, 77

ADDISON AND STEELE	Edward A. Bloom and Lillian D. Bloom
MATTHEW ARNOLD: THE POETRY	Carl Dawson
MATTHEW ARNOLD: PROSE WRITINGS	Carl Dawson and John Pfordresher
W. H. AUDEN	John Haffenden
JANE AUSTEN 1811-1870	B. C. Southam
JANE AUSTEN 1870-1940	B. C. Southam
SAMUEL BECKETT	L. Graver and R. Federman
ARNOLD BENNETT	James Hepburn
WILLIAM BLAKE	G. E. Bentley Jr
THE BRONTËS	Miriam Allott
BROWNING	Boyd Litzinger and Donald Smalley
ROBERT BURNS	Donald A. Low
BYRON	Andrew Rutherford
THOMAS CARLYLE	Jules Paul Seigel
CHAUCER 1385-1837	Derek Brewer
CHAUCER 1837-1933	Derek Brewer
CHEKHOV	Victor Emeljanow
CLARE	Mark Storey
CLOUGH	Michael Thorpe
COLERIDGE	J. R. de J. Jackson
WILKIE COLLINS	Norman Page
CONRAD	Norman Sherry
FENIMORE COOPER	George Dekker and John P. McWilliams
CRABBE	Arthur Pollard
STEPHEN CRANE	Richard M. Weatherford
DANTE	Michael Caesar
DEFOE	Pat Rogers
DICKENS	Philip Collins
JOHN DONNE	A. J. Smith
DOS PASSOS	Barry Maine
DRYDEN	James and Helen Kinsley
GEORGE ELIOT	David Carroll
T. S. ELIOT	Michael Grant
WILLIAM FAULKNER	John Bassett
HENRY FIELDING	Ronald Paulson and Thomas Lockwood
FORD MADOX FORD	Frank MacShane
E. M. FORSTER	Philip Gardner
GEORGIAN POETRY 1911-1922	Timothy Rogers
GISSING	Pierre Coustillas and Colin Partridge
GOLDSMITH	G. S. Rousseau
THOMAS HARDY	R. G. Cox
HAWTHORNE	J. Donald Crowley
HEMINGWAY	Jeffrey Meyers
GEORGE HERBERT	C. A. Patrides
GERARD MANLEY HOPKINS	Gerald Roberts
ALDOUS HUXLEY	Donald Watt
IBSEN	Michael Egan
HENRY JAMES	Roger Gard

FOR
Do No